ATTACKING COVERAGES WITH THE PASSING GAME

Steve Axman

Throughout this book, the masculine shall be deemed to include the feminine and vice versa.

ISBN: 978-1-58518-005-9
Library of Congress Control Number: 2006939950
Diagrams and book layout: Deborah Oldenburg
Cover design: Cheery Sugabo
Front cover photo: Getty Images

Coaches Choice
P.O. Box 1828
Monterey, CA 93942
www.coacheschoice.com

Dedication

To the memory of my wonderful father,
Julius O. Axman

Acknowledgments

I must first acknowledge both Coach Joe Scanella (Oakland Raiders) and Coach Dom Anile (Indianapolis Colts) for first whetting my appetite for passing football while at C.W. Post College. My most significant acknowledgment must go to my true mentor, Coach Homer Smith, my head coach during my years at the United States Military Academy at West Point, along with Army coaches Bruce Tarbox and Mike Mikolayunas. I was very fortunate to have worked with Coach Willie Peete at the University of Arizona. I learned much from Willie. I also must mention the valuable year I spent with Coaches Mouse Davis and Don Frease at the Denver Gold (USFL), learning the principles of the run-and-shoot offense. I was also able to learn much about the pass game from Coaches Jack Elway and Dave Baldwin during my time at Stanford University and from Joe Krivak while at the University of Maryland. And, I must acknowledge the great time I had developing potent, pass-oriented offenses while I was the head football coach at Northern Arizona University working with such great assistant coaches as Steve Kragthorpe, Karl Dorrell, Ken Zampese, Eric Price, and Marty Mornhinweg. Special acknowledgment goes to former Lumberjack offensive coordinator Brent Myers. My one year of working with Coach Steve Loney at the University of Minnesota was of great value to me. I also must acknowledge the extremely valuable time I spent working with Rick Neuheisel, Keith Gilbertson, John Pettas, and Bobby Kennedy while at the University of Washington. Most recently, I have had the great opportunity to become reacquainted with the run-and-shoot offense while working with Coach Rob Phenicie at the University of Montana. Thanks also go to Coaches John Reeves, Jim Brennan, and Lindy Infante. And, thanks to the many, many great coaches with whom I have had the great pleasure of talking about passing game X's and O's over the course of my career.

Contents

Preface

Attacking Coverages with the Passing Game analyzes the structure of eight basic pass coverages (four zone and four man-to-man) and ways to beat these coverages with pass routes, pass-route combinations, and integrated pass patterns. The four zone coverages are cover 2, cover 3, quarters coverage, and quarter-quarter-half coverage. The four man-to-man coverages are man-free, cover-2 man under, four-across man, and blitz-man coverage. Can defenses utilize more coverages? Certainly! However, other coverages are usually offshoots or modifications of these eight basic coverages.

When we train our quarterbacks, and the other players who make up the actual pass-game portion of our offense, we always start out by teaching these eight basic pass coverages. We thoroughly teach the basics of cover 3, and then help our players to understand that cover 3 weak, or strong, roll, or three-deep prevent are all derivations of the basic concepts of cover 3. The same is true for cover 1 man-free, cover 2, and all of the other basic eight coverages that this book will deal with. However, we always start out with the basic coverages and go from there. Is one safety in the middle of the field? Two? None? Such information quickly helps us to categorize the great multitude of pass coverages we may see during the course of a season so that we can effectively know what we're facing both in the coverage strengths and weaknesses. In addition, such analyses help us to understand which types of routes, route combinations, and pass patterns can most effectively attack such coverage structures.

Is *Attacking Coverages with the Passing Game* all-inclusive? Certainly not, and it is not meant to be. Chapter 5 offers 30 conceptual pass-game thoughts to attack cover-2 man under. More approaches are certainly possible, and many of those might be extremely effective in attacking cover-2 man under. What *Attacking Coverages with the Passing Game* is trying to do is present a solid understanding of the eight basic pass coverages, their strengths, their weaknesses, and their basic pass-route, pass-route-combination, and pass-pattern vulnerabilities. When learned and understood, such knowledge will help an offense to attack any (and all) coverage structures that might be thrown at it. So, yes, another way to execute a smash-route combination versus cover 2 may be possible. However, once an offense and its players understand the usage of the smash-route-combination concept, a multitude of possible executions can be realized. The purpose of this book is to help you, the coach/reader, understand the basics of pass coverage as a foundation from which to attack and dismantle pass coverages with a sound, effective pass offense.

Diagram Key

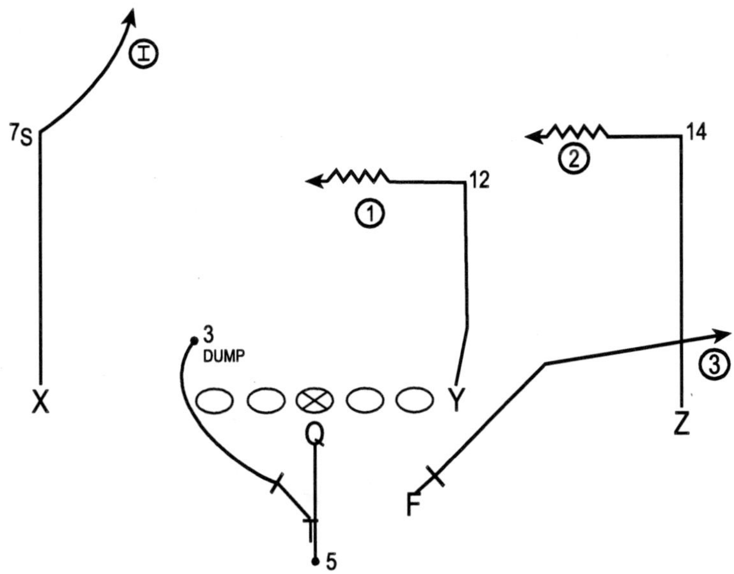

Ⓘ	Quarterback's *initial* read in case of defensive coverage presents a "gimme" (a clear, open throw).
① ② ③	Circled number is a quarterback read progression. Number(s) by itself on a receiver's route stem is yardage depth.
18	Number(s) by itself on a receiver's route stem is yardage depth.
7s	Number with an "S" to the bottom right of the number signifies the number of steps a receiver takes on his route stem.
3, 5 or 7	Number at the bottom of the quarterback dropback action telling the number of steps in the quarterback's drop.
—ww→	Squiggly portion of a route's line telling possible route "zone" throttle down action in zone void.

1

Understanding Pass-Coverage Structure

To attack pass coverages effectively, coaches and players must first understand the fundamental concepts of coverage structure. Cover 2, cover 3, quarters coverage, 2 man, Tampa 2, blitz man, quarter-quarter-half, 3 sky, 3 weak, 3 prevent, press-man free, off-man free, and so on—where does it all start? How is the coach in the press box able to quickly identify the coverages being used in a game in an effort to shut down his pass game so that he can effectively call his plays? More importantly, how does the quarterback, with a threatening stunt or blitz breathing down his neck, quickly identify the coverage being utilized to help him anticipate where he should be going with the ball in regard to the pass pattern being utilized? How are the wide receivers, the tight ends, and even the backs quickly able to discern the coverages in front of them to help them execute their pass routes correctly? Actually, such coverage-structure identification is simpler than it seems. If the quarterback, the potential receivers, and the coaching staff can understand the basic concepts of pass-coverage structure, then the offense will always have a good chance of identifying and understanding the multitude of defensive pass coverages it may face during the course of a season.

The 0-1-2 System

A very easy system can be utilized to help understand and teach pass-coverage structure. The system, known as 0-1-2, starts and bases the understanding and teaching of pass-coverage structure on the number of *deep* safeties in the middle of the field.

In the 0-1-2 system of identifying and understanding pass-coverage structure, "0" refers to no deep safeties in the middle of the field. You should categorize such pass coverages as being in the zero-safeties family. With no deep safeties in the middle of the field, you should anticipate either a four-across man coverage (cover zero) by the secondary with the probability of some form of frontal stunt pressure. Or, you might anticipate a three-across man coverage (blitz man) with a secondary blitzer and a probable tie into some form of frontal stunt pressure.

"1" refers to one deep safety in the middle of the field. Categorize such pass coverages as being in the one-safety family. With one deep safety in the middle of the field, you should anticipate either some form of three-deep zone coverage (cover 3) or man-free coverage (cover 1).

"2" refers to two deep safeties in the middle of the field. Categorize such pass coverages as being in the two-safeties family. With two deep safeties in the middle of the field, you should anticipate some form of a two-deep zone (cover 2) or man-under coverage (cover-2 man-under), four-across zone coverage (quarters), or a mixture of cover 2 and quarters coverages (quarter-quarter-half).

The 0-1-2 system is a starting point for identifying and understanding pass-coverage structure. A multitude of variations of the aforementioned coverages can certainly be implemented. However, if they are all explained as coming from the basics of the 0-1-2 system, such coverage variations or deviations become easy to identify and understand.

It is important to realize that in the identification and understanding of coverage structure, a coverage on the field can, very simply, be wrong. Players can make mistakes and align incorrectly. In addition, a coverage can be unsound or seem to be unsound. And, a defense can gamble using overloaded and seemingly unsound blitzes that leave a (or some) receiver(s) left uncovered. Once again, relying on the 0-1-2 system for identifying and understanding coverage structure will allow coaches and players a sound basis from which to analyze and quickly recognize any such coverage variation during the midst of a pressure-filled game. In this fashion, the offense can go on the attack immediately to exploit the weaknesses of any coverage structure.

Zero-Safeties Coverage Family

When no deep safeties are in the middle of the field, you should be thinking cover zero (four-across man coverage) with the strong possibility of some form of a frontal stunt pressure. Or, you should be thinking blitz man (three-across man coverage) with a secondary blitzer and the strong possibility of being tied into some form of a frontal stunt. Once you see no deep safeties in the middle of the field, think stunt and blitz pressure. If it's cover zero (four-across man coverage), think frontal stunts and pressures by the defensive line and the linebackers. If it's blitz man (three-across man coverage), think secondary blitzer. The blitzer might be the weakside cornerback, the weak safety, or the strong safety.

Cover Zero (Four-Across Man Coverage)

In cover zero (four-across man coverage), no deep safeties are in the middle of the field. All four defensive backs are positioned down low, camped by alignment on receivers in off-man coverage. Press-man coverage techniques are a possibility. More often, all four defensive backs show off-man-coverage techniques. They are usually down low, seven to nine yards off the line of scrimmage, in tightened off-coverage alignments. The man-alignment stances are angled out at the receivers. The defensive backs aligned in man-to-man coverage will probably be in a bent-legged stance and looking (or staring) directly at the receivers. As a result of the cover-zero (four-across man coverage) alignment and stance look, you should expect frontal stunts and pressures. Diagram 1-1 shows cover zero (four-across man) off-man coverage with a six-man frontal pressure stunt.

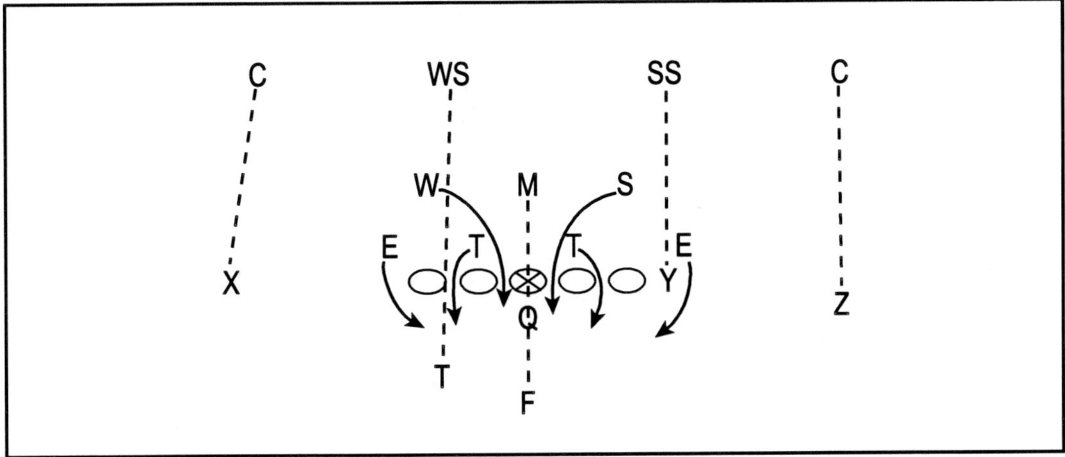

Diagram 1-1. Cover zero (four-across man) off-man coverage with a six-man frontal stunt

Blitz Man (Three-Across Man Coverage)

On blitz man (three-across man coverage), no deep safeties are in the middle of the field. Three defensive backs are eventually positioned down low, camped by alignment on receivers in off-man coverage as the fourth defensive back blitzes. Press-man-coverage techniques are a possibility. One safety, or the other, will often cheat his alignment to cover a specific receiver with a man-to-man coverage technique. The cheating of the man-coverage alignment, no matter how subtle the cheating action, often helps to tell where the secondary blitzer is coming from.

Three of the defensive backs show man-coverage techniques. They are usually down low, seven to nine yards off the line of scrimmage, in tightened off-man alignments. The man-alignment stances are angled out at the receivers. The man-to-man covering defensive backs will probably be in a bent-legged stance looking (or staring) directly at the receivers. As a result of the blitz-man (three-across man coverage) alignment and stance look, you would expect some type of blitz from the fourth secondary defender (he might be the weak corner, the weak safety, or the strong safety). In addition, the offense must also be aware of the strong possibility of frontal stunt action in combination with the secondary blitz action.

Diagram 1-2 shows blitz man (three-across man coverage) with a weak corner blitz in combination with a weakside frontal edge stunt pressure. Diagram 1-3 shows blitz man (three-across man coverage) with a weak safety blitz to the weakside of the

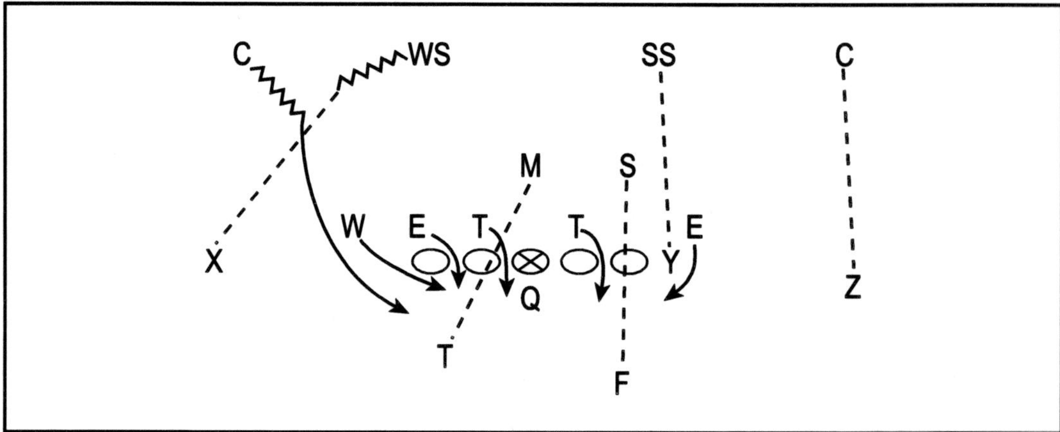

Diagram 1-2. Blitz man (three-across man coverage) with weak corner crash and weakside frontal edge stunt

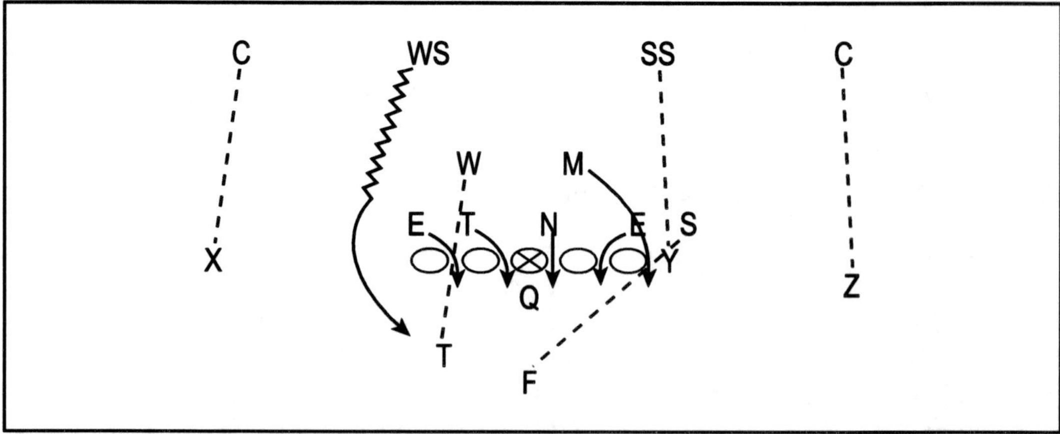

Diagram 1-3. Blitz man (three-across man coverage) with weak safety blitz and strongside linebacker cross stunt

offensive formation combined with a strongside linebacker cross stunt. Diagram 1-4 shows blitz man (three-across man coverage) with a strong safety blitz in combination with a strongside frontal "in" stunt.

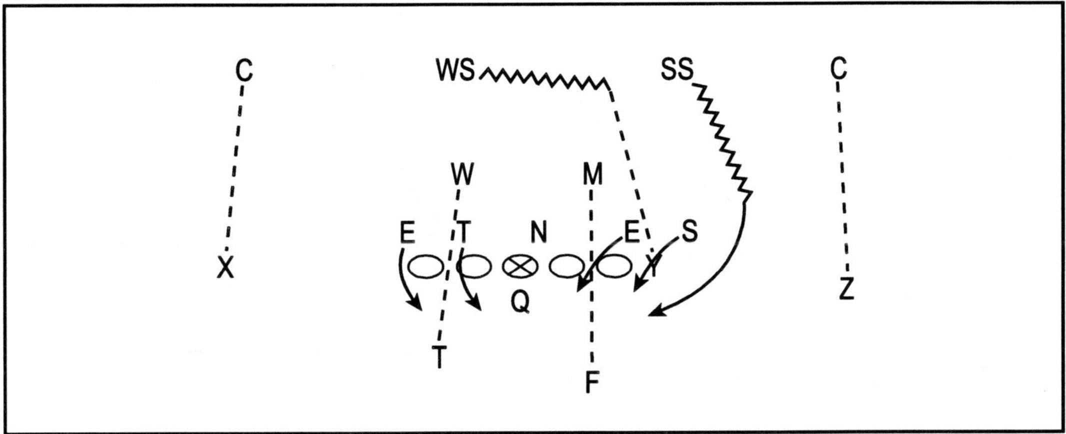

Diagram 1-4. Three-across man coverage with strong safety blitz and strongside frontal "in" stunt

One-Safety Coverage Family

When one deep free safety is in the middle of the field, you should be thinking some form of a three-deep zone coverage—the most common of which are cover 3. Or, you should be thinking cover 1 (man-free coverage). The key—once it has been determined that a one-deep free safety is in the middle of the field, making it part of the one-safety family—is to switch the key read from the one single safety in the middle of the field to the cornerbacks. You now want to see how the cornerbacks are aligned, and what type of coverage techniques they are showing. You want to see if the cornerbacks are playing zone-coverage alignments and techniques, which would tell you that it's probably some form of three-deep zone coverage (cover 3). Or, are the cornerbacks playing man coverage alignments and techniques, telling you it is cover 1 (man-free coverage)?

Cover 3 (Three-Deep Zone Coverage)

In cover 3 (three-deep zone coverage), one deep free safety is in the middle of the field. The cornerbacks are positioned off and deep normally aligned in a head-up to outside alignment on the widest receiver. The cornerbacks will probably be in more of a straight-legged, squared-up stance—and, rather than the man-coverage technique of looking (or staring) at the receiver, the cornerbacks will probably be looking ("peeking in") to the quarterback. Diagram 1-5 shows cover 3, the most basic three-deep zone coverage with four-underneath zone-coverage defenders.

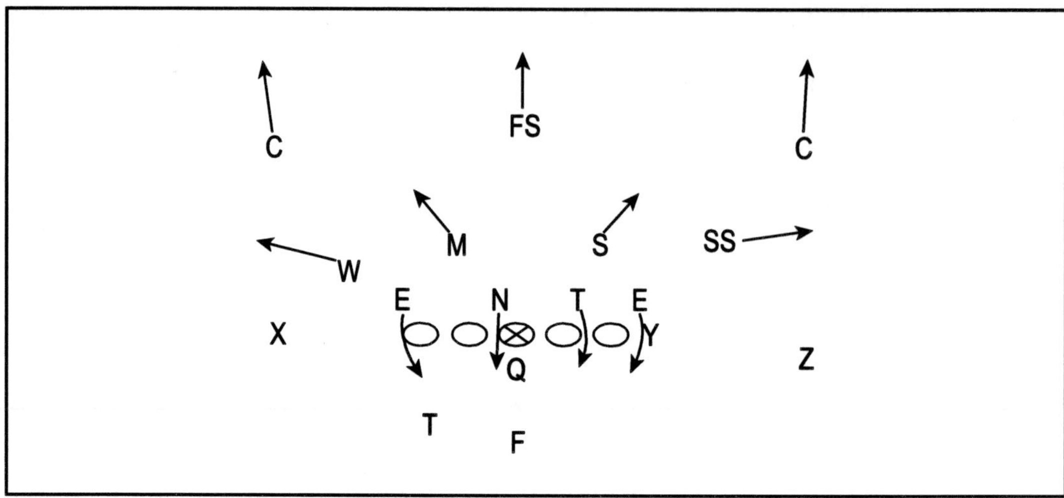

Diagram 1-5. Cover 3 three-deep, four-underneath zone coverage

Cover 1 (Man-Free Coverage)

In cover 1 (man-free coverage), one deep free safety is in the middle of the field. He is the deep-zone "free" safety backing up the underneath man coverage. The other three defensive backs and two linebackers—and possibly a fifth (nickel) and sixth (dime) defensive back substituting for the coverage linebackers—are positioned down low, tighter in alignment, seven to nine yards off the receivers in an off-man-free coverage alignment technique. They are camped down by alignment on the receivers in man coverage. Press man-free coverage is a popular part of the cover-1 (man-free coverage) package. Press techniques can be used in combination with off-man-free-coverage techniques in an effort to press specific or certain receivers while playing off-man-free-coverage techniques on others. In their man-coverage techniques, the man-coverage defenders are usually aligned in an inside-out alignment in more of a bent-legged stance, looking (or staring) at the receivers. Diagram 1-6 shows cover-1 (man-free) off-man-coverage techniques. Diagram 1-7 shows press cover 1 (man-free coverage).

Two-Safeties Coverage Family

When two deep safeties are in the middle of the field, think cover 2 (two-deep, five-under zone coverage). Or, think of coverages that are related to cover 2, such as cover-2 man under (two-man), quarters coverage, and quarter-quarter-half coverage. All of these coverages are related by the fact that they have two safeties in the middle of the field, making them all part of the two-safeties family. Once it has been determined that two deep safeties are in the middle of the field, check to see the depth of the safeties and the alignment depth and techniques of the cornerbacks. Doing so helps to determine if the two-safeties coverage is cover 2 or another coverage in the two-safeties coverage family.

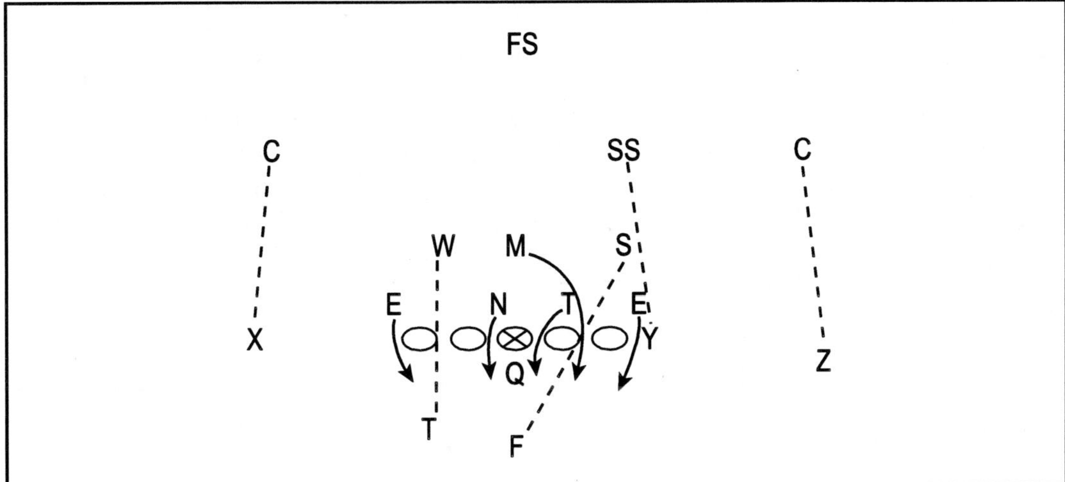

Diagram 1-6. Cover 1 (man-free coverage) with off-man-coverage techniques

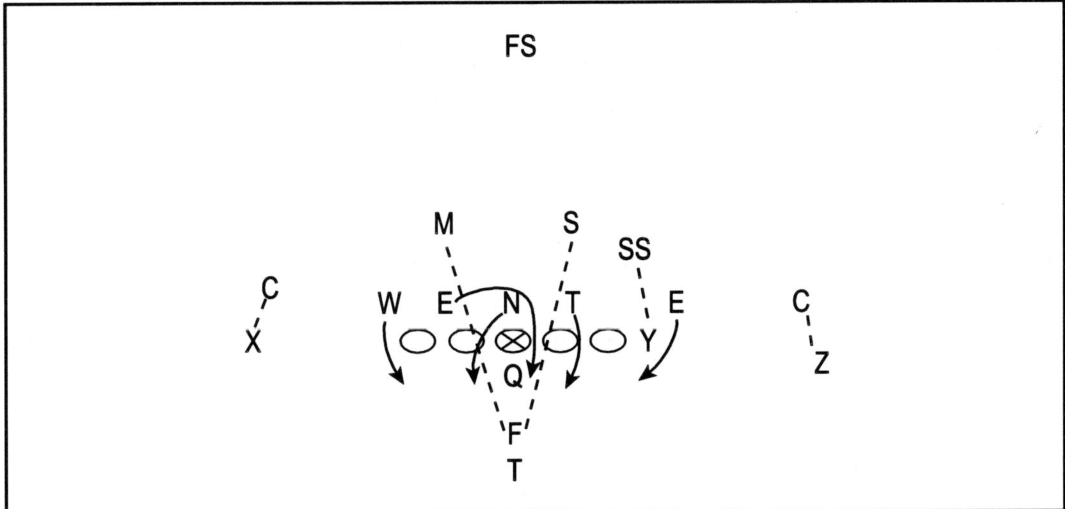

Diagram 1-7. Cover 1 (man-free coverage) with press-man-coverage techniques

Cover 2

In cover 2, the most common, or basic, coverage in the two-safeties family, two deep safeties are in the middle of the field. The two deep safeties are aligned deep and normally tight, or near, to the hashes. They play deep half-field zone coverage, approximately 14 yards deep.

The cornerbacks are low, or squatted, in alignment, five to six yards deep. They are normally aligned head-up to outside of the widest receivers. The cornerbacks will probably be in more of a straight-legged, squared-up stance. And, rather than the man-coverage technique of looking (or staring) at the receiver, the cornerbacks will look through the wide receiver in an effort to "peek in" towards the quarterback. Diagram 1-8 shows cover-2, two-deep, five-under zone coverage.

Diagram 1-9 shows cover-2, man-under (two-man) coverage. As in base cover 2, the two deep safeties are aligned deep and tight to the hashes playing deep, half-field coverage. The cornerbacks and other underneath coverage defenders (linebackers, nickel or dime secondary defenders), however, are aligned inside-out in press-man coverage.

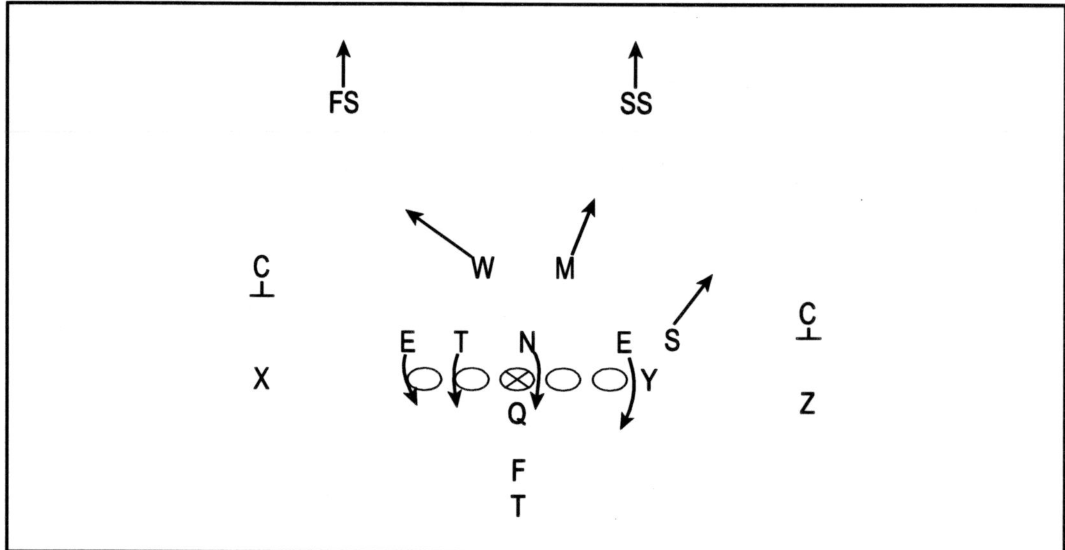

Diagram 1-8. Cover-2, two-deep, five-under zone coverage

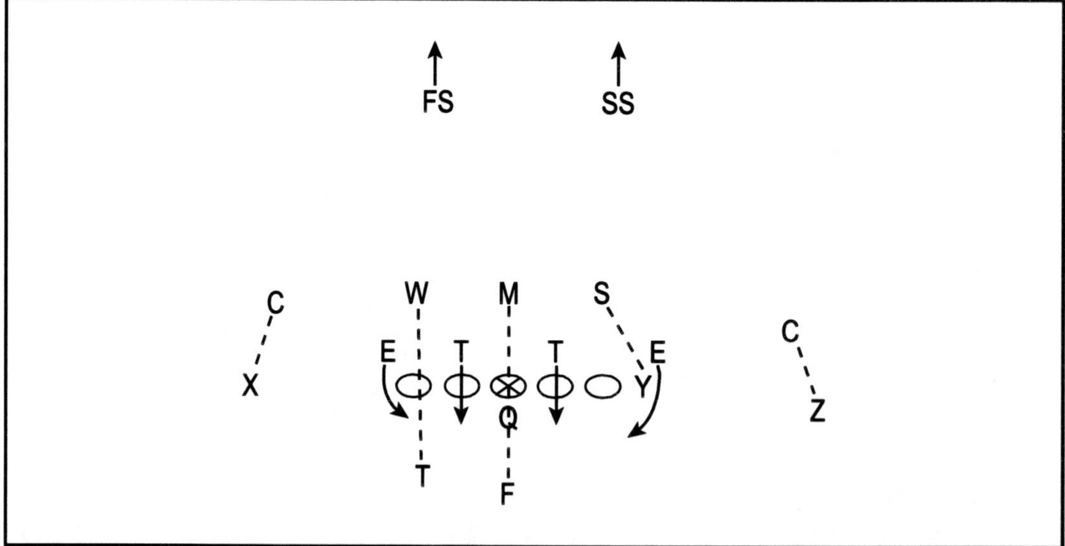

Diagram 1-9. Cover-2 man-under (two-man) coverage

Quarters Coverage

In quarters coverage, two deep safeties are in the middle of the field. The two deep safeties, however, are not aligned with discipline on or near the hashes, nor are they in the 12-14-yard cover-2 depth range. The quarters coverage safeties align lower (9 to 11 yards) and in more of a position that will allow them to become inside-out perimeter support defenders rather than as cover-2, deep-halves, zone-coverage defenders. And, rather than being deep-halves, zone-coverage defenders, the safeties are part of a four-across-zone, quarters (quarter-quarter-quarter-quarter) scheme with the cornerbacks.

In quarters coverage, the cornerbacks are aligned off, or deep, as part of the four-across, quarters-coverage scheme, also in the 9 to 11-yard range. The cornerbacks are positioned head-up to outside of the widest receivers in a straight-legged stance, but do not necessarily look in at the quarterback (because of the common use of inside-outside, brackets, or combination coverage keys between the cornerbacks and the safeties in quarters coverage on the first two receivers, outside-in, to their sides). Diagram 1-10 shows quarters coverage with three underneath-zone-coverage defenders.

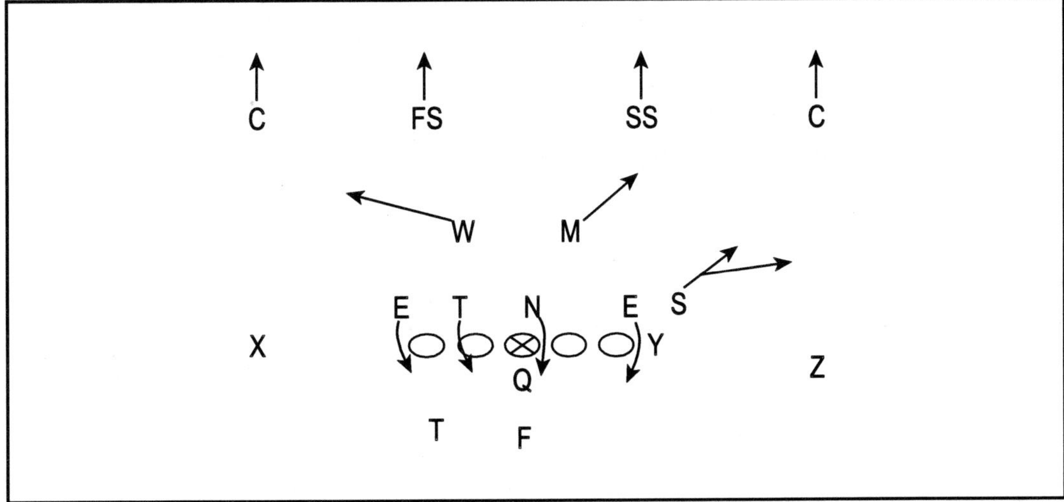

Diagram 1-10. Quarters coverage with three underneath-zone-coverage defenders

Quarter-Quarter-Half Coverage

In quarter-quarter-half coverage, two deep safeties are in the middle of the field. However, the two safeties play two different techniques in the quarter-quarter-half coverage scheme. The field/formationside strong safety plays normal quarters cover alignment and technique. The weak safety (i.e., the safety away from the formation strength side) plays a form of halves coverage that is approximately 12-14 yards deep, but slightly off the hash towards the sideline. This alignment is premised on the belief that considerable inside safety help is coming from the field/formation side quarters coverage strong safety.

Much like the safeties, the cornerbacks also play different techniques in the quarter-quarter-half coverage scheme. The field/formation-side cornerback plays normal off, head-up to outside-aligned, quarters coverage. The weakside cornerback (i.e., the cornerback away from the formation strength side) plays a normal squatted, cover-2 technique. Such action by the cornerbacks and the safeties helps to produce the combination of quarters coverage and cover 2 that produces the quarter-quarter-half coverage shown in Diagram 1-11.

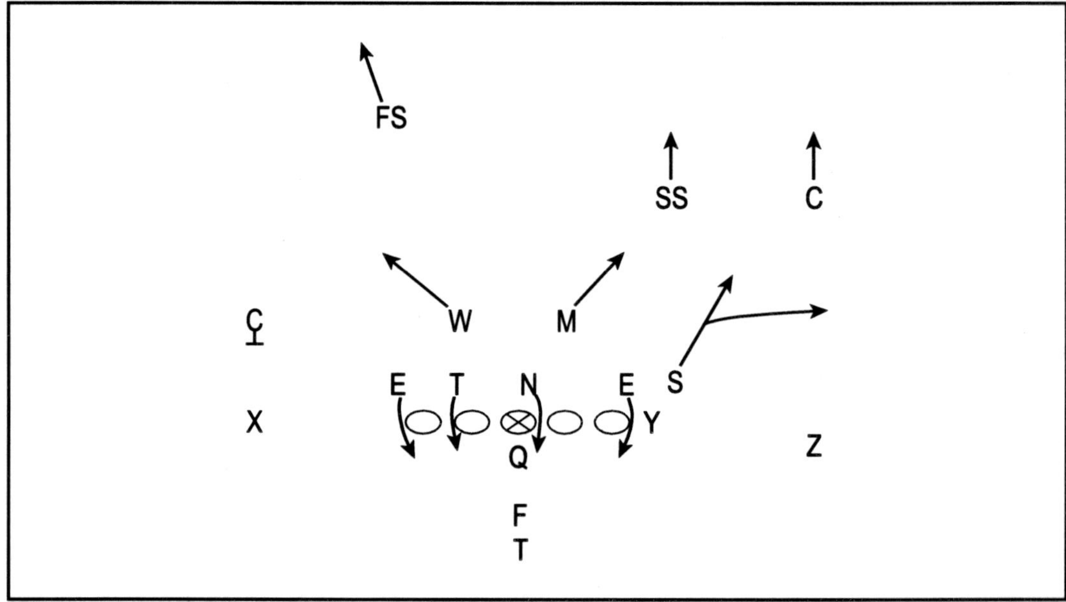

Diagram 1-11. Quarter-quarter-half coverage with four underneath-zone-coverage defenders

2

Pass Attack of Cover 3

Cover 3 is the most common, or basic, zone coverage in the one-safety family. One deep free safety is in the middle of the field. The one deep safety is normally aligned in deep center field. However, when the ball is on a hash mark, the one deep safety may be aligned tight to the hash, depending on the formation the coverage is facing and/or the split of the wide receivers—especially the spread receiver to the field. The one safety is responsible for the middle third of the field, aligning approximately 12 to 14 yards deep (however, the cover-3 safety's depth can vary greatly from team to team).

The cover-3 cornerbacks play deep-zone coverage, aligning approximately 10 to 12 yards deep (this depth can also vary greatly from team to team). They normally align head-up to outside of the widest receiver to their side. The cornerbacks will probably be in more of a straight-legged, squared-up stance. Unlike the man-coverage technique of looking or staring at the receiver they are aligned on, the cover-3 cornerbacks will normally look through their wide receiver to the inside in an effort to "peek in" toward the quarterback. Such "peek-in" action helps the cornerbacks to study the quarterback's eye focus on a pass pattern, helping to produce read keys for the cornerbacks as pass defenders.

A strong safety aligns to the field as the flat-pass-coverage defender and the coverage's perimeter-run-support defender. As a result, the front normally supplies a flat-zone-coverage defender to the weakside, away from the field strong safety. Diagram 2-1 shows cover-3 three-deep, four-under zone coverage.

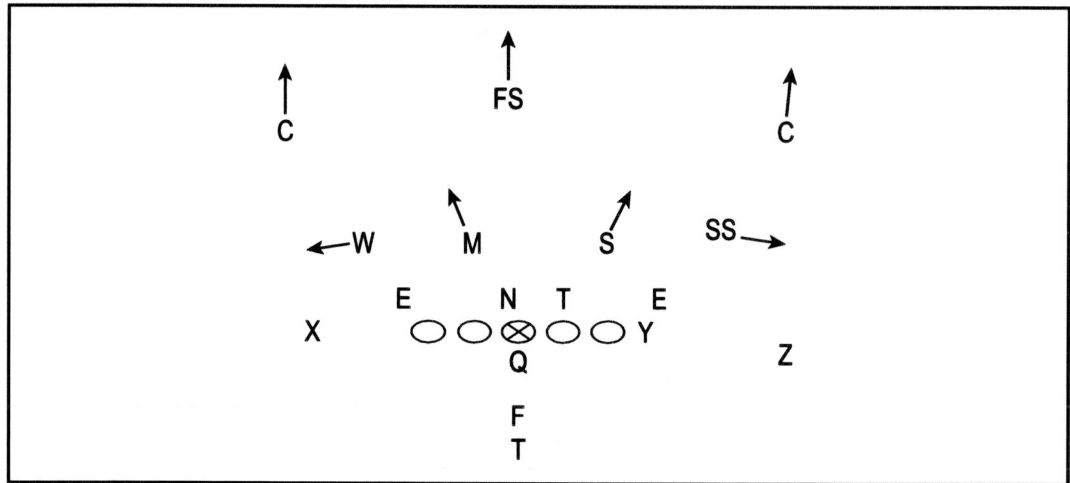

Diagram 2-1. Cover-3 three-deep, four-under zone coverage

Cover-3 Pass-Game Strengths

- Cover 3, with its three-deep, four-under zone coverage, is a balanced coverage. By design, one-and-a-half deep-zone defensive backs are assigned to each side of the field and two underneath-zone defenders are assigned to each side of the field.
- The three deep-zone defenders (the two cornerbacks and the middle safety) are considered the strength of the coverage, providing strong deep-pass coverage. The play of the three deep defenders is focused on staying as deep as the deepest receivers to prevent deep-pass completions. The deep-coverage emphasis is very much designed to force shorter, underneath throwing by an offense. In essence, cover 3 is designed to force passing offenses to patiently attack with the short, underneath throw game, something many pass-oriented teams are unwilling—or unable—to do.
- With the emphasis of the cover-3 cornerbacks staying as wide as (or wider than) the widest receivers, cover 3 does a good job of containing—or boxing in—pass completions to the inside, helping to prevent big gains.
- The four underneath-zone defenders (normally three linebackers and the strong safety) provide strong inside-out underneath-zone coverage. Many cover-3 teams feel that they are doing a good job of bunching up their under coverage to clog up middle routes and route combinations with their four underneath-coverage defenders.
- Depending on the technique utilized by the underneath-zone-coverage linebackers, the linebackers can run vertically with inside-receiver vertical-release routes. Doing so can force possible floating throws to such receivers, making such passes vulnerable to interceptions by the deep-middle-zone cover-3 free safety.

- Cover 3 is an excellent disguise coverage from which to stem to other coverages—especially cover 1 (man-free coverage). Cover 3 can also roll over to the frontside or backside to produce coverages in the two-safeties family.
- Substitution of an extra defensive back (strong-safety-type defender) for the weakside outside linebacker fits well for nickel-type pass coverage in the cover-3 scheme.

Cover-3 Pass-Game Weaknesses

The most basic pass-game weaknesses of cover 3 are the (initially) uncovered flat zones and the deep seams between the cornerbacks and the safety. Such cover-3 voids are shown in Diagram 2-2.

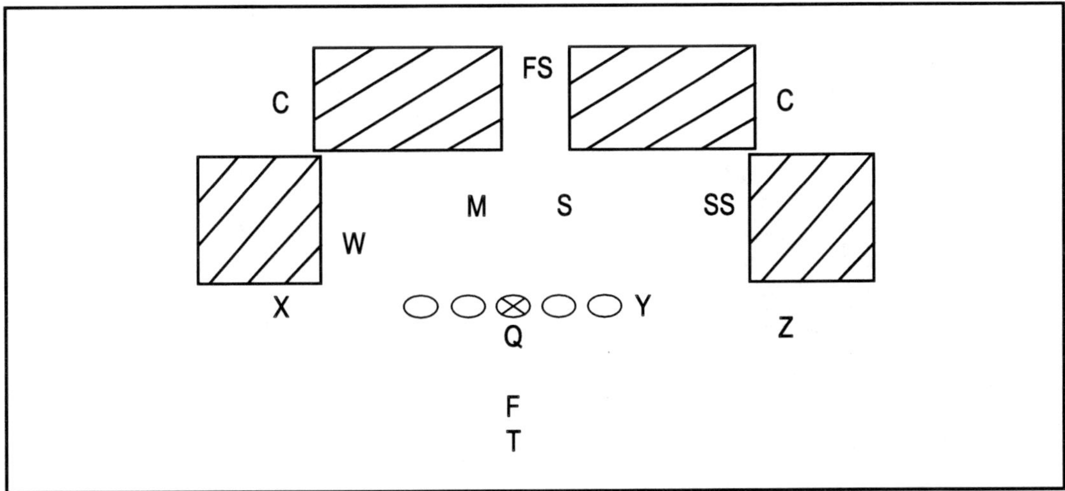

Diagram 2-2. Cover-3 voids

- Most pass attacks will focus on throwing in the short, underneath zones versus cover 3. The basic thinking is that cover 3 exposes itself to flat-zone throwing or opens itself up to inside routes and route combinations when the coverage works hard to cover the flats.
- Cover 3 gets most hurt by teams who are willing to patiently attack the coverage underneath when only four underneath defenders are covering the horizontal width of the field. Short, quick, underneath pass routes and pass-route combinations can effectively lead to sound, control-type passing that can successfully help "move the chains."
- Cover 3 is extremely susceptible to quick-game passing—especially in the flats (i.e., hitch and quick speed-out routes). The strong safety and weakside outside linebacker simply have a tough time covering such quickly-thrown outside-flat-area routes.

- Out-type routes also help to expose the vacated cover-3 flat-zone areas. Just as in quick-game passing, the strong safety and weakside outside linebacker have a tough time covering quickly-thrown outside flat routes.
- Cover 3 is especially vulnerable to side-by-side, lateral-read-route combinations, which are a big part of many offensive pass designs. Diagram 2-3 shows how the route combinations of a side-by-side lateral-read flanker (Z) rollaway and a tight-end (Y) alley route, and a split-end (X) curl and back flat can effectively attack cover-3 underneath coverage.
- Due to the heavy emphasis of the cover-3 strong safety and weakside outside linebacker in flying out hard to cover the flats, inside two-on-one and three-on-two

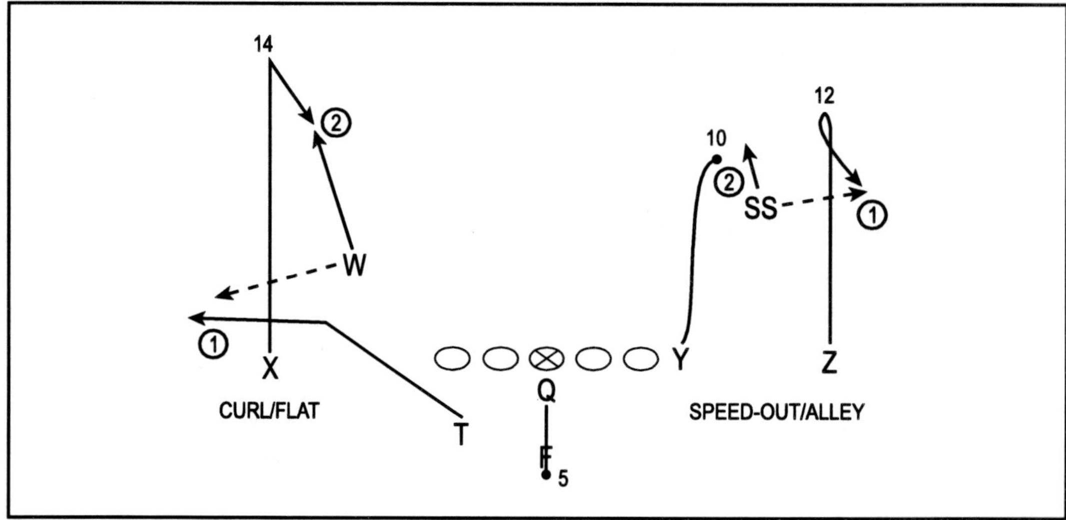

Diagram 2-3. Side-by-side lateral-read-route combinations versus cover 3

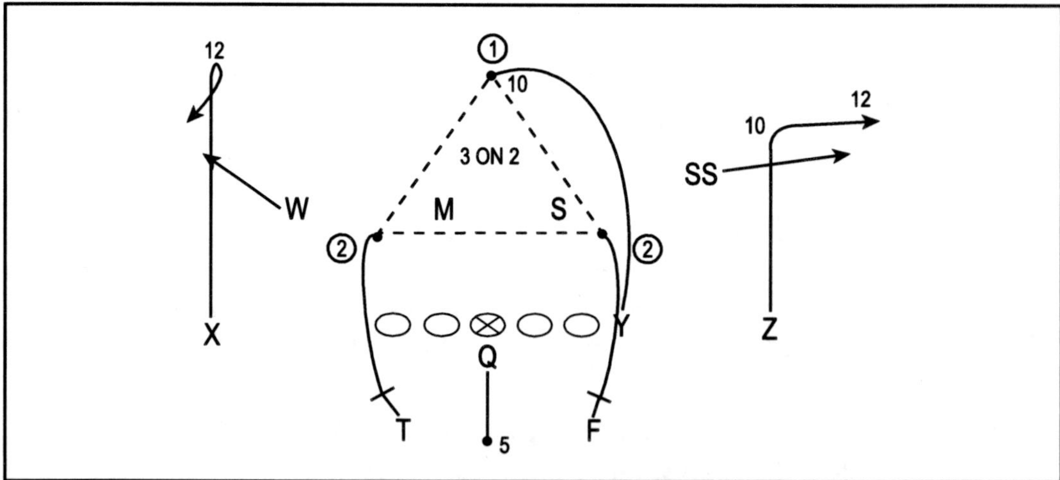

Diagram 2-4. Three-on-two isolation on two cover-3 inside linebackers

route isolations versus the weak and strong inside linebackers help to create excellent isolations in favor of the offense. Such a favorable three-on-two isolation on the two cover-3 inside linebackers is shown in Diagram 2-4.

- Deep intermediate holes can be produced in cover 3 to open up effective deep intermediate throws (such as comeback-outs and dig routes) by pushing the three-deep scheme vertically with streak-route threats and/or post/clear-out-type routes.
- Cover 3 can be exploited in the voids between the cornerbacks and the deep middle (or free) safety with the four-streak concepts. Two streaks occupy the outside cornerbacks, helping to create a two-on-one inside streak isolation on the middle (free) safety.
- Two-on-one high-low reads can be effectively executed on the cover-3 inside linebackers. A post or clear-out-type route helps to occupy the middle (free) safety and prevent him from interfering with the (high) dig route. Play-action helps to hold the isolated linebacker and open the desired throw to the dig route. Such a two-on-one high-low isolation on a cover-3 inside linebacker with play-action is shown in Diagram 2-5.

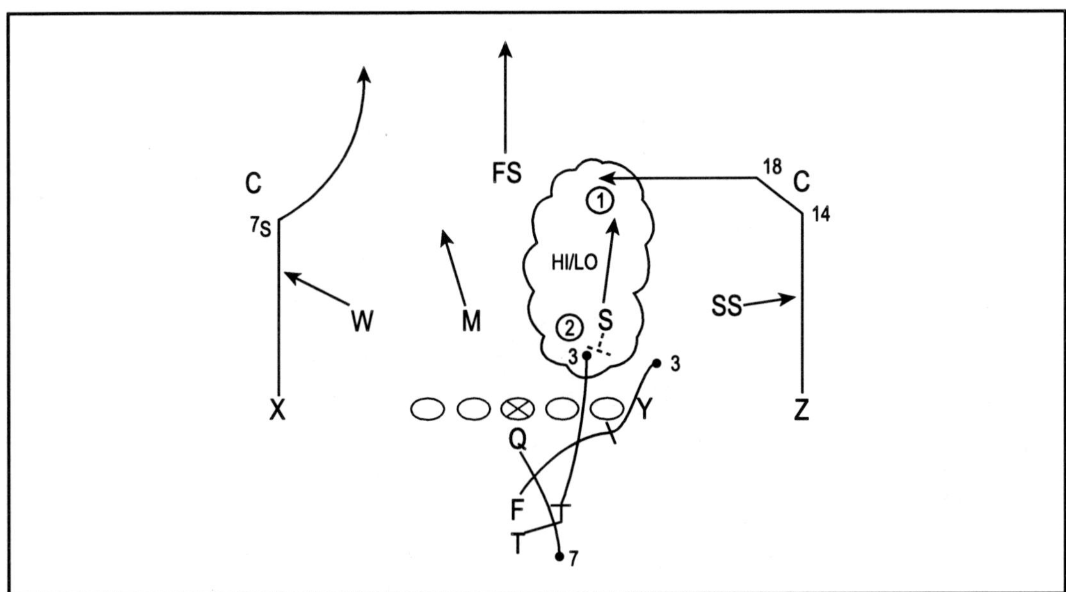

Diagram 2-5. Two-on-one high-low isolation on cover-3 inside linebacker

- One-on-one option-route isolations—such as a tight-end (Y) option route—can be very effective versus the two cover-3 inside linebackers, since the cover-3 strong safety and weakside outside linebacker are often forced to work out to the flats so heavily.
- Naked action can be very effective versus cover 3. The misdirection action can help the offense to outflank the cover-3 underneath coverage with flat routes and

comeback-out routes, while creating an excellent crossing naked-route isolation, as shown in Diagram 2-6.

- Screens of all types can be very effective versus cover 3. Formationing can help spread out the cover-3 underneath coverage to make such screens especially effective.

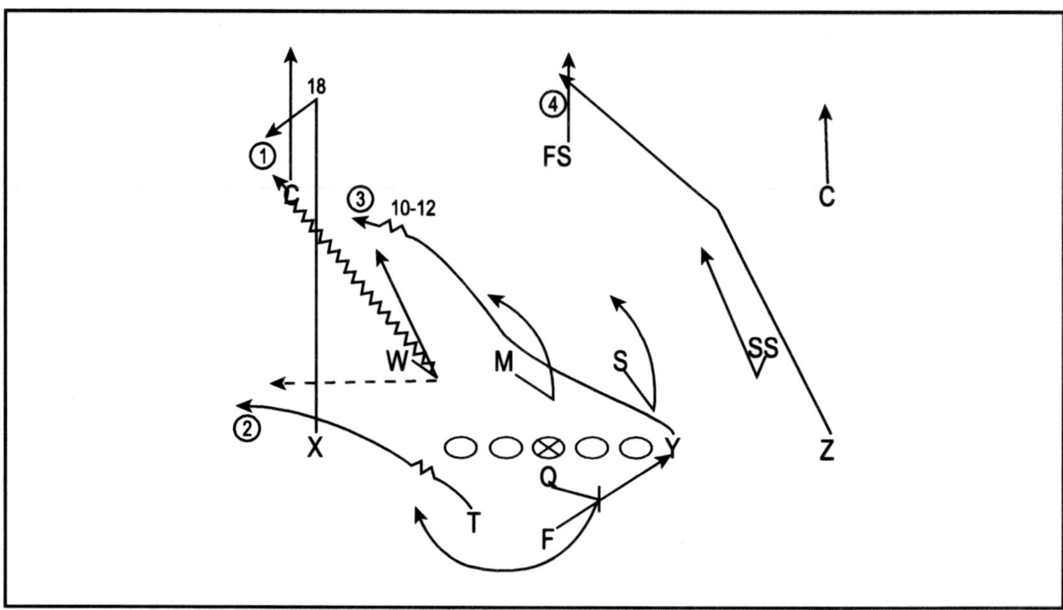

Diagram 2-6. Misdirection naked action versus cover 3

Route Combination and Pass-Pattern Attack of Cover 3

Quick-Game Hitch

The quick-game (three-step-drop-timed throw by the quarterback) hitch route is an excellent route concept versus cover 3. The hitch route helps to exploit the cover-3 flat-zone-coverage void. Diagram 2-7 shows hitch action versus cover 3 to both sides of the formation, allowing the quarterback to make a pre-read decision as to which side of the formation has the best hitch isolation throw opening

Quick-Game Double Hitch with Lateral Read

The quick-game double-hitch-route combination is an excellent concept versus cover 3—strong or weak. The two-on-one, side-by-side, lateral-read concept helps to isolate the strong safety or the weakside outside linebacker, forcing the defenders to cover either the inside or outside hitch route. The quick-game double-hitch-route concept with lateral-read action is shown in Diagram 2-8.

Quick-Game Speed-Out

The quick-game speed-out route is an excellent route concept versus cover 3. Just like the hitch route, the speed-out route helps to exploit the cover-3 flat-zone-coverage void, as shown in Diagram 2-9. The diagram also shows double-quick speed-out-route action to the strongside of the formation to produce effective double-quick speed-out, side-by-side, lateral-read action.

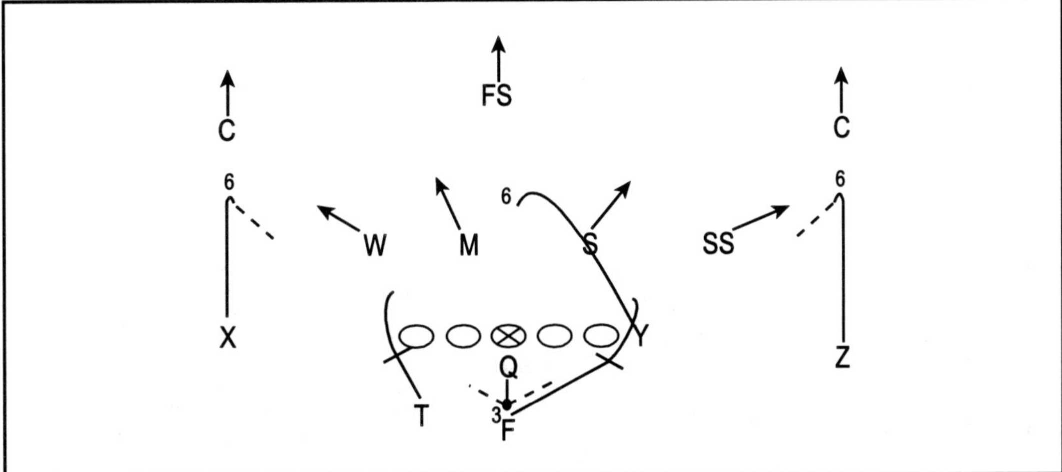

Diagram 2-7. Quick-game hitch action versus cover 3

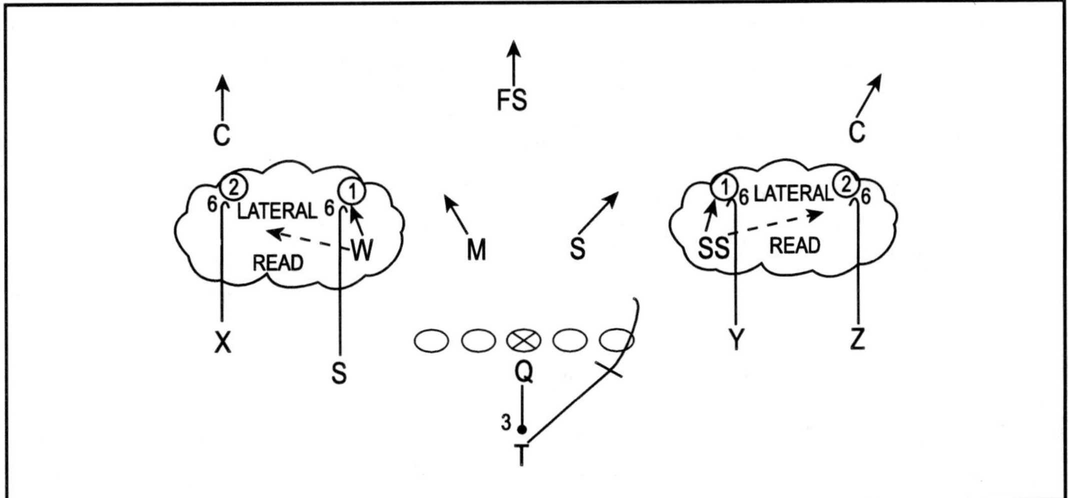

Diagram 2-8. Quick-game double-hitch action with lateral read versus cover 3

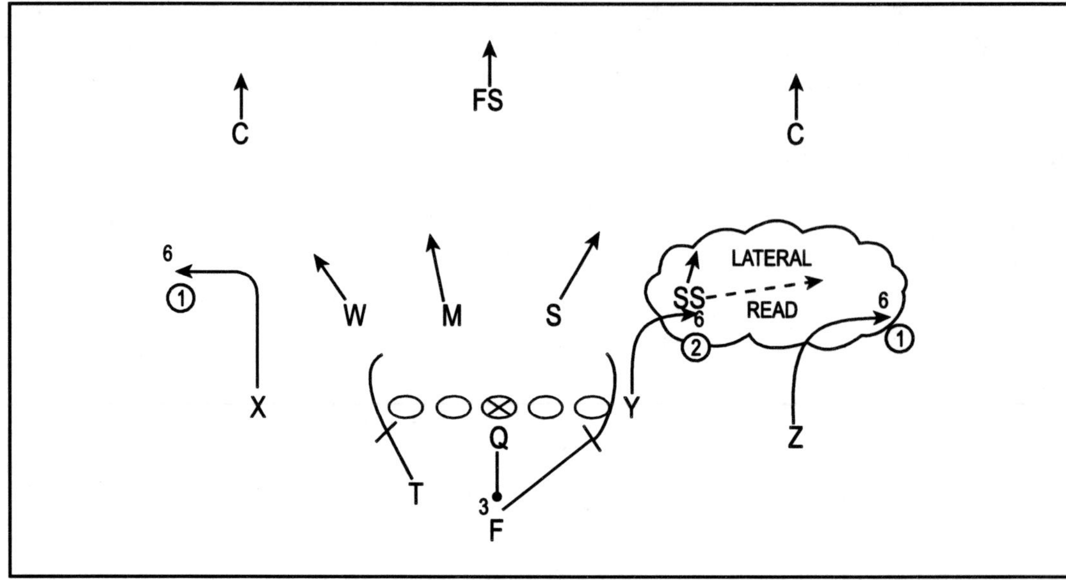

Diagram 2-9. Quick-game speed-out versus cover 3

Quick-Game Slant/Arrow Lateral Read

The quick-game slant/arrow lateral-read-route combination is an excellent concept to utilize versus cover 3. The arrow route is a special route to help accommodate a slant route in the side-by-side, lateral-read concept. The arrow route is a route run directly out to the sideline without any normal up-the-field flat-route buildup in an effort to influence the strong safety or the weakside outside linebacker to work quickly to the flat to open up the slant throw. Tell the quarterback to throw the arrow route until he can't. Doing so can help influence the strong safety or weak outside linebacker to drive on the arrow route as those defenders see the quarterback staring down the arrow route. The slant/arrow lateral-read-route concept versus cover 3 is shown in Diagram 2-10.

Quick-Game Inside-Receiver Stick-Route Isolation

The quick-game inside-receiver stick-route isolation can be a very effective concept versus cover 3. The flat route of the back can help to stretch the coverage of the cover-3 strong safety to help open up the tight-end (Y) stick-route isolation, as shown in Diagram 2-11.

Quick-Game Double-Move Route Isolations

Double-move action off of quick-game pass routes is an excellent way to attack cover-3 cornerbacks who try to jump the quick-game prime routes. Double-move route isolations off of the hitch and quick speed-out routes to produce hitch-and-go and quick speed-out-and-up routes are shown in Diagram 2-12.

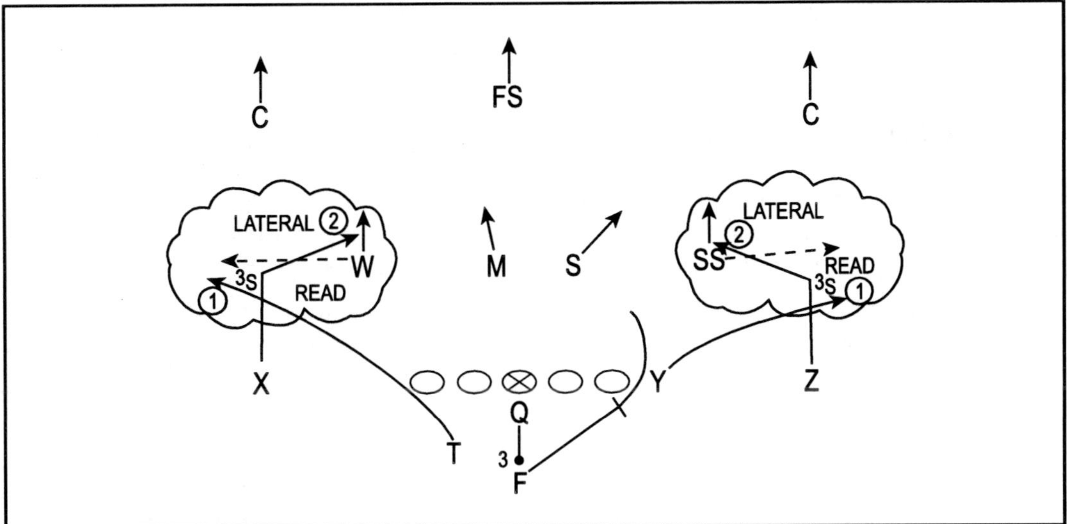

Diagram 2-10. Quick-game slant/arrow lateral-read-route combination versus cover 3

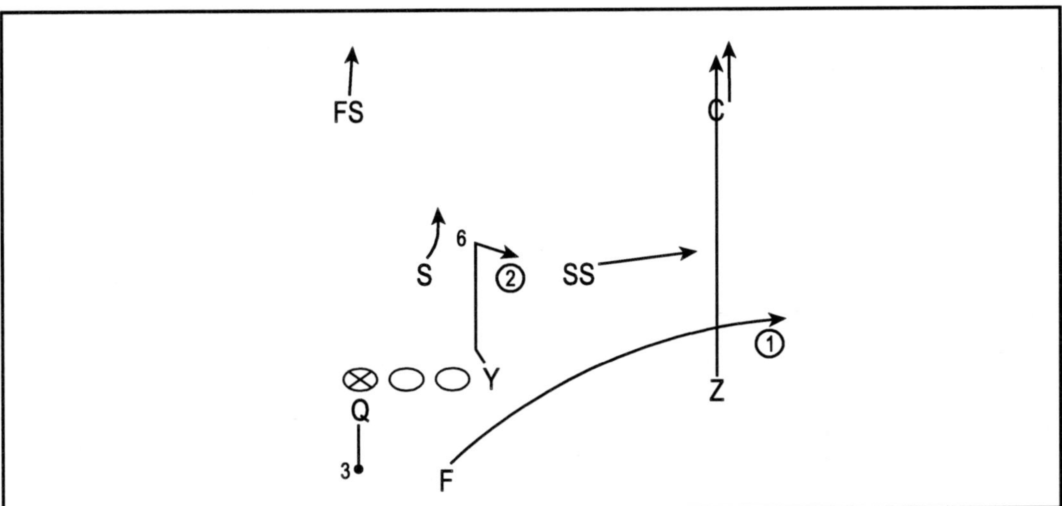

Diagram 2-11. Quick-game inside-receiver stick-route isolation versus cover 3

Speed-Out/Rollaway Lateral-Read Combinations

The five-step-quarterback-drop-timed speed-out and rollaway lateral-read-route combinations are excellent ways to attack cover 3. Both the prime-route speed-out and rollaway routes effectively attack the cover-3 flat-zone-coverage voids. As shown in Diagram 2-13, the tight-end (Y) alley route helps to create a true lateral read on the strong safety, while the back's seam route helps to hold the weakside linebacker from getting out to the rollaway route. The rollaway route is an excellent concept to use when the ball is on the hash into the boundary where the speed-out may not have enough room to operate. Diagram 2-14 shows a similar lateral-read concept with deeper, seven-step-quarterback-drop-timed comeback-out and deep rollaway routes.

Acute/Rollaway/Speed-Out Isolations with Middle-Read Action

Acute (short 10- to 12-yard comeback-out routes), rollaways, and speed-out routes work very well with an inside-receiver, middle-read-route concept versus cover 3. The middle-read route has the option of breaking into an open deep middle (i.e., cover 2), or the middle-read receiver breaks his middle-read route off into a short square-in-type dig route versus a coverage where a safety is in the middle of the field (such as cover

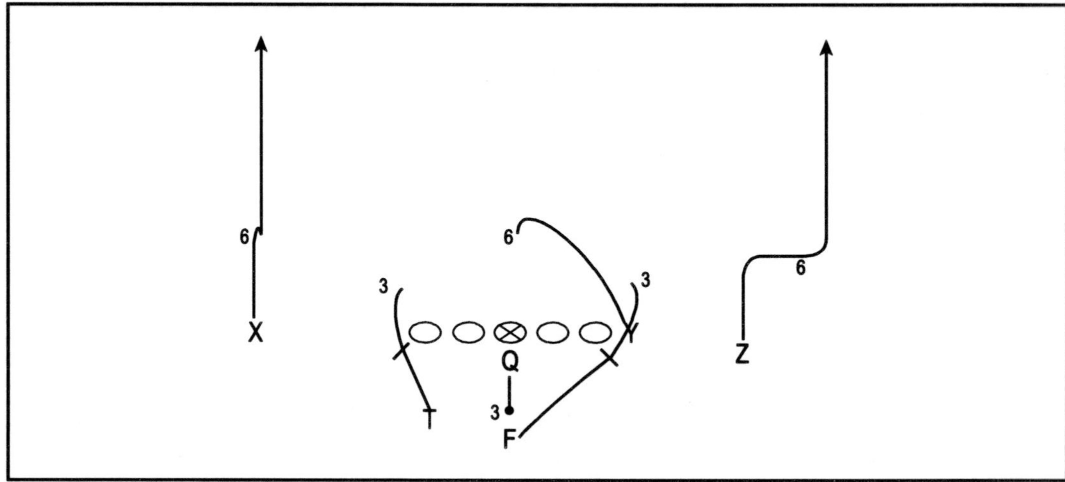

Diagram 2-12. Quick-game double-move routes versus cover 3

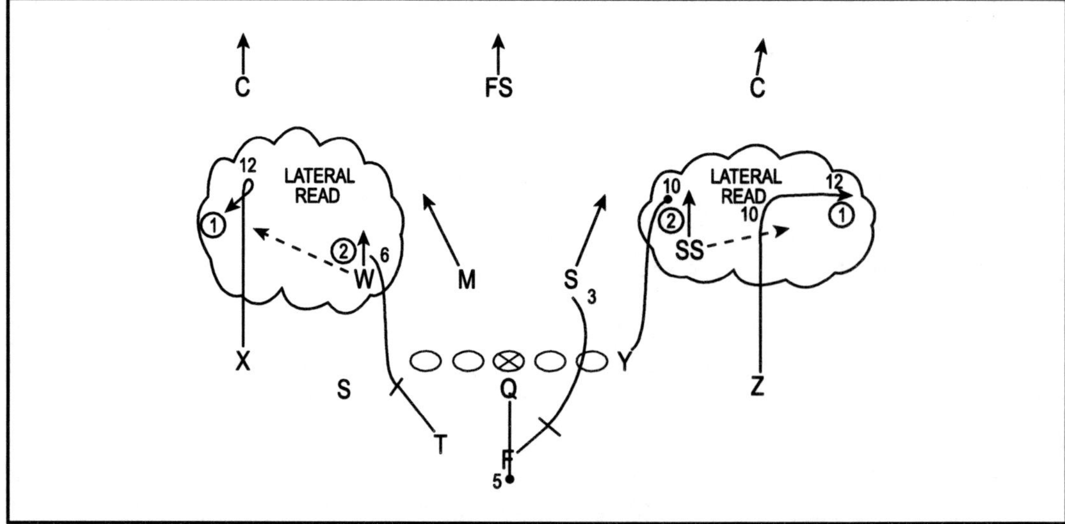

Diagram 2-13. Speed-out and rollaway lateral-read concepts versus cover 3

3). If the middle-read-route receiver sees "no-one deep" in front of him, he, simply, keeps on going deep. Versus deep-middle coverage, the outside acute, rollaway, or speed-out routes become the prime routes for the quarterback. The underneath back sit routes and the tight-end (Y) break-off route action on the tight end's middle-read route become the late-outlet routes, as shown in Diagram 2-15. Diagram 2-16 shows how the middle-read concept can be used with seven-step-quarterback-drop-timed comeback-out and deep-rollaway routes.

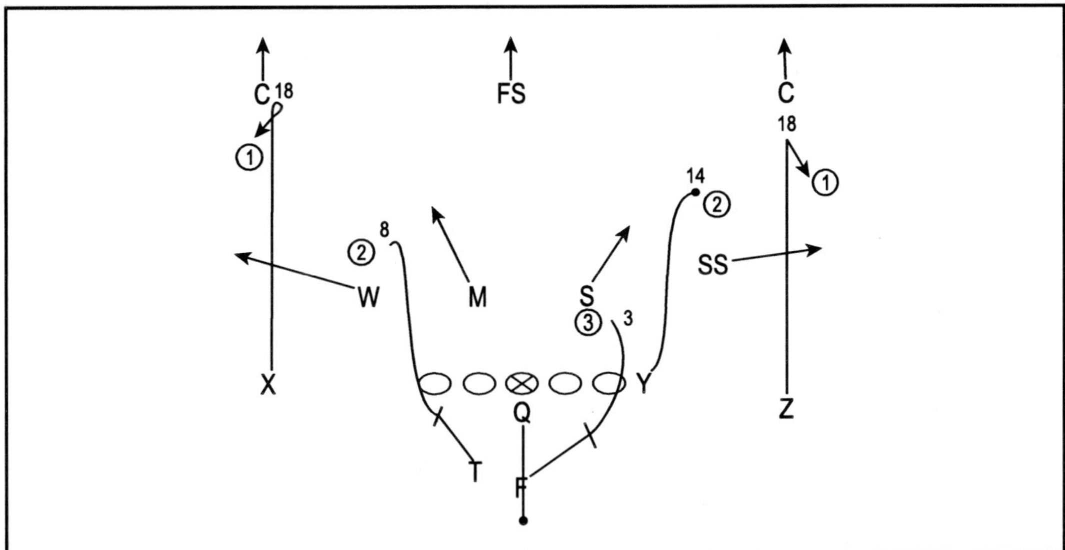

Diagram 2-14. Comeback-out and deep rollaway lateral-read concepts versus cover 3

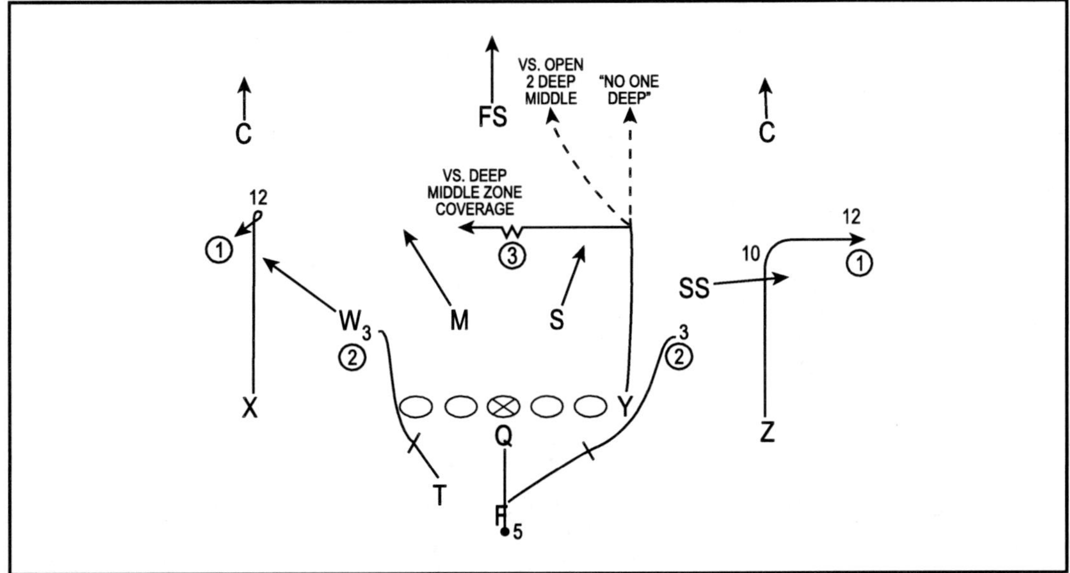

Diagram 2-15. Acute/rollaway/speed-out routes with middle-read route versus cover 3

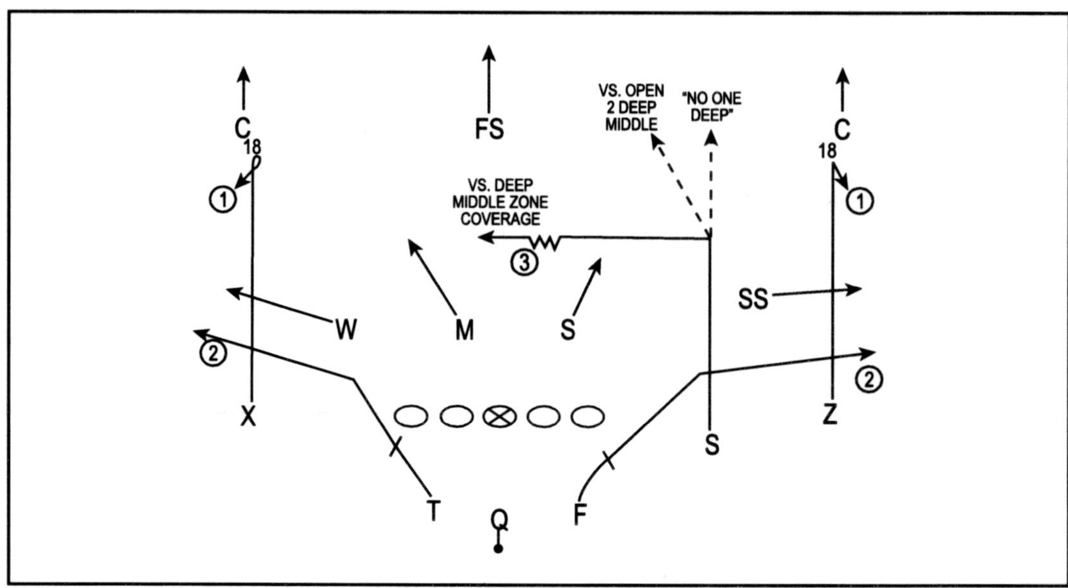

Diagram 2-16. Comeback-out and deep-rollaway routes with middle-read route versus cover 3

Comeback-Out Play-Action Pass

The comeback-out to the split end (X) in a pro-set formation with play-action faking is a very popular method of attacking cover 3. The route combination actually becomes a high-low read in relation to the action of the weakside outside linebacker as he covers the tight-end (Y) cross route or the split-end (X) comeback-out route, as shown in Diagram 2-17.

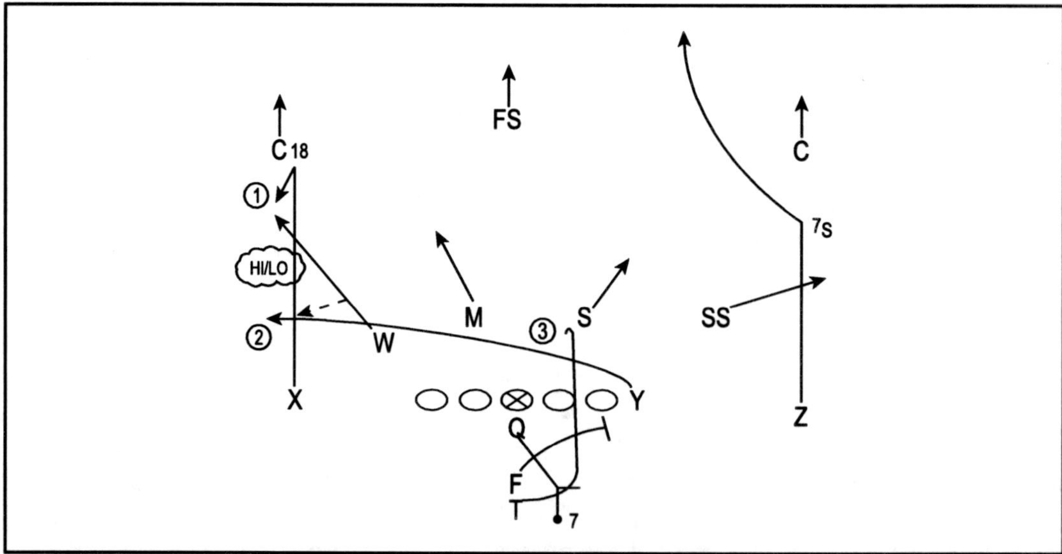

Diagram 2-17. Split-end (X) comeback-out isolation with play-action versus cover 3

Curl (or Hook)/Flat Lateral-Read Concept

The curl/flat (or deeper hook/flat) lateral-read concept is an excellent way to attack the lack of underneath coverage of cover 3. To the weakside, the lateral-read action isolates on the weakside outside linebacker, as shown by the split-end (X) curl route and the back's flat route in Diagram 2-18. To the strongside, the lateral-read action isolates on the strong safety, as shown by the flanker (Z) hook route and the tight-end (Y) flat route. The only difference between the curl and hook routes are the depths of the routes and the need for seven-step-timed drop action by the quarterback for the deeper hook route. Diagram 2-19 shows the use of curl (or deeper hook)/flat lateral-read action with middle-read thinking by an inside receiver.

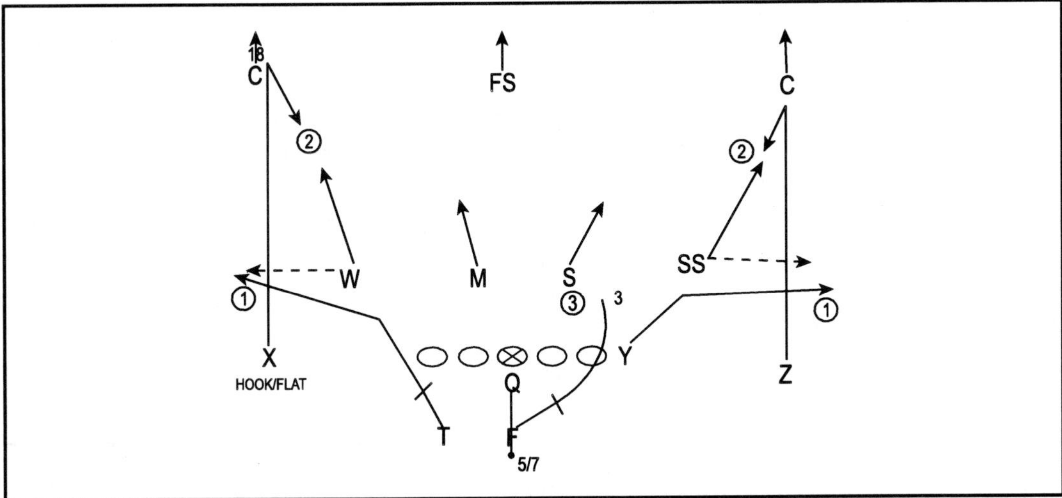

Diagram 2-18. Curl/flat or hook/flat lateral-read concept versus cover 3

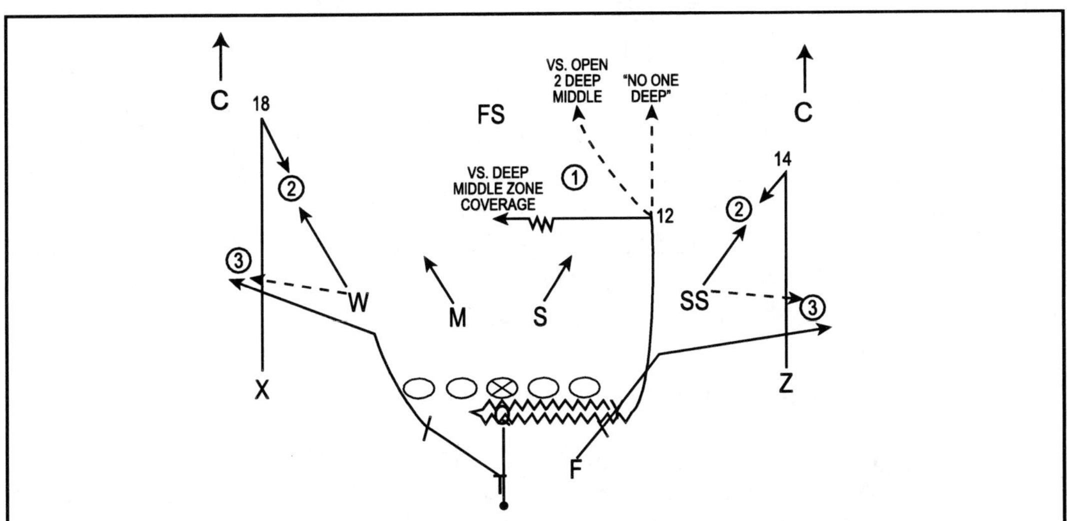

Diagram 2-19. Curl/flat or hook/flat lateral-read concept with middle read versus cover 3

Double Square-In Concept

Double square-in action is an excellent concept versus cover 3. The pattern concept helps to isolate the three receivers to the strongside on the two strongside underneath-coverage defenders (the strong safety and the strongside inside linebacker). The quarterback simply scans inside-out from the tight-end (Y) short square-in to the flanker (Z) square-in to the back's flat route, as shown in Diagram 2-20.

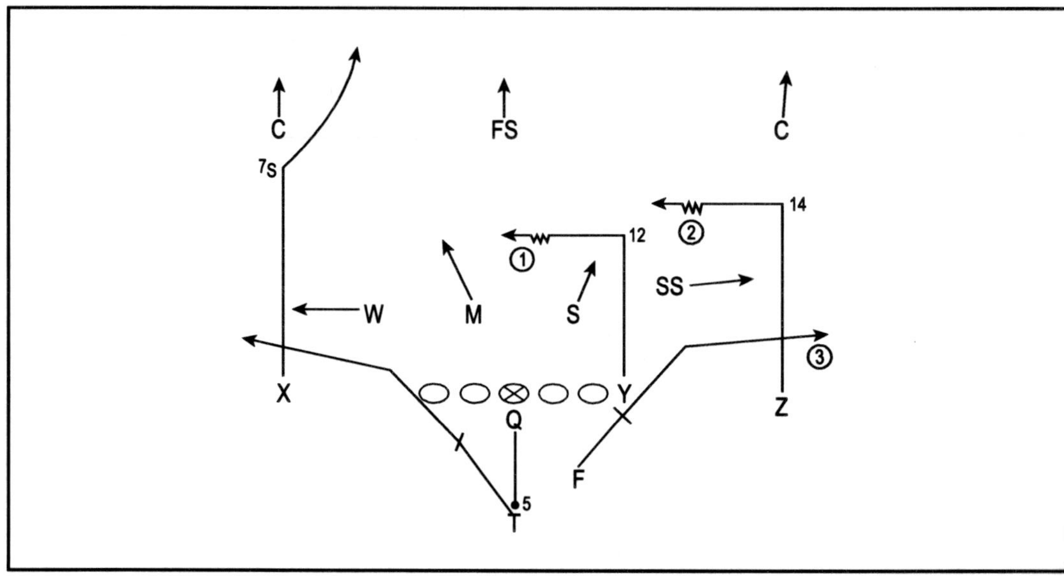

Diagram 2-20. Double square-in action versus cover 3

Speed-Out, Rollaway, Curl Double-Move-Route Concepts

As has been shown, speed-outs, rollaways, and curl routes are excellent ways to attack cover 3. Quite often, a cover-3 cornerback will try to jump such wide-receiver routes. As a result, double-move-route concepts can be very effective to create "home-run" deep-ball threats to combat aggressive cornerback play on such five-step-timed quarterback drop actions. Diagram 2-21 shows a rollaway- (fake-) and-go double-move action by the split end (X), and speed-out-and-up double-move action by the flanker (Z). Diagram 2-22 shows a curl-and-go double-move action by the split end (X), and a flat-and-up double-move action by the tight end (Y).

Deep-Hook/Flat-Route Combinations as Outlets

The deep-hook/flat-route outlet combination can be a very effective side-by-side, lateral-read concept in attacking cover 3, as shown in Diagram 2-23. Deep, longer-developing hook routes that push the cover-3 cornerbacks vertically can find excellent cover-3 void pockets to work into to effectively act as late outlets. Diagram 2-23 shows the quarterback reading the flanker (Z) curl/flat prime-route-read combination and scans back to the hook/flat outlet-route combination (reading the hook route first and the flat route second). The timing of the pattern is coordinated with the five-step timing of the prime-route curl/flat read and the backside seven-step timing of the hook/flat-route outlet combination.

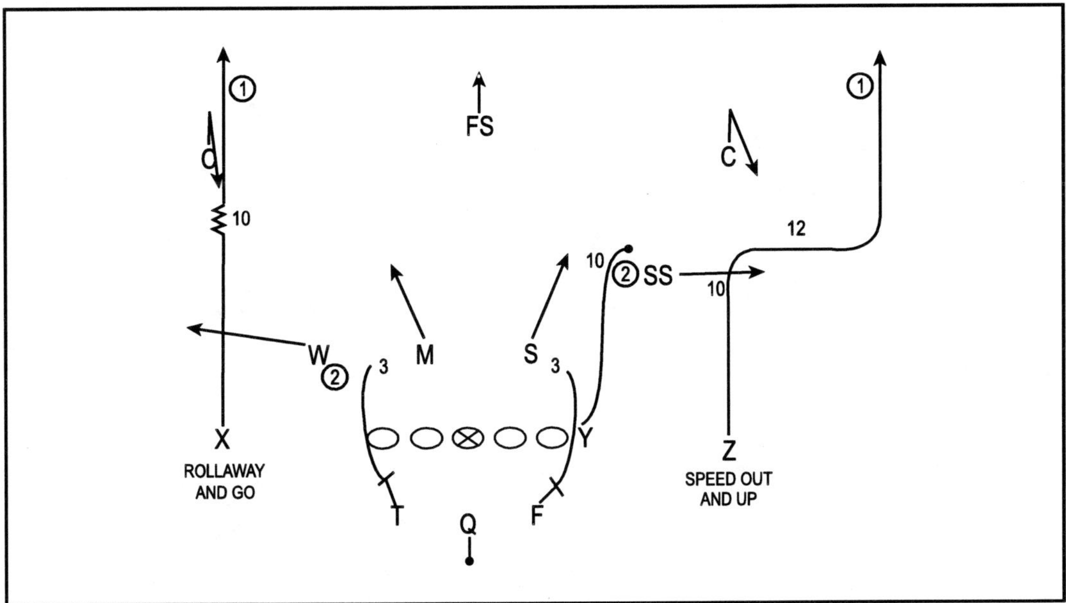

Diagram 2-21. Rollaway-and-go/speed-out-and-up double-move concepts versus cover 3

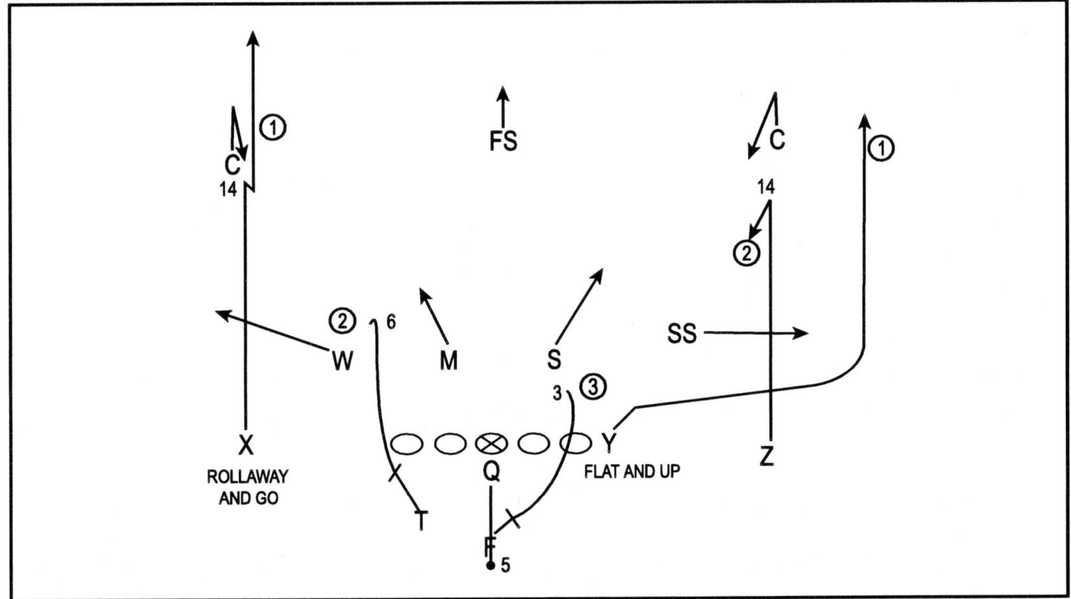

Diagram 2-22. Curl-and-go/flat-and-up double-move concepts versus cover 3

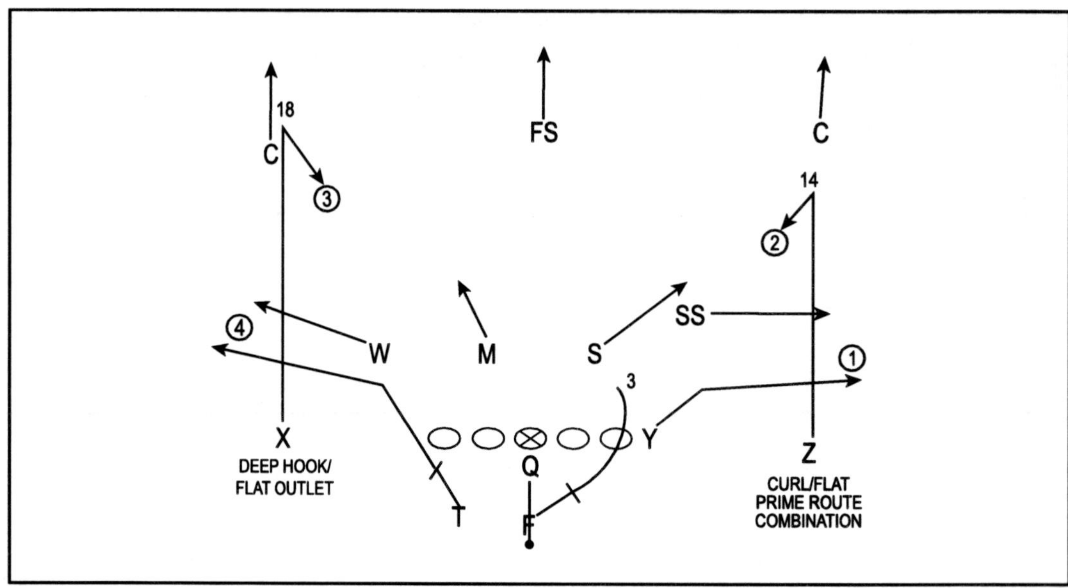

Diagram 2-23. Deep hook/flat outlet action versus cover 3

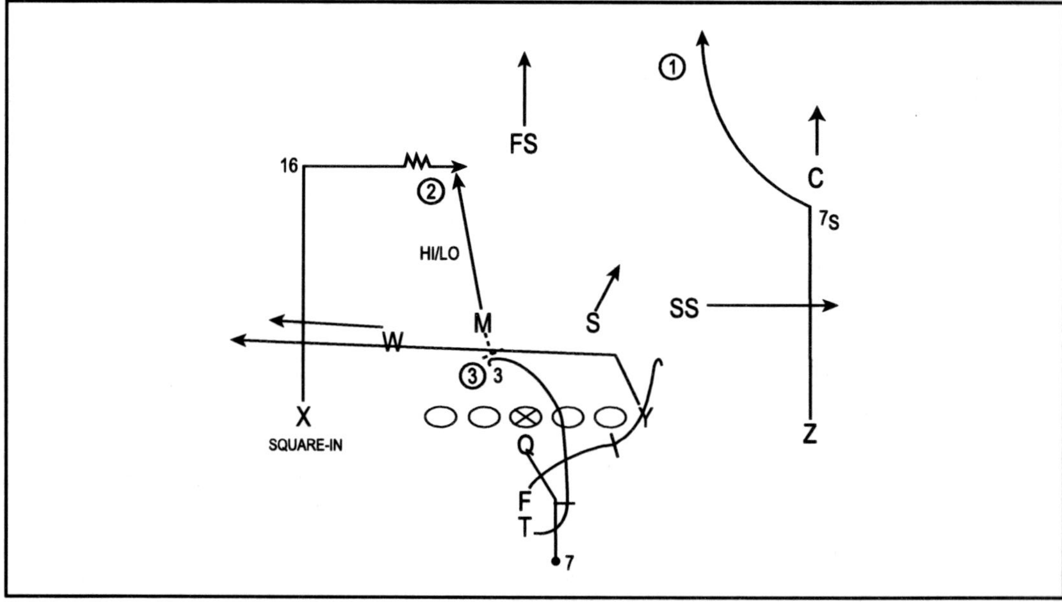

Diagram 2-24. Three-tiered dig/square-in concept versus cover 3

Three-Tiered Dig/Square-In High-Low Isolation

The three-tiered dig/square-in high-low-isolation concept presents an excellent high-to-low read action for the quarterback versus cover 3. As shown in Diagram 2-24 from a sprint-draw play-action fake, the flanker receiver (Z) runs a deep skinny-post clear-out route through the middle (free) safety to prevent that defender from being able to jump the dig (or square-in) route. The split end (X) runs a dig to produce a high-low read for the quarterback on the playside inside linebacker in combination with the tailback's sit route. If the quarterback has time, he should check the skinny post for a big play potential pass.

Four-Streaks Concept

The four-streaks concept is an extremely effective way of attacking cover 3 deep in the seams between the cornerbacks and the free safety. True four-streak action will definitely occupy the outside cornerbacks via the wide receivers' streak routes to help produce the inside two-on-one streak isolation on the middle (free) safety. However, the outside receivers may be better off running deep rollaway routes or comeback-out routes as outlets if the cornerbacks are aligned deeply, as shown by the dotted lines of the outside-wide-receiver streaks in Diagram 2-25. The deep rollaways or comeback-out routes do, however, still come off of the deep-streak threats.

If the two-on-one, inside-streak-read isolation does not look good, the quarterback can dump the ball off to the back, or the quarterback could go to the outside to the outlet deep rollaways or comeback-outs if they are being utilized instead of outside-streak routes.

Under Concept

The under concept is a decent concept versus cover 3. Often, the lack of cover-3 flat coverage has the under route turn into a hitch route, as the under route stays out wide in the coverage void rather than unnecessarily working to the inside to produce a high-

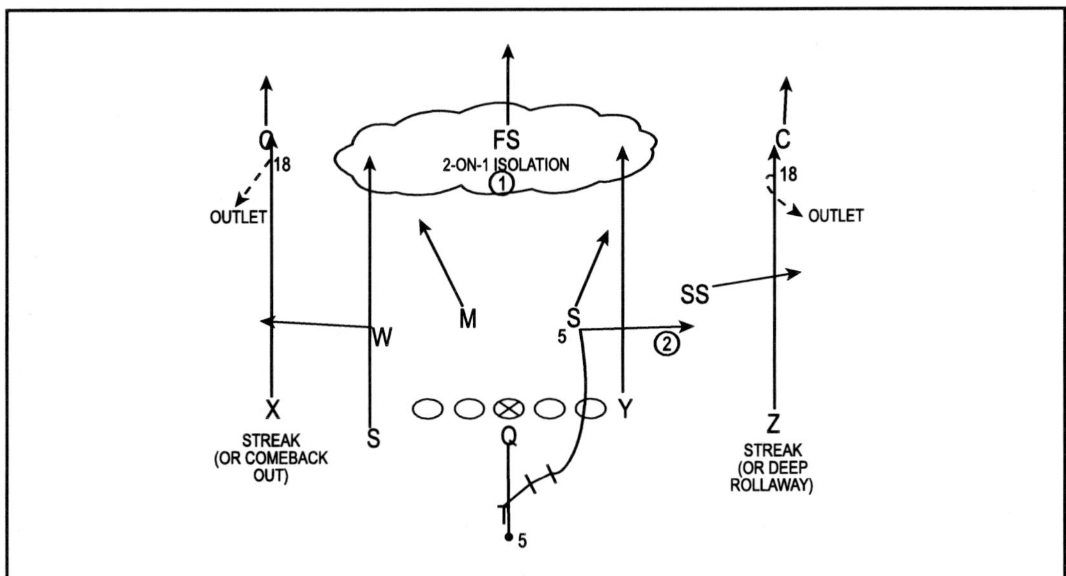

Diagram 2-25. Four-streaks concept versus cover 3

low read on the inside linebacker. However, the under-route receiver will work inside if the strong safety or weak outside linebacker drives out hard to the flat. The under concept versus cover 3 is shown in Diagram 2-26 from a no-backs set—both weak and strong.

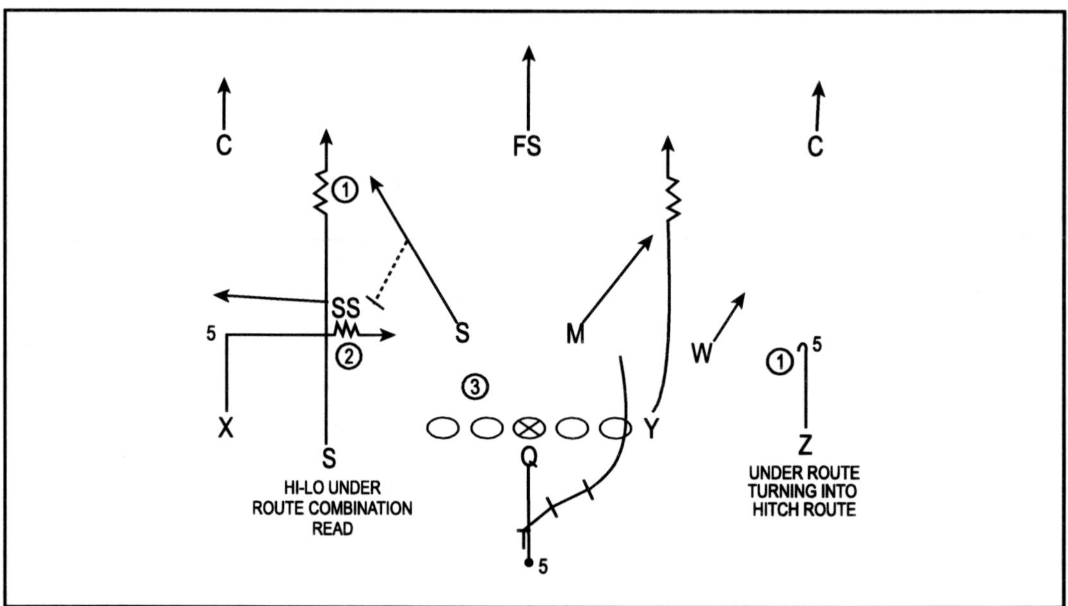

Diagram 2-26. Under concept versus cover 3

Drive Concept

The drive concept helps to create a three-on-two flood isolation on the two inside cover-3 linebackers. The drive-route wide receiver, the tight end, and the back form a triangle-alignment position to help create the three-on-two isolation advantage. The drive concept versus cover 3 is shown in Diagram 2-27.

Cross Concept

Versus cover 3, the cross concept also helps to create a three-on-two flood isolation on the two inside linebackers. The slot receiver, tight end, and back form a triangle-alignment position to help create the three-on-two isolation advantage. The cross concept, from a balanced doubles set with a tight-end cross and a slot short-dig action, is shown in Diagram 2-28.

Texas Concept

The Texas concept helps to create a two-on-one crossing isolation on the cover-3 strongside inside linebacker. The underneath cross route stretches the cover-3 strong safety with an initial flat-route stem and threat. He then breaks underneath and crosses the square-out action of the tight end. If the inside linebacker runs out with the tight end's square-out route, the underneath cross route should be open underneath. If the tight end is able to wall off the inside linebacker, the quarterback can stick a tight throw in to the tight end before the tight end works out wide toward the coverage of the cover-3 strong safety. The Texas concept versus cover 3 is shown in Diagram 2-29.

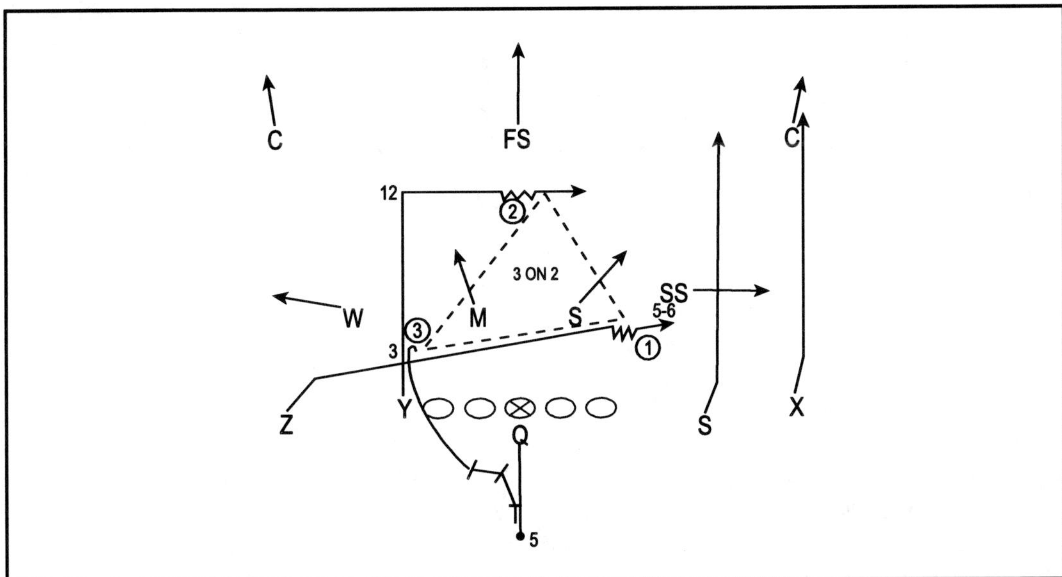

Diagram 2-27. Drive concept versus cover 3

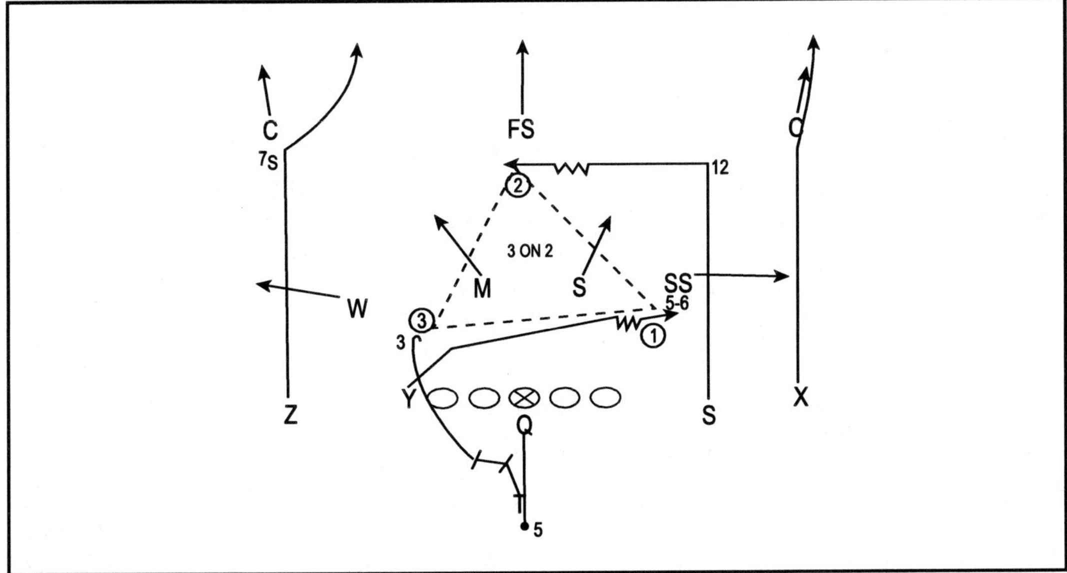

Diagram 2-28. Cross concept versus cover 3

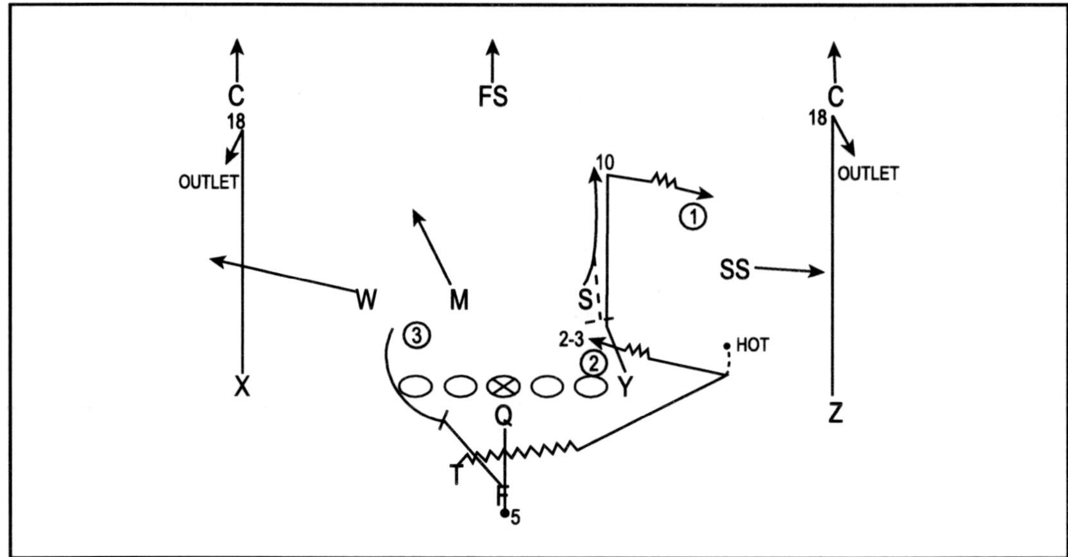

Diagram 2-29. Texas concept versus cover 3

Option-Isolation Concept

Option-isolation routes help to produce excellent one-on-one isolations on cover-3 linebackers. Option routes can help to produce one-on-one size, talent, and speed mismatches. Option routes are best run off of five-step-drop timing by the quarterback. This timing allows for option routes to be run in the 8- to 12-yard range, giving the option-route receivers time to properly maneuver and execute their option-route man- or zone-separation techniques. Diagram 2-30 shows a tight-end (Y) option and a halfback (H) option versus cover 3.

High-Low Delay-Route Isolations

High-low delay-route isolations can be very effective against cover 3. With a vertical read route (with a strong chance of the inside receiver's read route breaking off into a square-in route if the read-route receiver does not read open space in front of him) and a delay route working underneath, the quarterback simply throws off of the two-on-one coverage reaction of the isolated strongside inside linebacker. A high-low-read fullback delay versus cover 3 is shown in Diagram 2-31.

High-Low Pivot and Break Route Isolations

Just like delay-route high-low isolations, tight-end (Y) pivot and break route isolations can be very effective versus cover 3. Since the vertical route is run by a back who takes greater time to work through the line of scrimmage, the back isn't given an inside-break square-in outlet-route option versus deep, middle, free-safety coverage. As a result, the quarterback reads the high-low action of the back's streak route and the Y-pivot or Y-break route off of the reaction of the isolated strong inside linebacker. Of course, if the read is high, the quarterback *must* be aware of the position of the cover-3 free safety. As a result, the quarterback is primarily thinking Y-pivot or Y-break action with the hope that the back's streak route will pull the inside linebacker out of the Y-pivot or Y-break area. The pivot and break routes are run in the six- to seven-yard range. Diagram 2-32 shows both a Y-pivot and high-low-read isolation action to attack cover 3. Diagram 2-33 shows Y-break action versus cover 3.

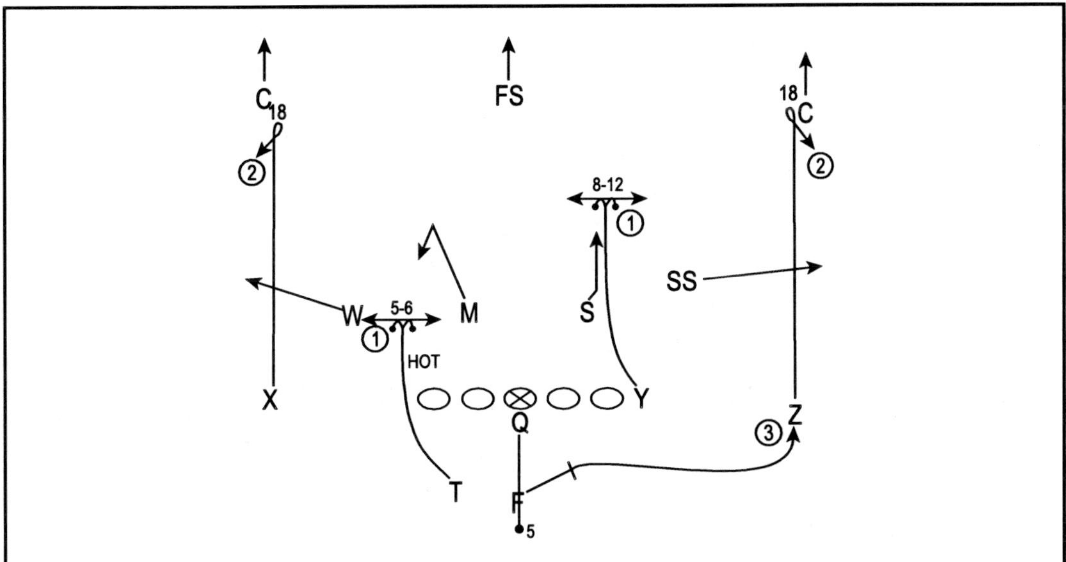

Diagram 2-30. Option isolation routes versus cover 3

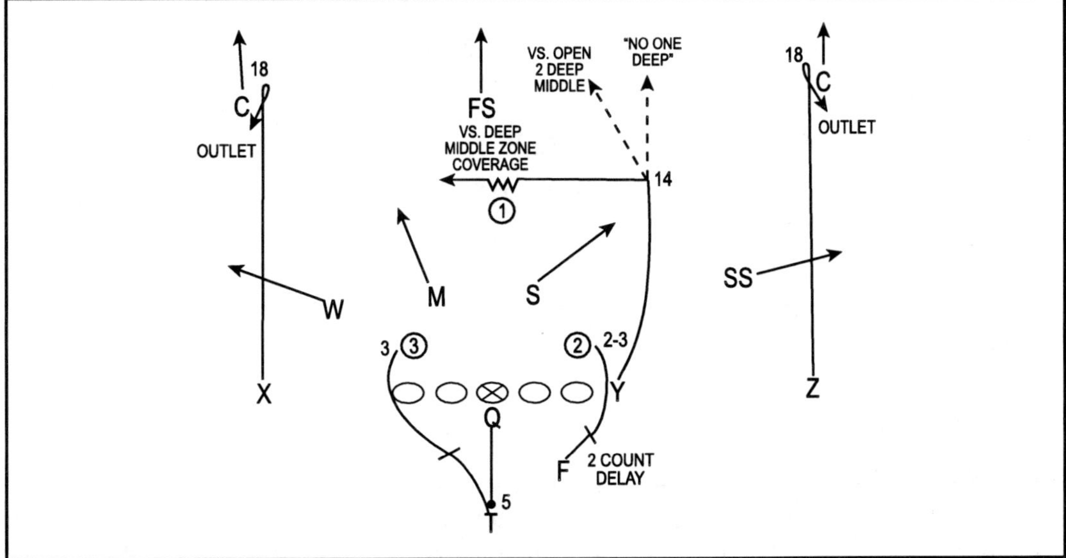

Diagram 2-31. High-low-read fullback-delay route isolation versus cover 3

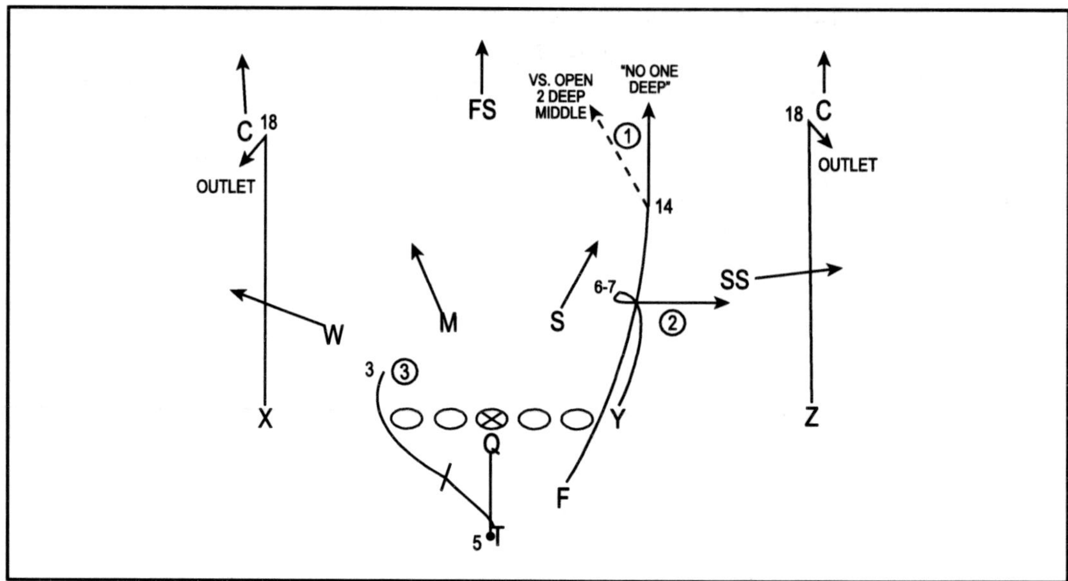

Diagram 2-32. High-low-read Y-pivot isolation versus cover 3

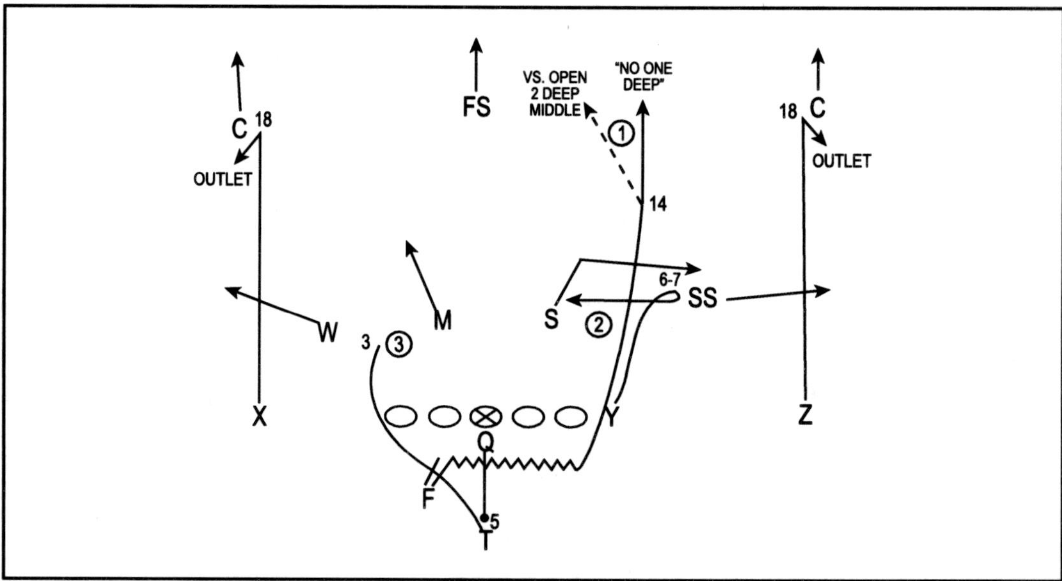

Diagram 2-33. High-low-read Y-break isolation versus cover 3

Post Isolation

Many coaches believe that a highly timed five-step-drop, skinny-post throw is a very effective way to beat cover 3 deep. As a result, many passing offenses will tack on skinny-post routes to the backside of a pattern to give the quarterback a potential "home-run" throw if the middle (free) safety does not honor the coverage of the skinny-post seam. Such backside skinny-post action versus cover 3 is shown in Diagram 2-34 with a frontside speed-out/alley prime-route-read combination.

Double-Post Concept

An excellent quick, post-throw action versus cover 3 is the double-post-isolation concept. The pattern concept is a two-on-one double-post isolation on the middle

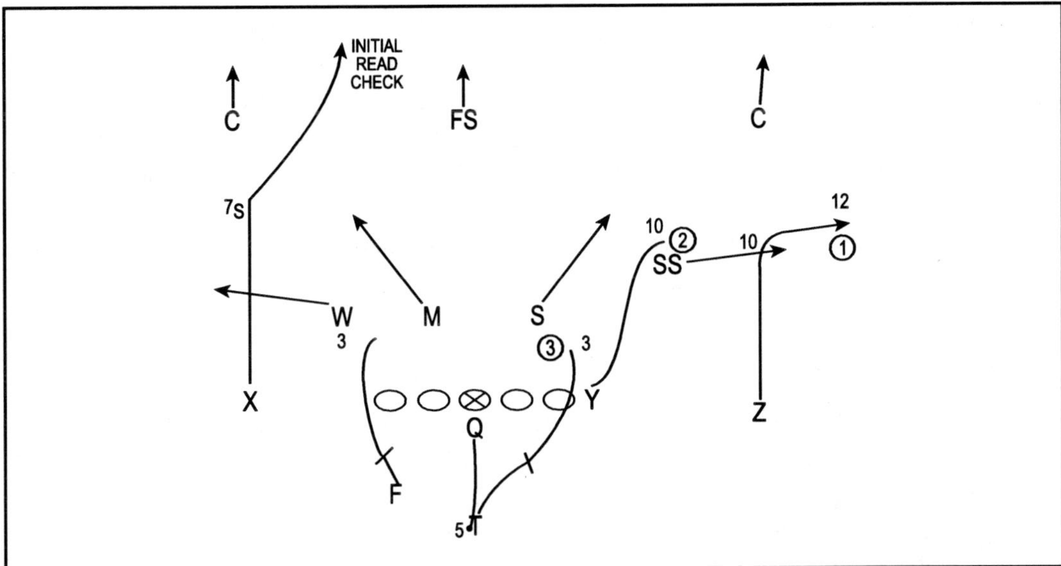

Diagram 2-34. Backside skinny-post-route concept versus cover 3

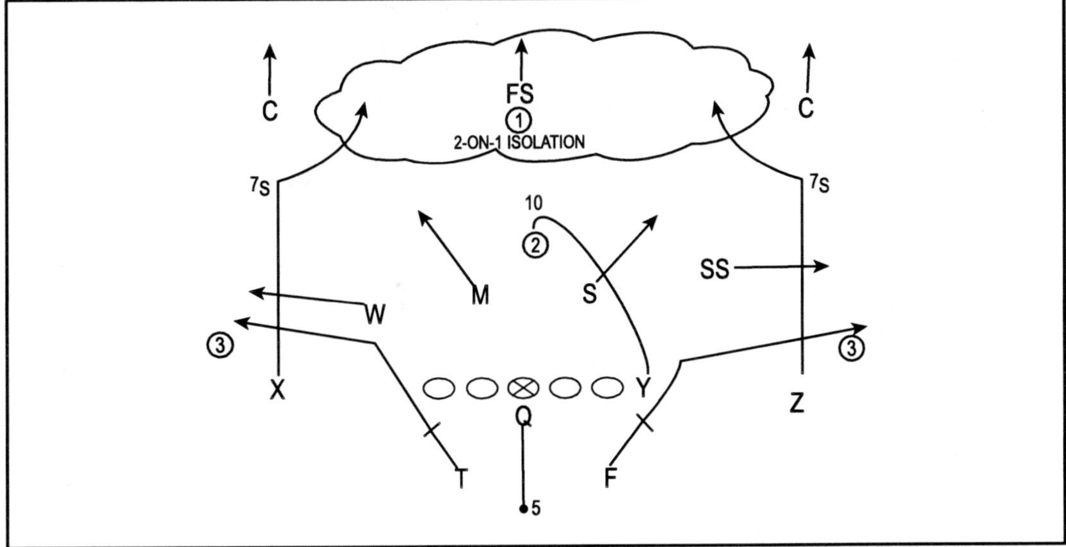

Diagram 2-35. Double-post-isolation concept versus cover 3

(free) safety. Both wide receivers run skinny-post routes in the cornerback/safety seams. The quarterback throws off of the positioning of the middle (free) safety to the most open skinny-post route. The double-post concept is shown versus cover 3 in Diagram 2-35.

Post Isolation with Backside Read/Curl Concept

Another excellent means of attacking the seams between the cover-3 cornerbacks and the middle (free) safety is a post isolation with a backside read/curl-route combination. The read/curl route receiver, recognizing a middle (free) safety, runs the seam route aspect of the read route between the cornerback to his side and the middle (free) safety. The quarterback throws off of the position of the middle (free) safety to either the skinny-post route or the seam-route action of the read route. (The read/curl route would become a broken arrow versus an open, two-deep-safety middle.) The curl/flat-route combination acts as the pattern's outlet. The post isolation with the backside read/curl-route combination is shown in Diagram 2-36.

Three-Tiered Outside-Flood Concept

The three-tiered outside-flood concept is an excellent means of attacking cover 3. The concept pushes the playside cornerback deep and floods the strong safety with a two-on-one flood isolation. The flat route stretches the strong safety to open up a hole for the tight end (Y) to work his flood route into. The flood-route-pattern concept versus cover 3 is shown in Diagram 2-37.

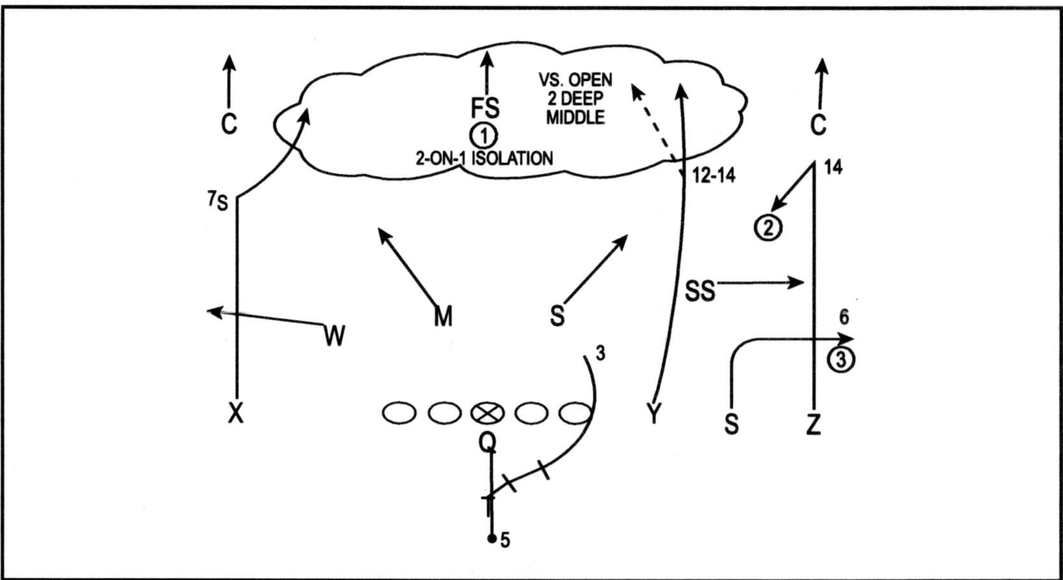

Diagram 2-36. Post isolation with backside read/curl concept versus cover 3

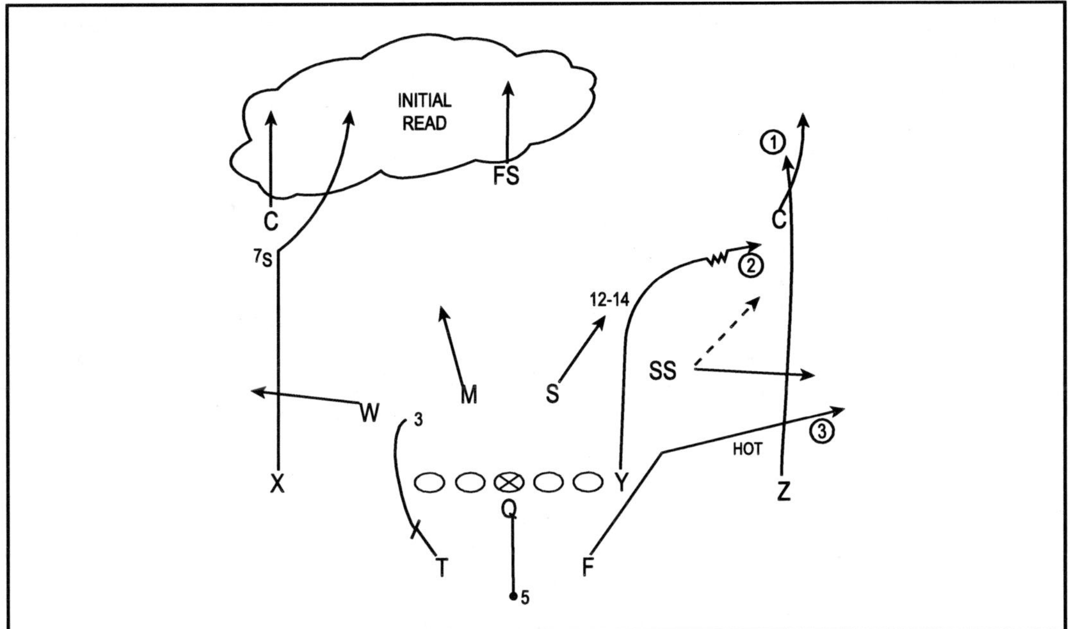

Diagram 2-37. Flood-pattern concept versus cover 3

Naked-Bootleg Concept

The naked-bootleg concept can be an effective way to attack cover 3. The naked-bootleg action refers to the fact that no fakeside lineman is pulling to the backside to block protect for the bootlegging quarterback. The naked-bootleg pattern works to pull out the weakside outside linebacker or the strongside strong safety with flat-route action so that the naked-route receiver can work to get open off of the playside inside linebacker. In addition, comeback-out routes can be extremely effective additions to naked action versus cover 3. Naked-bootleg action is shown in Diagram 2-38 in its effort to attack cover 3, with a comeback-out route added to the basic naked pattern.

Wide-Receiver Screens

Outside-wide-receiver screens that work to the inside can be very effective versus cover 3. The weakside outside linebacker and the strong safety, in their efforts to work out hard to cover the flats, are very susceptible to inside-breaking wide-receiver screens with kick-out action, as shown in Diagram 2-39.

Inside-Backfield and Tight-End Screens

Inside-backfield and tight-end screen action can be very effective versus cover 3. With the hard flow to the outside flats by the weakside outside linebacker and the strongside strong safety, inside screen blocking can be very effective versus the lone remaining screenside inside linebacker. A naked-action screen to the faking back is shown in Diagram 2-40.

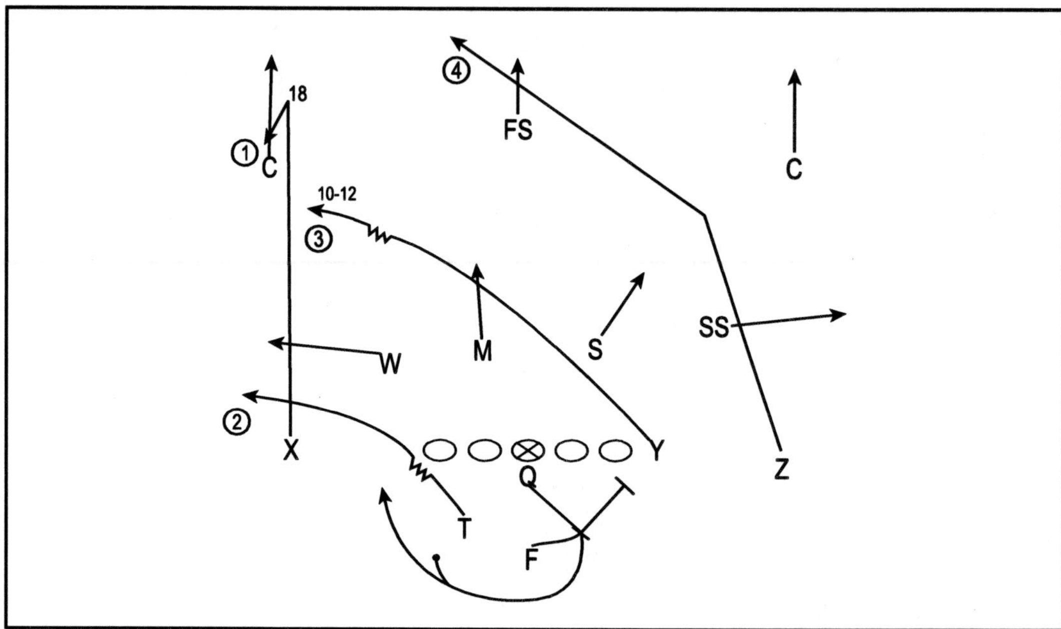

Diagram 2-38. Naked-bootleg action with a comeback-out route versus cover 3

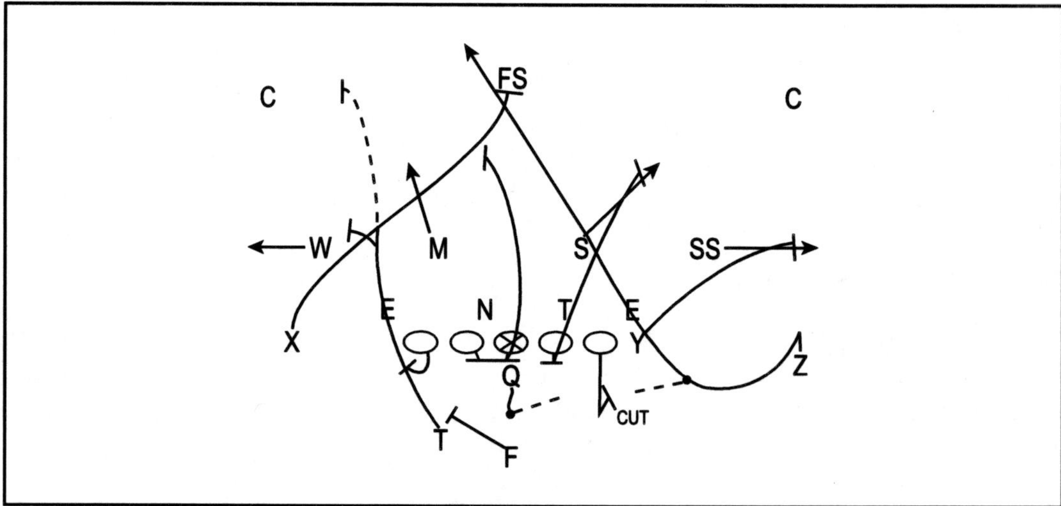

Diagram 2-39. Wide receiver screen versus cover 3

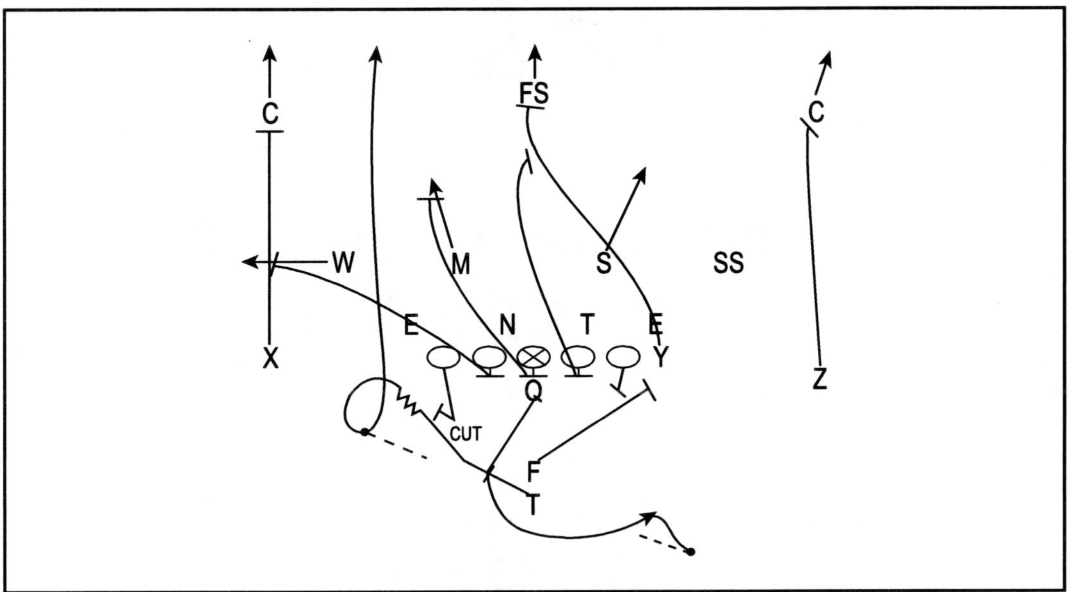

Diagram 2-40. Inside naked screen action versus cover 3

3

Pass Attack of Cover 1 (Man Free)

Cover 1 (man-free coverage) is one of the most basic man coverages used in football today. Man free plays man-to-man coverage underneath in either a press or an off-coverage mode. A single, deep-zone free safety is in the middle of the field to back up the underneath-man-coverage defenders. In this sense, man-free coverage is most similar to cover-2 man-under coverage in that it has a deep-zone-coverage component backing up its man-coverage defenders. In cover-2 man-under coverage, two deep-zone defenders back up five man-under-coverage defenders most often in an up press-man-coverage mode.

Man free readily lends itself to nickel- and dime-coverage substitutions. A second (nickel) and third (dime) secondary defender can be easily substituted for linebackers to provide more—and better—pass-coverage defenders. In man free, the one deep free safety plays a center-field position to back up all of the underneath-man-coverage defenders. Man-free coverage is illustrated in Diagram 3-1, showing both up press-man coverage and off-man coverage.

Chapter 3 will focus on man-free press-man coverage, the more difficult aspect of the man coverage to attack. Off-man-coverage attack will be the focus of Chapter 8.

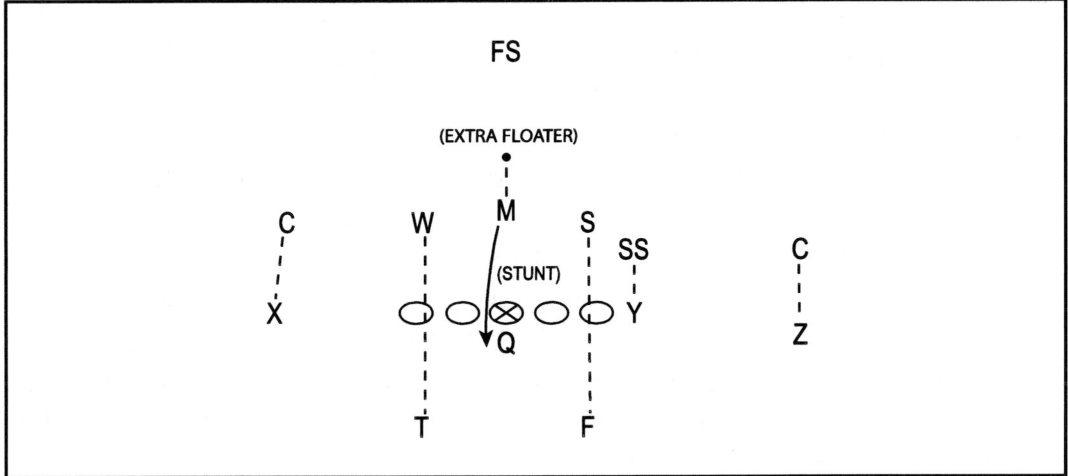

Diagram 3-1. Man-free coverage

Man-Free Coverage Pass-Game Strengths

Man-free coverage plays man-to-man coverage on all five potential receivers of the offense—whether the man-coverage defenders are in an up position in press-man coverage, or aligned in an off (or loose) man-coverage position.

- The use of press-man coverage is a definite strength of man-free coverage. Press-man-coverage techniques can be very difficult to beat if an offense's receivers are not well-versed and practiced to do so.
- The five underneath-man-coverage defenders of man-free coverage can do a great job of disrupting pass-route releases—especially routes that work upfield vertically.
- The five underneath-man-coverage defenders of man-free coverage take away easy, quick, or short pass-game routes and patterns.
- Since man-free coverage takes away easy, quick, or short pass-game routes and patterns, the coverage is an excellent third-and-medium down coverage.
- The one deep-zone-coverage free safety acts as an excellent back-up security player to assist with the coverage of any deep routes.
- The one deep-zone-coverage free safety acts as excellent back-up for any short-route completions in helping to prevent such short completions from turning into big gains.
- The man-under aspect of the coverage makes it very easy for the coverage to fortify its man-coverage abilities by substituting extra (nickel and dime) defensive backs for normal coverage linebackers.

- The man-free man-under linebackers (or nickel/dime defenders) can run vertically with any inside-receiver vertical-release routes. Doing so can force possible floating throws to such receivers making such passes vulnerable to interceptions by the one deep-zone-coverage free safety.
- The man-free man-under-coverage defenders easily fit to any formation, shift, and motion variations.
- The man-under-coverage aspect of man-free coverage easily ties into frontal stunt pressure of up to five rush defenders. For this major reason, man-free coverage readily fits the double-eagle (bear) front package, as shown in Diagram 3-2.
- Man-free coverage can allow the front to rush only four frontal defenders to provide the defense with five underneath-man-coverage defenders and an extra free underneath "floater" or "hole" defender.
- If the offense's backs and/or tight ends don't release into pass routes, extra floaters (or hole players) can be provided for the defense. Such floaters (or hole defenders) can sit for short crossing or in-breaking routes.
- Man-free coverage can provide a designated robber coverage defender to cover the dig hole area underneath the deep free safety by rushing only four frontal defenders. All five potential offensive receivers are still able to be fully covered man-to-man.
- The structure of man-free coverage allows for a great deal of coverage flexibility.

Man-Free Coverage Pass-Game Weaknesses

- Two of the most basic premises of attacking man (man-to-man) coverage holds true for the attack of man-free coverage: isolate and cross. In both concepts, it's

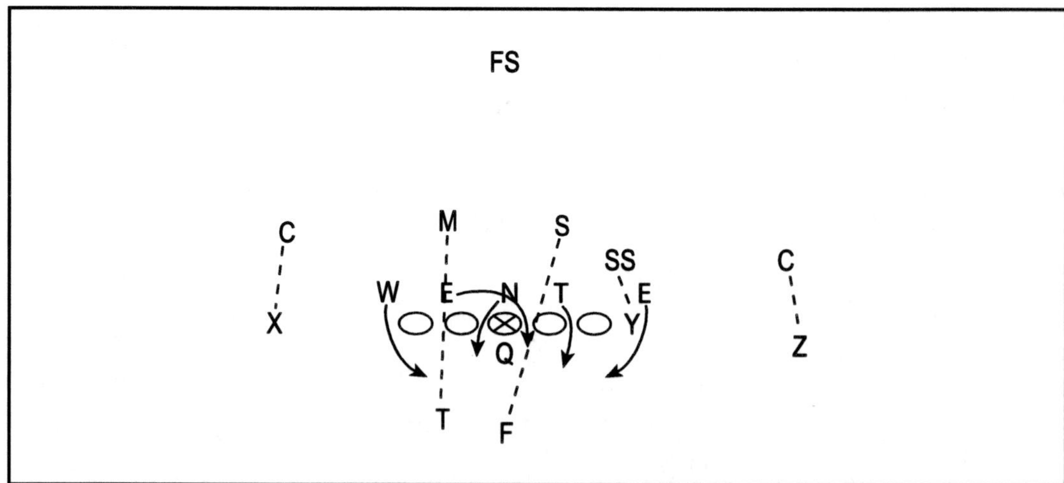

Diagram 3-2. Double eagle (bear) front with man-free coverage

extremely important for the receivers to man-separate and then to be sure to maintain such separation from the man-to-man coverage.

- Beating tight man-to-man press coverage can easily lead to big gains. A major reason for this is that the other coverage defenders (other than the free safety) may be chasing/covering other receivers. As a result, the area around the receiver making the reception may be well cleared out, allowing the receiving ballcarrier to run for a big gain. In addition, with only one deep free safety behind the man coverage, a lot of deep safety help to support receptions by the receivers may not be available.
- The total man-coverage design can only be as strong as the weakest man-coverage defender—much as a chain is only as strong as its weakest link. An offense can quickly focus on attacking—or isolating—the weakest man-coverage defender(s).
- Quick-game isolations—such as slants, inside-receiver speed-outs, and fades—can be very effective versus man-free coverage.
- Underneath-smash and under-route isolations offer the offense quick, inside crossing routes to help beat the man-under coverage to the inside.
- Option-isolation routes (Y-options, H-options, slot-options) help to exploit possible one-on-one mismatches in favor of the offense in the attack of man-free coverage.
- Y-pivot and Y-break routes also help create one-on-one isolation routes in favor of the offense versus man-free coverage. Stick routes and the square-out route on a Texas concept also do the same.
- Post-corner isolations by both outside- and inside-aligned receivers can help to exploit both the one-on-one underneath-man-under coverage as well as the normal deep-outside-zone voids left by the single free-safety coverage of man-free coverage. Such deep post-corner-isolation action by an inside receiver into the outside single-safety deep man-free void (as well as the excellent underneath-lateral-dragging action of the smash route versus the man-under coverage) is shown in Diagram 3-3.
- Deeper digs and square-ins can help to isolate man-under coverage and utilize the crossing action of such routes. It is very important, however, to be sure that some form of a clear-out or post route is working through the middle of the field to hold the single deep man-free free safety. Diagram 3-4 shows the use of a clear-out route to blow the top off of the man-free coverage so that the single deep free safety cannot help to cover the deep square-in route.
- Cross-the-field route actions—such as drives and drag routes—can be very effective man-free-coverage underneath-isolation routes. Such routes have much (or all) of the width of the field to beat the man-under coverage and get open to receive a pass.

- Crossing action is an excellent way to attack the man-under aspect of man-free coverage. Cross-route-pattern concepts and the Texas concepts are excellent examples. Backs cross and back-fake-cross action are also excellent man-under-attack concepts that can be used to attack man-free coverage. Backs-cross action versus man free is shown in Diagram 3-5.

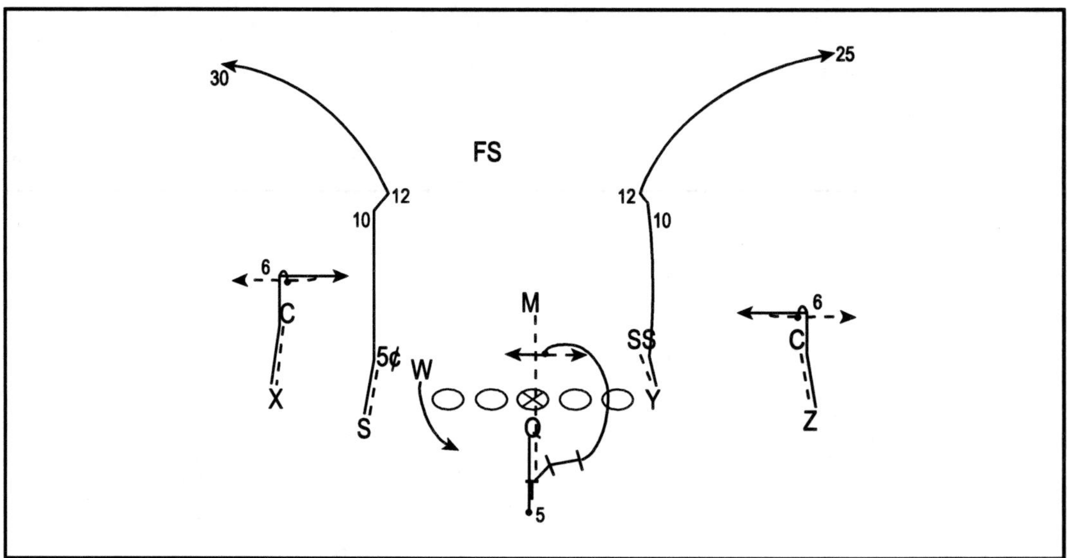

Diagram 3-3. Smash-pattern attack of deep man-free outside voids (plus underneath-smash-route drag action versus man-under coverage)

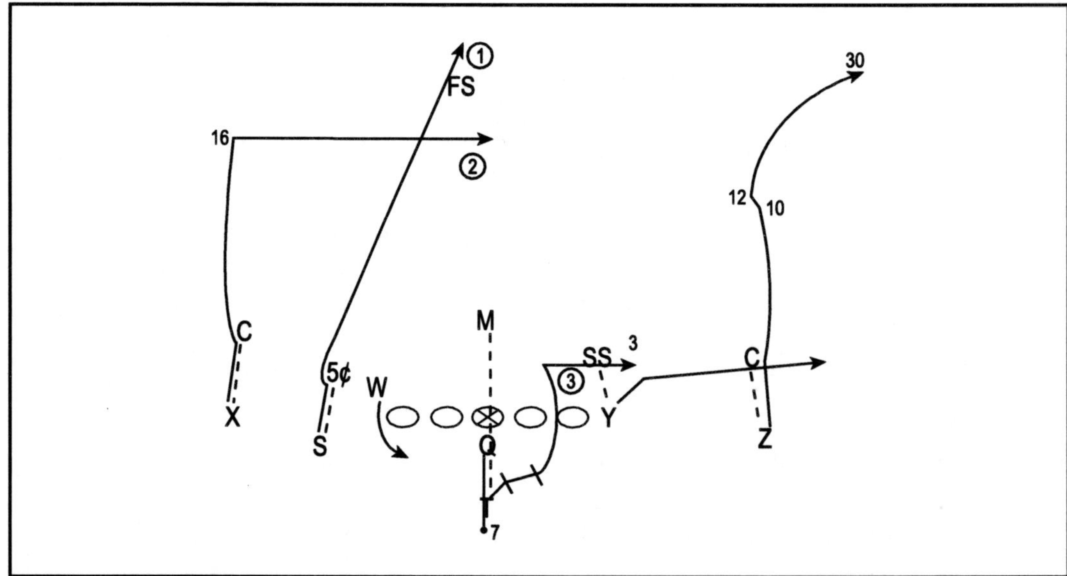

Diagram 3-4. Clear-out route used to blow the top off of the man-free coverage for deep square-in or dig-route action

- Picks and rubs are excellent route combinations to attack man-free coverage. Of course, such pick and rub action must be executed off of legal picking action. A slot/slash pick-route combination from a trips to the split-end (X) formation is shown in Diagram 3-6.
- Picking screens thrown to backs and receivers behind the line of scrimmage can also be very effective in defeating the man-under aspect of man-free coverage.
- Four-streaks-type designs can hold the inside defenders of man-free coverage to help produce excellent outside one-on-one isolations as shown in Diagram 3-7.

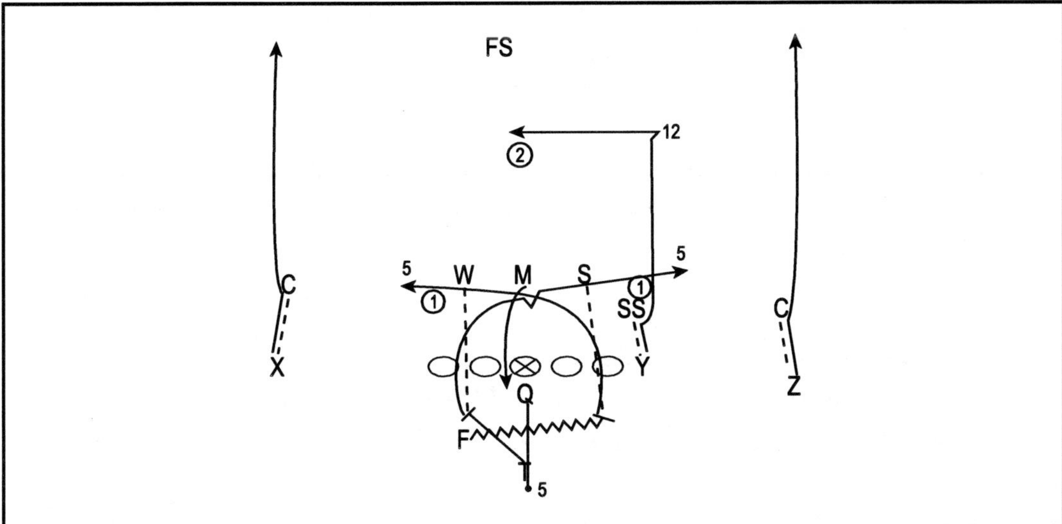

Diagram 3-5. Backs-cross pattern versus man-free coverage

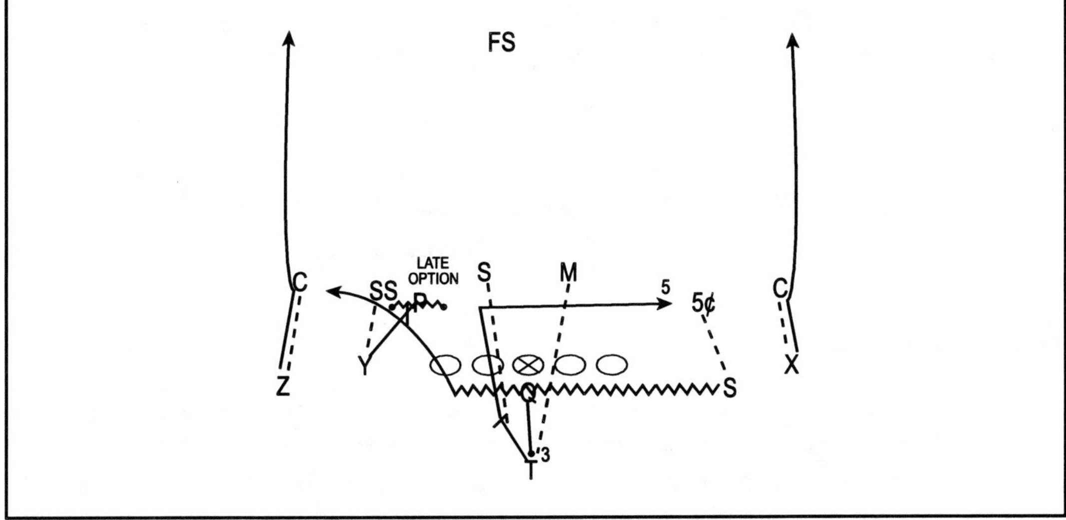

Diagram 3-6. Slot-pick action versus man-free coverage

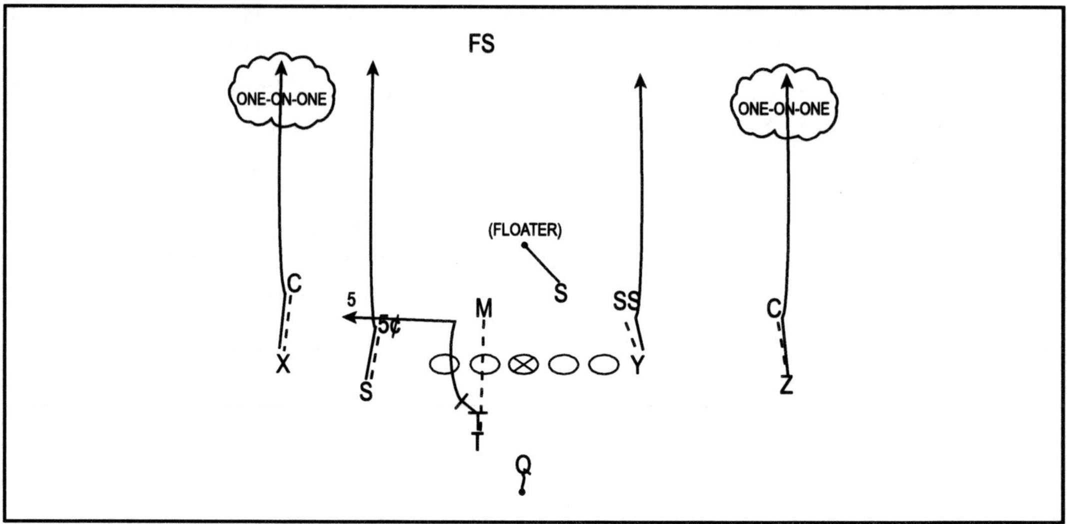

Diagram 3-7. Four-streaks design creating excellent outside one-on-one deep isolations versus man-free coverage

- Tight man-to-man press coverages can be extremely vulnerable to outside acute, rollaway, and comeback-out routes off of deep-streak-threat action.
- Outs (square-outs) can be very effective versus man-free one-on-one man coverage, which is especially true when executing such square-out routes by inside receivers.
- Curl-route and deeper hook-route isolations can be very tough on man-free one-on-one man coverage if the receivers can effectively get separation.
- Double-move routes are an excellent way to attack man-free coverage. This technique holds true whether the double-move action is off of quick-game three-step-drop-timed routes (quick hitch, slants, outs) or five-step-drop-timed routes (outs, flats, curls, rollaways).

Route Combination and Pass-Pattern Attack of Man-Free Coverage

Quick-Game Slant

Slant-route isolations and double-slant actions can be very effective versus man-free coverage. The major change in executing the slant route as compared to attacking zone coverage is the pressing, tight release of the slant receiver. This release is done in an effort to work the hips of the press-coverage defender to get the coverage defender's hips turned. The slant receiver initially sticks/attacks the press-coverage defender's outside hip. The slant receiver then drives back tightly, pressing on the defender with a north-south course to influence the defender to work upfield. The slant receiver then breaks his slant action hard to the inside getting separation and staying on the move at top speed to be sure to maintain such man separation. Slant and double-slant action versus man-free coverage is shown in Diagram 3-8.

Diagram 3-9 shows slant/arrow action versus man-free coverage. The crossing action of the slant and arrow actions can help to actually produce a quick crossing/picking action of the two routes, helping to free one route or the other versus the press-man coverage.

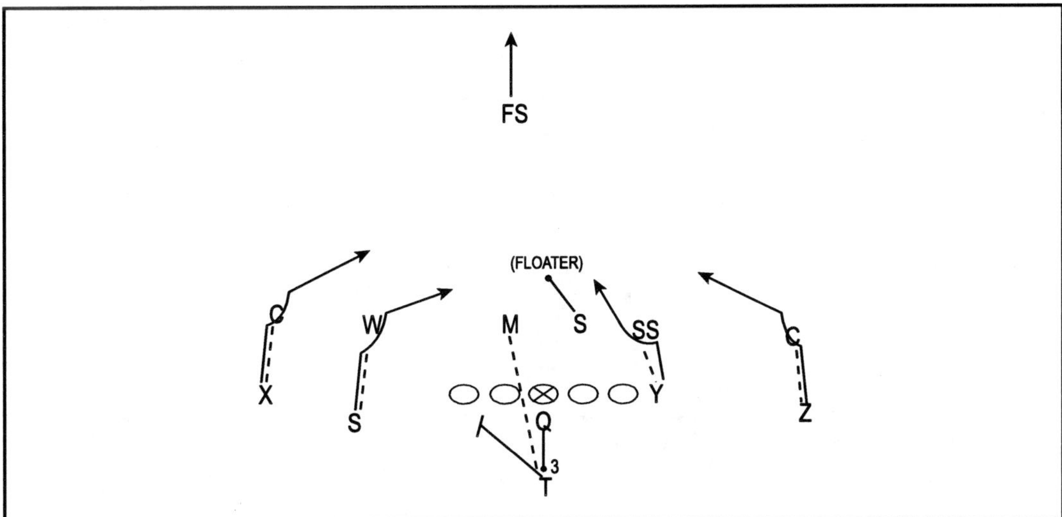

Diagram 3-8. Quick-game slant-route and double-slant-route action versus man-free coverage

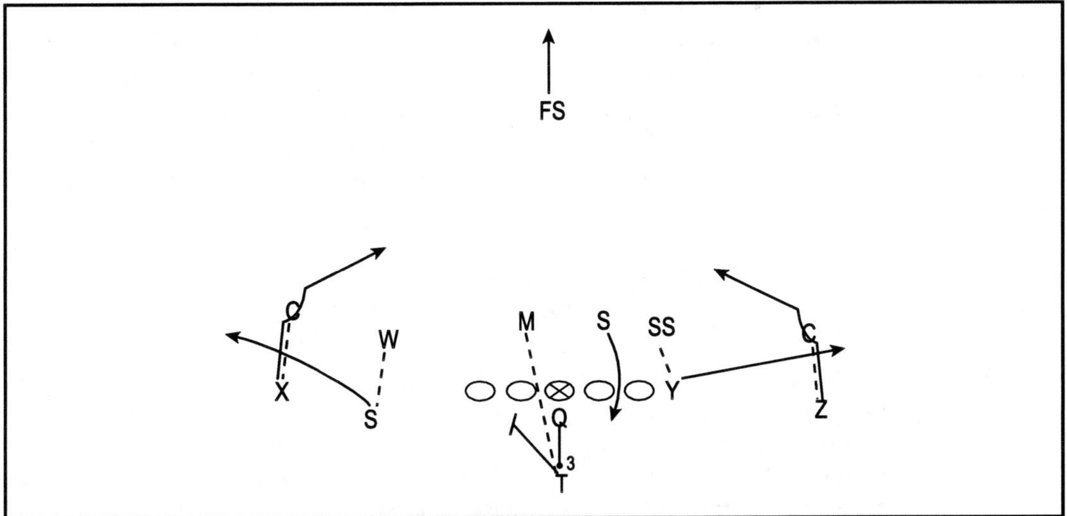

Diagram 3-9. Quick-game slant-/arrow-route combination versus man-free coverage

Quick-Game Speed-Out

The quick-game speed-out route can be a good concept versus man-free coverage. The quick speed-out route actually becomes a quick square-out route versus press coverage techniques by initially releasing into and threatening the man-coverage technique of his man-coverage defender as shown in Diagram 3-10.

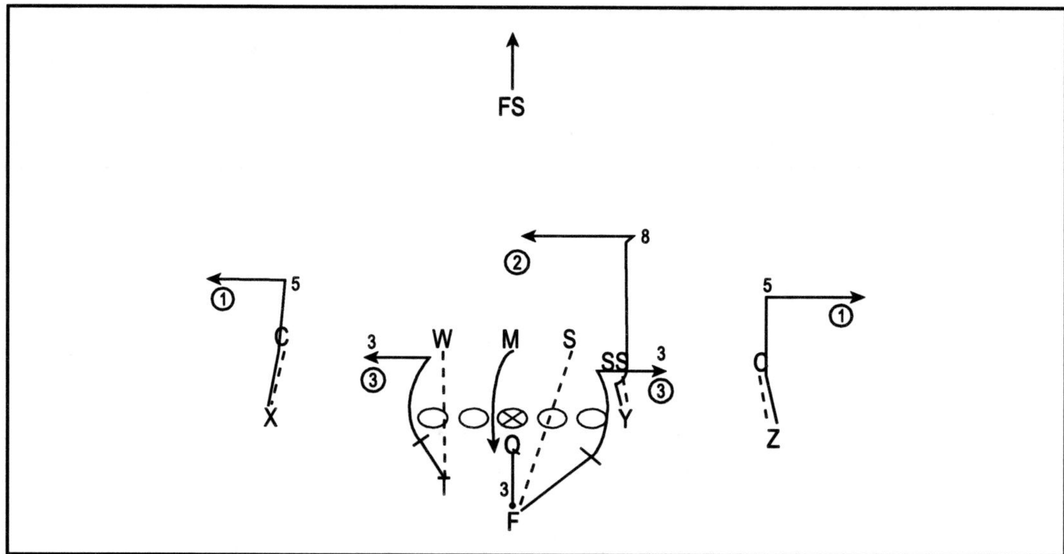

Diagram 3-10. Quick-game speed-out versus man-free coverage

Quick-Game Inside-Receiver Speed-Out and Fade

The quick-game inside-receiver speed-out and fade-route combination presents two excellent man isolations to help defeat man-free coverage. The wide receiver works a fade-route isolation versus the cornerback, while the inside receiver squares his speed-out route (actually becomes a quick square-out route) after initially releasing into and threatening the man-coverage technique of his man-coverage defender. Such quick-game inside-receiver speed-out action versus man-free coverage is shown in Diagram 3-11.

An excellent supplemental concept to utilize when a man-free man-coverage defender starts to overplay a quick-game speed-out is the spin route as shown in Diagram 3-12. The speed-out receiver, running the route as a quick-game square-out versus the press coverage, simply plants his upfield foot and spins back to the inside versus the defender's over play-action.

Versus the man-under coverage of man-free coverage, deeper, five-step-quarterback-drop-timed speed-outs by an inside receiver are also very effective. The widest receiver must outside release. The inside receiver attacks the technique of the man-under defender covering him, separates, and squares out to the sideline. As with all man-coverage wide-receiver separation techniques, the inside receiver must get separation and then be sure to run at top speed to maintain such separation. The deeper, five-step-drop-timed square-out concept versus man-free coverage is shown in Diagram 3-13.

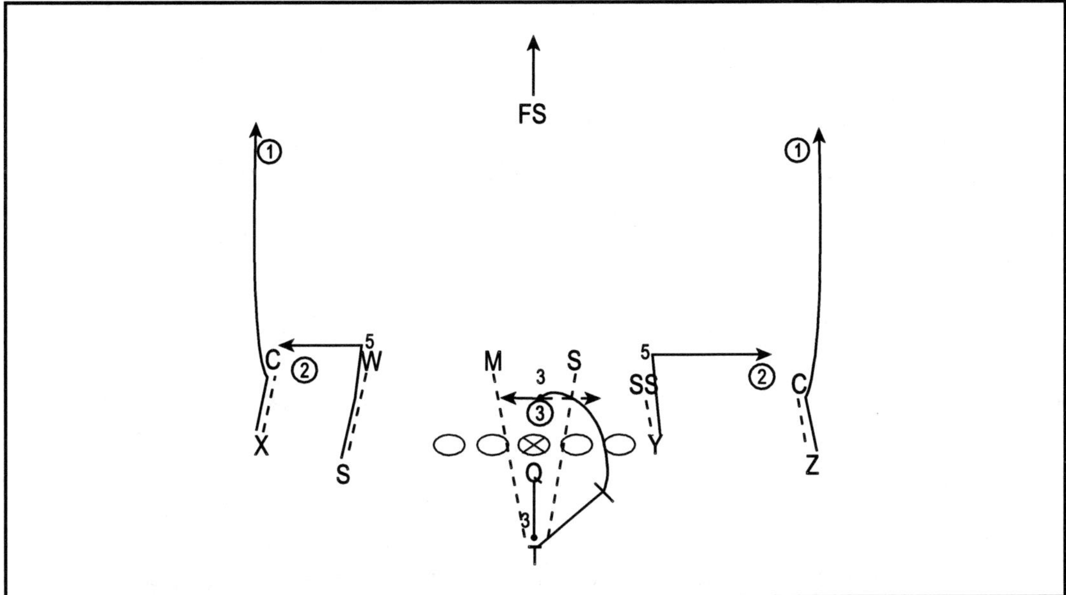

Diagram 3-11. Quick-game inside-speed-out action versus man-free coverage

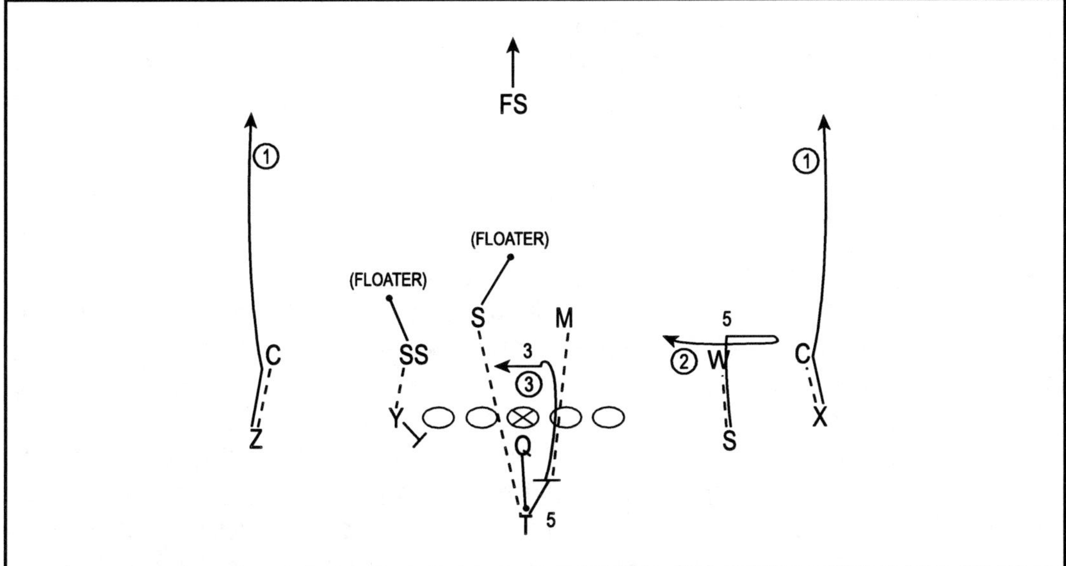

Diagram 3-12. Quick-game spin route versus man-free coverage

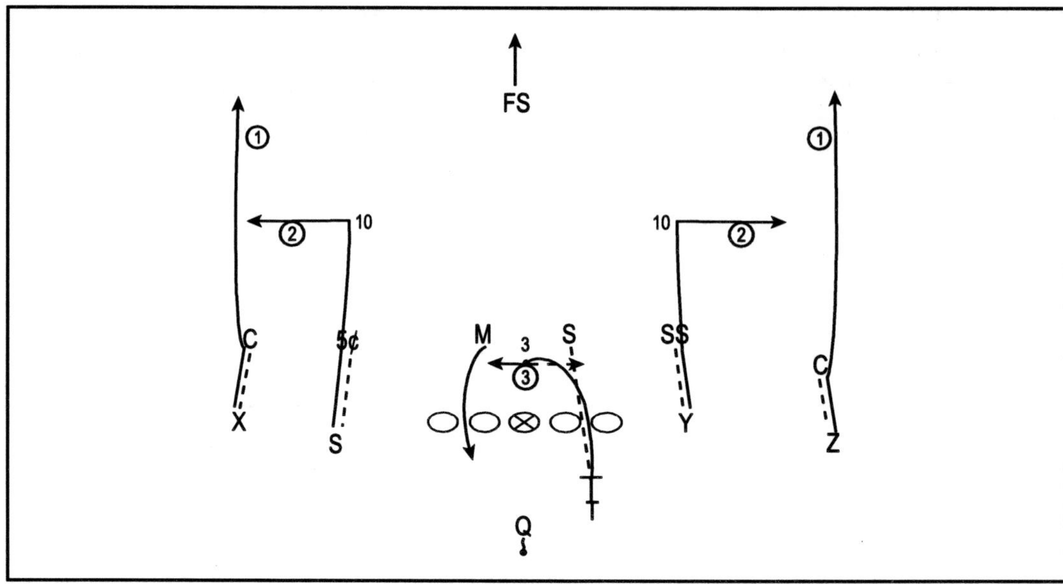

Diagram 3-13. Five-step timed inside receiver speed-out concept versus man-free coverage

Quick-Game Fade

The quick-game fade route requires special consideration in the attack of man-free coverage. Whether called in the play call, signaled to by the quarterback, or as a hitch-route adjustment, the fade route is a very effective route versus press-man-coverage techniques. It is very important for the fade receiver to attack the technique of the press defender covering him in an effort to push the press defender back on his heels. The receiver then tightly drives north-south through the defender in an effort to blow past the press coverage defender. It is also important for the fade receiver to leave four yards of width on the sideline for the quarterback to effectively throw a fade pass. Diagram 3-14 shows such fade-route action versus a man-free press defender.

Quick-Game Deep Hitch

The quick-game deep-hitch route can be very effective versus man-free press coverage. The difference in running a deep hitch compared to a normal hitch is an eight-yard hitch rather than a six-yard hitch. The extra two yards of stem can do much to help influence the covering press defender that the receiver is beyond hitch depth and is at this point working his stem for a fade or a route run deeper than six yards. As a result, the receiver can work the eight-yard hitch route tightly to the inside back into the quarterback to help the receiver body up on the deep-hitch route. The quarterback adjusts to fast five-step-drop timing to accommodate the extra two yards of hitch depth. Deep fades are not fade-adjusted versus press coverage. Quick-game deep-hitch action versus man-free coverage is shown in Diagram 3-15.

Quick-Game Double-Move Routes

Quick-game double-move routes can be very effective versus man-free press coverage. Hitch-and-go and speed-out-and-go routes are shown in Diagram 3-16. Diagram 3-17 shows slant-and-go action versus man-free coverage.

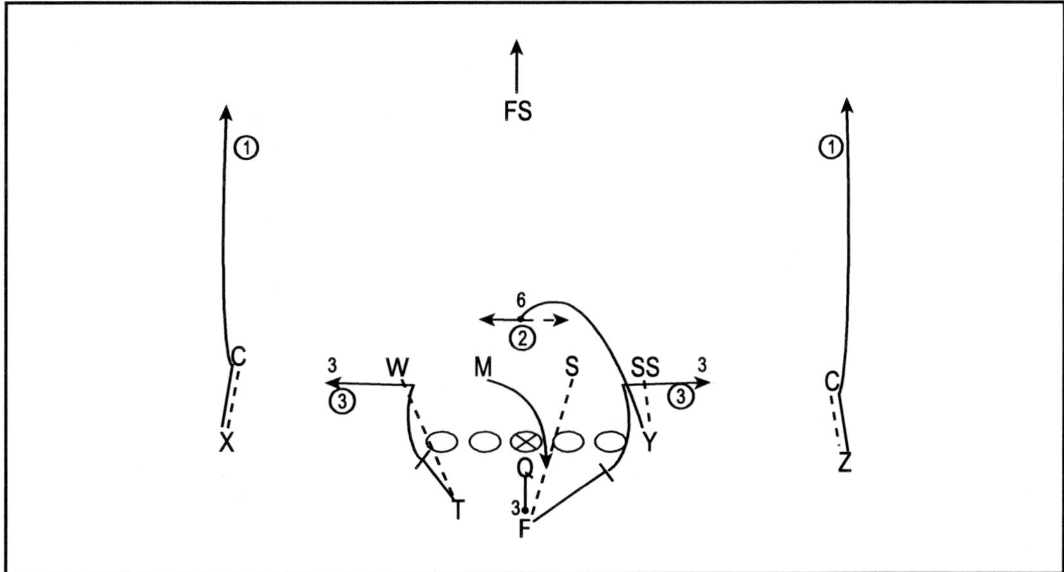

Diagram 3-14. Fade route versus man-free press defender

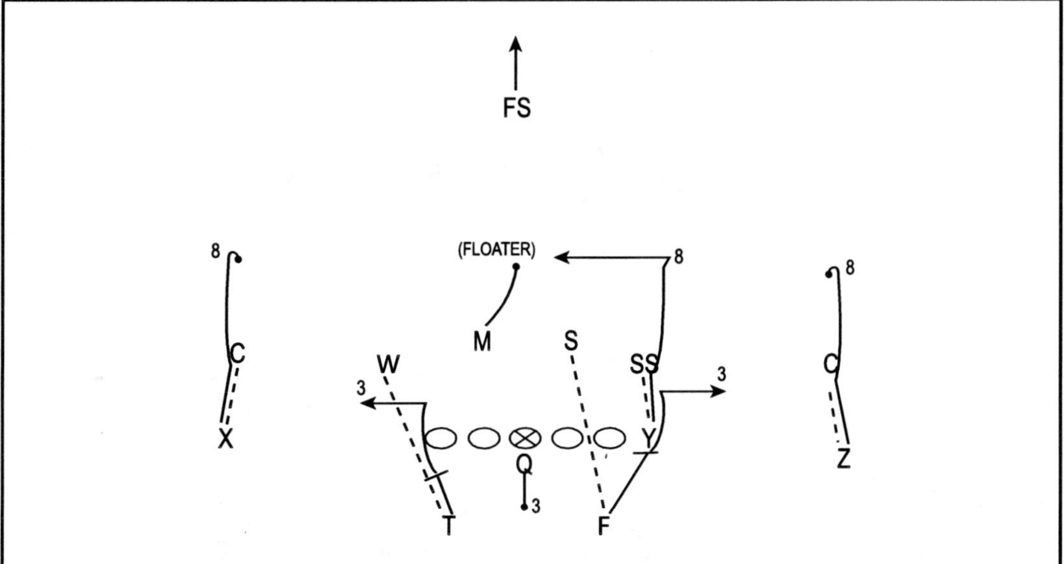

Diagram 3-15. Quick-game deep-hitch route versus man-free coverage

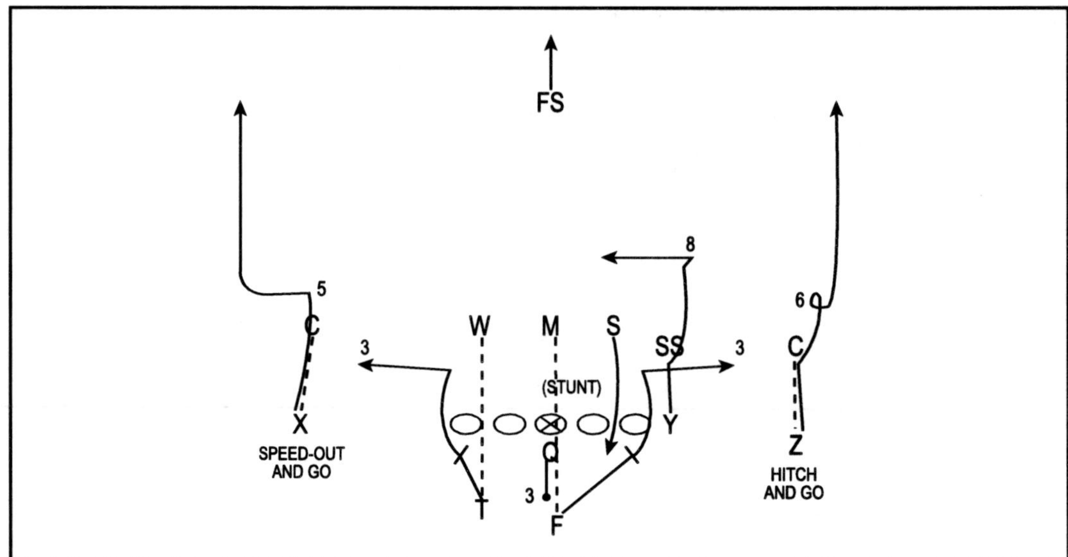

Diagram 3-16. Quick-game double-move hitch-and-go and speed-out-and-go routes versus man-free coverage

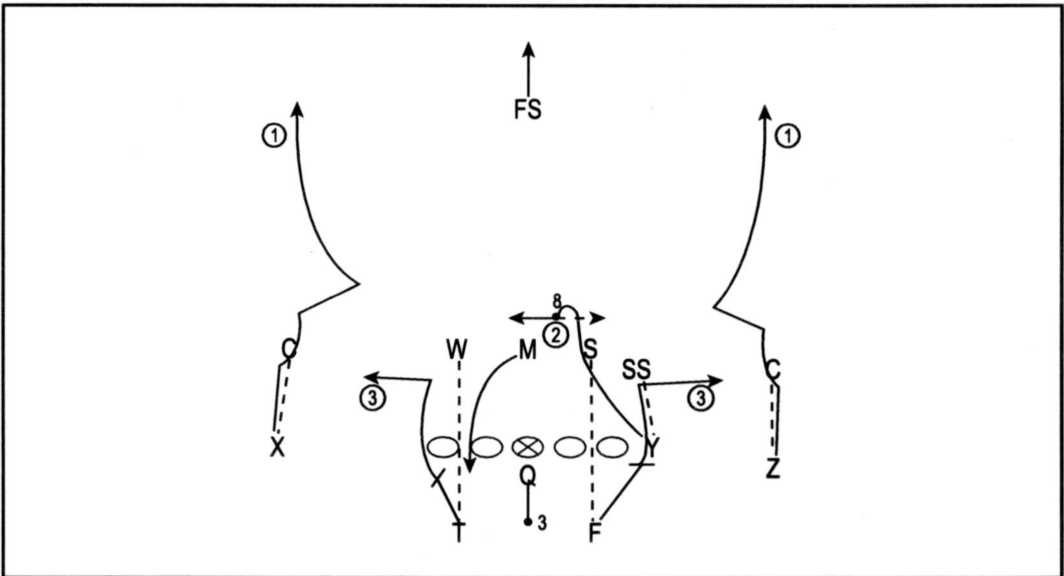

Diagram 3-17. Quick-game double-move slant-and-go action versus man-free coverage

Quick-Game Stick

The quick-game stick-route concept is an excellent isolation-type route versus man-free coverage. The flat route in front of the stick route helps to open up the stick area for the stick-route receiver to work into. The stick receiver initially works tightly into the technique of the defender man-covering him and then snaps to the outside to get separation. The stick receiver must then be sure to work hard to the outside, losing ground slightly, to help maintain such separation. The quick-game stick-route concept versus man-free coverage is shown in Diagram 3-18.

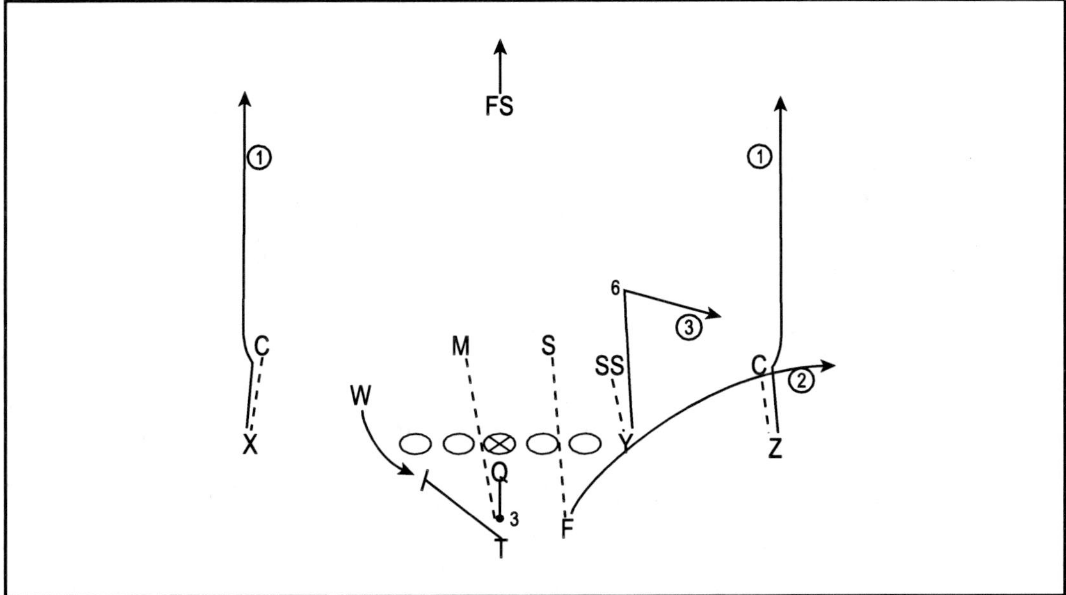

Diagram 3-18. Quick-game stick route versus man-free coverage

Quick-Game Double Under With Slot Fades

An excellent concept to attack the man-free coverage deep-outside voids is the quick-game double-under-with-slot-fades concept. The inside receivers (the slots) actually run fade routes on their press-man-coverage defenders. The quarterback works opposite the positioning of the free safety. The under routes underneath the fade routes act as outlets if the inside-receiver fade-route reads don't look good, as shown in Diagram 3-19.

Under Concept

The under concept presents an excellent underneath isolation of a wide receiver working underneath a clear route by the adjacent receiver to the inside versus man-free coverage. The clear route gets eaten up by the man-under coverage—and possibly the deep man-free safety. The under route must beat the man coverage by man-separating and maintaining such separation to the inside underneath the clear route by staying on the move. Diagram 3-20 shows an under-route isolation versus man-free coverage.

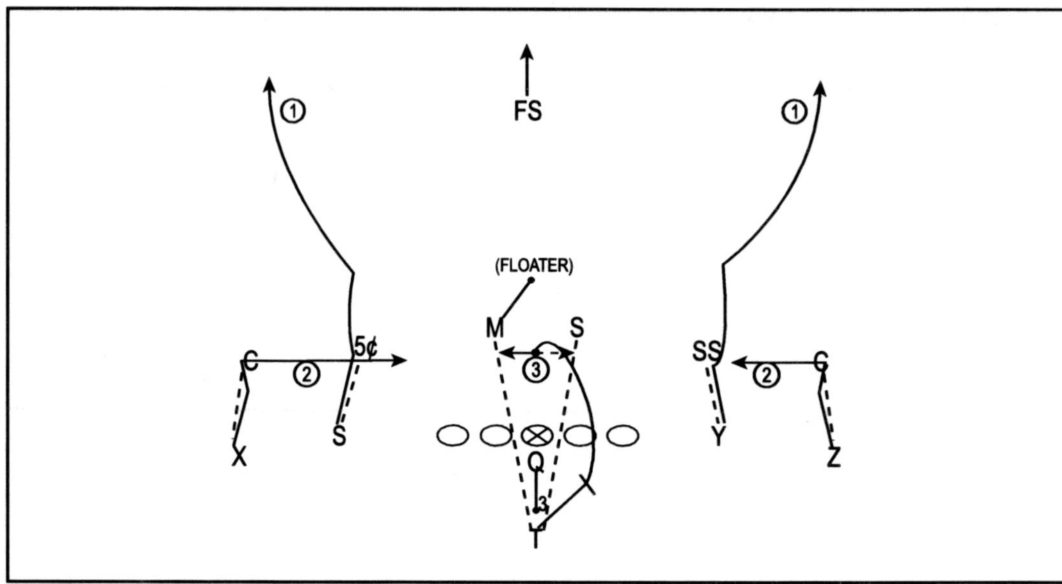

Diagram 3-19. Quick-game double under with slot fades versus man-free coverage

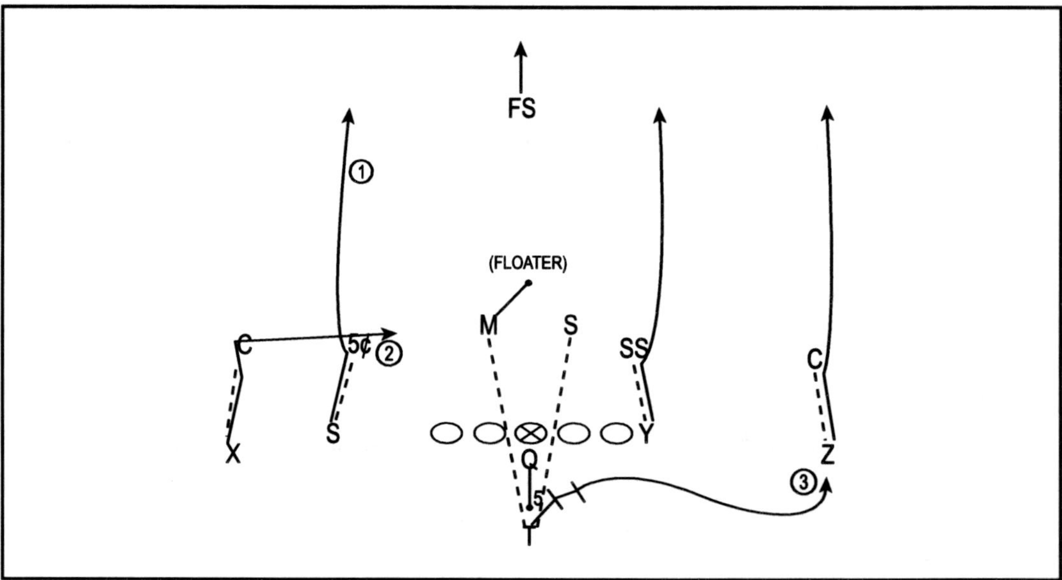

Diagram 3-20. Under concept versus man-free coverage

High-Low-Read Smash Isolation

The high-low-read smash isolation gives an offense an excellent ability to attack man-free coverage. The inside receiver post-corner route must beat the man-under coverage. However, the post-corner route is still able to work away from the man-free deep-zone free safety into the deep-outside man-free void. When run as a hitch-option route, the smash route has the ability to beat the press-man-under coverage across the field to the inside or back outside to the sideline if the man-coverage cornerback overplays the inside break of the smash route. Such man-breaking actions of the smash concept versus man-free coverage is shown in Diagram 3-21.

Bunch-Formation Post-Corner Flood-Isolation Concept

A bunch-formation post-corner flood-isolation concept is an excellent way of attacking man-free coverage. The flood concept is normally thought of as an action to overload zone coverages. However, the picking/crossing action of the post-corner bunch concept helps to condense the man-free coverage and actually outflank the coverage with the outside man-breaking flood routes as shown in Diagram 3-22.

Post-Corner High-Low Isolation

A very similar concept to the smash high-low isolation versus man-free coverage is the post-corner high-low isolation. The post-corner isolation of the widest receiver helps to produce an excellent deep isolation versus man free as shown in Diagram 3-23. This action gives the pass offense a chance to attack the coverage in the deep outside zone away from the free safety in an area that is a coverage void. In addition, the inside receiver is shown running a spin-route action back to the inside off of his flat-route stem to give that receiver an excellent chance to man-separate and to beat press coverage to the inside.

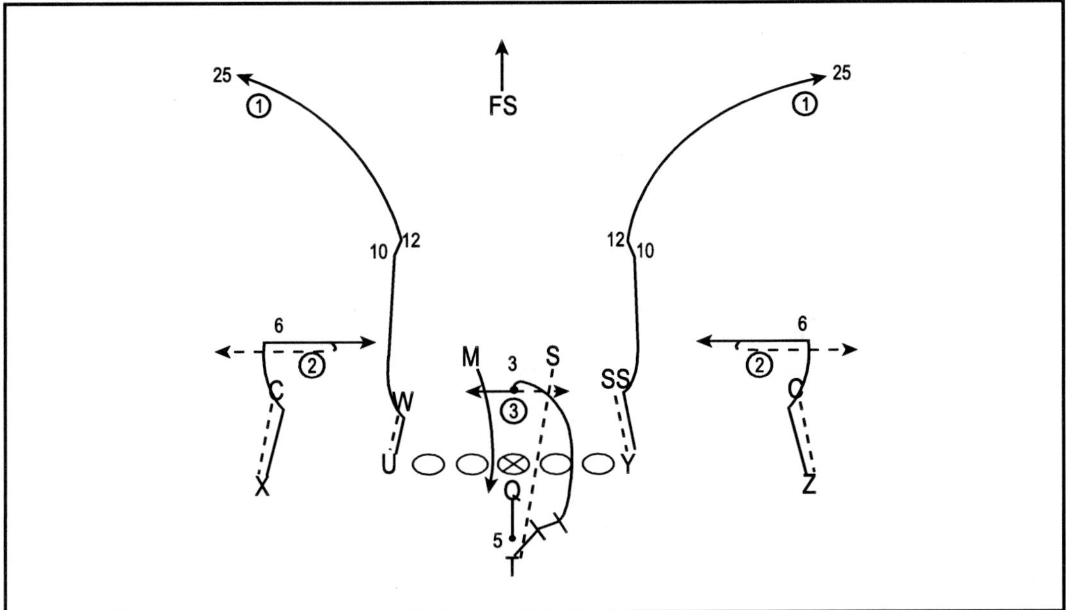

Diagram 3-21. Smash concept versus man-free coverage

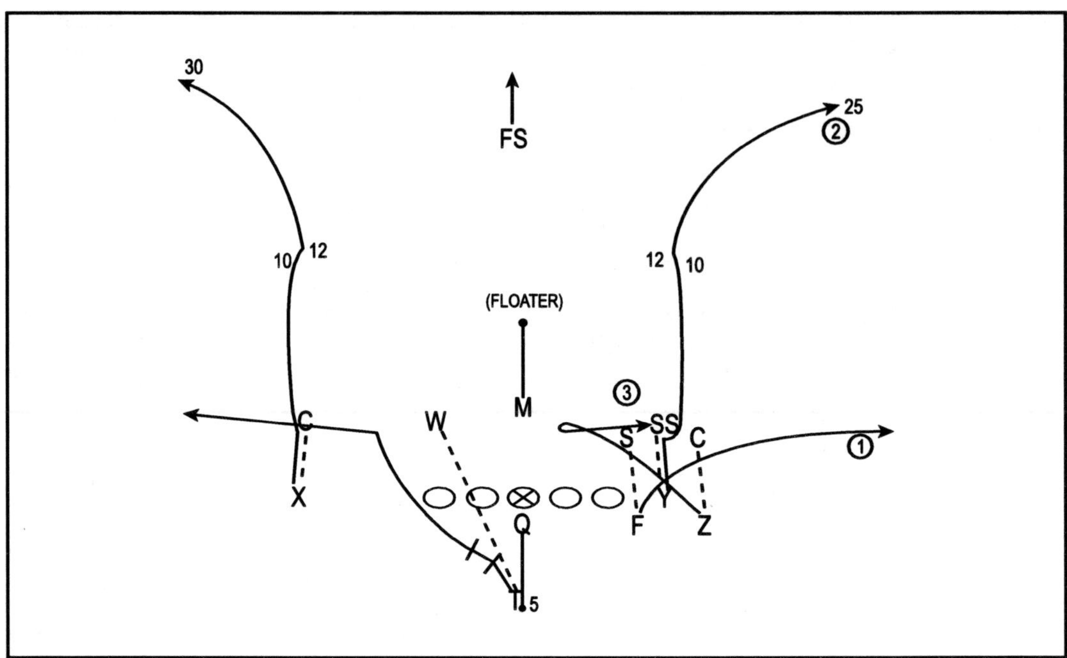

Diagram 3-22. Bunch-formation post-corner flood-isolation concept versus man-free coverage

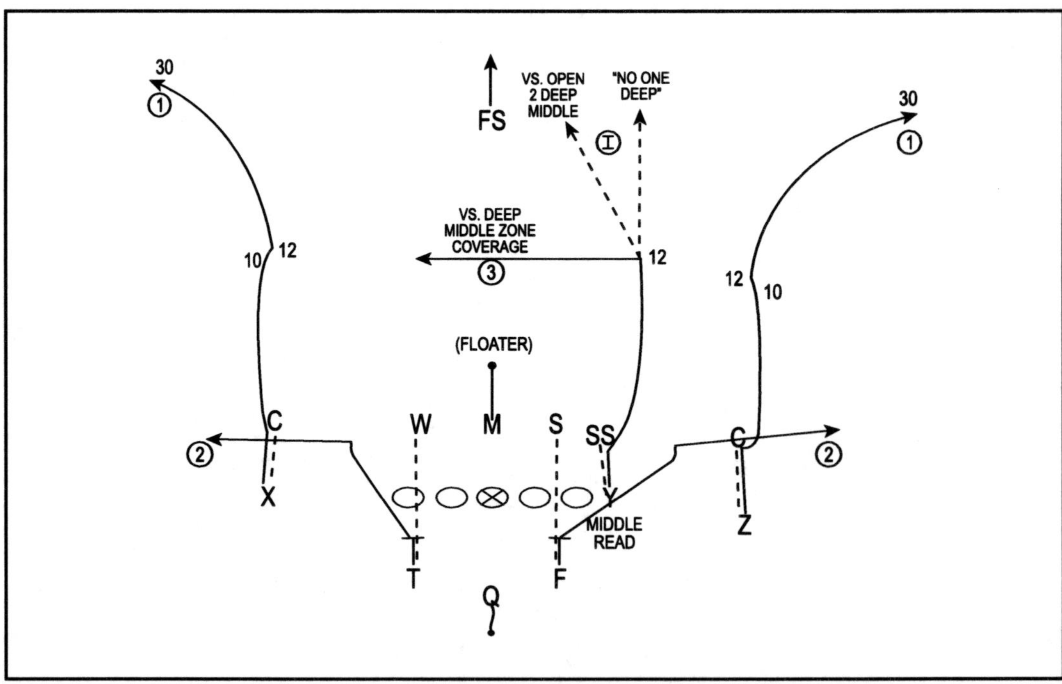

Diagram 3-23. Post-corner high-low isolation concept versus man-free coverage

Post-Corner Deep Across

The post-corner deep across concept also does a good job of attacking man-free coverage. The post-corner route attacks the outside man-free void, while the deep-drag route has room all the way across the field to separate from his man-under coverage and get open. Diagram 3-24 shows a split-end (X) deep-across pattern versus man-free coverage. The major concern for using longer developing routes, such as the deep over versus man free, is pass-protection time needs versus the potential of five pass rushers.

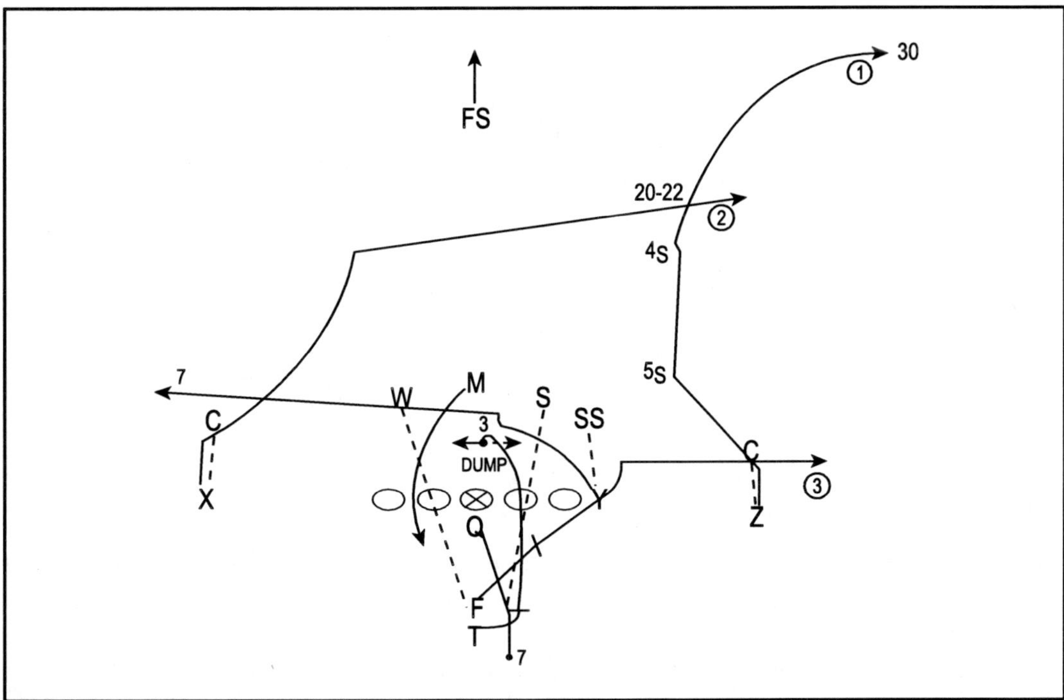

Diagram 3-24. X-deep-across concept versus man-free coverage

Three-Tiered Dig Concept

The three-tiered dig concept is set up by having the wide receiver opposite the dig run through the middle of the field to push the man-free free safety deep to open up a void for the dig route to work into. Doing so helps eliminate the deep-safety-coverage threat so that the dig receiver can focus on beating the one-on-one press-man-under coverage. The pattern concept versus man-free coverage is shown in Diagram 3-25. Once again, the pass-protection time needed for the execution of a long-developing pass route, such as a dig route, can be a major concern of the total pass pattern in regard to the potential of five pass rushers that can so often be associated with man free.

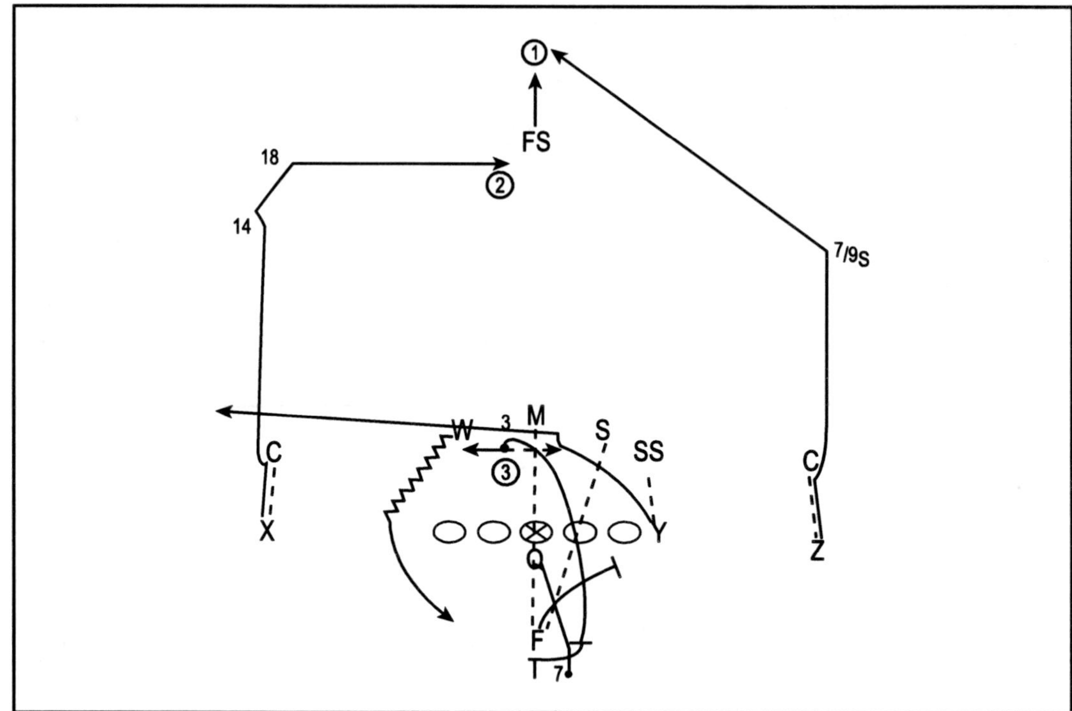

Diagram 3-25. Three-tiered X dig concept versus man-free coverage

Four-Streaks Concept

The four-streaks concept is an excellent way of attacking man-free coverage if the offense feels it has a good outside, one-on-one isolation. The two inside streaks help to hold their man-under-coverage defenders and the single deep free safety. The quarterback must understand that an unfavorable three-on-two ratio exists inside, with an excellent one-on-one ratio to the outside. The four-streaks concept, with its excellent outside one-on-one streak isolation, is shown in Diagram 3-26.

Rollaway/Acute Routes

Rollaway and acute routes are excellent isolation actions versus man-free coverage. They are especially effective when they develop off of strong streak-threat fakes pushing the man-free press cornerbacks deep. Rollaway-/acute-route action versus man-free coverage is shown in Diagram 3-27 from a four-streaks design.

Diagram 3-28 shows comeback-out and deep rollaway routes versus man-free coverage with middle-read action. The quarterback drop timing for such deeper developing routes is seven steps.

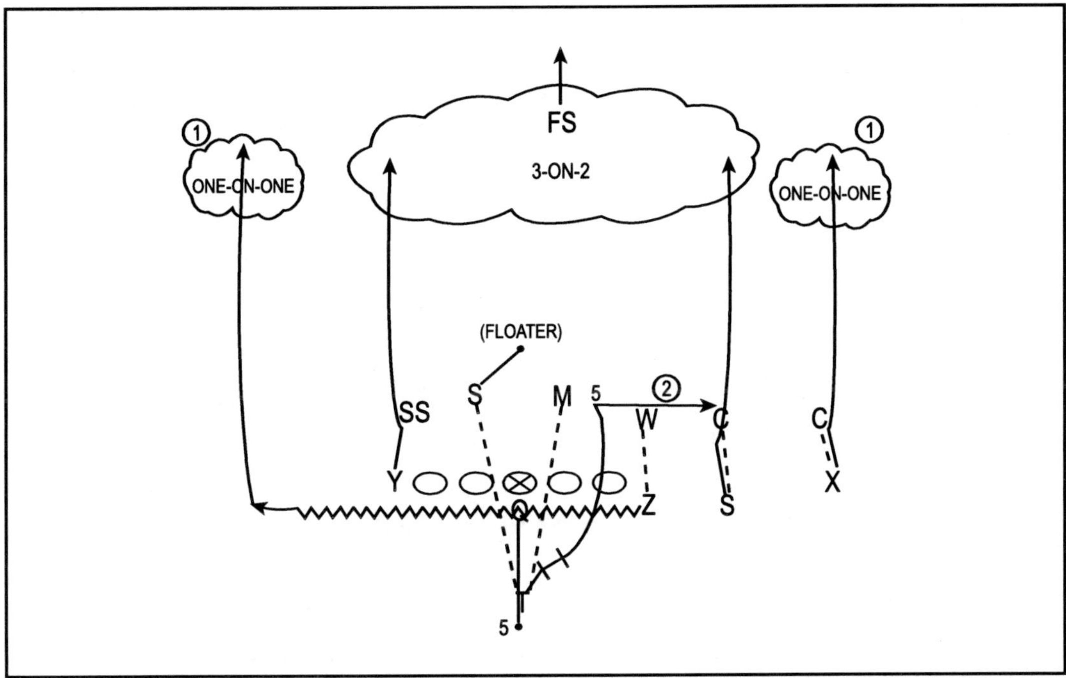

Diagram 3-26. Four-streaks concept outside one-on-one isolations versus man-free coverage

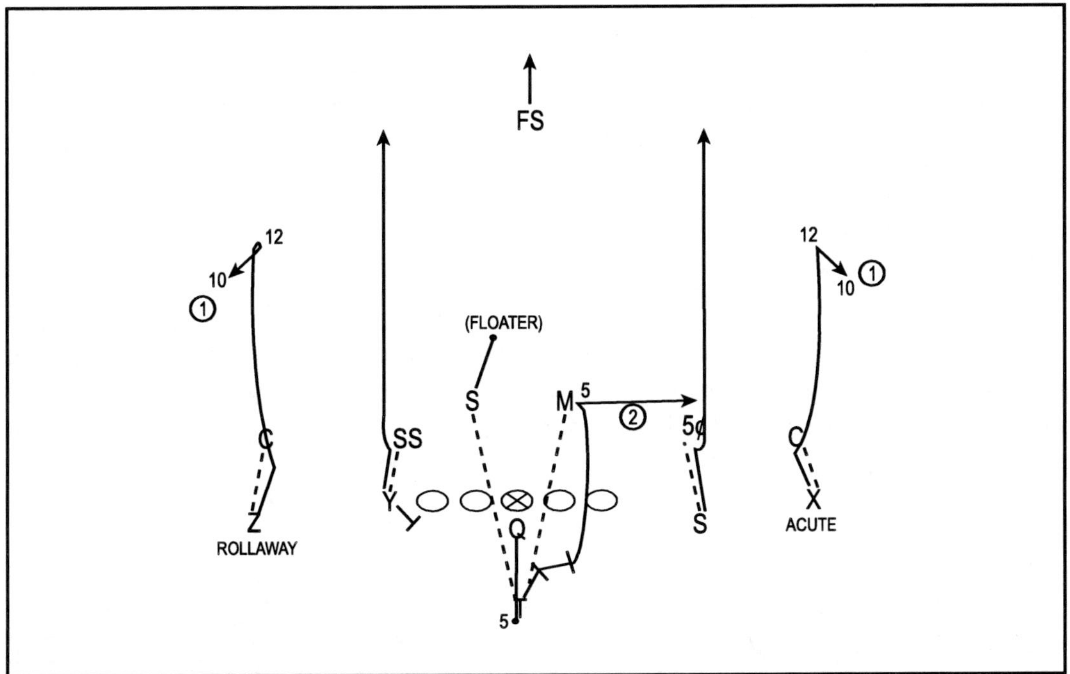

Diagram 3-27. Rollaway/acute routes versus man-free coverage

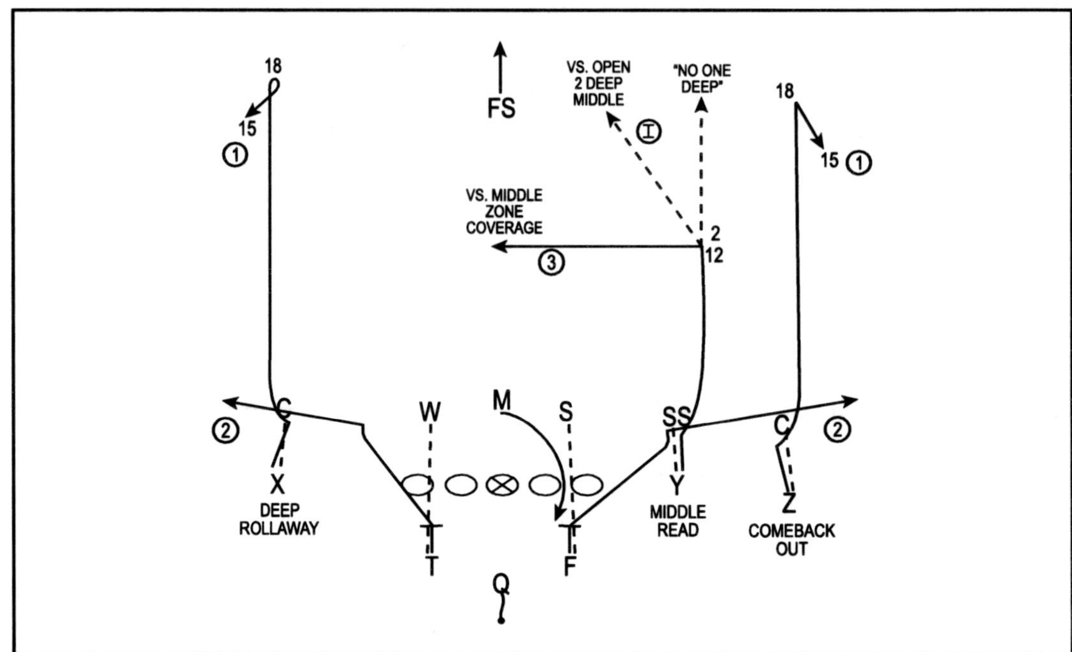

Diagram 3-28. Comeback-out and deep rollaway route action versus man-free coverage

Speed-Outs

Speed-out routes are not a high priority versus man-free coverage. However, it's important to note that if speed-outs are called versus man-free press-man coverage, the speed-out routes must be adjusted to square-out routes "on the run" as shown in Diagram 3-29.

Switch Acute

The switch-acute concept is an excellent concept versus man-free coverage. The switching action on the stem of the two receivers involved in the route combination helps to produce a picking/crossing action that helps combat the press-man coverage as shown in Diagram 3-30 with sprint-out quarterback action. The route can be deepened by having the route be a comeback-out at 18 yards.

Curl/Hook

Curl- and hook-route concepts can be very effective versus man-free coverage, with or without flat-route thinking in combination. The key is the beating of the press-man coverage with the curl and hook routes. The receivers must learn to throw their defenders by them as they aggressively work back to the quarterback and body up on the ball. Curl and hook action versus man-free coverage is shown in Diagram 3-31.

Diagram 3-32 shows sprint-out curl action versus man-free coverage. Note that the curl route must work to the outside if the pass is late developing so that the receiver works in special coordination with the quarterback as the play takes more time to develop. The curl route can also be deepened to 18 yards to be run as a hook route.

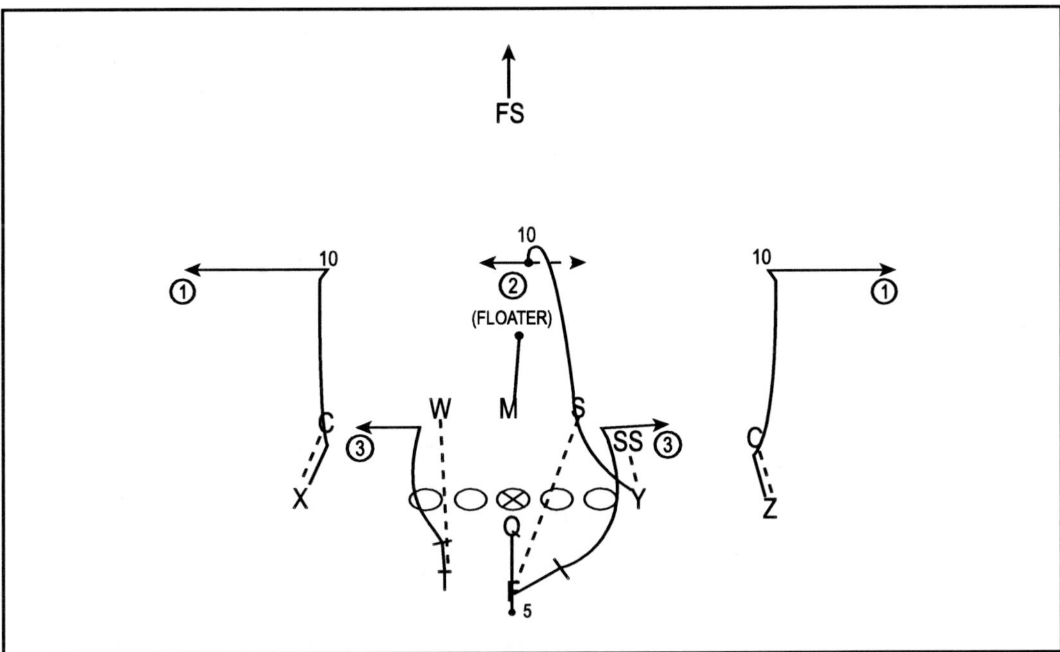

Diagram 3-29. Adjusting speed-outs into square-outs versus man-free coverage

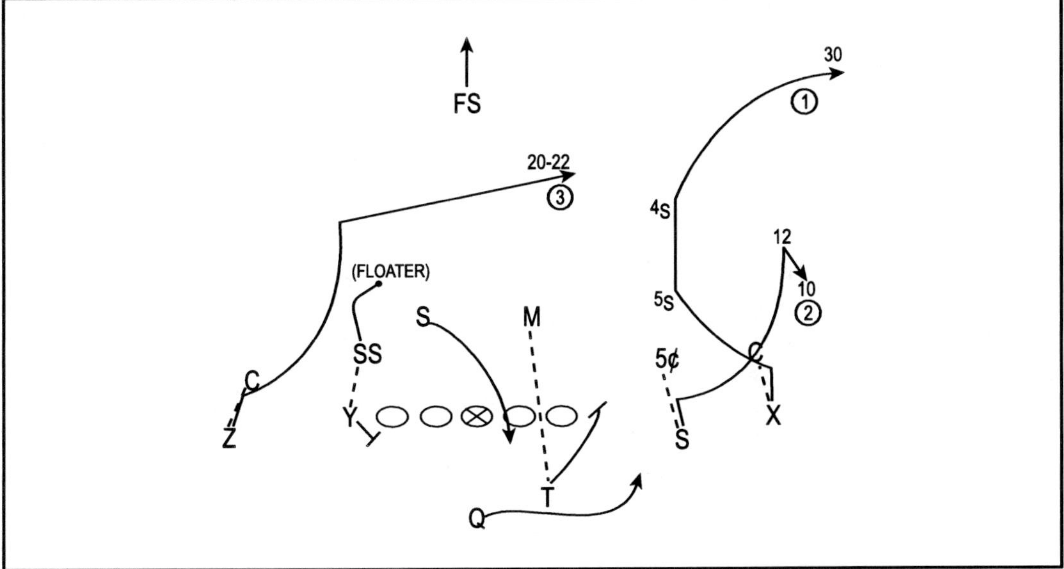

Diagram 3-30. Switch-acute-route combination versus man-free coverage

Speed-Out, Rollaway, Double-Move Curl-Route Concepts

As has been shown, acutes, speed-outs, and curl-route concepts are excellent ways to attack man-free coverage. Quite often, a man-free cornerback will try to jump such wide-receiver routes. As a result, double-move-route concepts can be very effective to

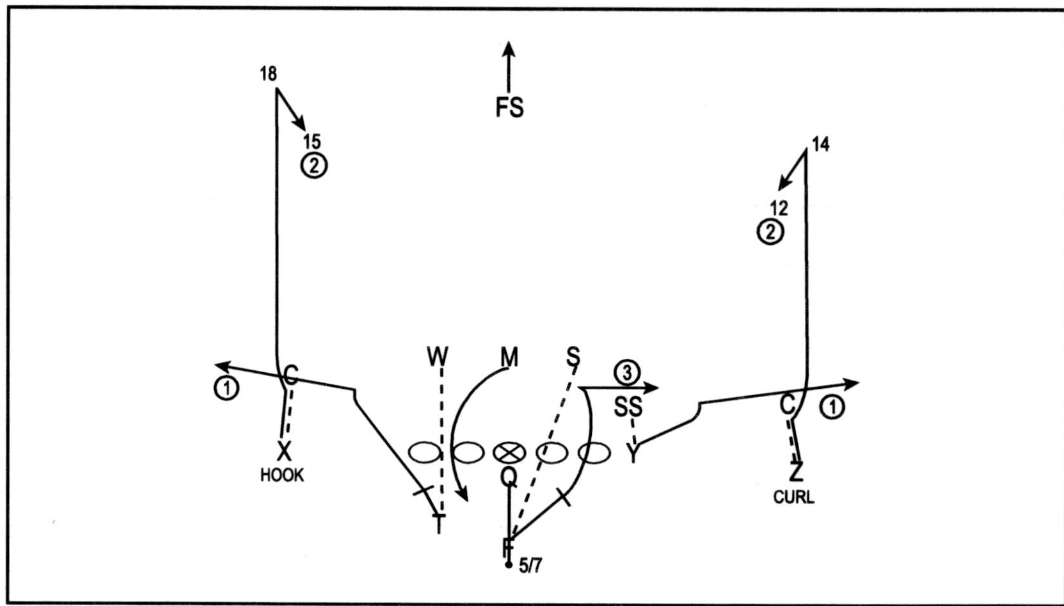

Diagram 3-31. Curl- and hook-route action versus man-free coverage

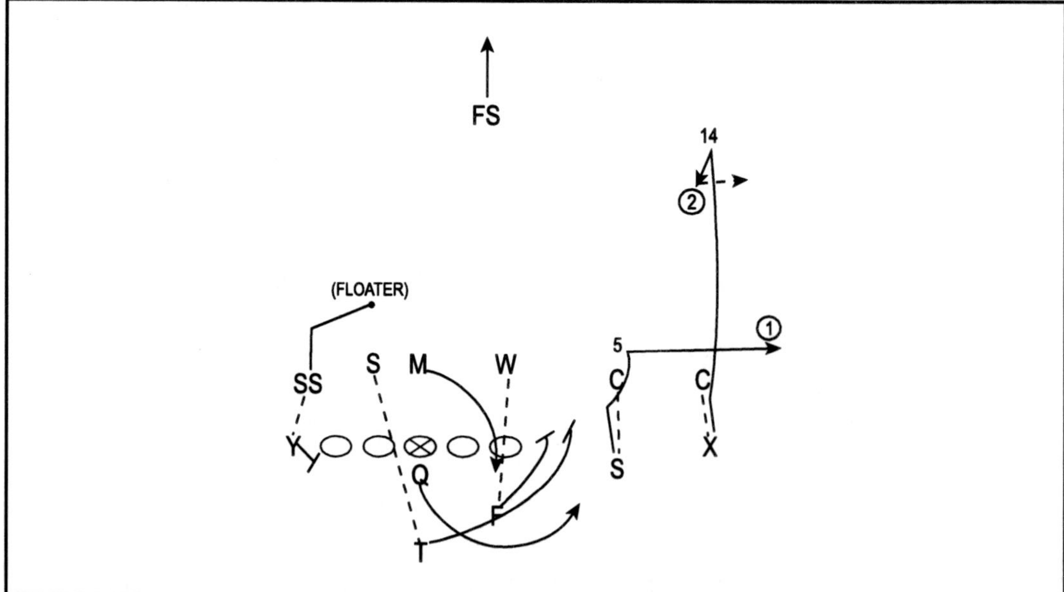

Diagram 3-32. Sprint-out curl action versus man-free coverage

create "home-run" deep-ball threats to combat aggressive cornerback play on such five-step-timed-quarterback-drop actions. Diagram 3-33 shows an acute- (fake-) and-go double-move action by the split end (X), and speed-out-and-up double-move action by the flanker (Z). Diagram 3-34 shows a curl-and-go double-move action by the split end (X), and a quick speed-out-and-up double-move action by a slotback (S).

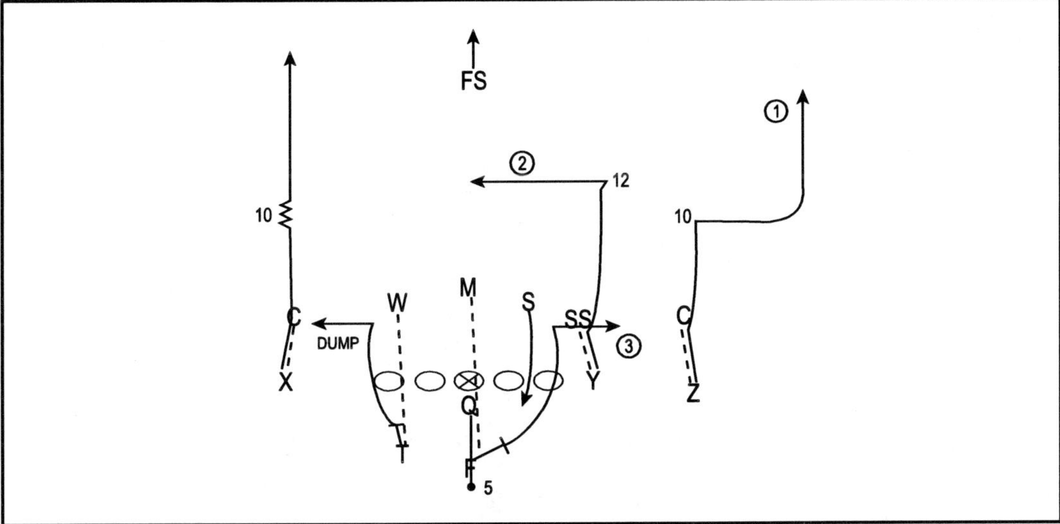

Diagram 3-33. Acute-and-go/speed-out-and-up double-move concepts versus man-free coverage

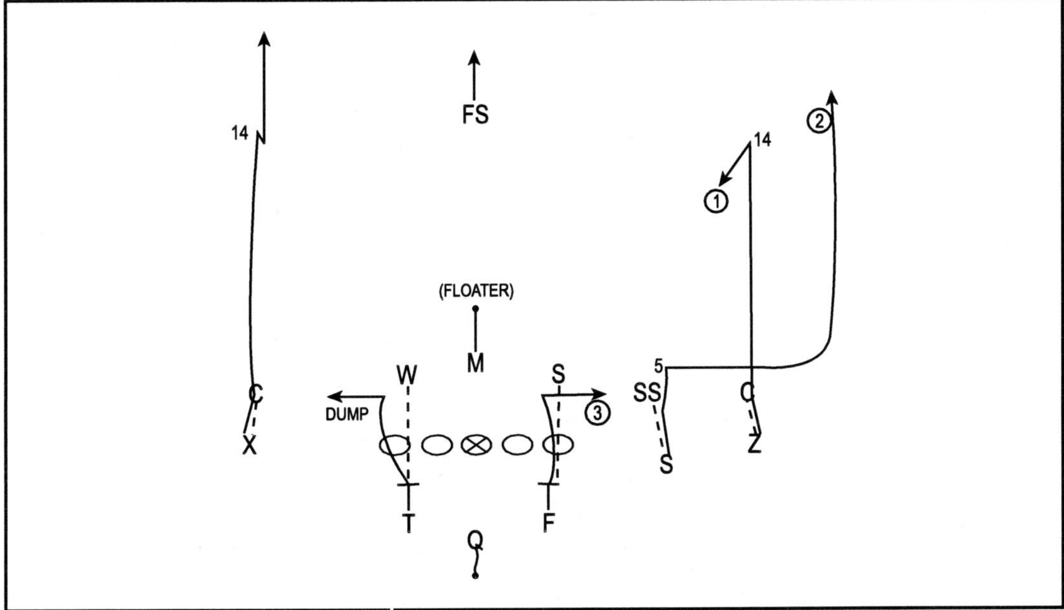

Diagram 3-34. Curl-and-go/quick speed-out-and-up double-move concepts versus man-free coverage

Square-In/Flat Combination

Many coaches prefer running square-ins versus man-free coverage rather than curls and hooks. The feeling is that the receiver has a better chance of producing man-to-man separation versus press-man coverage with square-in routes as shown in Diagram 3-35. Diagram 3-36 shows double square-in action versus man-free coverage.

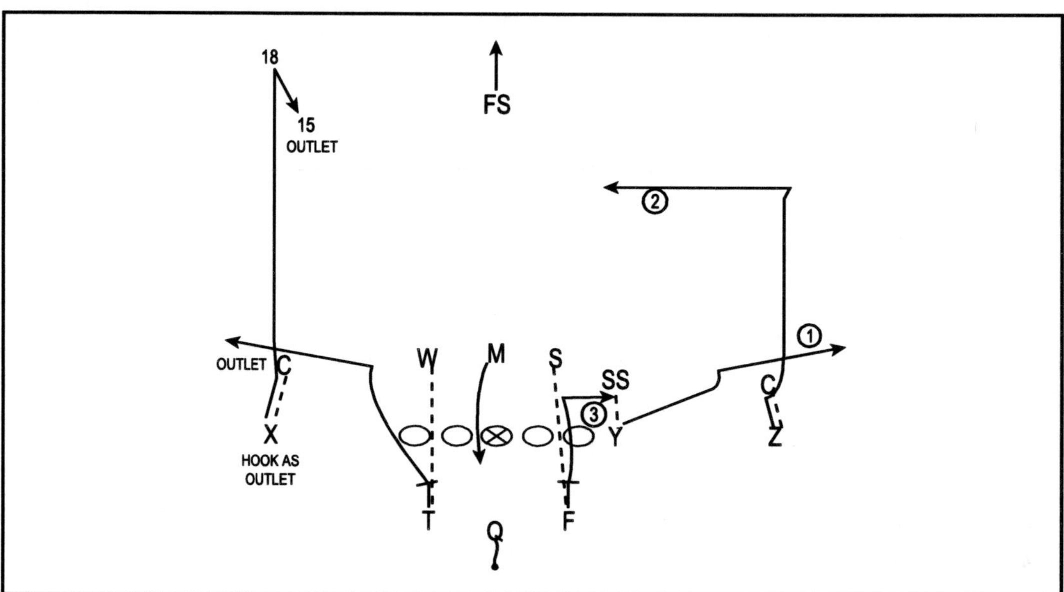

Diagram 3-35. Square-in/flat-route combination versus man-free coverage

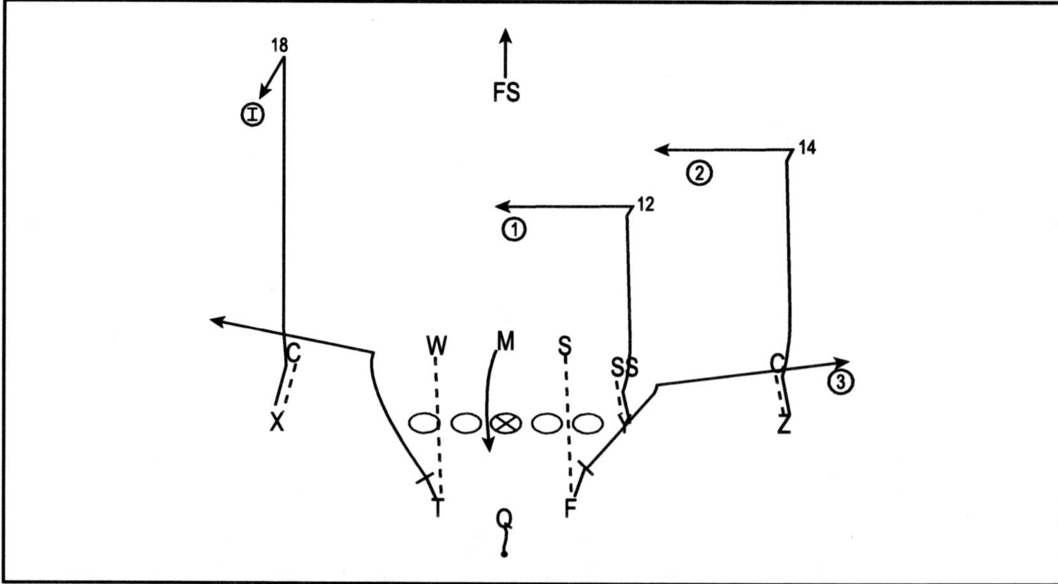

Diagram 3-36. Double square-in action versus man-free coverage

Shallow Cross/Replacement Curl

The shallow cross/replacement curl concept helps to produce an excellent crossing/picking action to attack man-free coverage. The inside, hard-breaking shallow route helps to produce an excellent man, stunt, and blitz-beater-type route. The replacement curl (replacing the original alignment of the outside receiver) has an excellent chance of man-separating to break back into the quarterback due to the crossing/picking action of the two receivers. The replacement curl is shorted to 10 yards to help produce consistent quarterback-drop timing. The shallow cross/replacement curl-combination-route concept is shown in Diagram 3-37 versus man-free coverage.

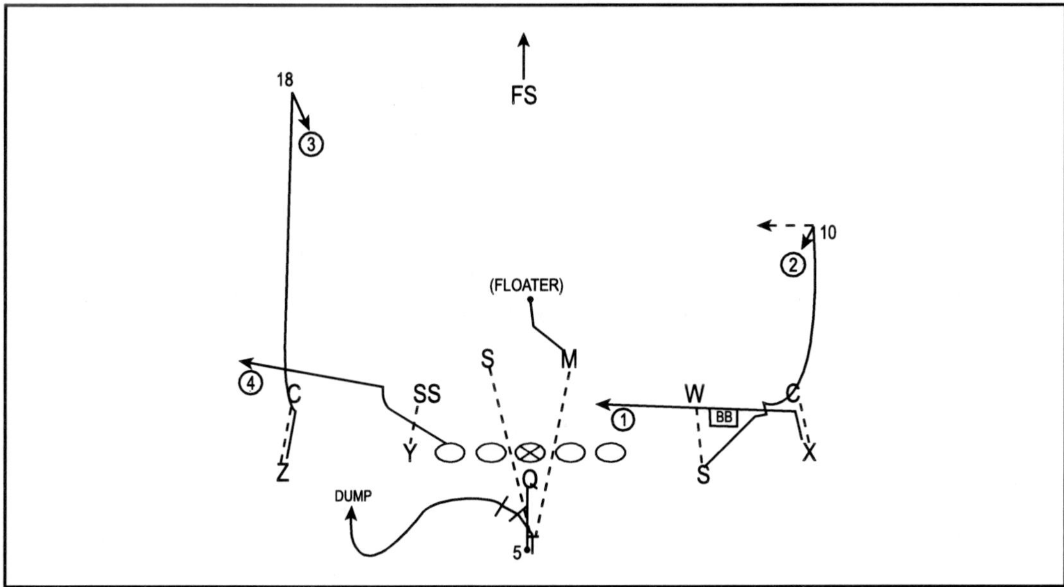

Diagram 3-37. Shallow cross/replacement curl concept versus man-free coverage

Curl/Hook/Square-In Routes as Outlets

Curls, hooks, and square-in routes can be very effective outlet routes to the backside of a pattern versus man-free coverage. Although such routes can have a tough time separating from press-man coverage, those routes are often given more time to accomplish such tasks as a result of being outlets. Once such receivers are able to separate, they are given plenty of room to maneuver as they work across the field to the inside as shown in Diagram 3-38. And, with two side-by-side in-breaking outlet routes, the free safety's ability to assist in stopping both routes is eliminated.

Drive Concept

The drive concept helps to create three excellent man-to-man coverage isolations—isolation on two of the inside man-free linebackers, and a similar isolation on one of the cornerbacks. The drive route by one of the wide receivers is, in itself, an excellent man-beater route. The same can be said for the tight end's short-dig route. The back, on his break-to-the-inside aspect of his sit route (which he must be sure to execute patiently to be sure to follow the execution of the tight end's short-dig route) also presents an excellent man-beater route for the quarterback to go to, as shown in Diagram 3-39. The main concern of the drive concept versus man free is the possibility

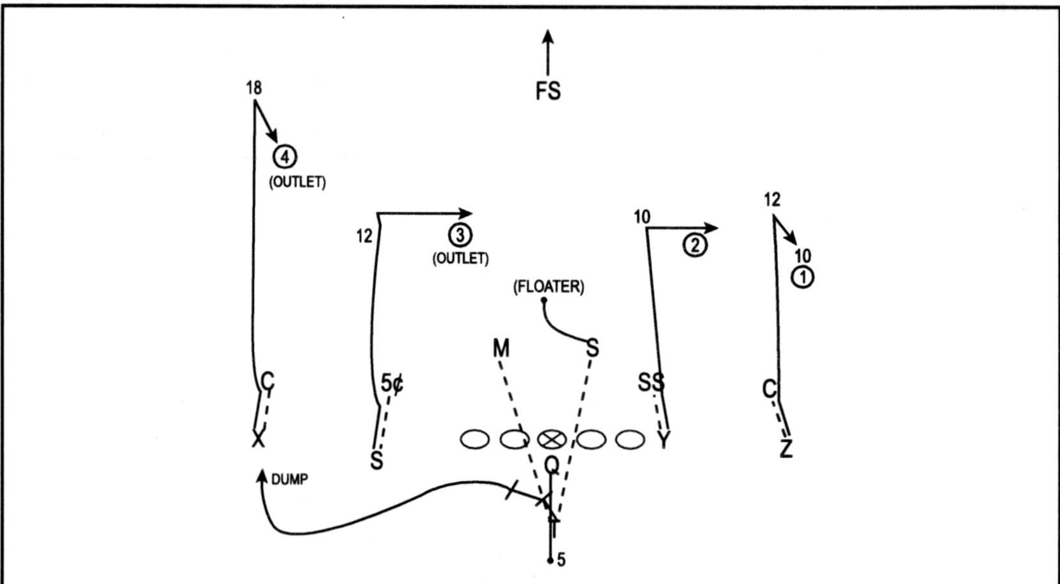

Diagram 3-38. Curls, hooks, and square-ins as backside outlets versus man-free coverage

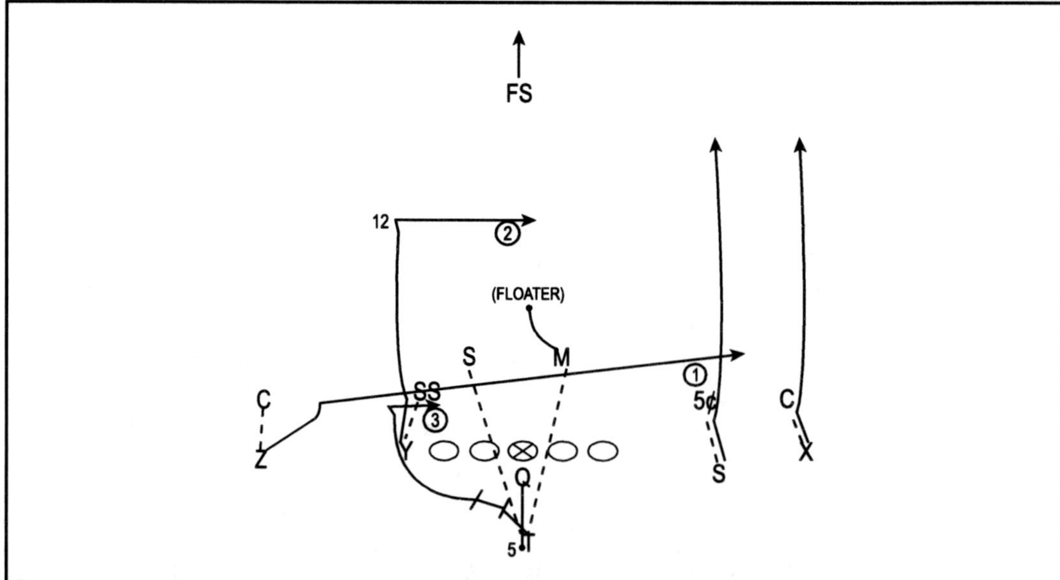

Diagram 3-39. Drive concept versus man-free coverage

of underneath floaters or hole defenders who may be free to jump routes of the drive concept—especially the drive route itself. Working the drive concept back to a two-receiver slotted side is shown in Diagram 3-39.

Cross Concept

The crossing-route action of the cross concept is an excellent man-free-coverage beater. As in the drive concept, the cross, short dig, and the man-adjustment aspect of the sit route help to create excellent man-under-beater possibilities. Crossing receivers, themselves, are also excellent man-beater actions as shown in Diagram 3-40 versus man-free coverage.

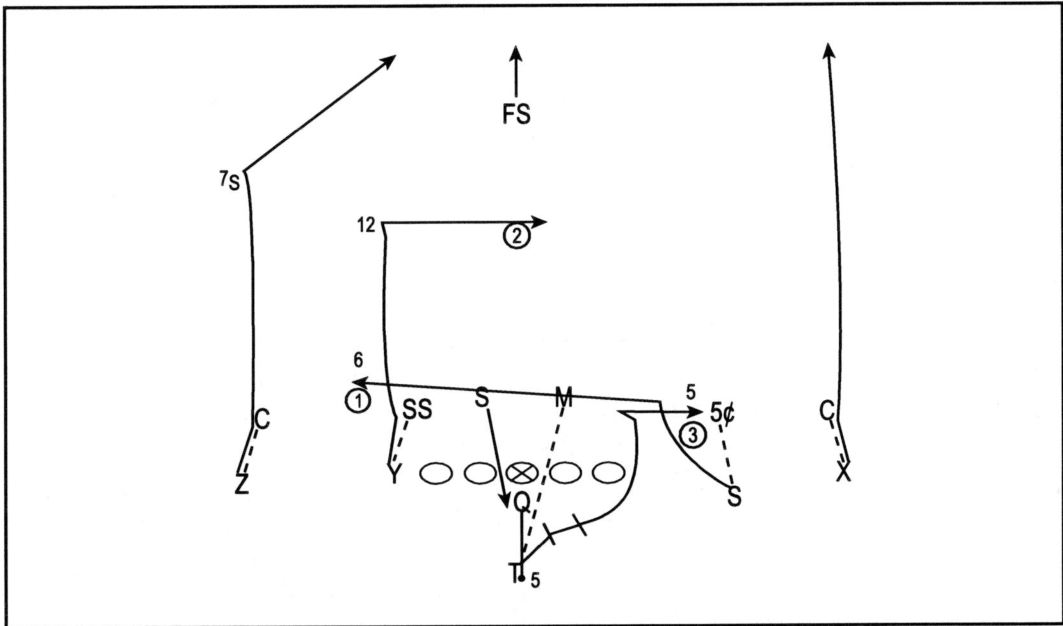

Diagram 3-40. Slot-cross concept versus man-free coverage

Double-Cross Concept

The double-cross concept is an extremely popular method of attacking man-free coverage. Two inside receivers execute picking/rubbing cross-route action with a dig-type route that works into the center of the field to act as an outlet if one of the two crossing routes don't open up. A post route by the wide receiver opposite the dig route works to blow the man-free free safety deep so that the safety cannot jump on the inside man-breaking dig route. The double-cross concept versus man-free coverage is shown in Diagram 3-41.

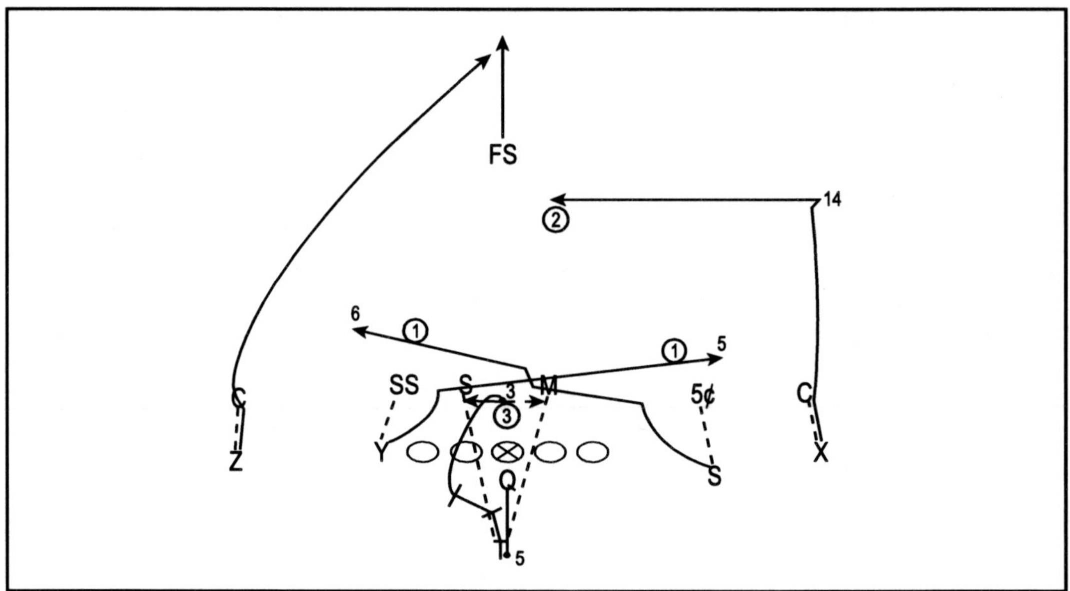

Diagram 3-41. Double-cross concept versus man-free coverage

Texas Concept

The Texas concept helps to create a crossing isolation on two of the underneath-man man-free defenders. The tight end works to pin the strong safety to the inside for his outside square-out-type man-break. The back drives to the flat to produce hard outside flow by his covering linebacker, and then works back inside hard underneath to separate from that linebacker. The major complication for the Texas concept versus man free can be the possibility of a floater or hole defender sitting in the short middle zone in a position to jump on the back's inside-breaking Texas route. The Texas concept versus man-free coverage is shown in Diagram 3-42. Note that outside streak routes are shown to act as excellent outside one-on-one deep isolations versus man free.

Option-Isolation Concept

Option-isolation routes help to produce excellent one-on-one isolations on man-free under-coverage defenders. Option routes can help to produce one-on-one size, talent, and speed mismatches. Option routes are best run off of five-step-drop timing by the quarterback. Five-step-drop-quarterback timing allows for option routes run in the 8- to 12-yard range, giving the option-route receivers time to properly maneuver and execute their option-route man- or zone-separation techniques. Diagram 3-43 shows a tight-end (Y) option and a halfback (H) option versus man-free coverage. Note that to the outside of the option routes, deep rollaway and comeback-out routes are shown to act as excellent late-developing outlet routes versus man free.

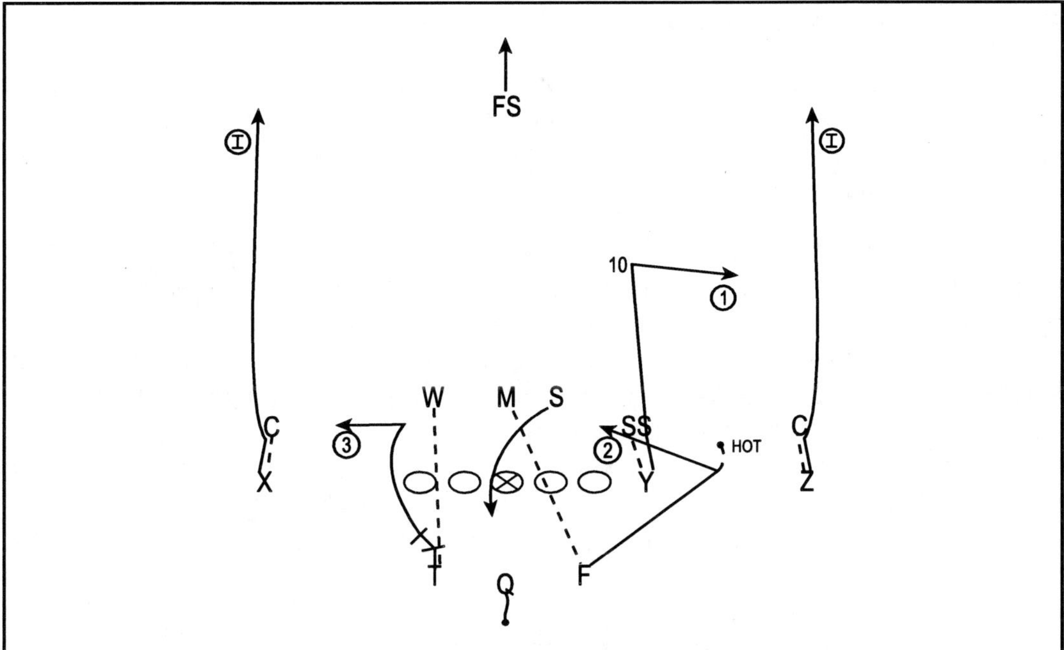

Diagram 3-42. Texas concept versus man-free coverage

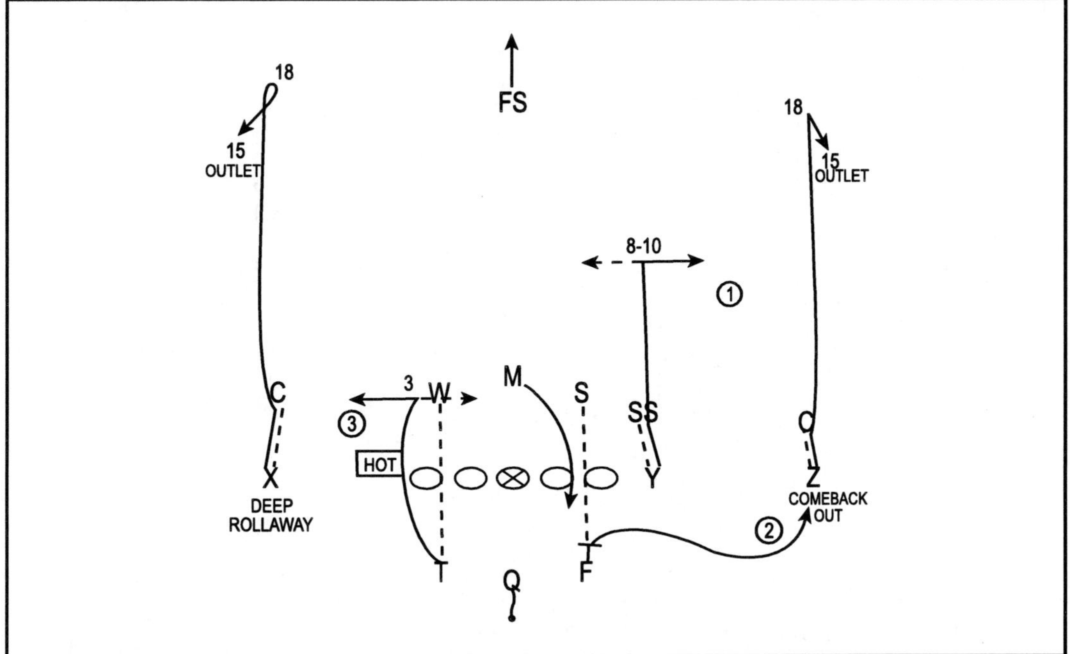

Diagram 3-43. Option-isolation routes versus man-free coverage

Pivot- and Break-Route Isolations

Tight-end (Y) pivot- and break-route isolations can be very effective versus man-free coverage. Such routes can often help produce mismatches in favor of the offense—especially if the linebacker is bigger and more physical than the man-free strong safety that may be covering him.

The pivot and break routes are run in the six- to seven-yard range. Versus a normal inside-out man-coverage alignment by the covering strong safety, the Y-pivot route may be the better route of the two, allowing the tight end to wall off the covering defender by alignment. However, versus an active, fast-flowing linebacker, the break route can help the tight end to separate by breaking back to the inside. Diagram 3-44 shows a Y-pivot high-low-read-isolation action to attack man-free coverage. More often than not, the back's route becomes a clear-type route, since the back is not given the option to man-break to the inside, due to the fact that he has to start from a deepened backfield alignment. The Y-pivot route is the safer concept to use versus man free in that the tight-end (Y) pivot route works to the outside, away from any potential man-free hole or floater defenders who may be sitting in the short-underneath-middle zone. Diagram 3-45 shows Y-break action versus man-free.

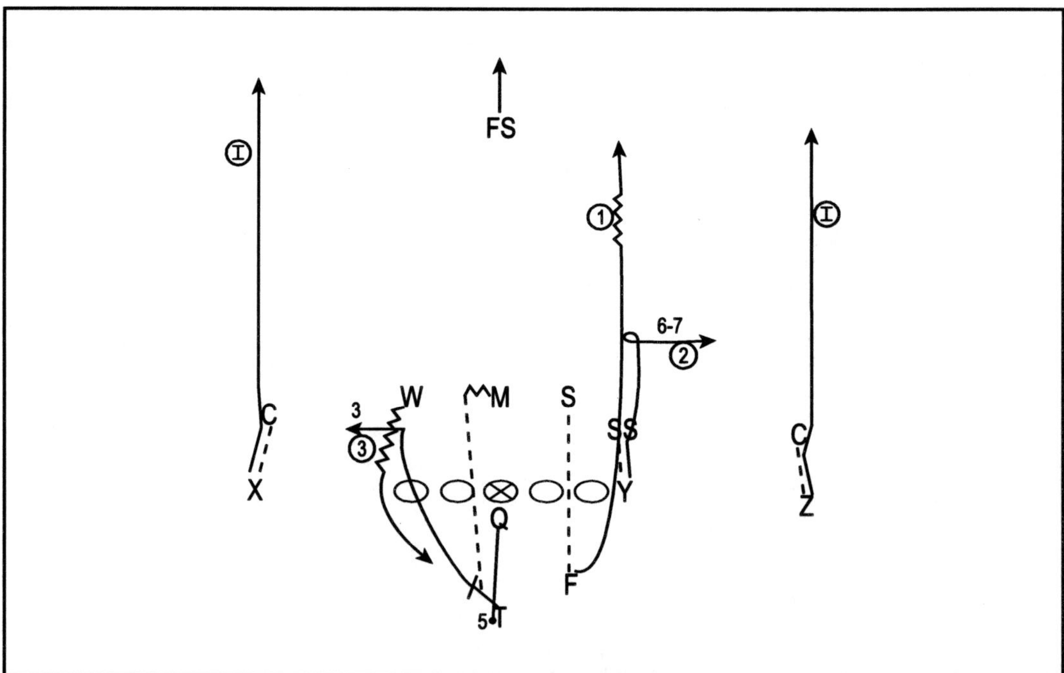

Diagram 3-44. Y-pivot isolation versus man-free coverage

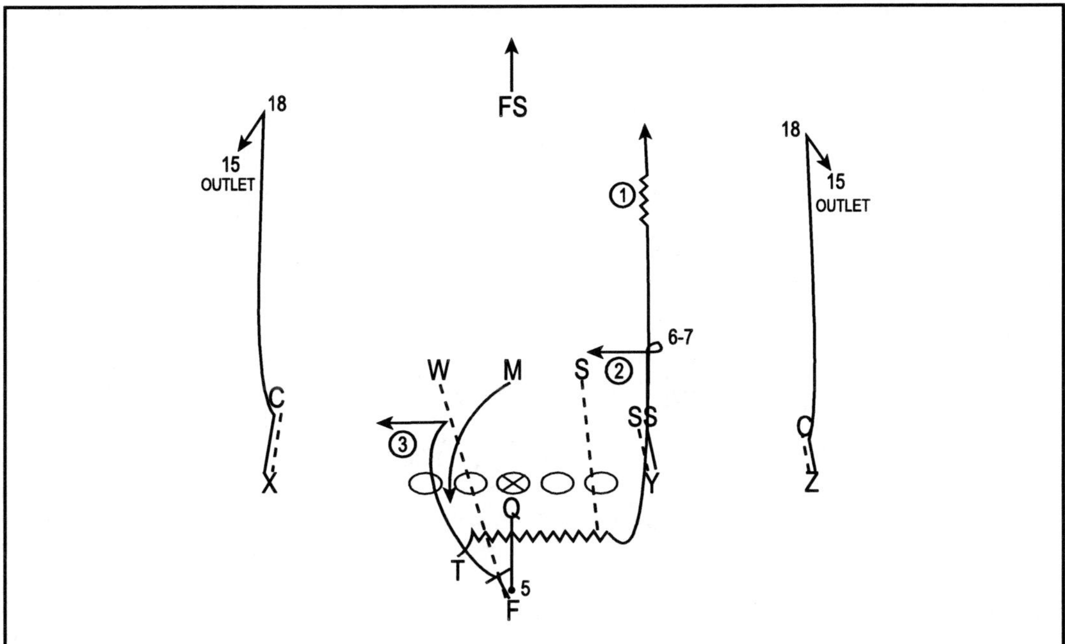

Diagram 3-45. Y-break isolation versus man-free coverage

Backs-Cross and Fake-Cross Isolations

Short inside backs-cross and fake-cross isolations are very effective versus man-free coverage. On backs cross, the quarterback reads the mesh of the crossing backs to see if one or both of the backs pop open versus the man-under coverage. If they don't, the tight-end route over the middle becomes the come-open-late route to go to. Between the crossing/picking action of the backs and the man-separating short-dig route of the tight end, a good chance exists that at least one of the three receivers will pop open. The backs-cross concept versus man-free coverage is shown in Diagram 3-46.

In backs-fake cross, the backs fake cross action once the linebackers start to play the cross action and man-break back out towards the sidelines. Again, the quarterback reads to see if one, or both, of the backs pop open. If not, the tight end's short-dig route then becomes the come-open-late route to go to. The backs-fake-cross concept versus man-free coverage is shown in Diagram 3-47.

Pick and Rub Concepts

Pick and rub concepts can be excellent man-free-coverage-beater route combinations. Of course, any pick or rub must be legally executed. Receivers cannot run into and/or block coverage defenders as a part of the pick or rub concept. Diagram 3-48 shows a pick-route combination with an inside receiver working to the outside versus man-free coverage.

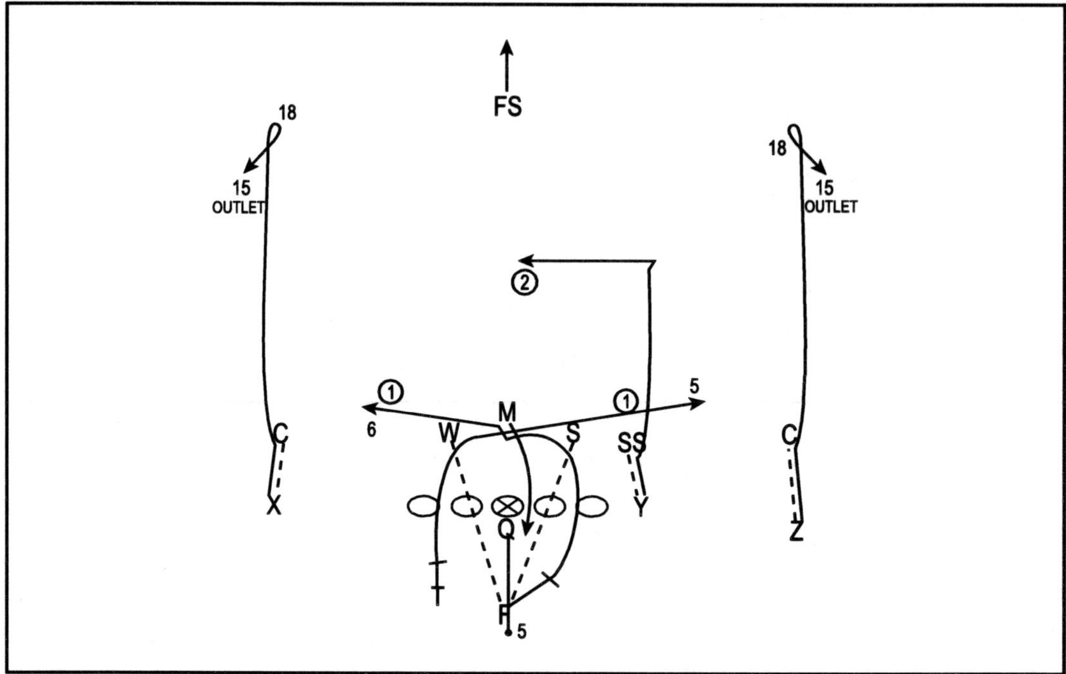

Diagram 3-46. Backs-cross concept versus man-free coverage

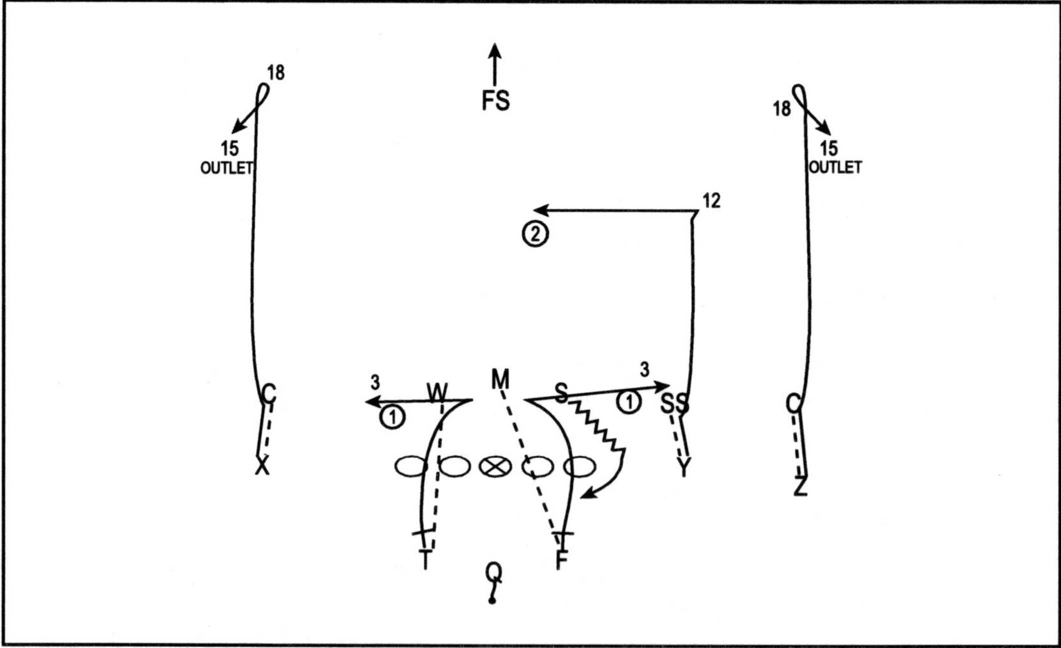

Diagram 3-47. Backs-fake-cross concept versus man-free coverage

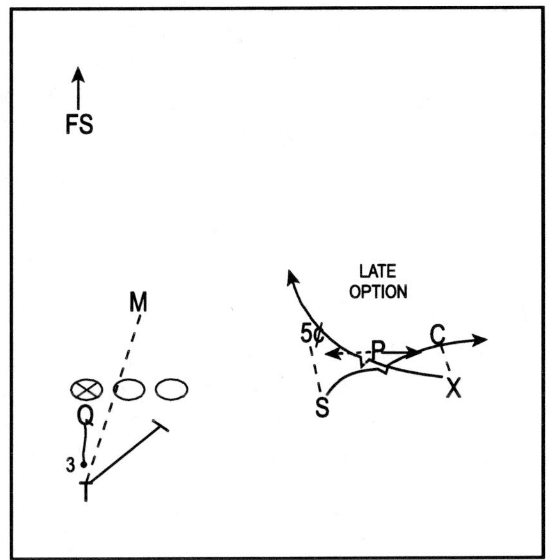

Diagram 3-48. Pick-route combination versus man-free coverage

An interesting idea is to have the receiver who actual sets up the pick for the prime pick, rub, or slice route run a modified option route if the quarterback snaps his eyes to that receiver. In this fashion, if the pick, rub, or slice receiver is covered, the quarterback has a delayed timed route to work to as an outlet.

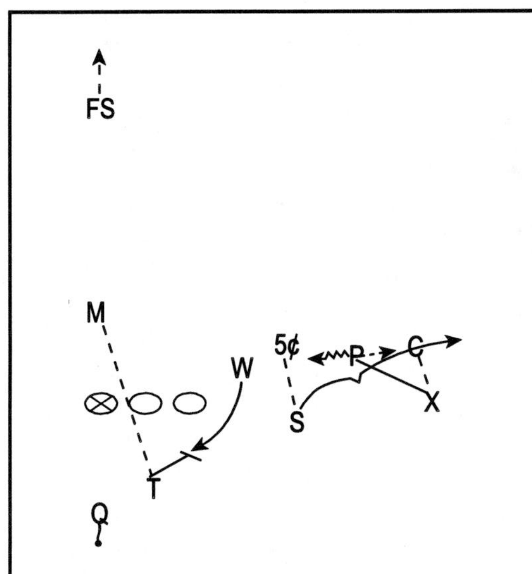

Diagram 3-49. Rub-route combination versus man-free coverage

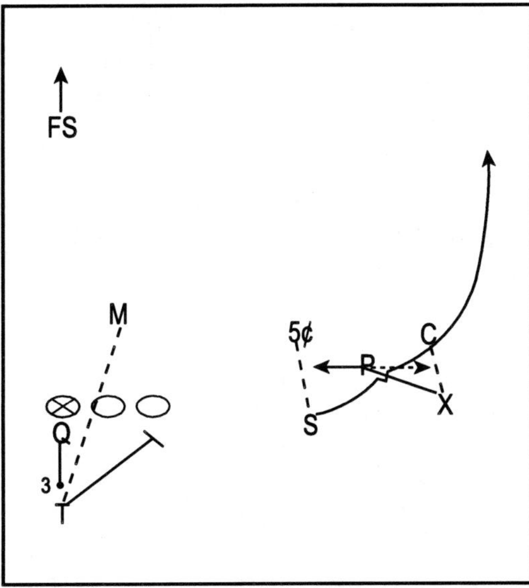

Diagram 3-50. Slice-route combination versus man-free coverage

Diagram 3-49 shows a rub-route combination with an outside receiver working to the inside. In rub action, the offense always has to be worried about the depth and activity of the deep, man-free free safety to the side of the rub. Diagram 3-50 shows a slice-route combination with an inside receiver working off a pick set-up and executing a fade route.

Picking Screens

Picking-type screens—legal when the ball is thrown behind the line of scrimmage—are very effective versus man-free coverage. Diagram 3-51 shows a wide-receiver screen with the slotback blocking out on the man-free cornerback man-covering the split end. Diagram 3-52 shows a pick screen to a back versus man-free coverage as the tight end blocks the linebacker assigned to man-cover the back.

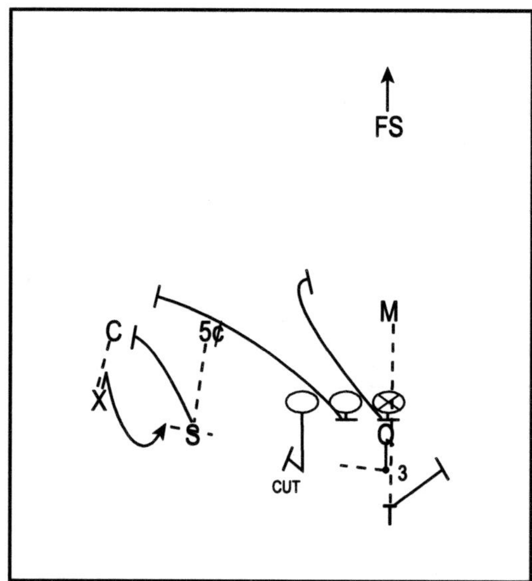

Diagram 3-51. Wide-receiver-pick screen versus man-free coverage

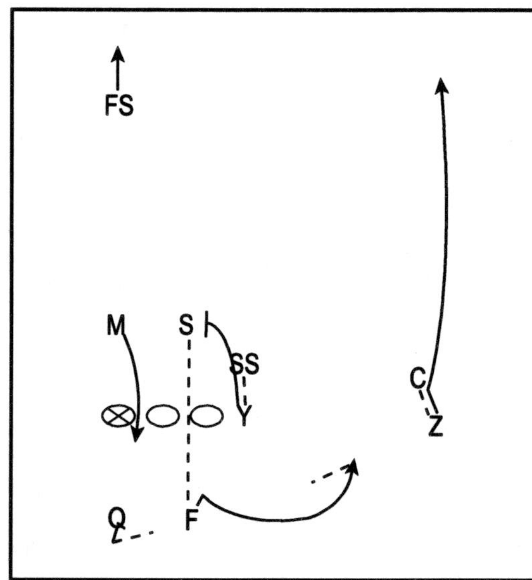

Diagram 3-52. Back-pick screen versus man-free coverage

4

Pass Attack of Cover 2

Cover 2 is the most common (or basic) coverage in the two-safety family. Two deep safeties are in the middle of the field. The two deep safeties are aligned deep and are usually tight, or near the hashes. They play deep half-field zone coverage, aligning approximately 14 yards deep. The cornerbacks are low, or squatted, in alignment, five to seven yards deep. They are usually aligned head-up to outside of the widest receiver. The cornerbacks will probably be in more of a straight-legged, squared-up stance. Rather than the man-coverage technique of looking or staring at the receiver, the cornerbacks will look through the wide receiver in an effort to "peek in" toward the quarterback. Diagram 4-1 shows cover-2 two-deep, five-under zone coverage.

Cover-2 Pass-Game Strengths

The five underneath-zone-coverage defenders are the strength of cover 2. In essence, cover 2 is a tilted coverage strong, to the strength of the formation or to the field. The three underneath-zone-coverage defenders to the strongside (one extra underneath-zone defender) is what produces the tilted aspect of cover 2. Diagram 4-2 shows the tilted strength aspect of cover 2.

- The five underneath-zone-coverage defenders of cover 2 produces a crowded "small field" for the underneath-pass game to throw into.

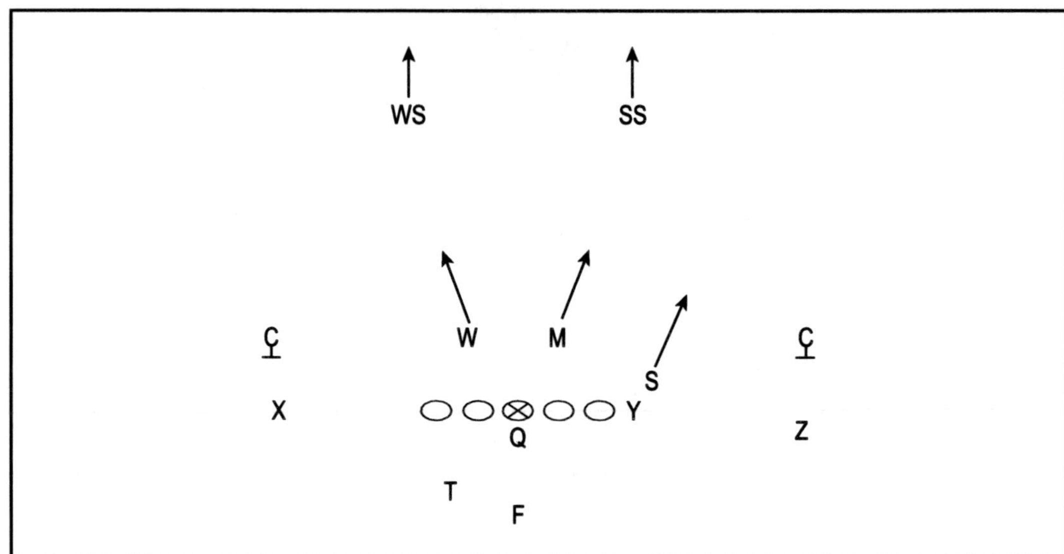

Diagram 4-1. Cover-2 two-deep, five-under zone coverage

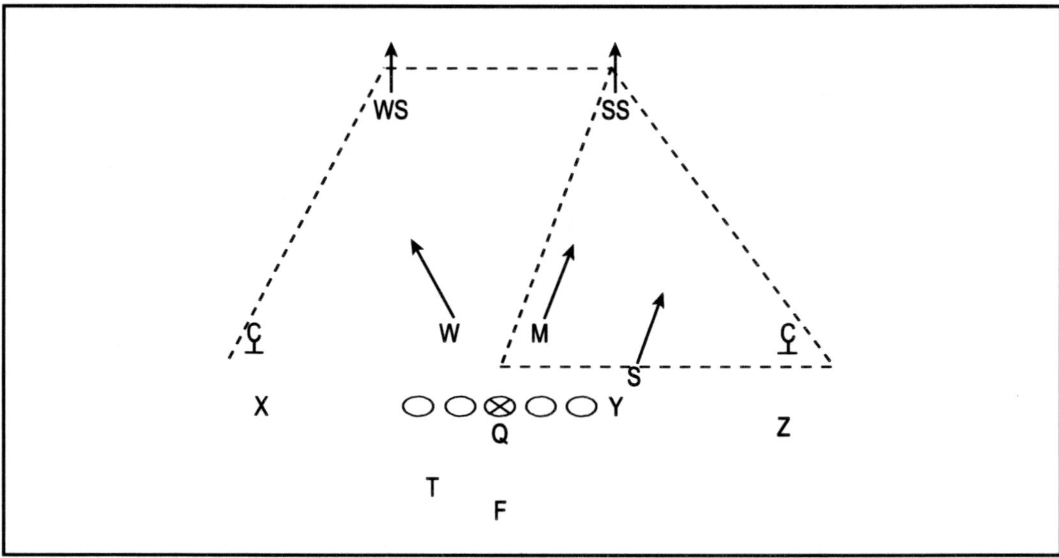

Diagram 4-2. Tilted aspect of cover 2

- The five underneath-zone-coverage defenders of cover 2 can do a great job of disrupting pass-route releases—especially routes that attack upfield vertically.
- The five underneath-zone-coverage defenders of cover 2 take away easy, quick, or short pass-game routes and patterns—which is a major strength of the coverage.
- Cover 2 especially eliminates side-by-side, lateral-read-route combinations, which are a big part of many offensive-pass designs. Diagram 4-3 shows how a side-by-

side lateral-read-hitch-route combination and a curl/flat-route combination are covered by the underneath-zone coverage of cover 2.

- Cover 2 does a good job of eliminating out-route concepts due to the squatted-cornerback-coverage play. Diagram 4-4 shows the elimination of a speed-out route due to squatted, cover-2 coverage of the cornerback. (Diagram 4-4 also provides another example of how cover 2 does an excellent job of taking away the side-by-side, lateral-read out-route combination of the flanker's speed-out route and the tight end's alley route, as discussed in the previous bullet point.

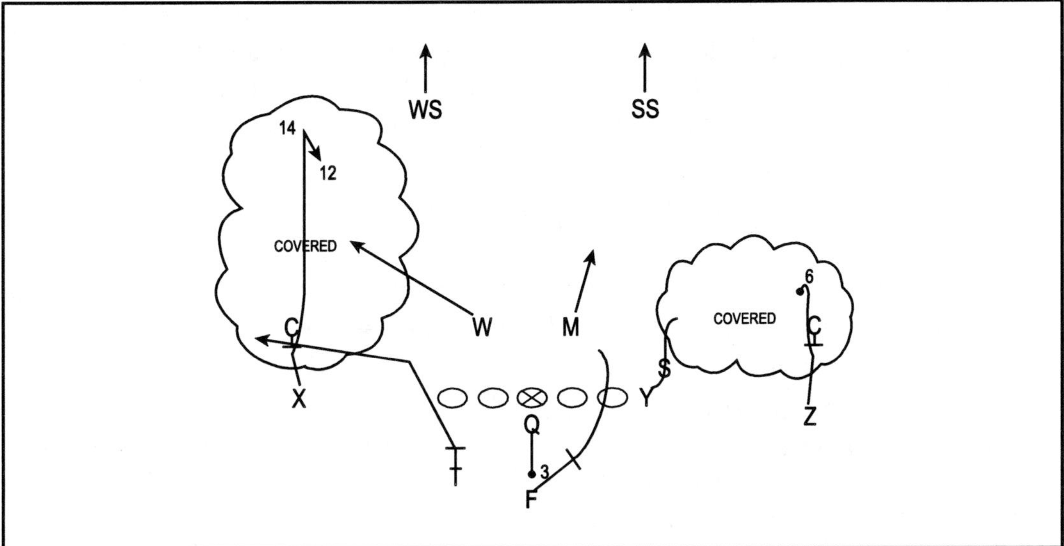

Diagram 4-3. Side-by-side, lateral-read-route combinations taken away by cover

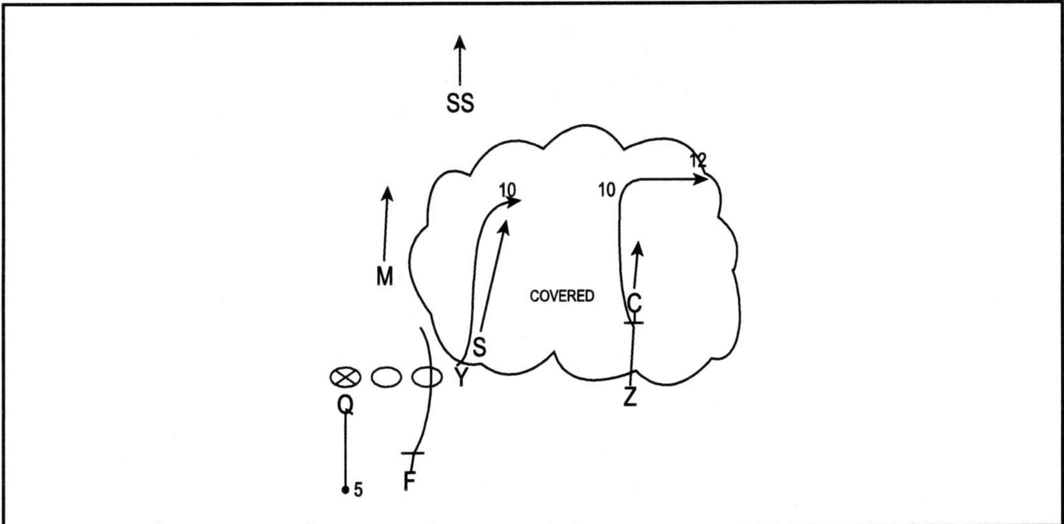

Diagram 4-4. Cover-2 elimination of out routes

- Depending on the technique utilized by the underneath-zone-coverage linebackers, the linebackers can run vertically with any inside-receiver vertical-release routes. This technique can force possible floating throws to such receivers, making such passes vulnerable to interceptions by the deep cover-2 safeties.
- Cover 2 is an excellent disguise coverage from which to stem to other coverages due to the easy ability of the deep cover-2 safeties to rotate up, back deep to the middle of the field, or deep to the outside.
- Cover-2 cornerbacks can help to do a great job of containing and pushing pass-pattern routes to the inside toward the cover-2 hash-mark-aligned safeties.
- Cover 2 is considered one of the hardest coverages to throw into because cover-2 pass-game vulnerabilities are difficult to attack, necessitating more difficult, deeper throws down the deep middle of the field and to the deep outside.

Cover-2 Pass-Game Weaknesses

- The basic pass-game weaknesses of cover 2 are the deep outside holes from the hash to the sideline and the deep middle zone between the hashes. Cover-2 voids are shown in Diagram 4-5.
- Cover 2 is susceptible to high-low isolation reads to the outside. Such isolations put a receiver high and a receiver low on the cover-2 cornerback, then throw opposite to the cornerback's coverage reaction. The outside cover-2 high-low isolation versus the cornerback is shown in Diagram 4-6.

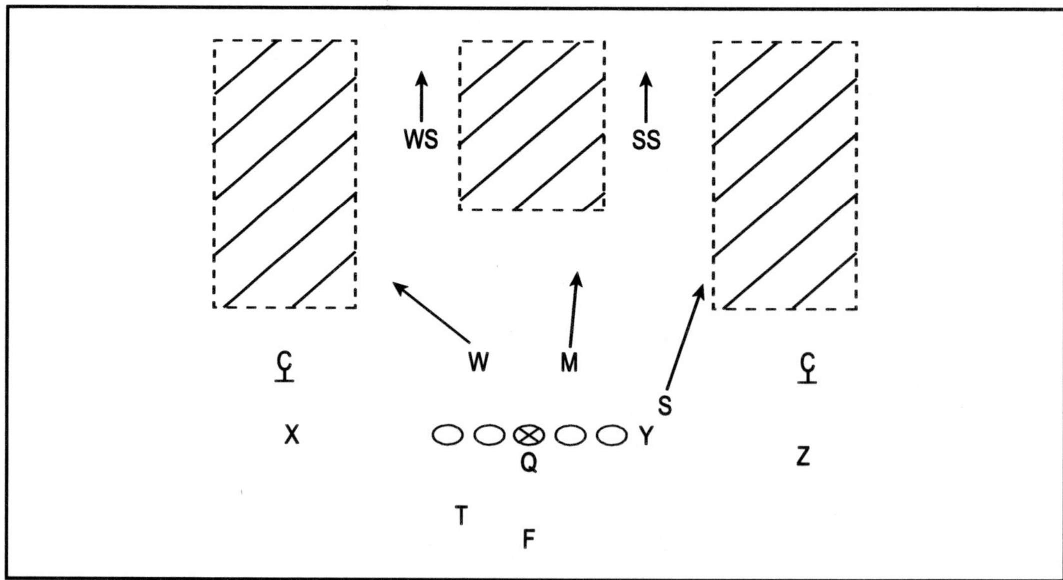

Diagram 4-5. Cover-2 voids

- Three streak routes (two up the sideline, and one down the middle of the field) create a three-on-two isolation on the two deep-halves cover-2 safeties. A three-on-two streak isolation is most effective versus hard-squat cornerbacks where the outside streaks can more easily find the deep outside-coverage voids.
- Two-on-one deep isolations can also be placed on one of the two deep safeties—either with an outside and an inside receiver, or with two inside receivers. Both concepts are shown from a four-streaks pattern with a skinny-post-read route by an inside receiver. Once again, the outside-streak route of the widest receiver is most effective versus a hard-squat cornerback who opens up void for a stick-it-in-the-hole-type throw on the sideline.

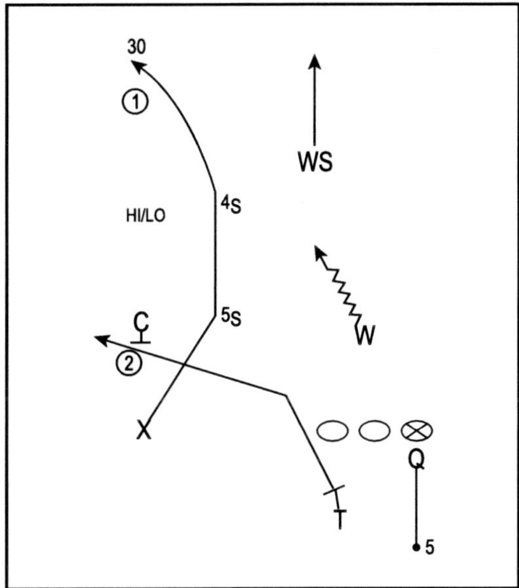

Diagram 4-6. Outside high-low isolation on cover-2 cornerback

- Route combinations that clear one or both deep cover-2 safeties and run a deep dig-type route underneath the clear route helps to open up a coverage void in the cover-2 structure that can be exploited. The clear routes help to blow the top off of cover 2 by pushing the cover-2 safeties deep to help create the deep dig-route-coverage voids as shown in Diagram 4-7.
- Spot-dropping and vertical-route-carrying cover-2 linebackers help to create excellent high-low isolations on the linebackers. Flood-route combinations and isolation-option routes also effectively attack cover-2 linebacker play. The "shell" aspect of the cover-2 safeties and cornerbacks helps prevent the four defensive backs from effectively helping the coverage roles of the linebackers.
- Widening the cover-2-under coverage and working the spaces in between the cornerbacks and the cover-2 linebackers (i.e., short hooks) is an excellent way to attack cover 2. This technique helps create an effective attack of a cover-2 area that the defense thinks is a strength of the coverage.
- Man-coverage cover-2 linebackers within the zone scheme become extremely vulnerable to crossing routes and patterns and isolation routes. The crossing routes can help to create natural picking actions to help free a man-covered receiver. Isolation routes, such as option routes, can help to create mismatches in favor of the receivers.
- Play-action passing helps to greatly distort cover-2 linebacker-coverage play. The freezing of a linebacker by forcing him to react up to a play-action-run fake can

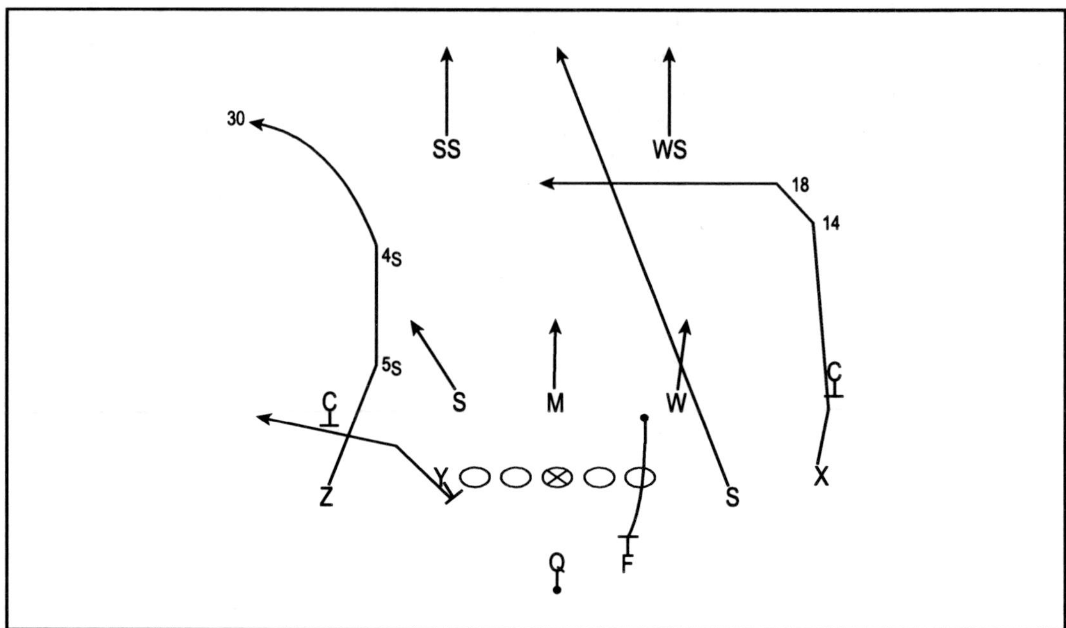

Diagram 4-7. Clear/dig-route combination to create deep cover-2-coverage void

greatly help to create and/or increase cover-2 voids. Play-action-run faking helps to hinder the abilities of the cover-2 linebackers to run with receivers and/or disrupt their releases.

- Cover 2 is especially vulnerable to misdirection play-action bootleg or naked-bootleg passes. The lack of secondary run support of the cover-2 secondary shell makes a cover-2 defensive seven-man front all the more run-conscious. Play-action passing—especially the misdirection play-action passing or a bootleg (or naked-bootleg) pass—helps to create cover-2 weaknesses.
- Screens can be very effective versus cover 2. Formationing can help to create screen numbers (i.e., three-on-two) mismatches in favor of the offense.

Route Combination and Pass-Pattern Attack of Cover 2

Quick-Game Double Slant

The quick-game (three-step-drop-timed drop throw by the quarterback) double-slant-route combination places a two-on-one isolation on the linebacker aligned on the slotted receiver. If the linebacker (S) in Diagram 4-8 follows the inside slant, a throw lane is opened up to the outside slant. If the linebacker tries to work outside to the outside slant, the inside slant receiver bends his slant upfield to make the reception. The quick-game double-slant-route combination action is shown in Diagram 4-8.

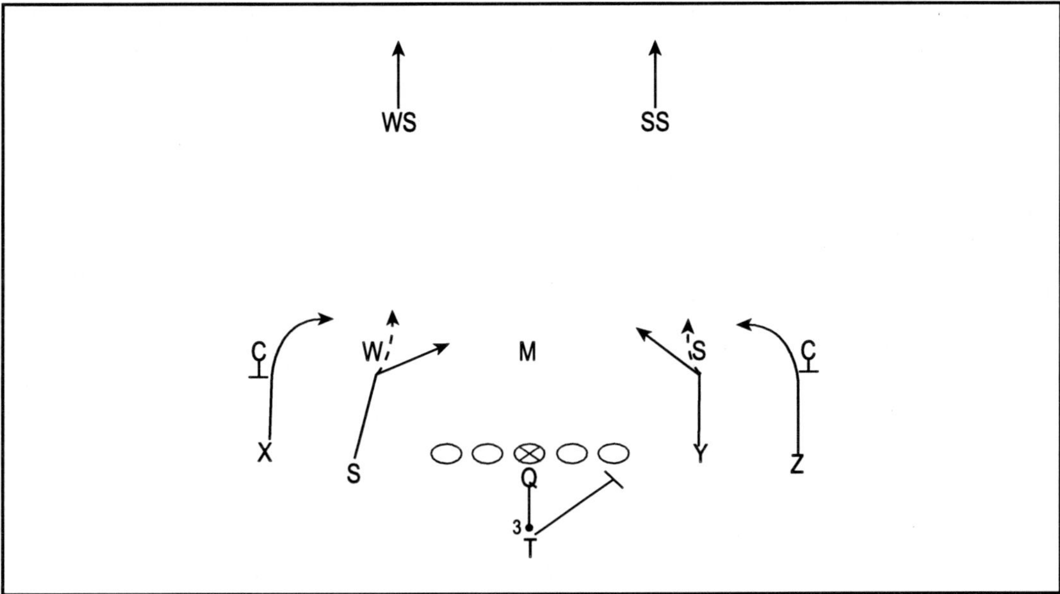

Diagram 4-8. Quick-game double-slant combination versus cover 2

Quick-Game Slant Isolation

Quick-game slant-isolation routes can be very effective versus cover 2, especially if combined with a quick, play-action fake away from the slantside to hold the linebacker(s) from getting in the slant-throw lane. Such isolation-slant action is enhanced by having plenty of field room to work in (i.e., throwing to the flanker to the field or to the split end when in the middle of the field). Maximum splitting by the isolation-slant receiver also helps to spread the field and give the slant action more room to work in. Isolation-slant action with a quick play-action fake away from the slantside is shown in Diagram 4-9.

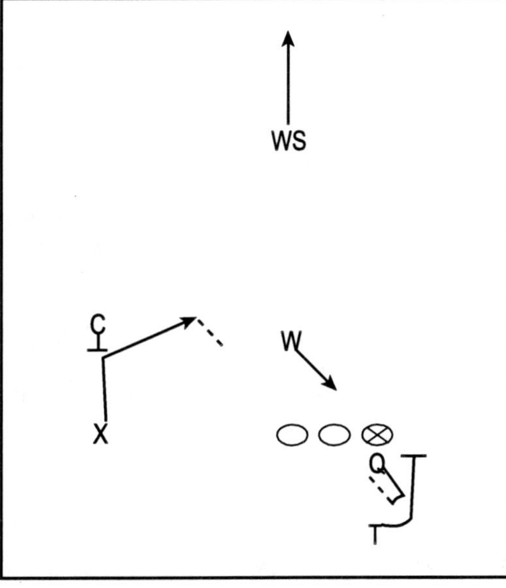

Diagram 4-9. Quick-game isolation-slant action with quick play-action fake away from slant versus cover 2

Quick-Game Inside-Receiver Speed-Out

The quick-game inside-receiver speed-out-route combination is a quick, high-low fade/speed-out isolation on a cover-2 cornerback. The widest receiver must outside release in an effort to get the cornerback to turn his back to the inside receiver's speed-out route. If the cornerback runs with the fade route, the quarterback quickly throws low to the inside receiver's speed-out route. If the cornerback stays squatted waiting on the in speed-out route, the throw is made over the cornerback's head in the hole to the fade route. If in doubt, the quarterback should throw the ball "low" to the inside receiver's speed-out route quickly to give the speed-out receiver the ability to make the catch and knife upfield quickly before he gets out to the cornerback. Diagram 4-10 shows the quick-game inside-receiver speed-out-route combination.

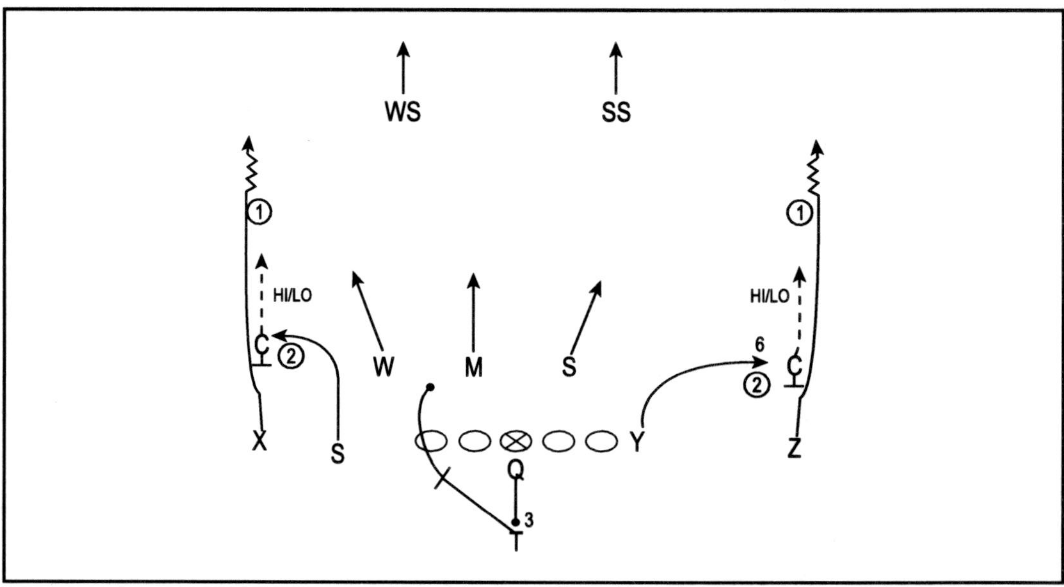

Diagram 4-10. Quick-game inside-receiver speed-out versus cover 2

Quick-Game Inside-Receiver Stick-Route Isolation

The quick-game inside-receiver stick-route isolation can be very effective versus cover 2. As shown in Diagram 4-11 from a two-tight-end, two-wide-receiver formation, the quarterback simply works to the tight end to the one-linebacker side.

Diagram 4-12 shows quick-game double-slant action with a backside flanker (Z) slant-and-go-route action. The slant-and-go route is an excellent double-move route to utilize off of slant action if a deep cover-2 safety tries to jump a wide receiver's slant route. The slant-and-go receiver breaks his slant-and-go route to the outside fade-throw area.

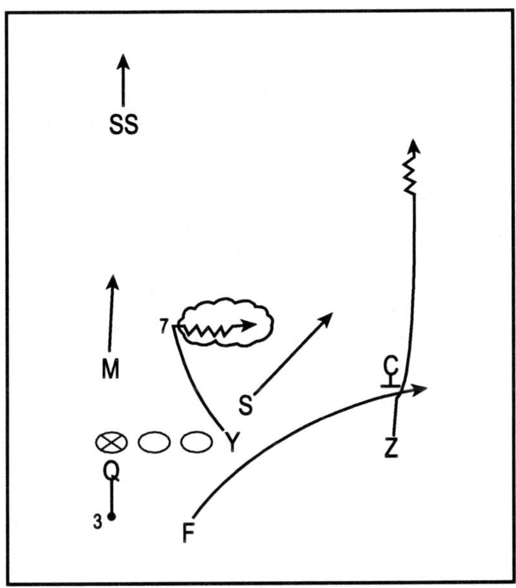

Diagram 4-11. Quick-game inside-receiver stick-route isolation versus cover 2

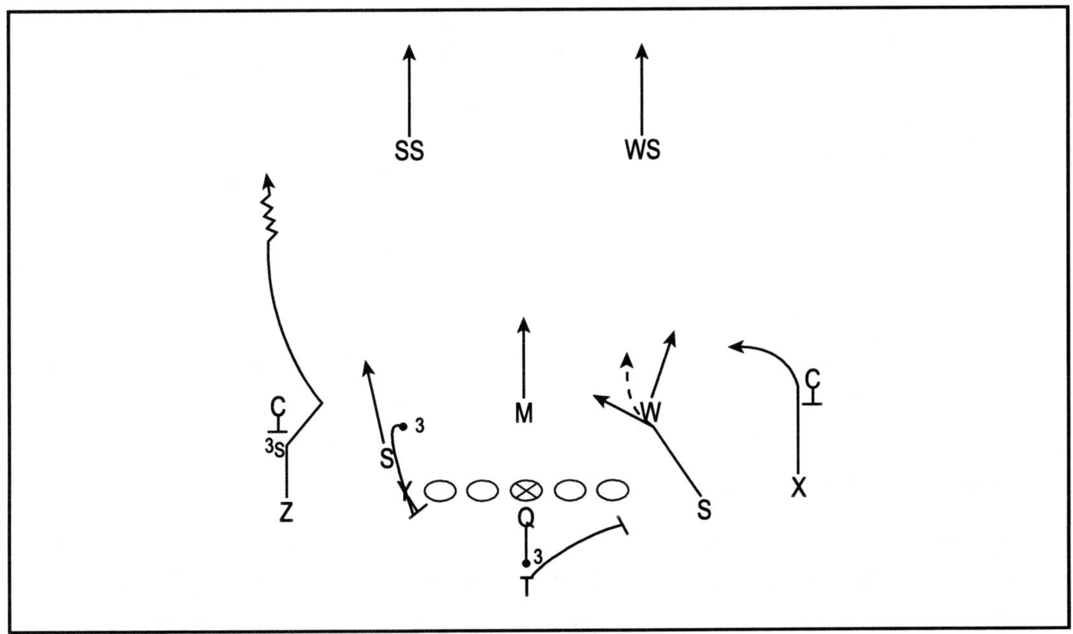

Diagram 4-12. Quick-game double-slant combination and backside slant-and-go versus cover 2

Smash High-Low Isolation

The high-low-read smash isolation attacks one of cover 2's biggest weaknesses, the deep outside area from the hash to the sideline. The smash-route combination puts a (high) post-corner route over the top of the cover-2 cornerback and a (low) smash (hitch-option) route underneath the cornerback. The quarterback throws high or low off of the action of the cornerback. If in doubt (the cornerback splitting the difference between the inside receiver post-corner and the smash routes), the quarterback should always throw low. A retreating cornerback will usually be able to react to a deep post-corner throw to a greater degree because of the extended time it will take a pass to get to the post-corner than it will to get to the (low) smash route. A high-low smash-route pattern versus cover 2 is shown in Diagram 4-13.

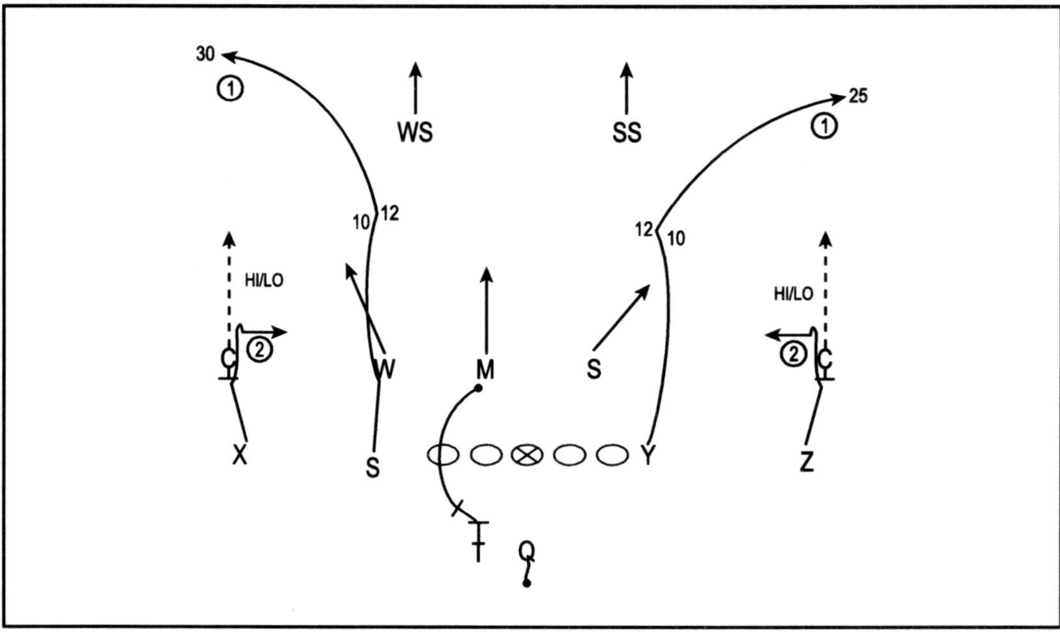

Diagram 4-13. High-low-read-smash concept versus cover 2

Post-Corner High-Low Isolation

A very similar concept to the smash high-low isolation is the post-corner high-low isolation. The difference of the two concepts is that in the post-corner isolation, it is the widest receiver that runs the (high) post-corner route with a back running a (low) flat route to control the cornerback. The post-corner route is run off of a cover-2 post-corner stem adjustment in which the wide receiver breaks inside for five steps, breaks straight upfield for four steps, head nods to the post route, and then breaks to the corner. In addition, running the post-corner routes with the widest receivers allows the tight end to run a streak route down the middle of the field to split the two deep cover-2 safeties.

The middle-streak route will help hold the deep cover-2 safeties from flying out wide to cover the post-corner routes or present the quarterback with a excellent deep middle route if the two deep cover-2 safeties do widen. Diagram 4-14 shows a high-low-read post-corner pattern versus cover 2.

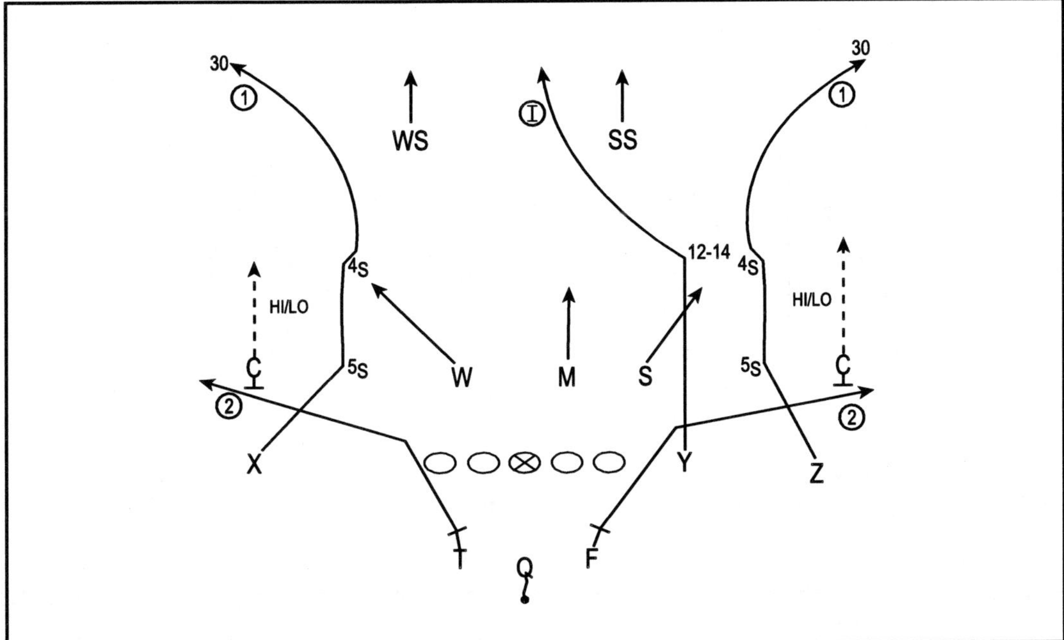

Diagram 4-14. High-low-read post-corner concept versus cover 2

Post-Corner Adjustment Concept

Some offenses will use the cover-2 high-low post-corner route as an adjustment route to be run instead of running lateral-read-route combinations that are extremely well-defensed if the coverage is cover 2. As a result, such offenses will adjust such lateral-read-route combinations as a speed-out/alley combination or a curl/flat combination, and instead adjust on the run to a cover-2 post-corner/flat combination. Such cover-2 post-corner-adjustment action is shown in Diagram 4-15.

Post-Corner Deep Across

The post-corner deep-across pattern is an excellent concept versus cover 2. However, instead of a two-receiver high-low read, the wide receiver opposite of the cover-2 post-corner route runs a deep-over route to produce a three-tiered high-low read, as shown in Diagram 4-16. Play-action, as shown, helps the across route to effectively get across the field. The pattern can be easily flipped over in design having the opposite wide receivers run the cover 2 post-corner and deep-over routes.

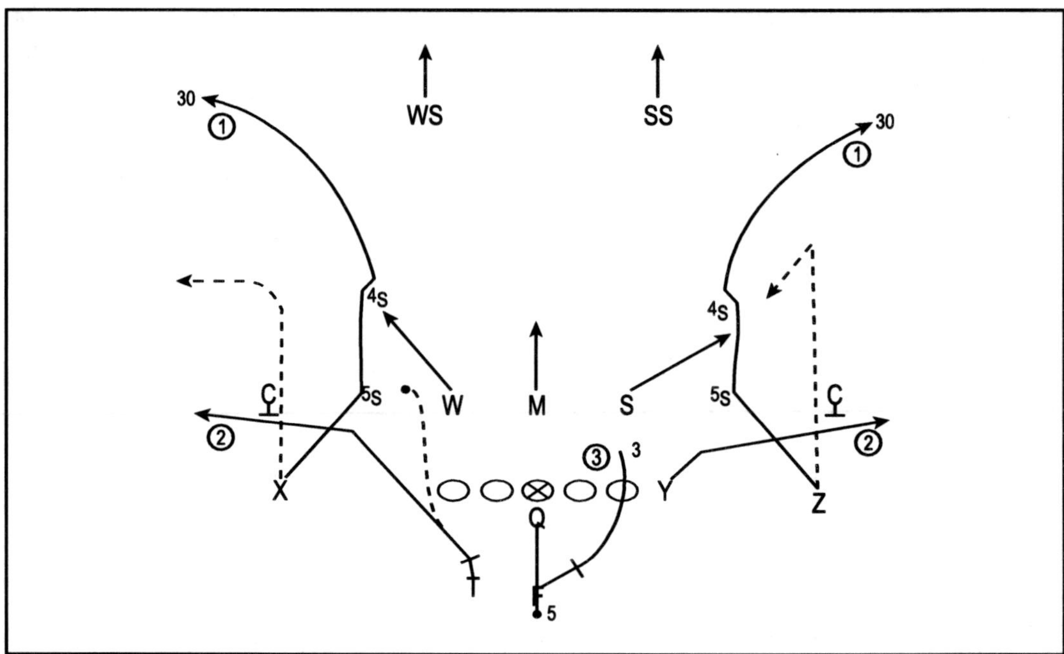

Diagram 4-15. Post-corner adjustment concept versus cover 2

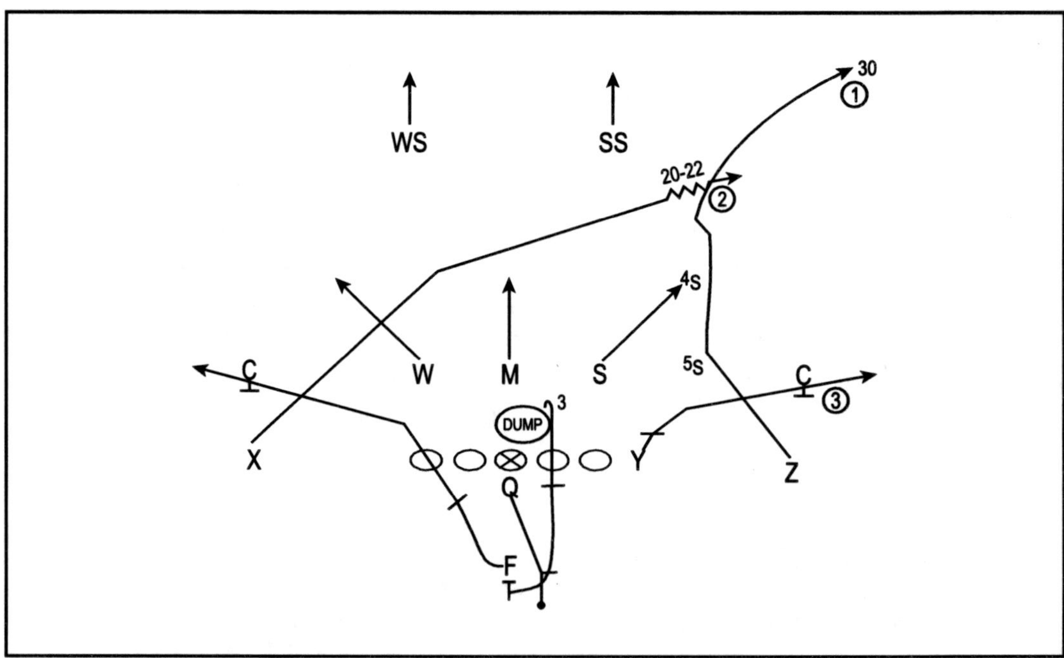

Diagram 4-16. Cover 2 post-corner, split-end (X) deep-over pattern versus cover 2

Three-Tiered-Dig Concept

The three-tiered-dig concept is set up by having the wide receiver opposite the dig run through the middle of the field to push the two cover-2 safeties deep to open up a void for the dig route to work into. This technique helps to create a high-low, dig/sit-route combination isolating on the inside linebacker to the side of the dig. Play-action greatly helps hold the linebackers from getting underneath the dig routes. The pattern concept, with a flanker (Z) dig, as shown in Diagram 4-17, can be easily flipped over in design having the opposite wide receivers run the cover-2 post-corner and dig routes.

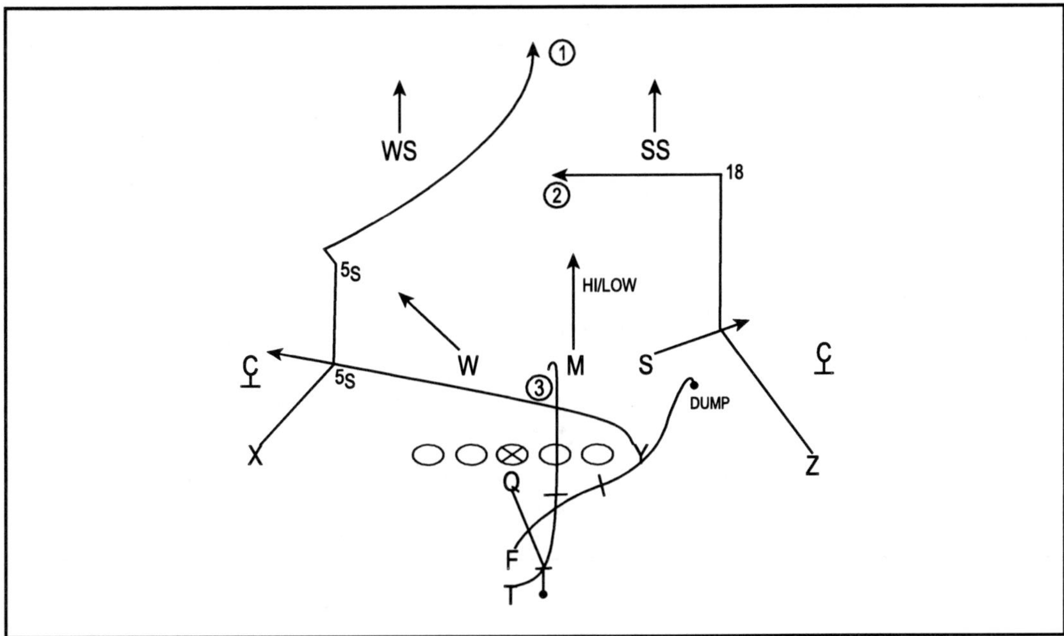

Diagram 4-17. Three-tiered high-low-read flanker (Z) dig pattern versus cover 2

Three-Streaks Concept

The three-streaks concept is an excellent way to attack cover 2 in which the cornerbacks play a hard-squat technique. The pattern produces a three-on-two route ratio versus the two cover-2 deep safeties. If the ball is thrown to the outside, the receivers should expect a throttled down-hole throw on the sidelines 18 to 22 yards deep. The three-streaks concept to attack cover 2 is shown in Diagram 4-18.

Four-Streaks Concept

The four streaks concept is an excellent way of attacking cover 2 when the cornerbacks play a soft cover-2 technique. Since the soft cover-2 technique takes away outside-streak-hole throws, the pattern relies on an inside receiver who, on the run, breaks off a broken-arrow route to split the two deep safeties as the inside receiver on the opposite side holds the cover-2 safety to his side. A sit route is run by the single back to hold the linebacker to the side of the read route so he can't drop underneath the cover-2 broken-arrow aspect of the route. The four-streaks concept versus cover 2 is shown in Diagram 4-19.

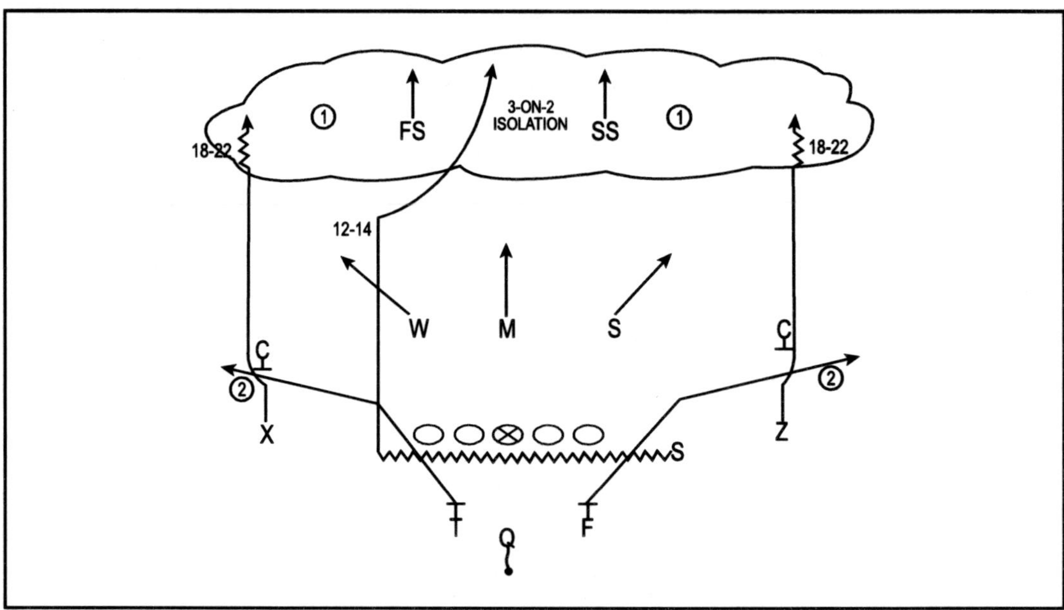

Diagram 4-18. Three-streaks concept versus cover 2

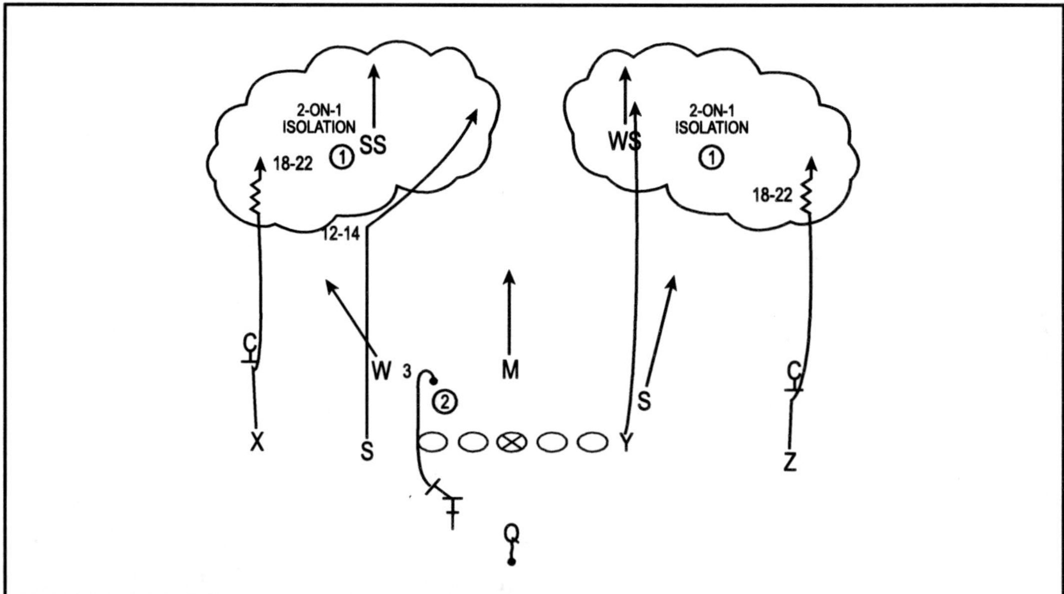

Diagram 4-19. Four-streaks concept versus cover 2

Under Concept

The under concept presents an excellent short high-low-read isolation on an inside linebacker. The clear route attempts to get to the second level for a possible hole throw just behind the cover-2 pass-dropping linebacker who is being isolated. The under route works underneath the isolated linebacker for the high-low isolation read. The under concept is best to the two linebacker side, as shown in Diagram 4-20 with a flanker (Z) under route.

If run to the cover-2 three-linebacker side, a trips formation of one sort or another helps to occupy the innermost cover-2 linebacker of the three to help produce a clean under high-low-read isolation. This concept is shown in Diagram 4-21.

Drive Concept

The drive concept helps to create a three-on-two flood isolation on the two inside cover-2 linebackers. The drive-route wide receiver, the tight end, and the back form a triangle-alignment position to help create the three-on-two advantage. The drive concept versus cover 2 is shown in Diagram 4-22.

Cross Concept

The cross concept also helps to create a three-on-two flood isolation on the two inside cover-2 linebackers. The slot receiver, tight end, and back form a triangle-alignment

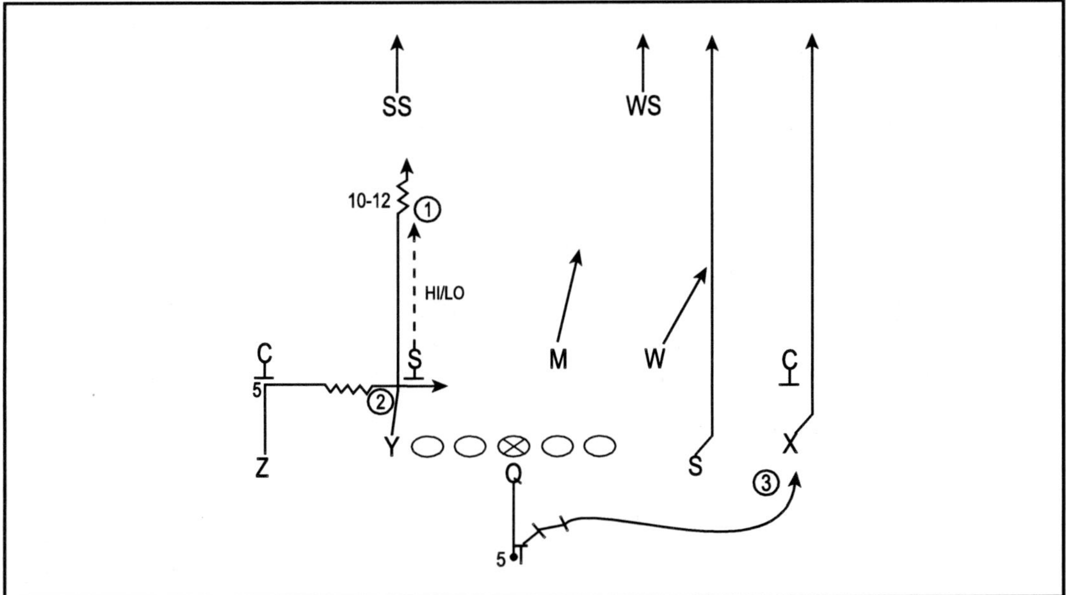

Diagram 4-20. Under concept to two-linebacker cover-2 side

position to help create the three-on-two advantage. The crossing action helps the effectiveness of the cross pattern versus zone or man action. The cross concept is from a balanced doubles set with a tight-end drag, slot short-dig action as shown in Diagram

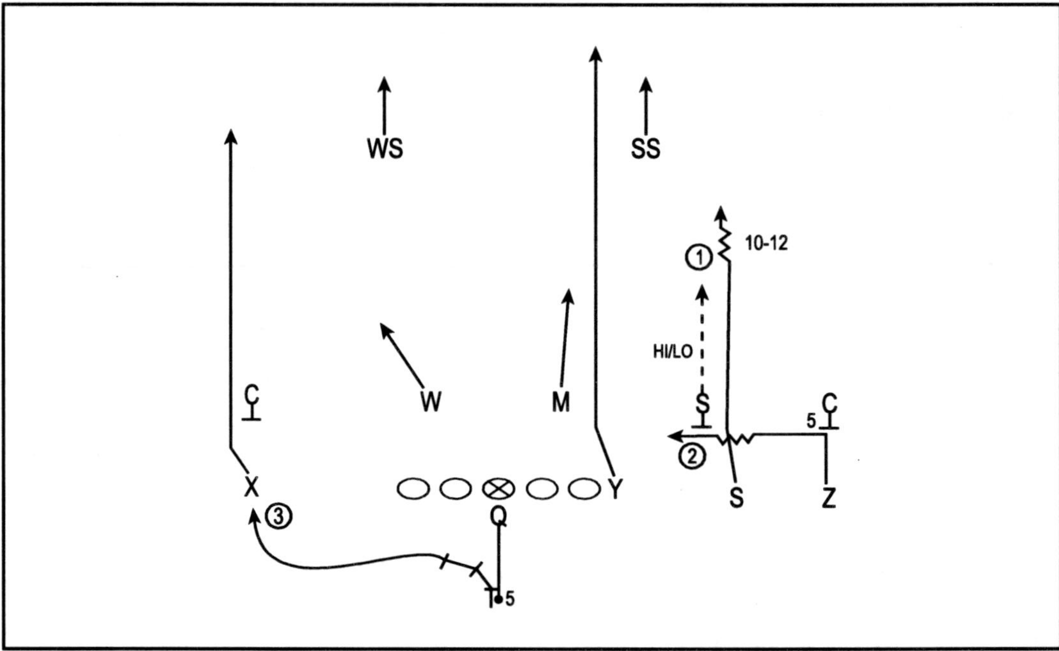

Diagram 4-21. Under concept to three-linebacker cover-2 side with trips formation

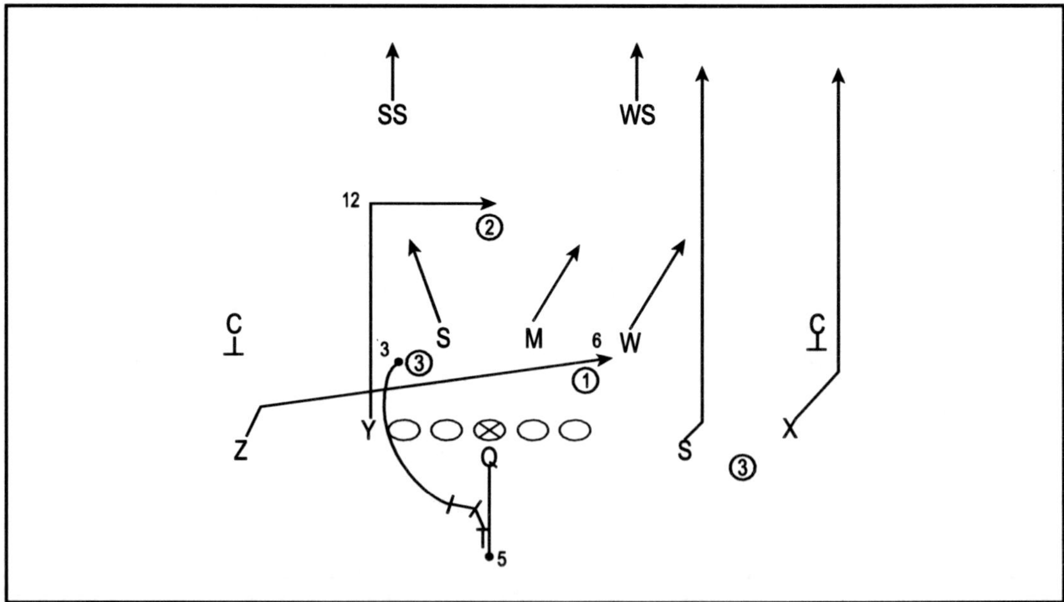

Diagram 4-22. Drive concept versus cover 2

4-23. The pattern can be easily flipped having the tight end run the short dig and the slot running the drag route. The back would then have to go to the side opposite the drag action.

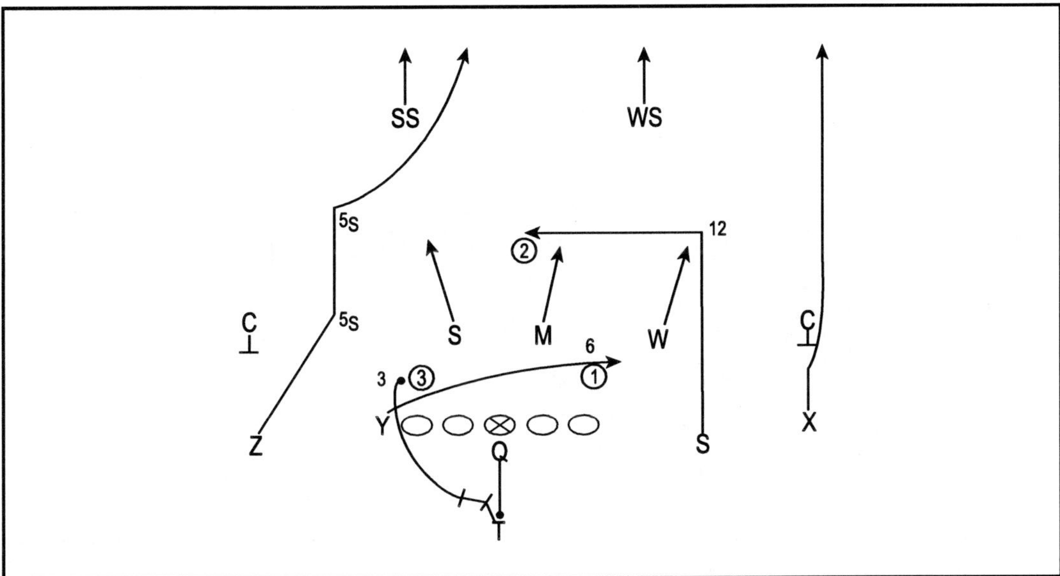

Diagram 4-23. Cross concept versus cover 2

Texas Concept

The Texas concept helps to create a two-on-one crossing isolation on the inside linebacker. The underneath cross route stretches the cover 2 outside linebacker with an initial flat route stem and threat. He then breaks underneath and crosses the square-out action of the tight end. If the inside linebacker runs out with the tight end's square-out route, the underneath cross route should be wide open. If the tight end is able to wall the inside linebacker off, the quarterback can stick a tight throw in to the tight end before the tight end works out wide into the cover-2 outside linebacker. The Texas concept versus cover 2 is shown in Diagram 4-24.

Option-Isolation Concept

Option-isolation routes help to produce excellent one-on-one isolations on cover-2 linebackers. Option routes can help to produce one-on-one size, talent, and speed mismatches. As previously mentioned, option routes are best run off of five-step-drop timing by the quarterback. Five-step-drop-quarterback timing is for option routes run in the 8- to 12-yard range, giving the option-route receivers time to properly maneuver and execute their option-route man- or zone-separation techniques. Diagram 4-25 shows a tight-end (Y) option and a split-end (X) option to attack cover 2 from a no-backs formation.

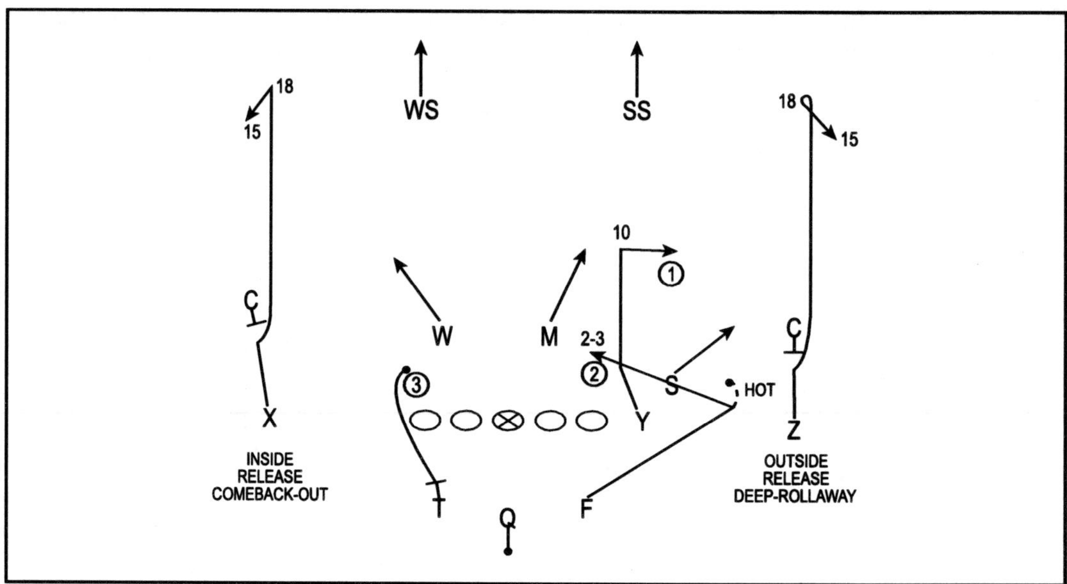

Diagram 4-24. Texas concept versus cover 2

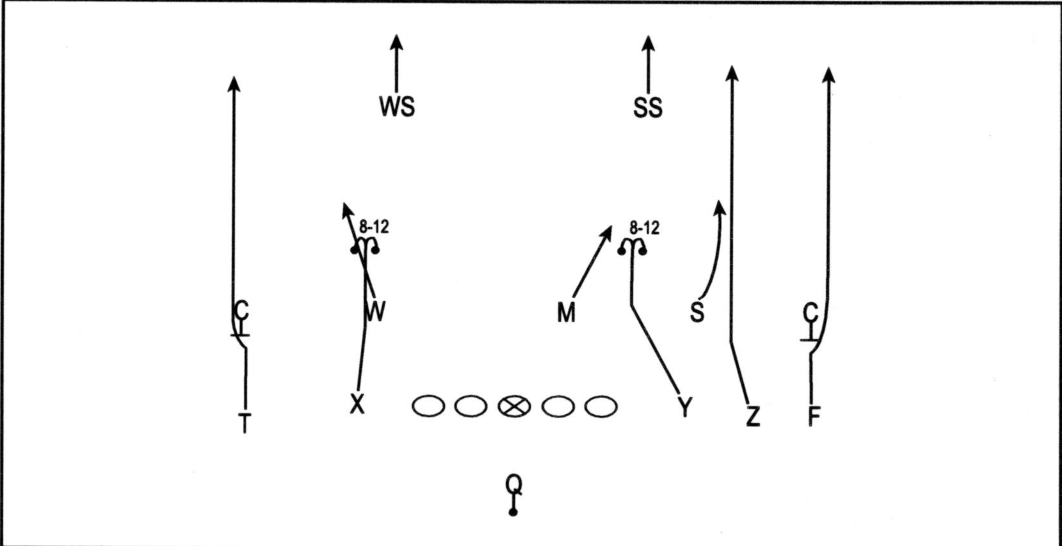

Diagram 4-25. Option-isolation routes versus cover 2

High-Low Delay-Route Isolations

High-low delay-route isolation can be very effective against cover 2—especially if the linebackers carry with vertical routes of the inside receivers. With vertical broken-arrow routes splitting the deep cover-2 safeties and a delay route working underneath, the quarterback simply throws off of the two-on-one coverage reaction of the isolated

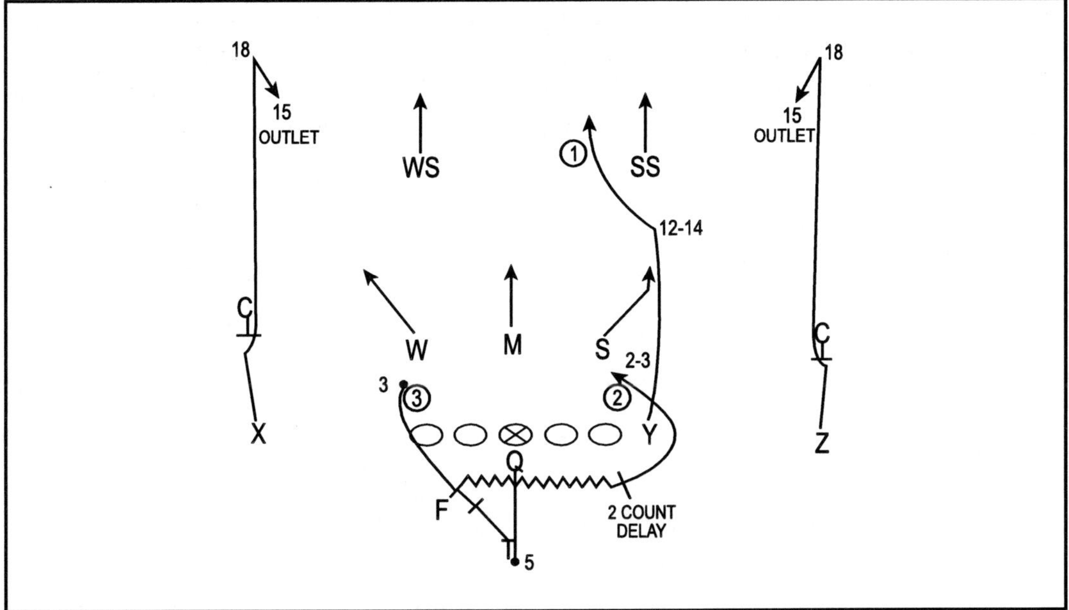

Diagram 4-26. High-low-read fullback-delay-route isolations versus cover 2

strong, inside linebacker. A high-low-read fullback delay versus cover 2 is shown in Diagram 4-26.

High-Low Pivot- and Break-Route Isolations

Just like delay-route high-low isolations, tight-end (Y) pivot- and break-route isolations can be very effective versus cover 2—especially if the linebackers try to carry with vertical routes of the inside receivers. With a vertical broken-arrow route by a back splitting the deep cover-2 safeties and a tight-end (Y) pivot or break route, the quarterback simply throws off of the two-on-one coverage reaction of the isolated strong, inside linebacker. The pivot and break routes are run in the six- to seven-yard range. Diagram 4-27 shows a Y-break high-low-read isolation action to attack cover 2. Diagram 4-28 shows a Y-pivot action to attack cover 2.

Naked-Bootleg Concept

The naked-bootleg concept is an excellent way to attack cover 2. The lack of secondary run support of the cover-2 secondary makes the cover-2 seven-man front vulnerable to the run game. Naked-bootleg action refers to the fact that no fake side lineman is pulling to the backside to block protect the bootlegging quarterback. Such run-game vulnerability helps to make play-action passing all the more effective versus cover 2 and its seven-man fronts. Naked-bootleg action is an extremely effective misdirection play-action concept that helps attack the weaknesses of cover 2.

Naked-bootleg action is shown in Diagram 4-29 in its effort to attack cover 2 with slam-flat route action by the backside back. It is extremely important for the widest spread receiver to the side of the misdirection naked bootleg to outside release on the cover-2 cornerback to open up area inside of the wide receiver's streak-clear route.

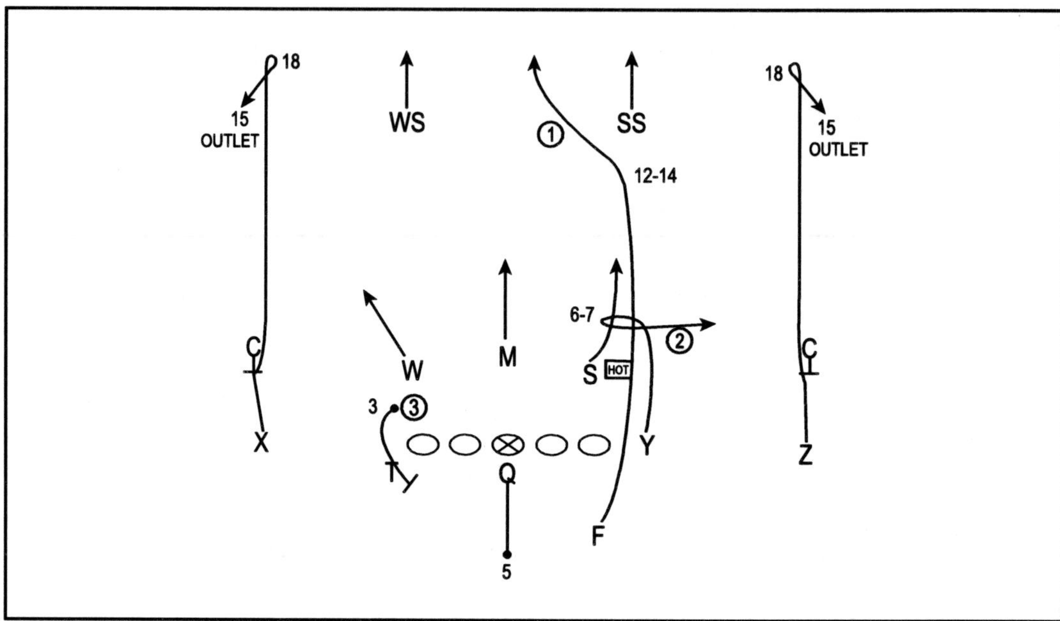

Diagram 4-27. High-low-read Y-break isolation versus cover 2

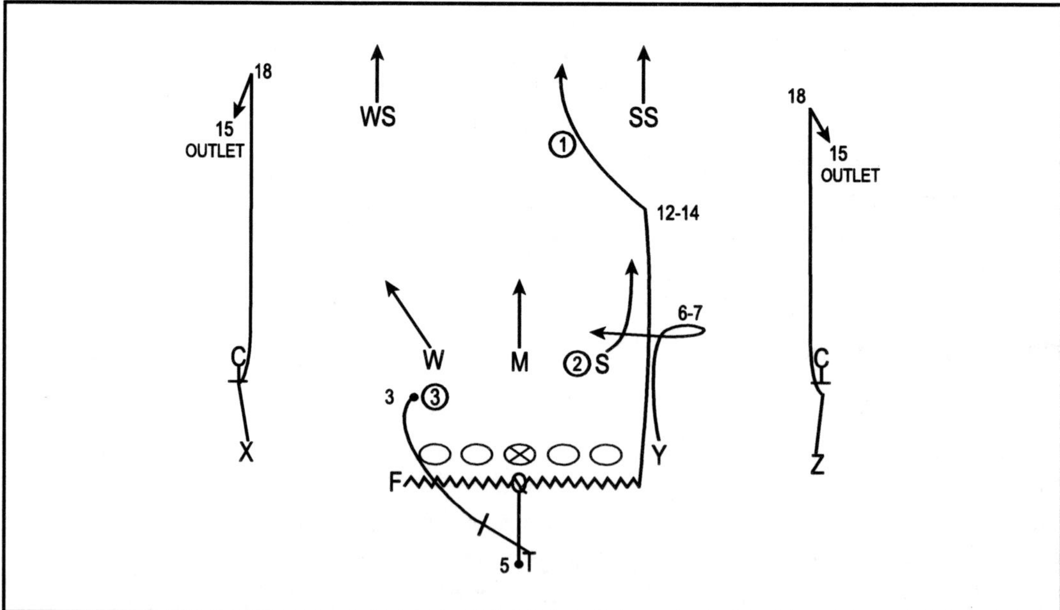

Diagram 4-28. High-low-read Y-pivot isolation versus cover 2

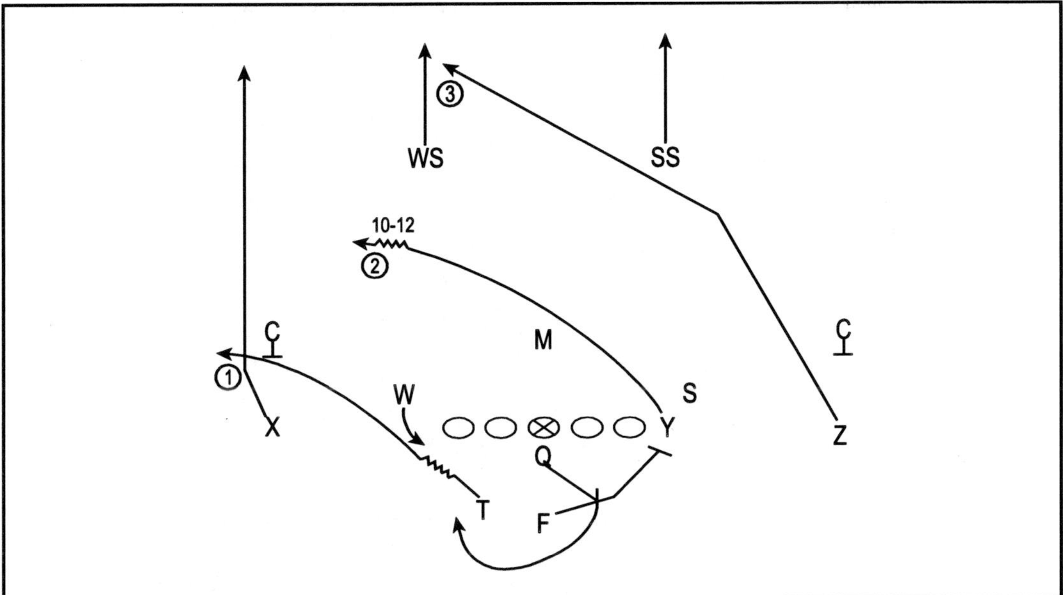

Diagram 4-29. Naked-bootleg action versus cover 2

Deep Curl/Hook Outlets

Deep curl/hook-outlet routes can be very effective concepts in attacking cover 2. The effectiveness of cover 2 in covering curl/hook-flat lateral-read-route combinations has been previously discussed. However, deep, longer-developing curl/hook routes that push the deep cover-2 safeties vertically can act as effective late outlets because they can find cover-2 void pockets to work into. Diagram 4-30 shows deep-curl/hook action used as late-developing pass-pattern outlets versus cover 2. An inside Y-option route-pattern concept is used for the example.

Some offenses are very effective using short curl routes (in the 10- to 12-yard range) to a well-spread wide receiver as a prime route versus cover 2. The feeling is that if the curl receiver can hold his ground (not get pushed to the inside on his short curl-route stem), a cover-2 void between the cornerback and the linebacker to the inside can be exploited. This concept is shown in Diagram 4-31 with a backside, deep-hook outlet versus cover 2.

Wide-Receiver Screens

Wide-receiver screens are very effective versus cover 2, which can be especially true from spread formations if the front tries to keep six front defenders in the box. As a result, the offense can gain a three-on-two advantage to, say, a trips-type set with a wide-receiver-screen concept. Such wide-receiver-screen action is shown in Diagram 4-32 versus cover 2.

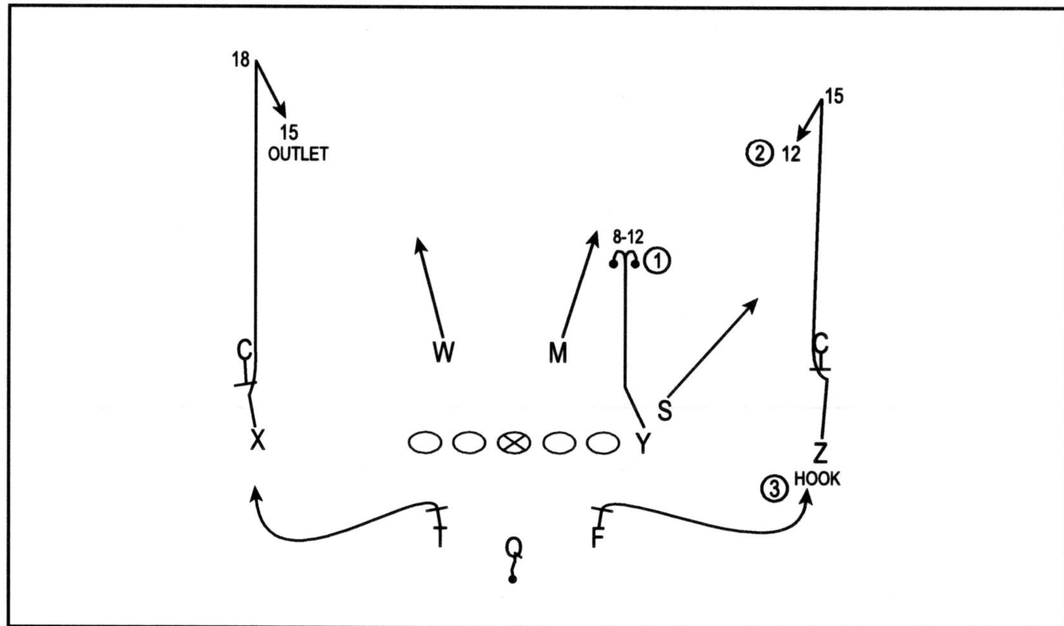

Diagram 4-30. Deep curl/hook-outlet action versus cover 2

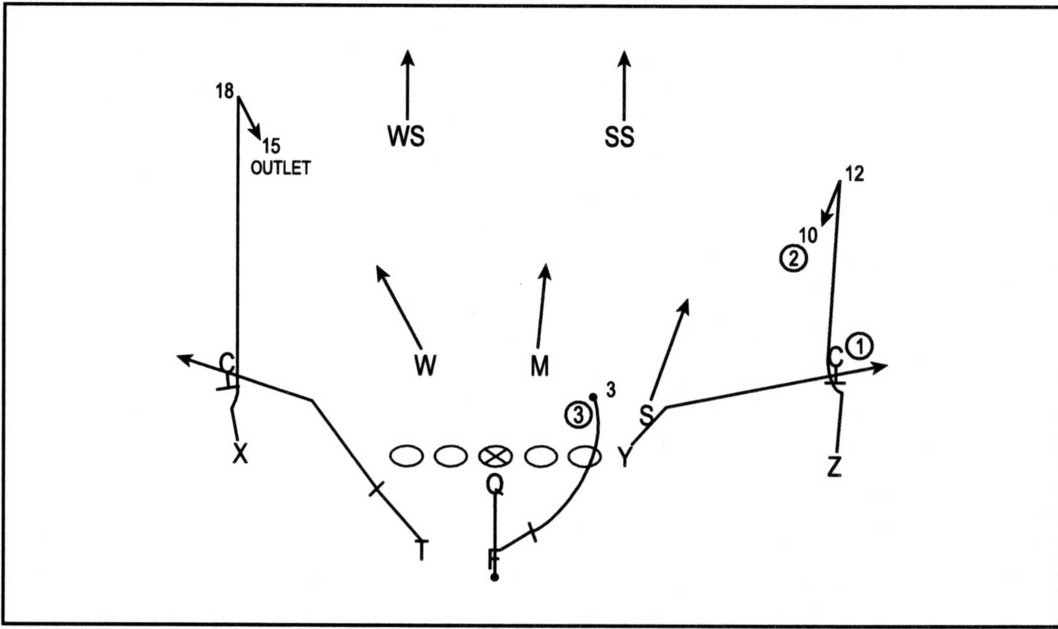

Diagram 4-31. Short curls as prime routes versus cover 2

Back Screens

Back screens can be very effective versus cover 2—especially if the linebackers are spot droppers. Back-screen action can allow the linebacker spot droppers to get depth to allow for the back-screen blockers to work up to the linebackers to block for the back's screen action, as seen in Diagram 4-33.

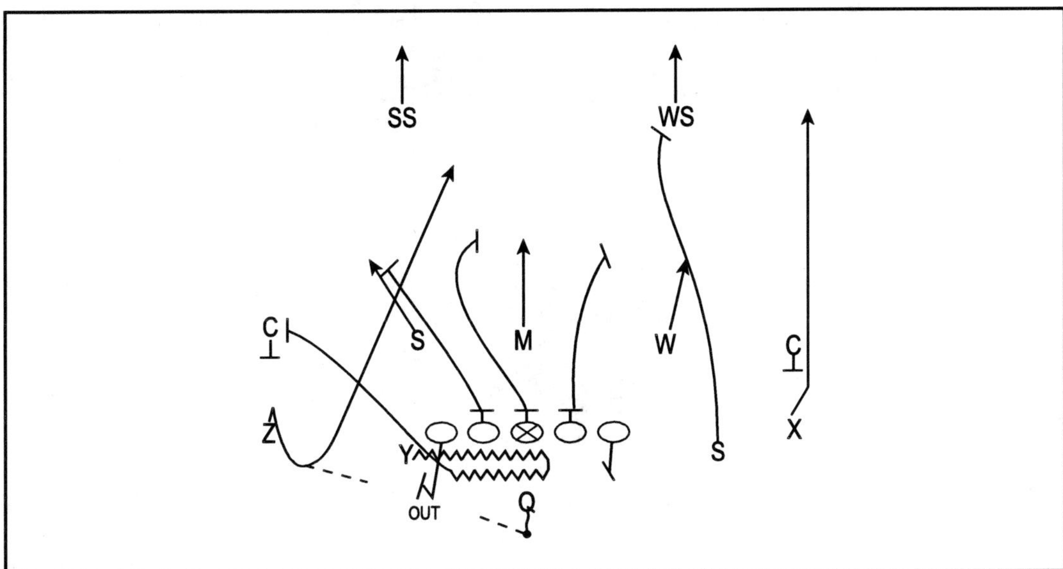

Diagram 4-32. Wide-receiver screen versus cover 2

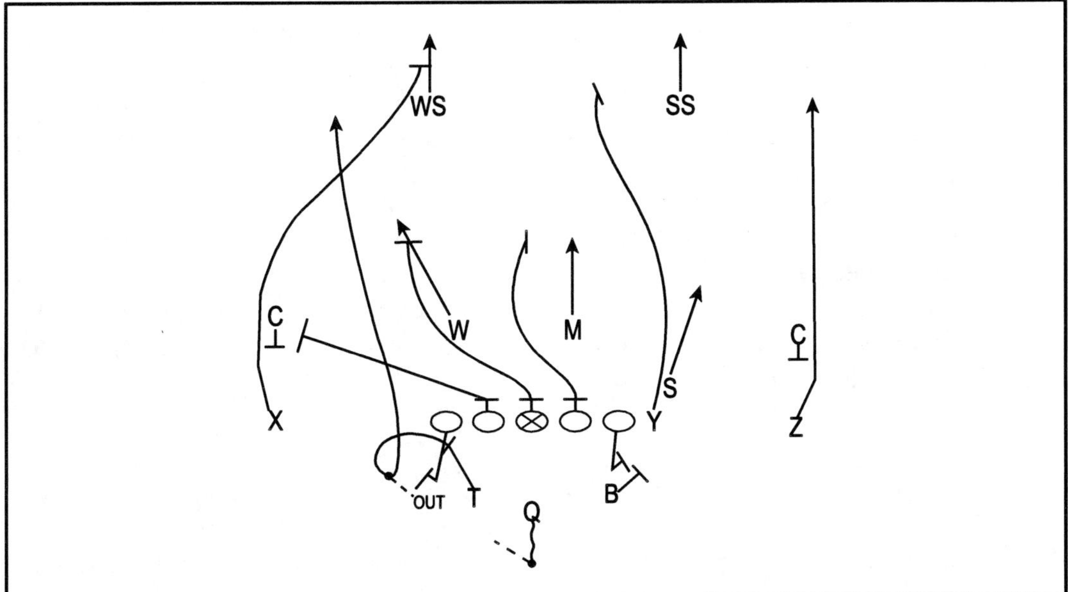

Diagram 4-33. Back screen versus cover 2

5

Pass Attack of Cover-2 Man Under

Cover-2 man under, or "2 man" as is it is often commonly called, is a widely used variation of cover 2. Just as the three cover-2 linebackers can spot drop and play true zone-underneath coverage, they can also zone drop and play a tight, man-to-man coverage technique on anyone who enters their zone—or they can play pure man coverage. Cover-2 man under is an extension of the linebackers playing man as all five cover-2 underneath defenders (the linebackers and the cornerbacks) play man-to-man coverage techniques. Extra nickel and dime secondary defenders can be substituted for one (or two) of the linebackers for extra underneath man-coverage strength.

The two deep cover-2 safeties in cover-2 man under play their normal half-field (or halves) zone coverage to back up the man-under aspect of cover-2 man under. Many of the attack concepts of cover 2 still remain intact, even though the five underneath-coverage defenders are using man-to-man coverage techniques in cover-2 man under. Cover-2 man under is shown in Diagram 5-1.

Cover-2 Man-Under Pass-Game Strengths

- The total pass-coverage structural design of cover-2 man under is a definite strength of the coverage. The man-to-man underneath coverage covers all five potential pass receivers backed up by two deep-zone halves-coverage safeties.

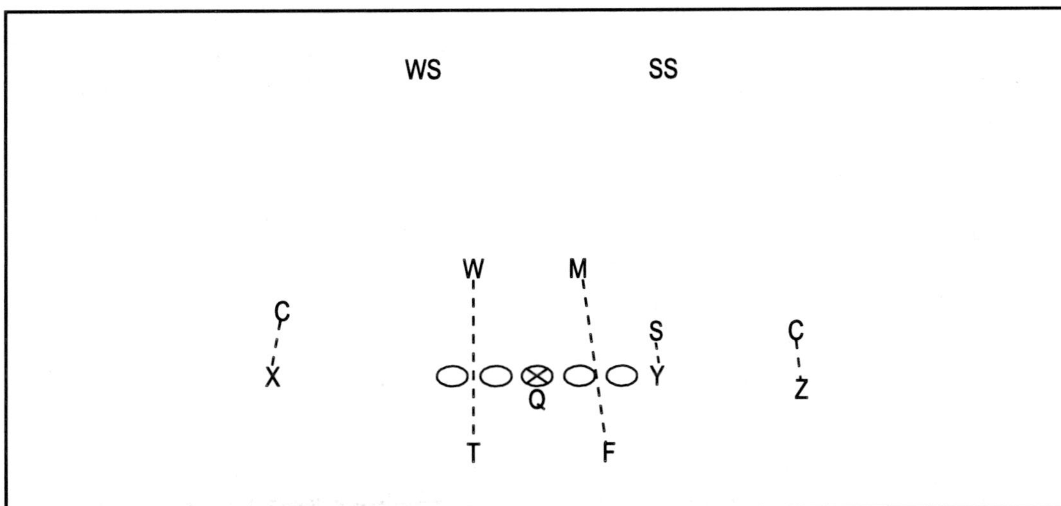

Diagram 5-1. Cover-2 man under

- The five underneath man-coverage defenders of cover-2 man under can do a great job of disrupting pass-route releases—especially routes that work upfield vertically.
- The five underneath man-coverage defenders of cover-2 man under take away easy, quick, or short pass-game routes and patterns.
- The two deep-zone halves-coverage safeties act as excellent backup security players to assist with the coverage of any deep routes.
- The two deep-zone halves-coverage safeties act as excellent backup for any short-route completions in helping to prevent such short completions from turning into big gains.
- The bump (or press) man-coverage techniques often associated with cover-2 man under can be very difficult to beat if a pass offense is not well prepared and practiced to do so.
- The man-under aspect of the coverage makes it very easy for the coverage to fortify its man-coverage abilities by substituting extra (nickel and dime) defensive backs for the normal cover-2 linebackers.
- Cover-2 man under is an excellent third-and-short- to medium-distance coverage. The press-man-coverage techniques help to take away any easy short underneath throws that may be able to get such short- and medium-yardage needs.
- The cover-2 man-under linebackers (or nickel/dime defenders) can run vertically with any inside-receiver vertical-release routes. This technique can force possible floating throws to such receivers making such passes vulnerable to interceptions by the two deep-zone halves-coverage safeties.

- Cover-2 man under is considered one of the hardest coverages to throw into due to the fact that cover-2 man under utilizes difficult-to-beat press-underneath man-coverage techniques and has two deep-zone halves-coverage safeties to back them up.

Cover-2 Man-Under Pass-Game Weaknesses

- Two of the most basic premises of attacking man (man-to-man) coverage holds true for the attack of cover-2 man under: isolate and cross.
- Quick-game isolations—such as slants, inside-receiver speed-outs, and fades—can all be very effective versus cover-2 man under.
- The total man-coverage design can only be as strong as the weakest man-coverage defender, much as a chain is only as strong as its weakest link. An offense can quickly focus on attacking, or isolating, on the weakest man-coverage defender(s).
- Underneath-smash isolations and under-route isolations offer the offense quick, inside crossing routes to help beat the man-under coverage to the inside.
- Option-isolation routes (Y-options, H-options, slot-options) help to exploit possible one-on-one mismatches in favor of the offense in the attack of cover-2 man under.
- Y-pivot and Y-break routes also help create one-on-one isolation routes in favor of the offense versus cover-2 man under . Stick routes and the square-out route on a Texas concept also do the same.
- Post-corner isolations by both outside- and inside-aligned receivers can help to exploit both the one-on-one underneath man-under coverage as well as the normal deep outside-zone voids left by the two-deep zone coverage of cover-2 man under. Such deep post-corner isolation action by an inside receiver into the outside two-deep cover-2 void (as well as the excellent underneath lateral dragging action of the smash route versus the man-under coverage) is shown in Diagram 5-2.
- Deeper digs and square-ins can help to isolate man-under coverage and utilize the crossing action of such routes. It is very important, however, to be sure that some form of a clear-out or post route is working through the middle of the field to hold the two deep cover-2 safeties. Diagram 5-3 shows the use of a clear-out route to blow the top off of the cover-2 coverage so that the two deep safeties cannot support the deep square-in route versus cover-2 man under.
- Cross-the-field route actions, such as drives and drag routes, can be very effective cover-2 man-under isolation routes. Such routes have much (or all) of the width of the field to beat the man-under coverage and get open to receive a pass.
- The crossing action is an excellent way to attack the man-under aspect of cover-2 man-under coverage. Cross-route-pattern concepts and the Texas concepts are

excellent examples. Diagram 5-4 shows a flanker (Z) cross pattern from a twins formation with backfield motion.

- Backs-cross and back-fake-cross action are also excellent man-under attack concepts that can be used to attack cover-2 man under.

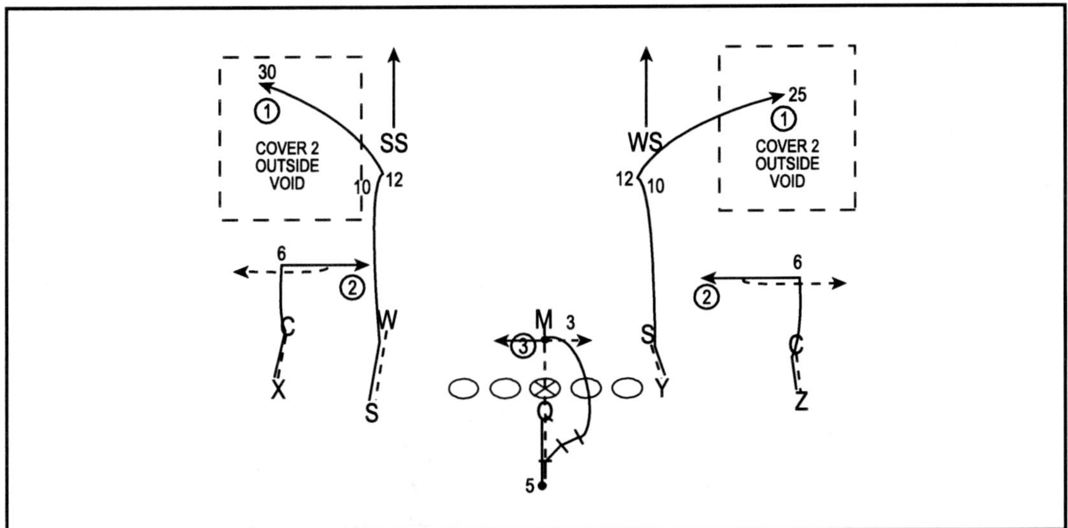

Diagram 5-2. Smash-pattern attack of deep cover-2-outside voids (plus underneath smash-route-drag action versus man-under coverage)

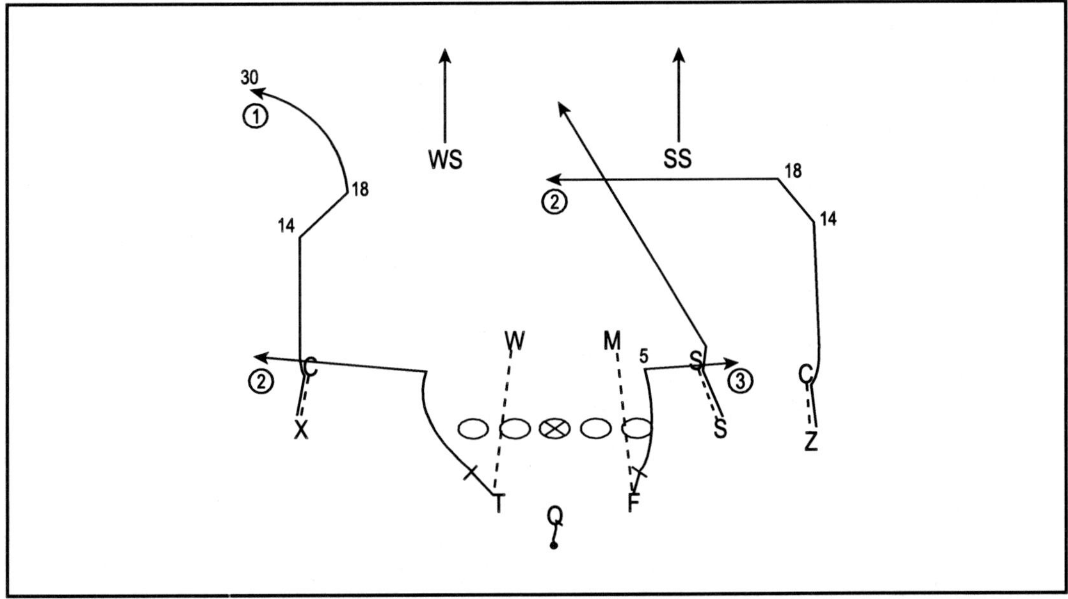

Diagram 5-3. Clear-out route used to blow off the top of the cover-2 man-under coverage for deep square-in or dig-route action

- Picks and rubs are excellent route combinations to attack cover-2 man under. Of course, such pick and rub action must all be executed off of legal picking action.
- Picking screens thrown to backs and receivers behind the line of scrimmage can also be very effective in defeating the man-under aspect of cover-2 man under. Diagram 5-5 shows backfield pick-screen action versus cover-2 man under.

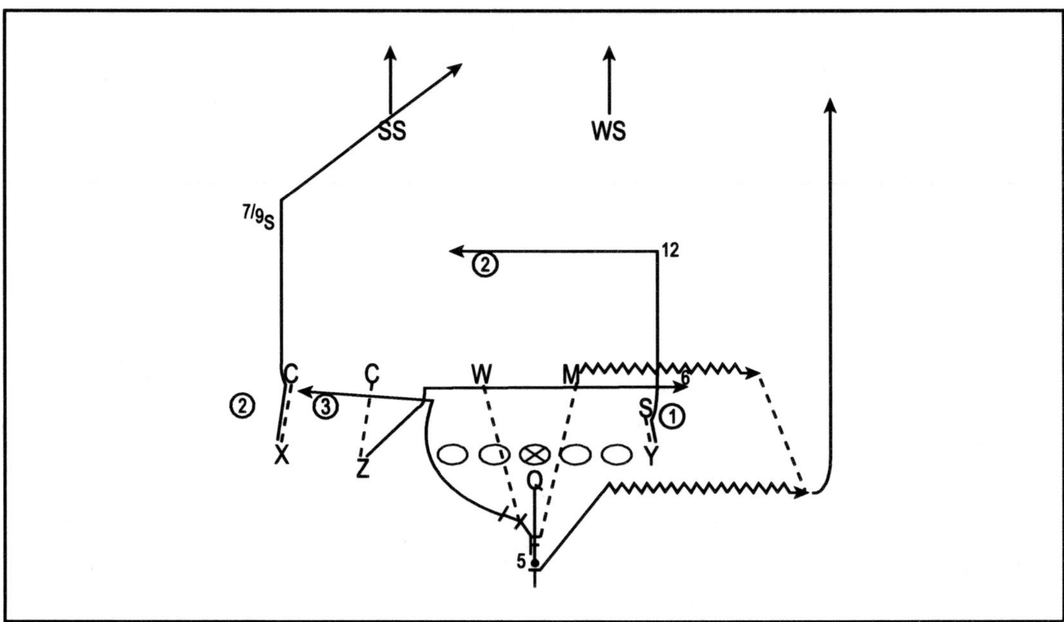

Diagram 5-4. Flanker (Z) cross pattern versus cover-2 man under

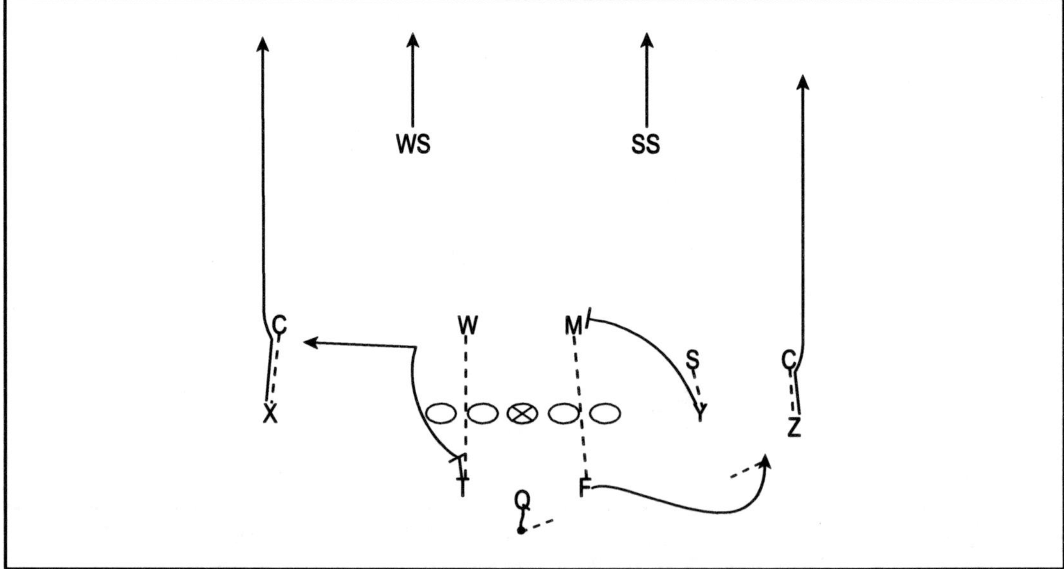

Diagram 5-5. Backfield pick-screen action versus cover-2 man-under

Route Combination and Pass-Pattern Attack of Cover-2 Man Under

Quick-Game Slant Routes

Slant-route isolations and double-slant actions can be very effective versus cover-2 man under, just as it is versus normal cover 2. The major change is the pressing, tight release of the slanting receiver in an effort to work the hips of the press-coverage defender to get the coverage defender's hips turned. The slant receiver initially sticks/attacks the press-coverage defender's outside hip. The slant receiver then drives back tightly, pressing on the defender with a north-south course to influence the defender to work upfield. The slant receiver then breaks his slant action hard to the inside, gets separation, and stays on the move at top speed to be sure to maintain such man separation. The slant versus cover-2 man under is shown in Diagram 5-6.

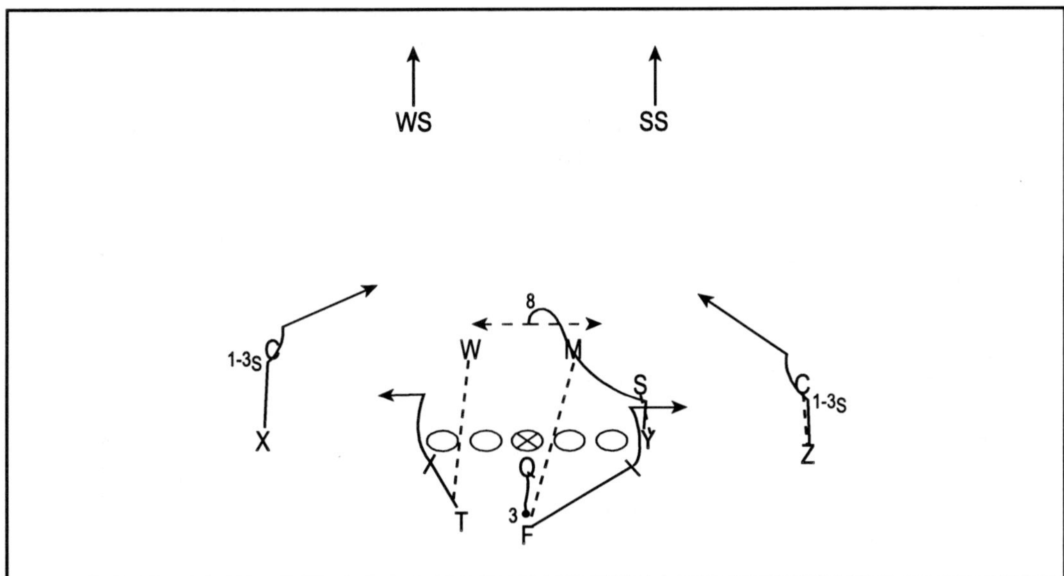

Diagram 5-6. Slant route versus cover-2 man under

Quick-Game Inside-Receiver Speed-Out-and-Fade

The quick-game inside-receiver speed-out-and-fade-route combination presents two excellent man isolations to help defeat cover-2 man under. The wide receiver works a fade-route isolation versus the cornerback, while the inside receiver squares his quick speed-out route after initially releasing into and threatening the man-coverage technique of his coverage defender. Such quick-game inside-receiver speed-out action versus cover-2 man under is shown in Diagram 5-7.

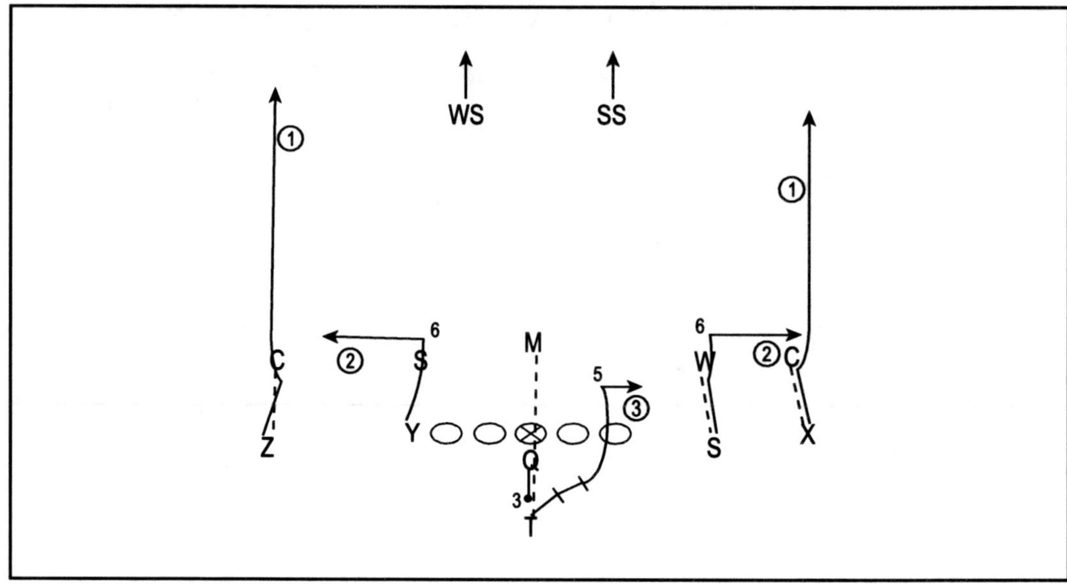

Diagram 5-7. Quick-game inside speed-out action versus cover-2 man under

An excellent supplemental concept to utilize when a cover-2-man-under coverage defender starts to overplay a quick-game speed-out is the spin route, as shown in Diagram 5-8. The speed-out receiver, running the route as a quick-game square-out versus the press-coverage, simply plants his upfield foot and spins back to the inside versus the defender's overplay action.

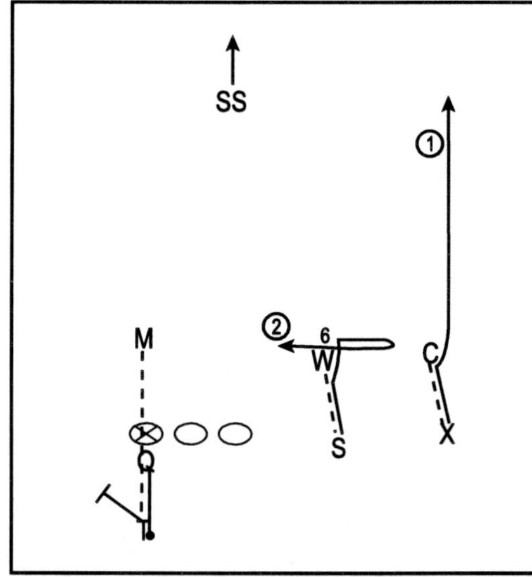

Diagram 5-8. Quick-game spin route versus cover-2 man under

Versus the man-under coverage of cover-2 man under, deeper, five-step quarterback-drop-timed speed-outs by an inside receiver are also very effective. The widest receiver must outside release. The inside receiver attacks the technique of the man-under defender covering him, separates, and squares out to the sideline. As on all man-coverage wide-receiver separation techniques, the inside receiver must get separation and then be sure to run at top speed to maintain such separation. The deeper, five-step drop-timed square-out concept versus cover-2 man under is shown in Diagram 5-9.

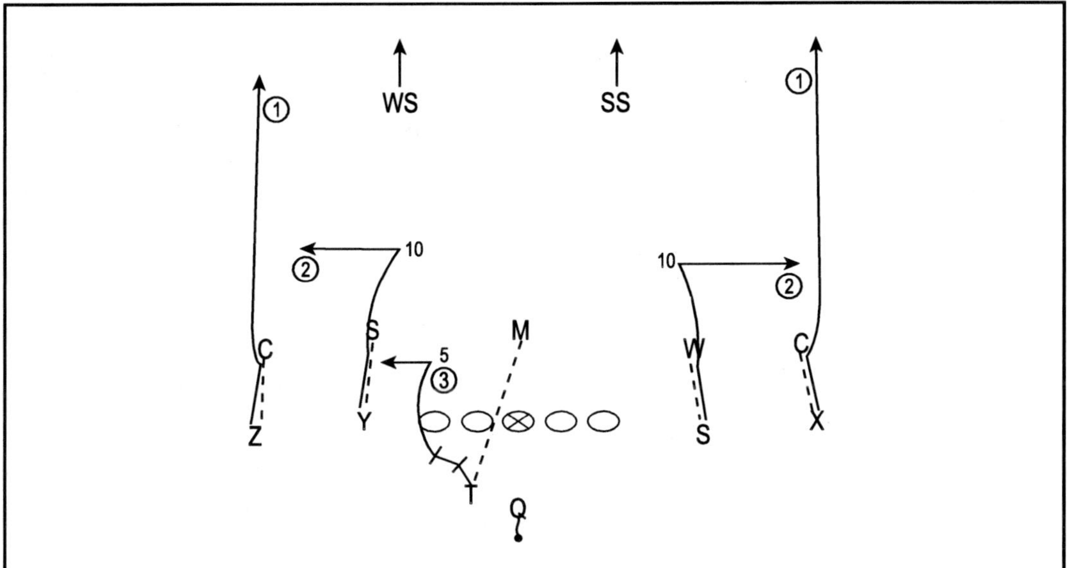

Diagram 5-9. Five-step-timed square-out concept versus cover-2 man under

Quick-Game Fade

The quick-game fade route requires special consideration in the attack of cover-2 man under. Whether called in the play call, signaled to by the quarterback, or as a hitch-route adjustment, the fade route can be a very effective route versus press-man-coverage techniques. It is very important for the fade receiver to attack the technique of the press defender covering him in an effort to push the press defender back on his heels. The receiver then tightly drives north-south through the defender in an effort to blow past the press-coverage defender. It is also important for the fade receiver to leave four yards of width (room) on the sideline for the quarterback to effectively throw a fade pass. A major concern of the quarterback is to analyze the alignment of the safety to the side of the fade-route throw. Unlike man-free coverage, cover-2 man-under safeties can get into an alignment position that can be a factor in defensing fade routes. Diagram 5-10 shows such fade-route action versus a cover-2 man-under press defender.

Quick-Game Deep Hitch

The quick game deep-hitch route can be very effective versus cover-2 man-under press coverage. The difference in running a deep hitch compared to a normal hitch is an eight-yard hitch rather than a six-yard hitch. The extra two yards of stem can do much to help influence the covering press defender that the receiver is beyond hitch depth and is now working his stem for a fade or a route run deeper than six yards. As a result, the receiver can work the eight-yard hitch route tightly to the inside back into the quarterback to help the receiver "body up" on the deep-hitch route. The quarterback adjusts to fast five-step drop-timing to accommodate the extra two yards of hitch depth. Deep hitches are not fade-adjusted versus press coverages. Quick-game deep-hitch action versus cover-2 man under is shown in Diagram 5-11.

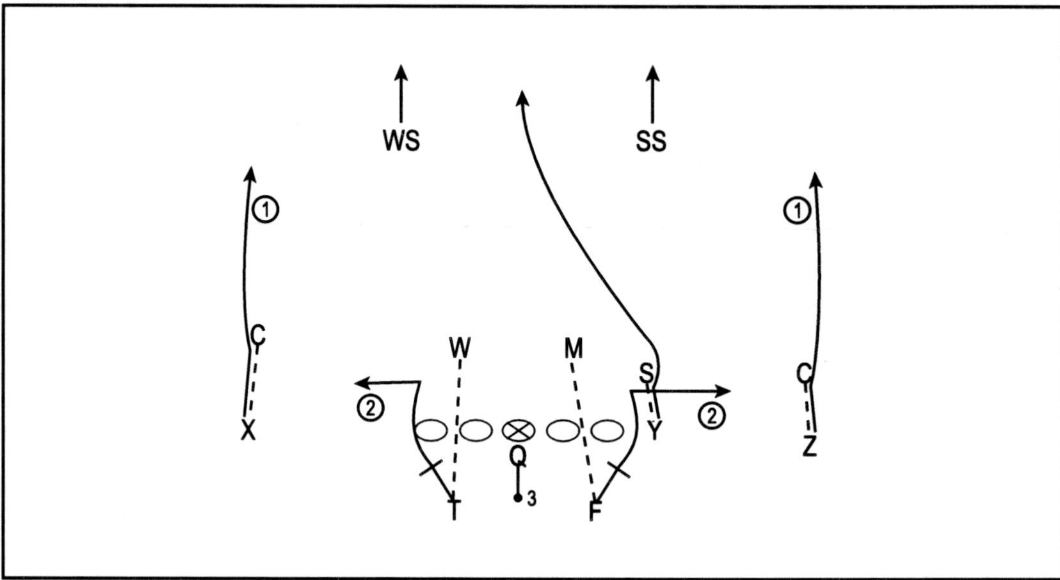

Diagram 5-10. Fade route versus cover-2 man-under press defender

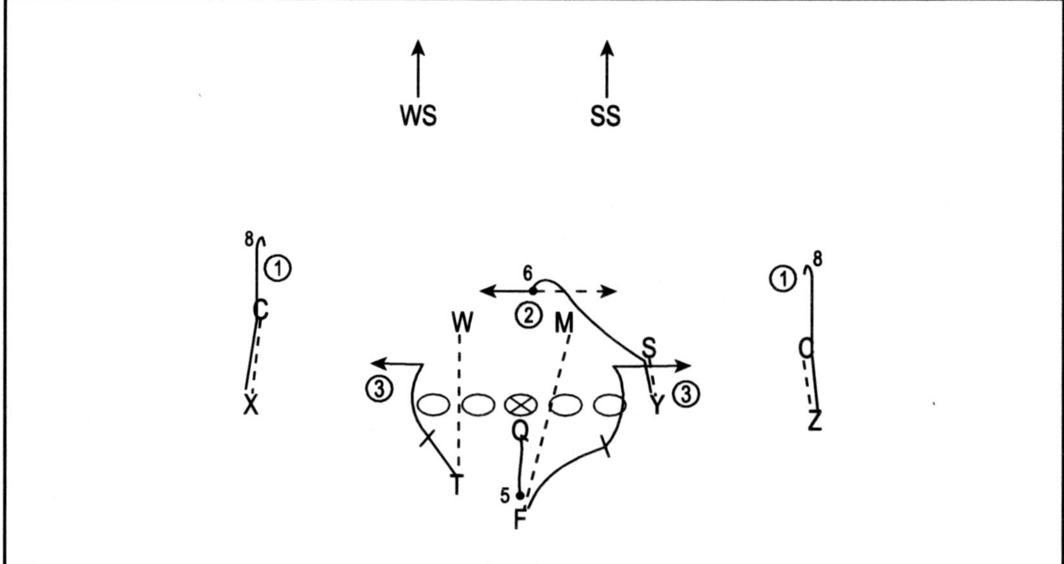

Diagram 5-11. Quick-game deep-hitch route versus cover-2 man under

Quick-Game Stick

The quick-game stick-route concept is an excellent isolation-type route versus cover-2 man under. The flat route in front of the stick route helps to open up the stick area for the stick-route receiver to work into. The stick receiver initially works tightly into the technique of the defender man-to-man covering him and then snaps to the outside to get separation. The stick receiver must then be sure to work hard to the outside, losing ground slightly, to help maintain such separation. The quick-game stick-route concept versus cover-2 man under is shown in Diagram 5-12.

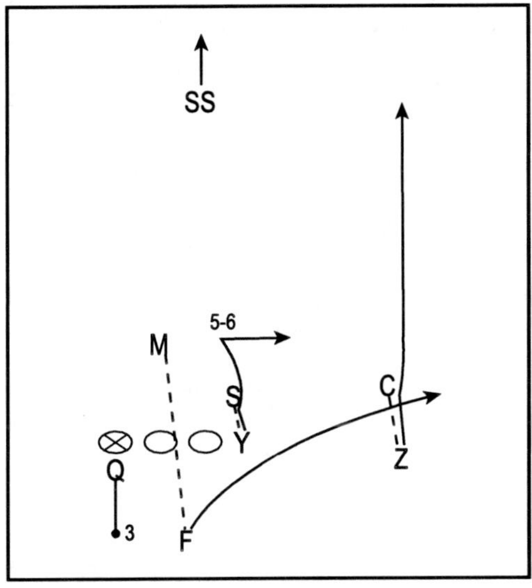

Diagram 5-12. Quick-game stick route versus cover-2 man under

Quick-Game Double-Move Slant Route

The quick-game double-move slant-and-go route can be very effective versus cover-2 man-under press coverage. The go aspect of the route and the throw to the go route must be sure to stay away from the cover-2 safety to the side of the throw by throwing into the fade area. Diagram 5-13 shows slant-and-go action versus cover-2 man under.

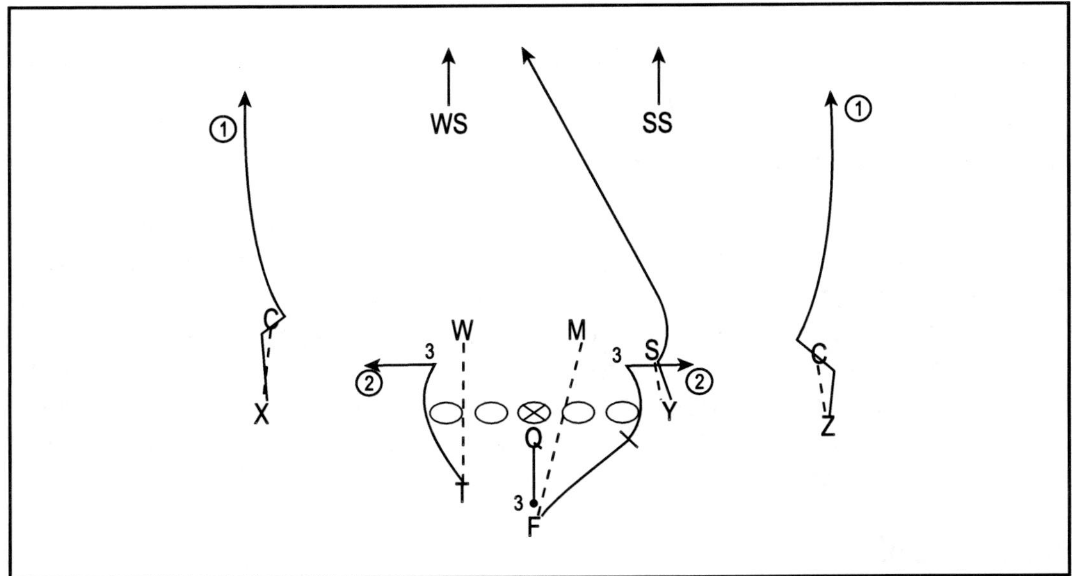

Diagram 5-13. Quick-game double-move slant-and-go action versus cover-2 man under

Under Concept

The under concept presents an excellent underneath isolation of a wide receiver working underneath a clear route by the adjacent receiver to the inside versus cover-2 man under. The clear route gets eaten up by the man-under coverage and (probably) the deep cover-2 safety to that side. The under route must beat the man coverage by man-separating and maintaining such separation to the inside underneath the clear route by staying on the move. Diagram 5-14 shows an under-route isolation versus cover-2 man under.

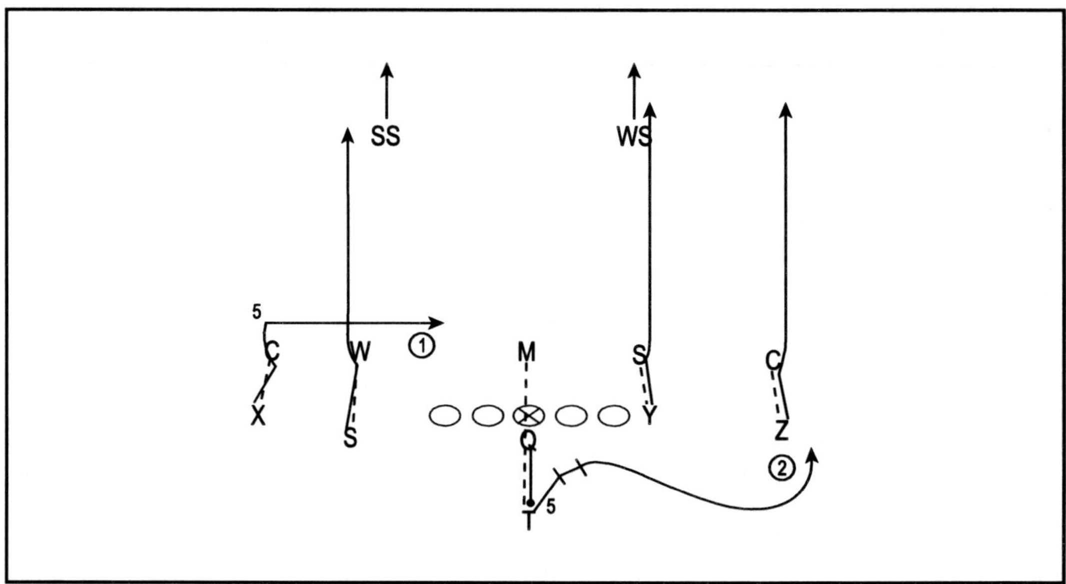

Diagram 5-14. Under concept versus cover-2 man under

High-Low-Read Smash Isolation

The high-low-read smash isolation gives an offense an excellent ability to attack cover-2 man-under deep. The inside-receiver post-corner route must still beat the man-under coverage. However, the post-corner route is still able to work away from the deep cover-2 zone safeties into the deep outside cover-2 voids. The smash route—run as a hitch-option route—gives the smash route the ability to beat the press-man-under coverage across the field to the inside or back outside to the sideline if the man-coverage cornerback overplays the inside break of the smash route. Such man-breaking actions of the smash concept versus cover-2 man under is shown in Diagram 5-15.

Switch Smash

The switch-smash concept is an excellent crossing action that helps produce a natural picking/rubbing action to help create separation from cover-2 man-under press coverage.

The inside receiver ends up running the get-open smash route off of his brushing-around-route stem. The outside receiver breaks into his post-corner route off of an inside, cover-2 post-corner stem, as shown in Diagram 5-16 versus cover-2 man under.

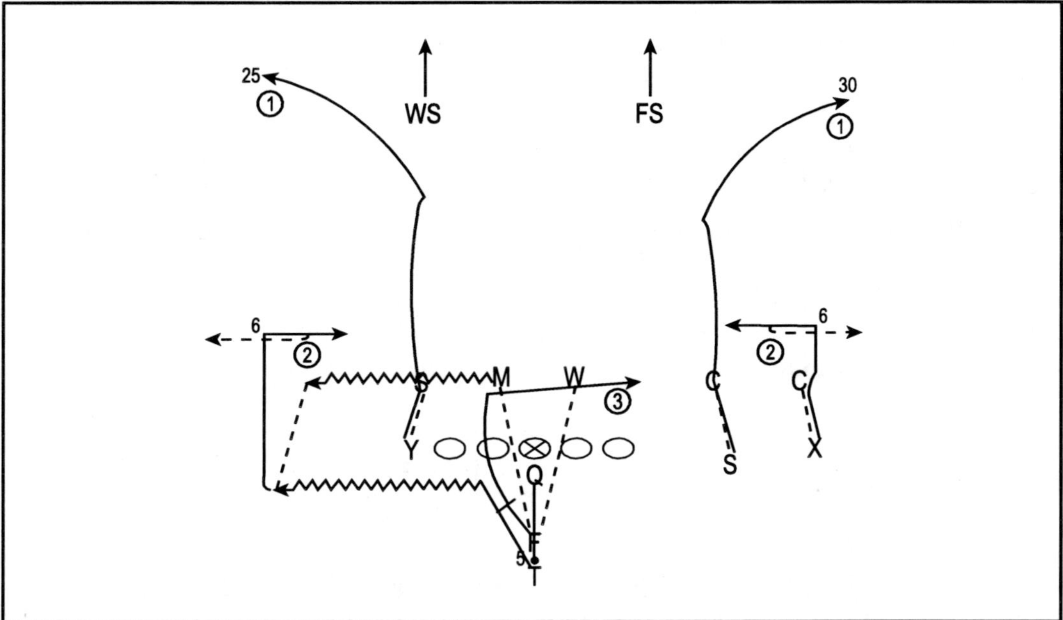

Diagram 5-15. Smash concept versus cover-2 man under

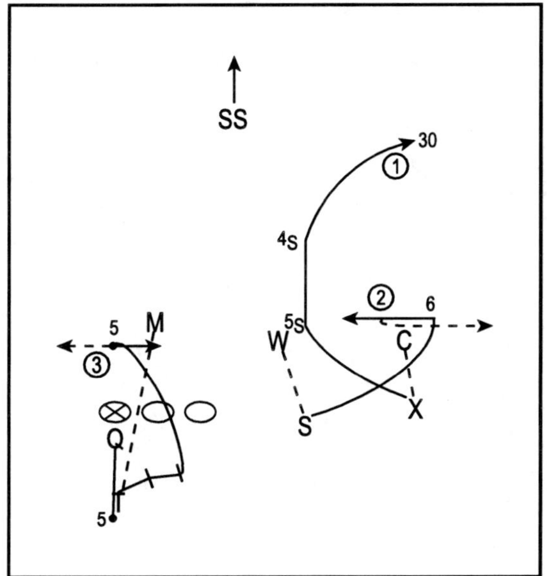

Diagram 5-16. Switch-smash concept versus cover-2 man under

Slant-Corner Sprint-Out

The slant-corner sprint-out concept is an excellent way to attack cover-2 man under. The prime slant-corner route works off of a slant-route stem. The timing of the slant-corner route does take time and is a reason why the route only works to 20 yards on the sideline. The inside receiver runs a squared-out, quick speed-out route. The quarterback's read thinking is the squared-out quick speed-out route to the slant-corner route, as shown in Diagram 5-17.

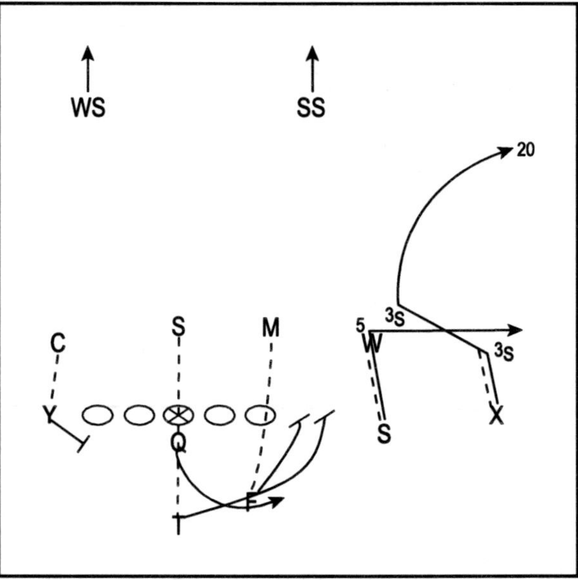

Diagram 5-17. Slant-corner sprint-out action versus cover-2 man under

Bunch-Formation Post-Corner Flood-Isolation Concept

A bunch-formation post-corner flood-isolation concept is an excellent way of attacking cover-2 man under. You might normally think of flood action to overload zone coverages. However, the picking/crossing action of the post-corner bunch concept helps to condense the cover-2 man-under coverage and actually out-flank the coverage with the outside, man-breaking flood-route action, as shown in Diagram 5-18.

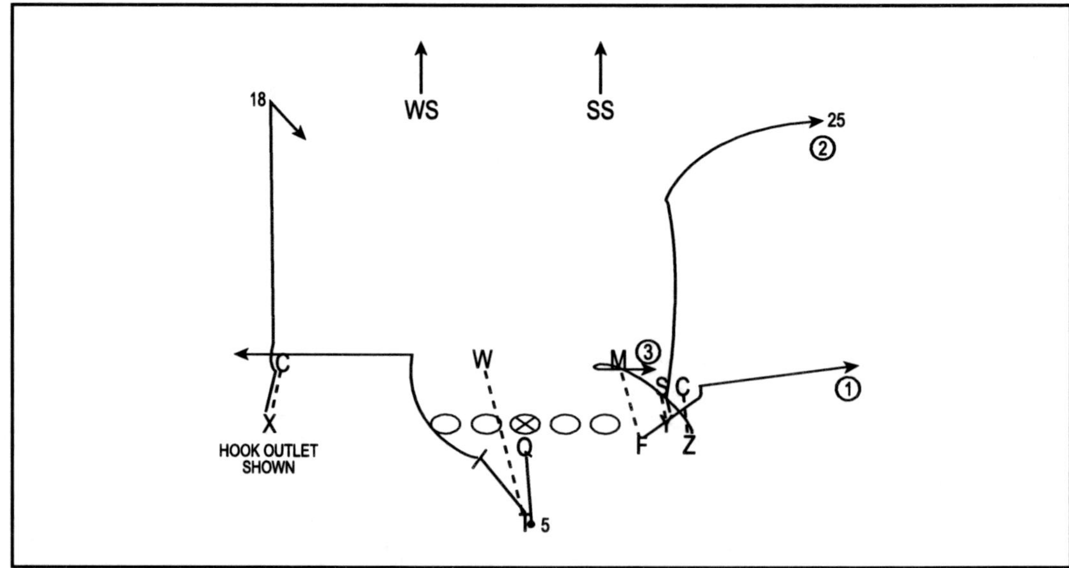

Diagram 5-18. Bunch-formation post-corner flood-isolation concept versus cover-2 man under

Post-Corner High-Low Isolation

A very similar concept to the smash high-low isolation versus cover-2 man under is the post-corner high-low isolation. The post-corner isolation of the widest receiver helps to produce an excellent deep isolation versus cover-2 man under, as shown in Diagram 5-19. This action gives the pass offense a chance to attack the coverage in the deep outside zone away from the safeties in an area that is a coverage void. Cover-2 post-corner adjustment routes (adjusting for such routes as outs and curls) similarly attack the structure of cover-2 man under.

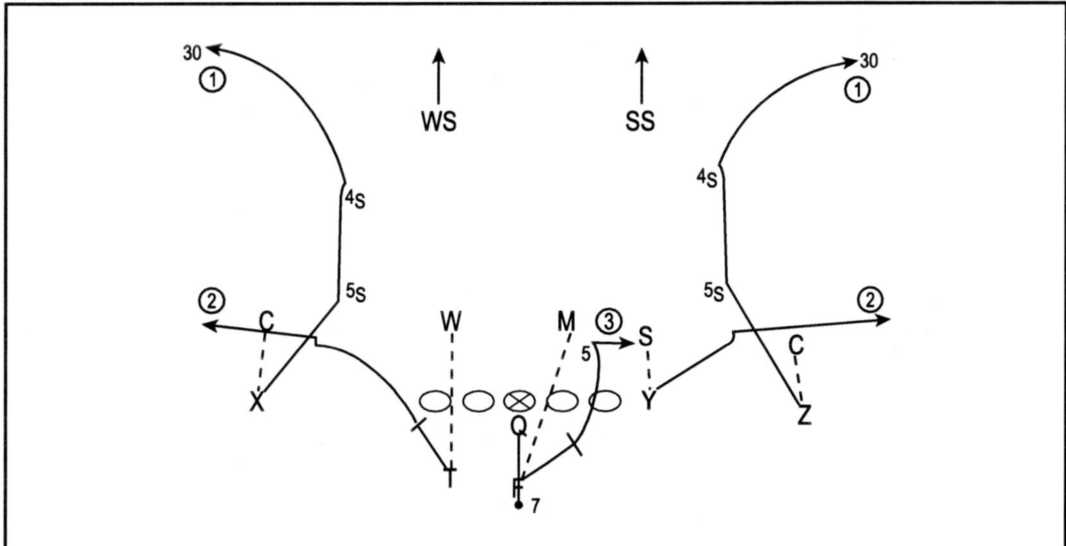

Diagram 5-19. Post-corner high-low-isolation concept versus cover-2 man under

Post-Corner Deep Across

The post-corner deep-across concept also does a good job of attacking cover-2 man under. The post-corner route attacks the outside cover-2 void while the deep-drag route has room all the way across the field to separate from his man-under coverage and get open. Diagram 5-20 shows a flanker (Z) deep-across pattern versus cover-2 man under.

Three-Tiered-Dig Concept

The three-tiered-dig concept is set up by having the wide receiver opposite the dig run through the middle of the field to push the two cover-2 safeties deep to open up a void for the dig route to work into. This technique helps eliminate the deep-safety-coverage threats so that the dig receiver can focus on beating the one-on-one man-under coverage. The pattern concept is shown in Diagram 5-21 versus cover-2 man under.

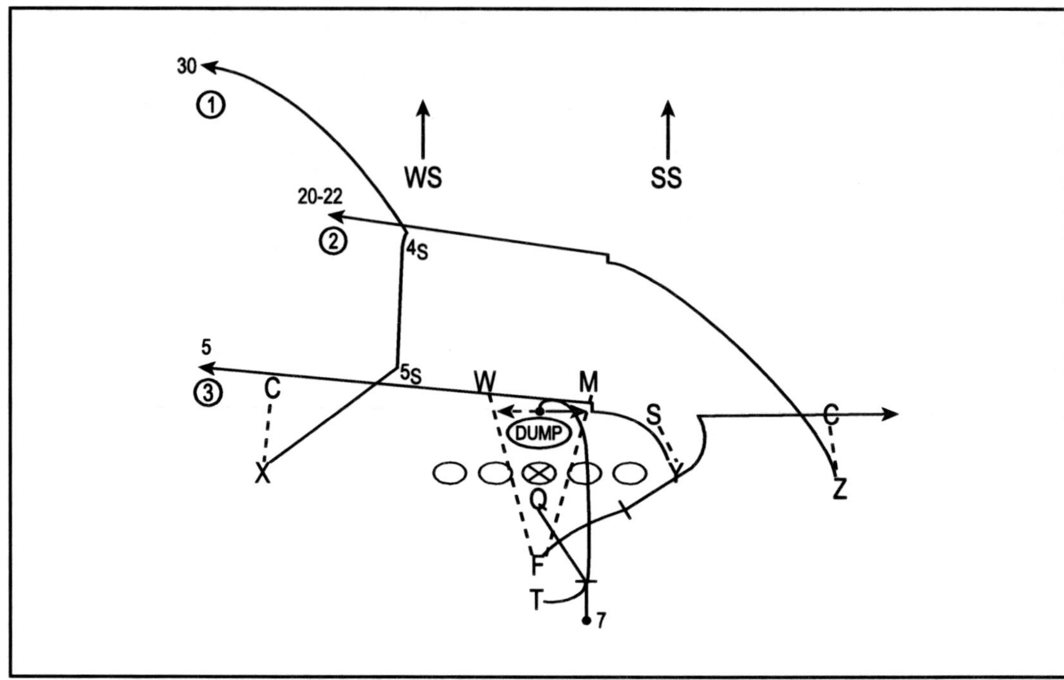

Diagram 5-20. Z-deep-across concept versus cover-2 man under

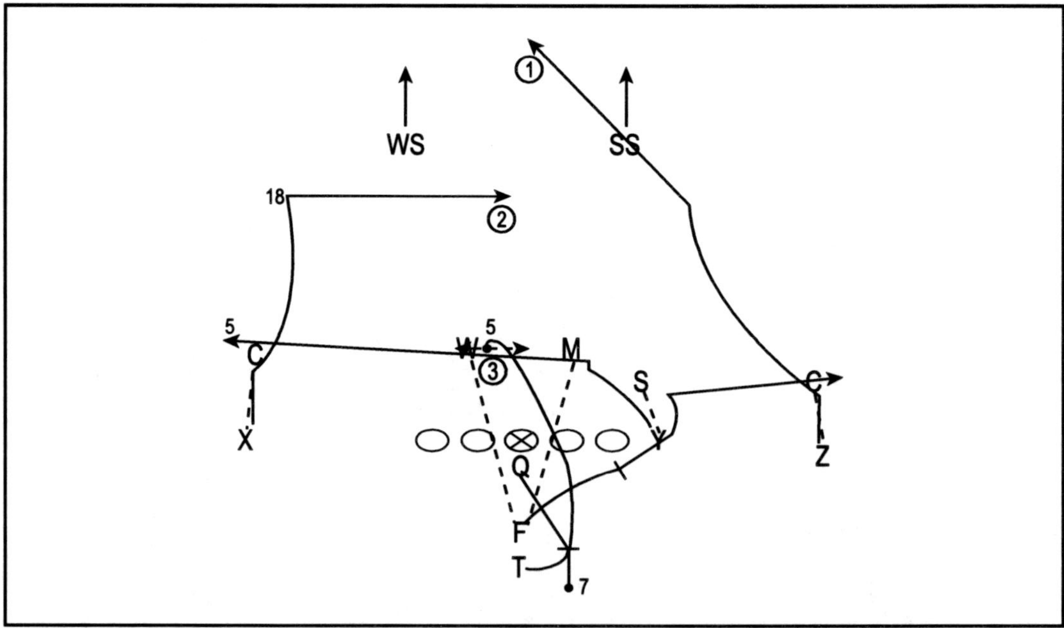

Diagram 5-21. Three-tiered split-end (X) dig concept versus cover-2 man under

Four-Streaks Concept

The four-streaks concept is a decent way of attacking cover-2 man under. However, it is only for outside, deep-streak, or fade throws to the two outside wide receivers. The two inside streaks help to hold their man-under-coverage defenders, and the two deep safeties as well. The quarterback must understand the unfavorable four-on-two ratio in favor of the defense to the inside with a much better one-on-one isolation ratio to the outside. The quarterback must, however, still be sure to be leery of a deep cover-2 safety working off the hash to support an outside streak or fade throw. The four-streaks concept with its outside one-on-one streak/fade-throw isolations is shown in Diagram 5-22 versus cover-2 man under.

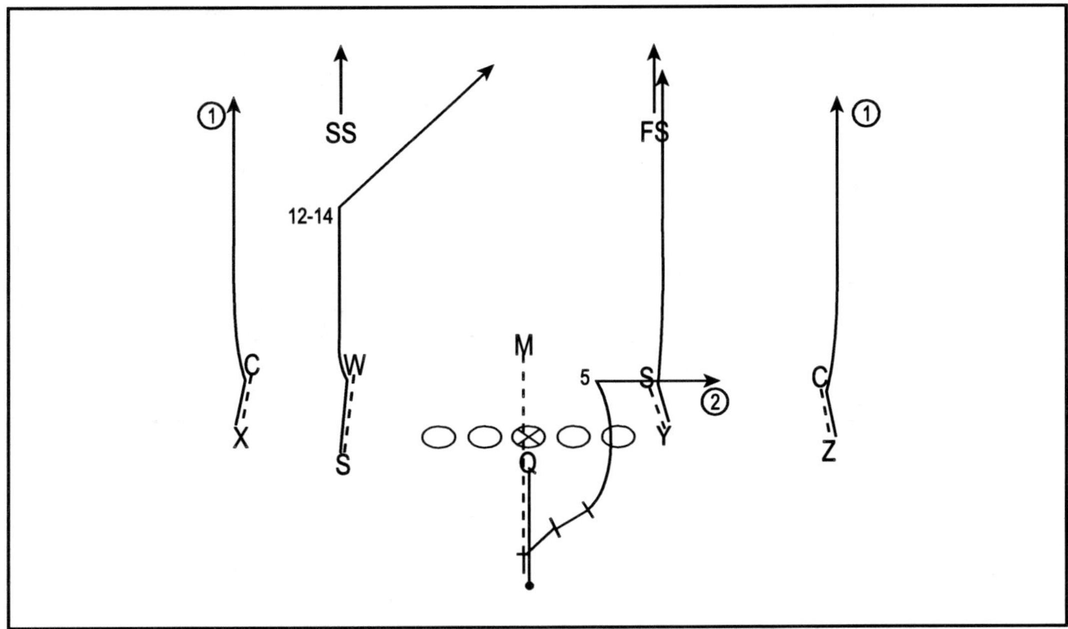

Diagram 5-22. Four-streaks concept outside one-on-one isolations versus cover-2 man under

Rollaway/Acute Routes

Rollaway and acute routes are excellent isolation actions versus cover-2 man under. These routes are especially effective when they develop off of strong, deep-streak-threat fakes pushing the cover-2 man-under press cornerbacks deep. Rollaway/acute-route action versus cover-2 man under is shown in Diagram 5-23 with middle-read action.

Comeback-Out/Deep Rollaway Routes

Diagram 5-24 shows the use of comeback-out and deep rollaway routes as outlet routes versus cover-2 man under with fullback-delay prime-route action. However, the quarterback could take a seven-step drop and treat the deep comeback-out or deep rollaway routes as prime routes if he feels he has a good one-on-one isolations to the outside.

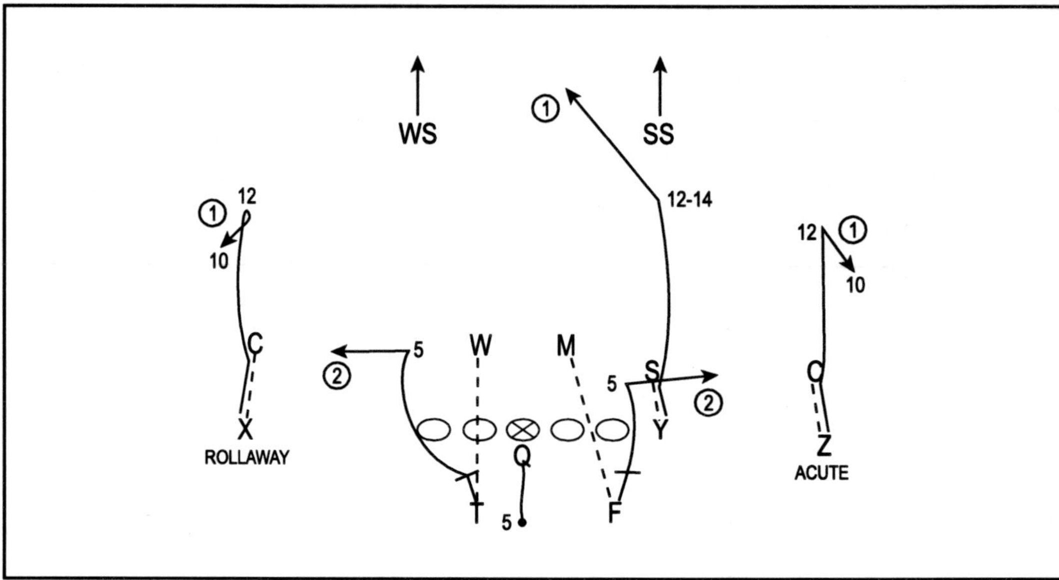

Diagram 5-23. Rollaway/acute-routes with middle-read action versus cover-2 man under

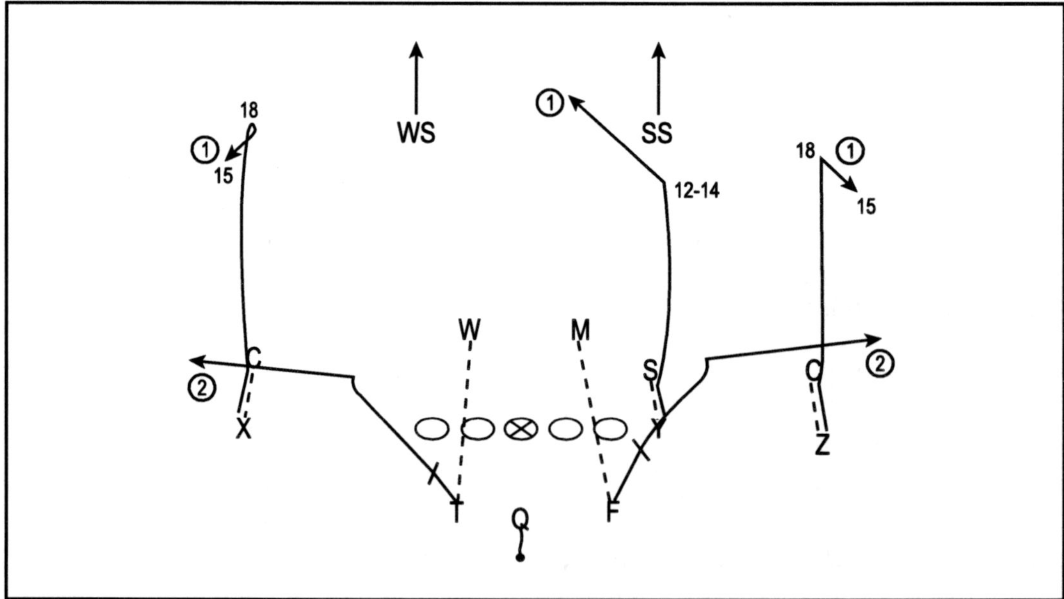

Diagram 5-24. Comeback-out and deep rollaway route action versus cover-2 man under

Switch Acute

The switch-acute concept is an excellent concept versus cover-2 man under. The switching action on the stem of the two receivers involved in the route combination helps to produce a picking/crossing action that helps combat the press-man coverage, as shown in Diagram 5-25 with sprint-out quarterback action. The route can be deepened by having the prime route become a comeback-out route at 18 yards.

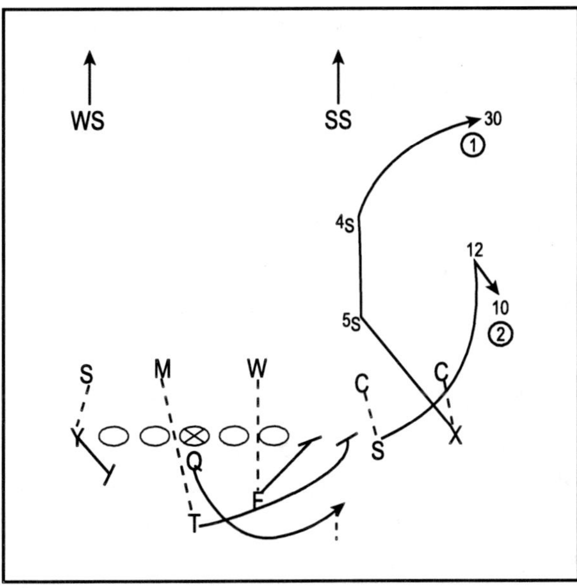

Diagram 5-25. Switch-acute route combination versus cover-2 man under

Double-Move Routes

As in the quick-pass game, some double-move routes from five-step drop-timing are extremely effective concepts to utilize versus cover-2 man under. Diagram 5-26 shows rollaway-and-go and acute-and-go double-move-route action versus cover-2 man under from four-streaks action.

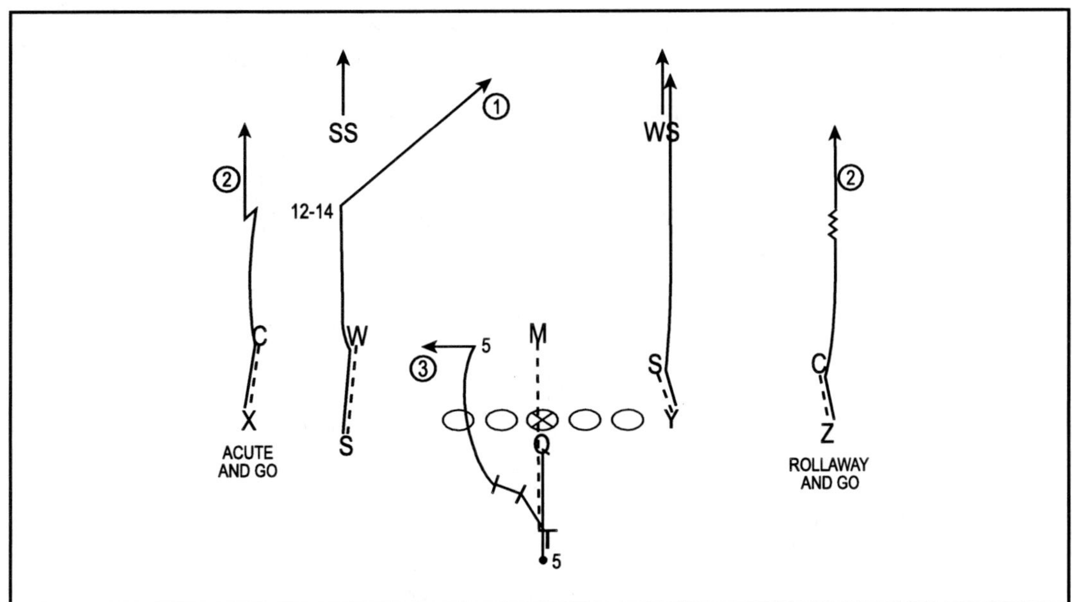

Diagram 5-26. Rollaway-and-go and acute-and-go double-move concepts versus cover-2 man under

Shallow-Cross Smash

Diagram 5-27 shows the use of shallow-cross smash action versus cover-2 man under. The shallow route provides an excellent man and stunt/blitz-beater route. The post-corner route does an excellent job of attacking the cover-2 man-under deep-outside-coverage void.

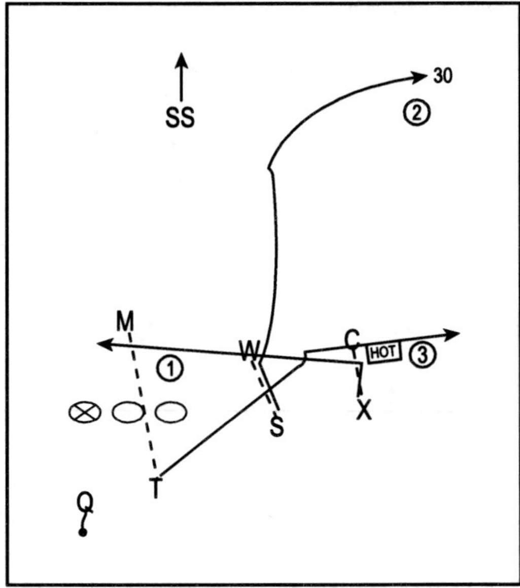

Diagram 5-27. Shallow-cross-smash concept versus cover-2 man under

Hooks as Outlets

Deeper developing hook routes can be effective outlet routes to the backside of a pattern. Although hook routes can have a tough time separating from press man coverage, such routes are often given more time to accomplish such tasks as a result of being outlets. Once such receivers are able to separate from the man coverage, they are able to work back toward the quarterback effectively without working into the cover-2 safety to their side. This route is shown in Diagram 5-28 versus cover-2 man under.

Diagram 5-29 shows the switch-read route backside-outlet concept that can be effectively used versus cover-2 man under. The crossing/switching action helps to create

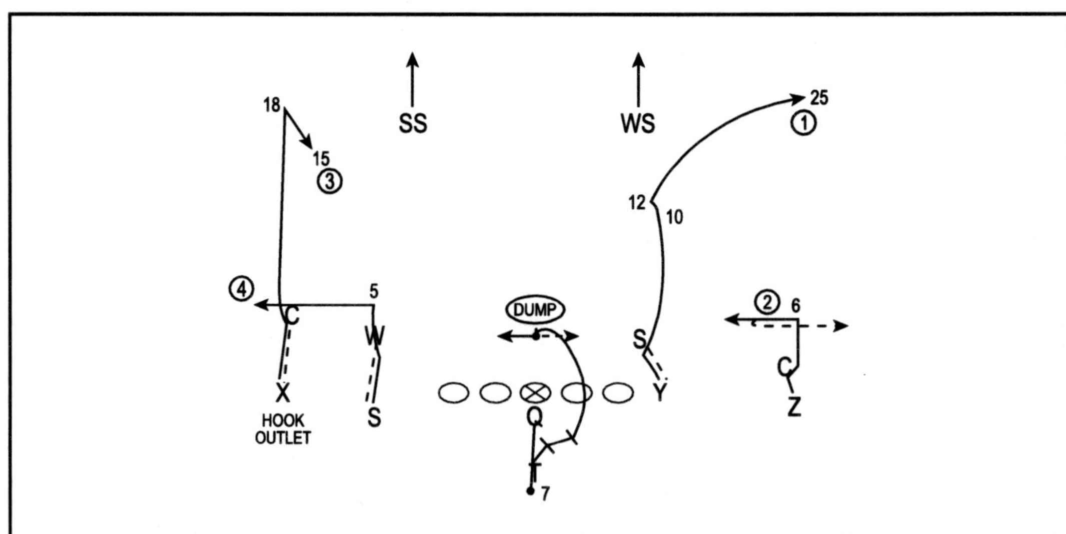

Diagram 5-28. Hook backside outlets versus cover-2 man under

natural, crossing, man separation for the outlet receivers. The outside receiver runs a read route off of the play of the cover-2 safety to his side with regard to being able to break the route deep into the middle of the cover-2 void—or he may have to square the route off to the inside if he were to see deep middle-zone coverage. The inside receiver takes his around route deep if he can beat his press-man-coverage defender. If he can't, he breaks his around route back underneath and drives across the field.

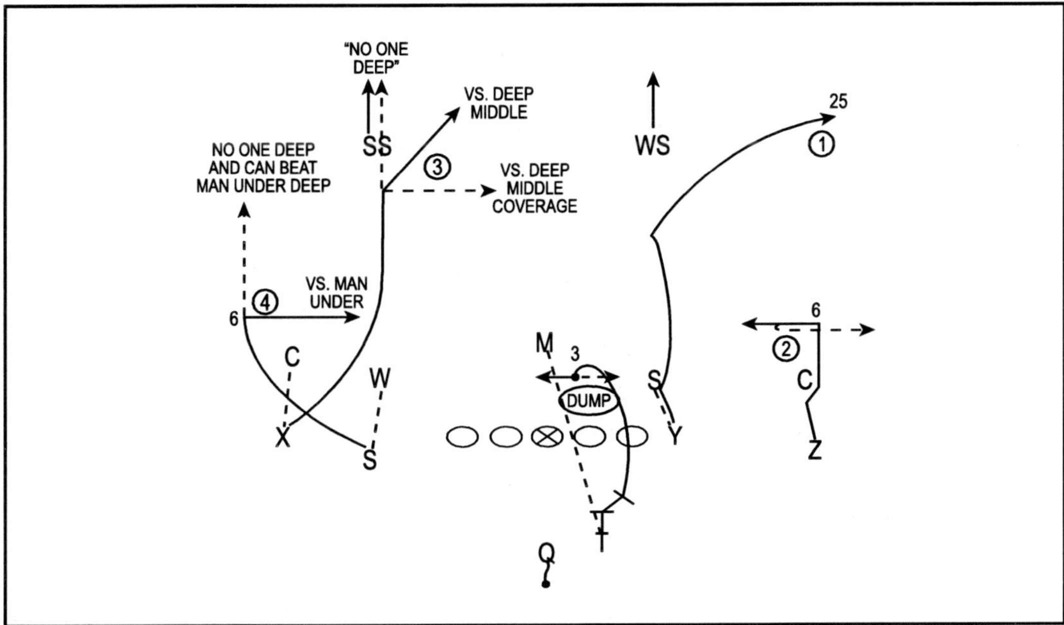

Diagram 5-29. Switch-read route backside outlet versus cover-2 man under

Drive Concept

The drive concept helps to create three excellent man-to-man coverage isolations on two (possibly three) of the inside cover-2 linebackers and a similar isolation on one of the cornerbacks. The drive route by one of the wide receivers is, in itself, an excellent man-beater route. The same can be said for the tight-end (Y) short-dig route. The back, on his break-to-the-inside aspect of his sit route, also presents an excellent man-beater route for the quarterback to go to. The back must, however, be sure to patiently execute the inside, man-breaking action of his sit route so that he can sequentially follow the tight-end (Y) short-dig route with proper spacing. This concept is shown in Diagram 5-30 versus cover-2 man under.

Cross Concept

The crossing action of the cross concept is an excellent cover-2-man-under beater action. As in the drive concept, the cross, the short dig, and the man-breaking adjustment aspects of the sit route (this time to the outside) help to create excellent man-under beater possibilities. And, crossing receivers, in themselves, are excellent man-beater action, as shown in the tight-end (Y) cross pattern in Diagram 5-31 versus cover-2 man under.

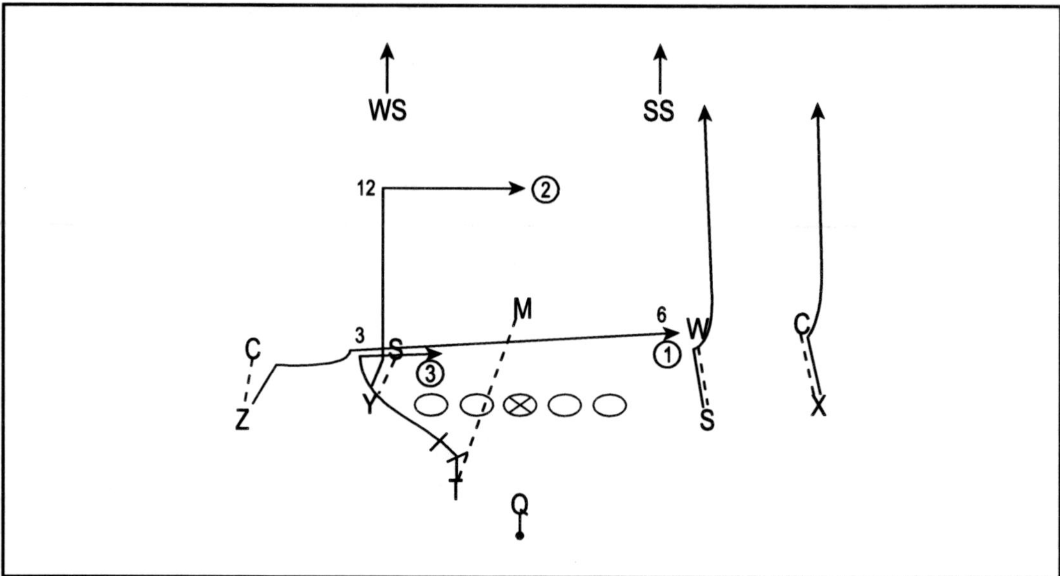

Diagram 5-30. Drive concept versus cover-2 man under

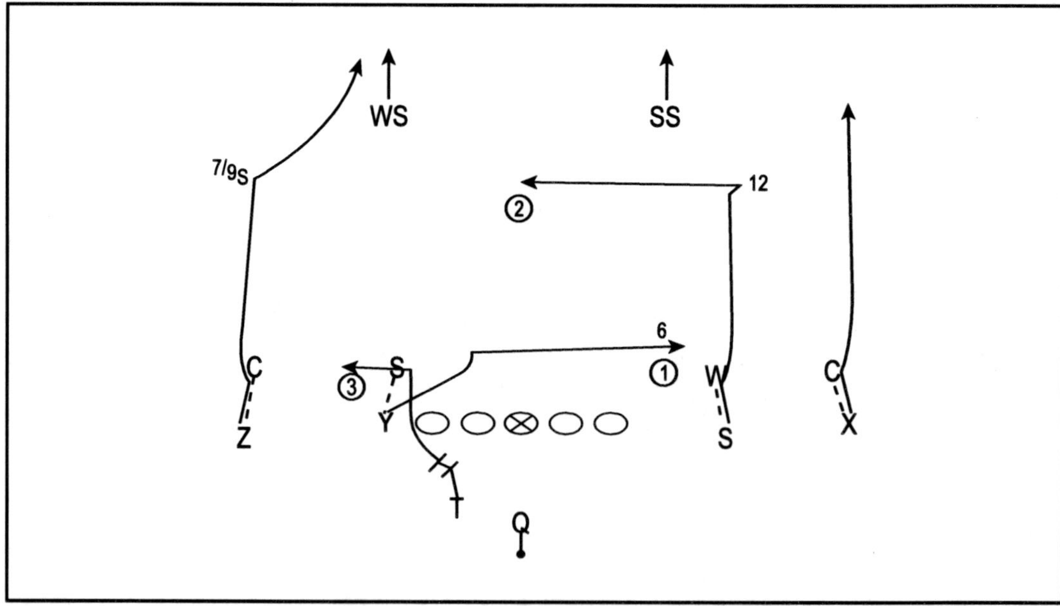

Diagram 5-31. Tight-end (Y) cross concept versus cover-2 man under

Double-Cross Concept

The double-cross concept is an extremely popular method of attacking cover-2 man under. Two inside receivers execute picking/rubbing cross-route action with a dig-type route that works into the center of the field. The dig route acts as an outlet if one of the two crossing routes do not open up. A post route by the wide receiver opposite the dig route works to blow the top off of the cover-2 safeties so that they cannot jump on the inside man-breaking dig route. The double-cross concept versus cover-2 man under is shown in Diagram 5-32.

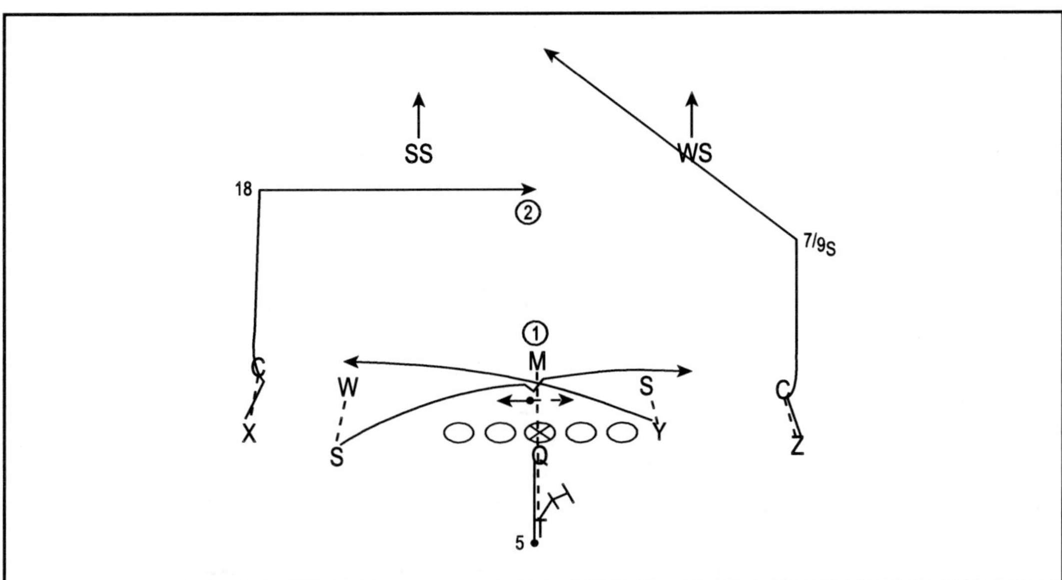

Diagram 5-32. Double-cross concept versus cover-2 man under

Texas Concept

The Texas concept helps to create a crossing isolation on the two linebackers to the cover-2, two-linebacker side. The tight end works to pin the inside linebacker to the inside for his outside square-out-type man break. The back drives to the flat to influence hard outside flow by his covering outside linebacker and then works back inside hard underneath to separate from that linebacker. The Texas concept versus cover-2 man under is shown in Diagram 5-33.

Option-Isolation Concept

Option isolation routes help to produce excellent one-on-one isolations on cover-2 man-under linebackers. Option routes can help to produce one-on-one size, talent, and speed mismatches. Option routes are best run off of five-step drop-timing by the quarterback. Five-step-drop quarterback timing allows for option routes to be run in the 8- to 12-yard range. This technique gives the option-route receivers time to properly maneuver and execute their option-route man- or zone-separation techniques. Diagram 5-34 shows a tight-end (Y) option and a halfback (H) option versus cover-2 man under.

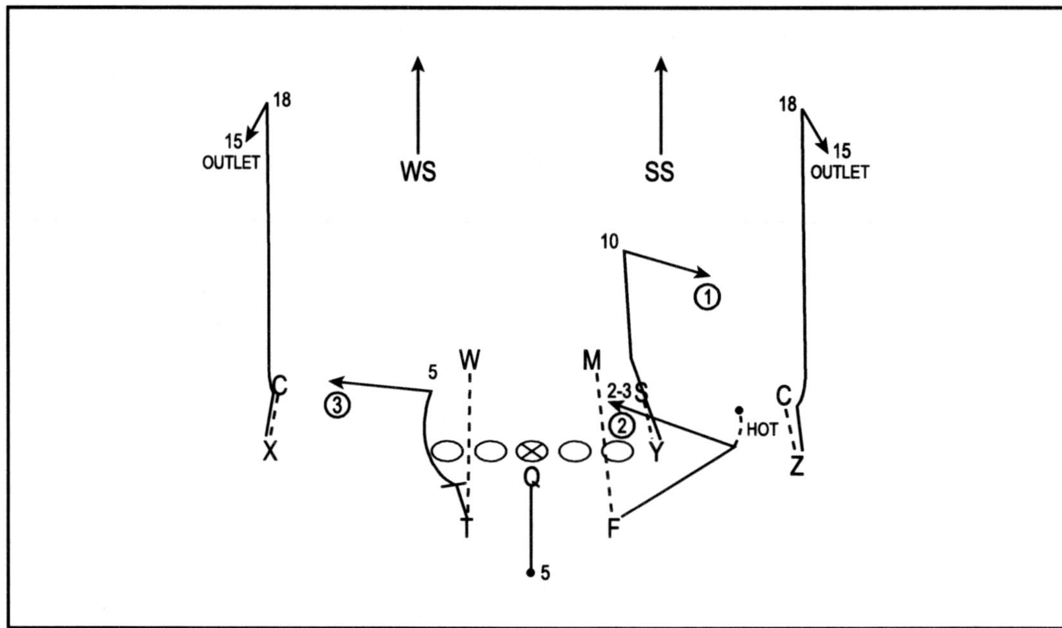

Diagram 5-33. Texas concept versus cover-2 man under

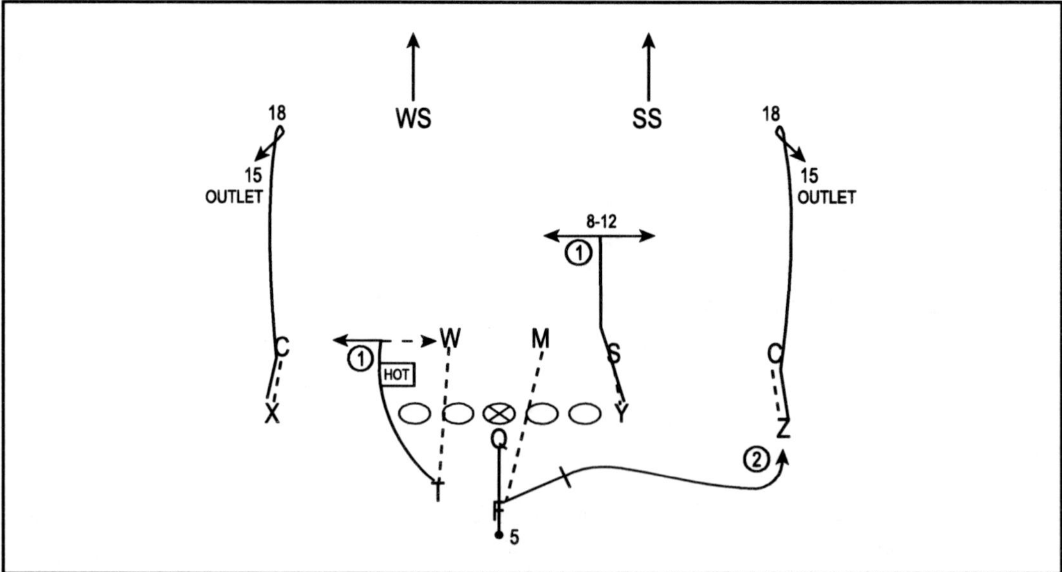

Diagram 5-34. H-option and Y-option isolation routes versus cover-2 man under

Pivot- and Break-Route Isolations

Tight-end (Y) pivot- and break-route isolations can be very effective versus cover-2 man under. Such routes can often help produce mismatches in favor of the offense—especially if the linebacker is bigger and more physical than the linebacker, or if the tight end is more athletic. The pivot and break routes are run in the six- to seven-yard range. Versus a normal inside-out man-coverage alignment by the covering linebacker (or, possibly, nickel defender), the Y-pivot route may be the better route of the two, allowing the tight end to wall off the covering defender by alignment. However, versus an active, fast-flowing linebacker, the break route can help the tight end to separate by breaking back to the inside. Diagram 5-35 shows a Y-pivot high-low-read isolation action to attack cover-2 man under. Diagram 5-36 shows a Y-break isolation versus cover-2 man under.

Backs-Cross and Fake-Cross Isolations

Short, inside backs-cross and fake-cross isolations are very effective versus cover-2 man under. On backs cross, the quarterback reads the mesh of the crossing backs to see if one (or both) of the backs pop open versus the man-under coverage. If they don't, the tight-end route over the middle becomes the come-open-late route to go to. Between the crossing/picking action of the backs and the man-separating short-dig route of the tight end, a good chance exists that at least one of the three receivers will pop open. The backs-cross concept versus cover-2 man under is shown in Diagram 5-37.

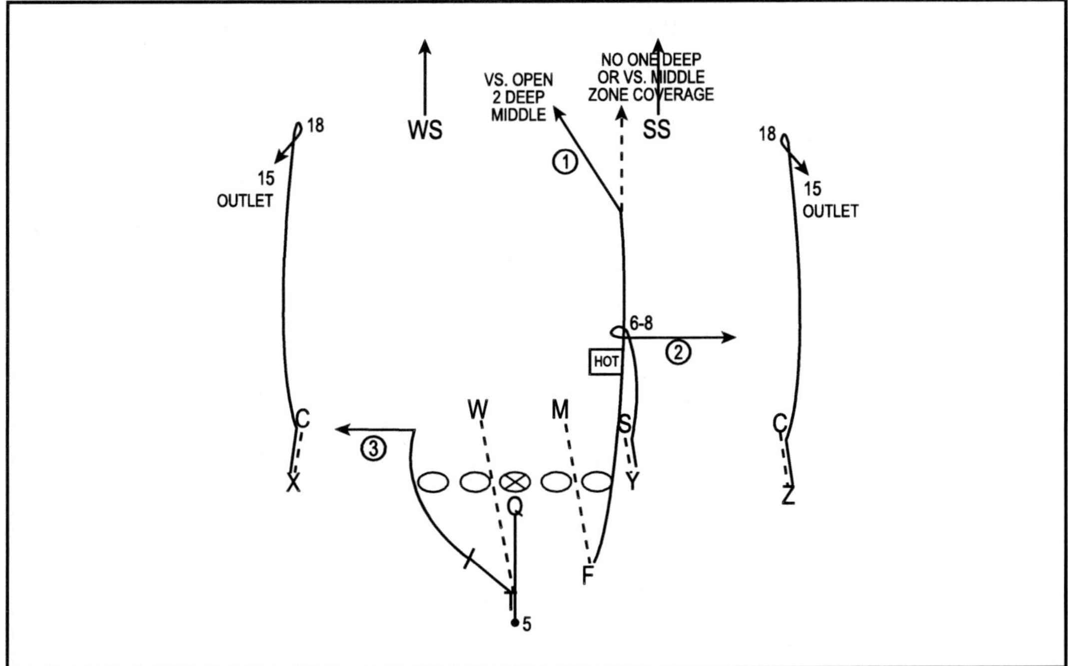

Diagram 5-35. Y-pivot isolation versus cover-2 man under

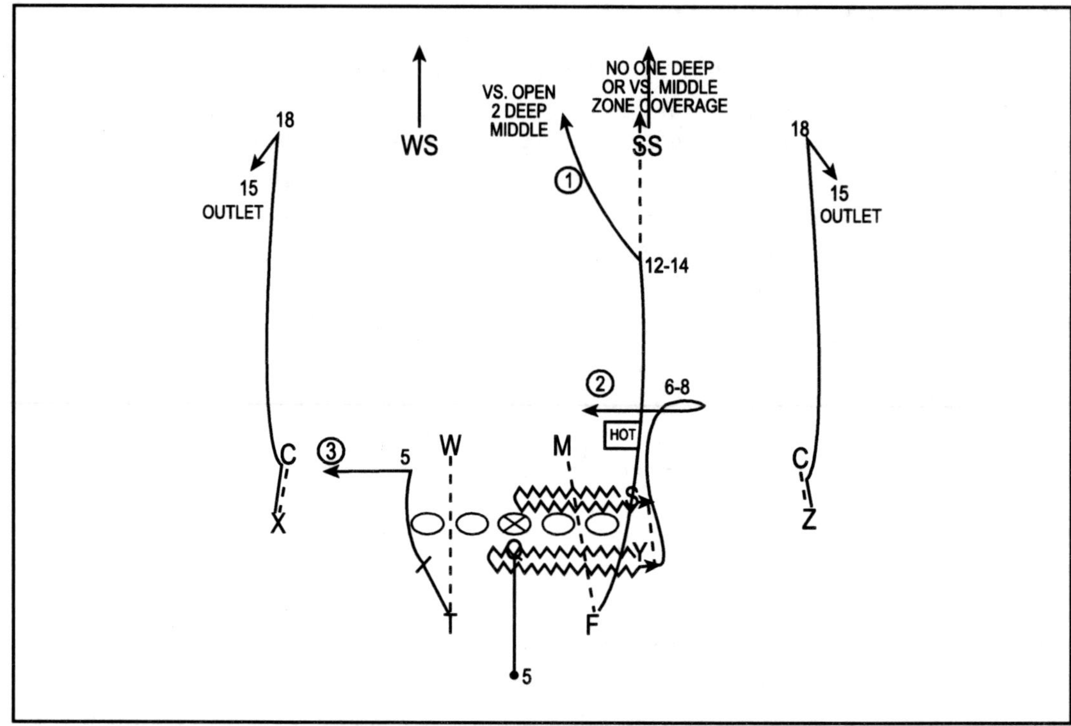

Diagram 5-36. Y-break isolation versus cover-2 man under

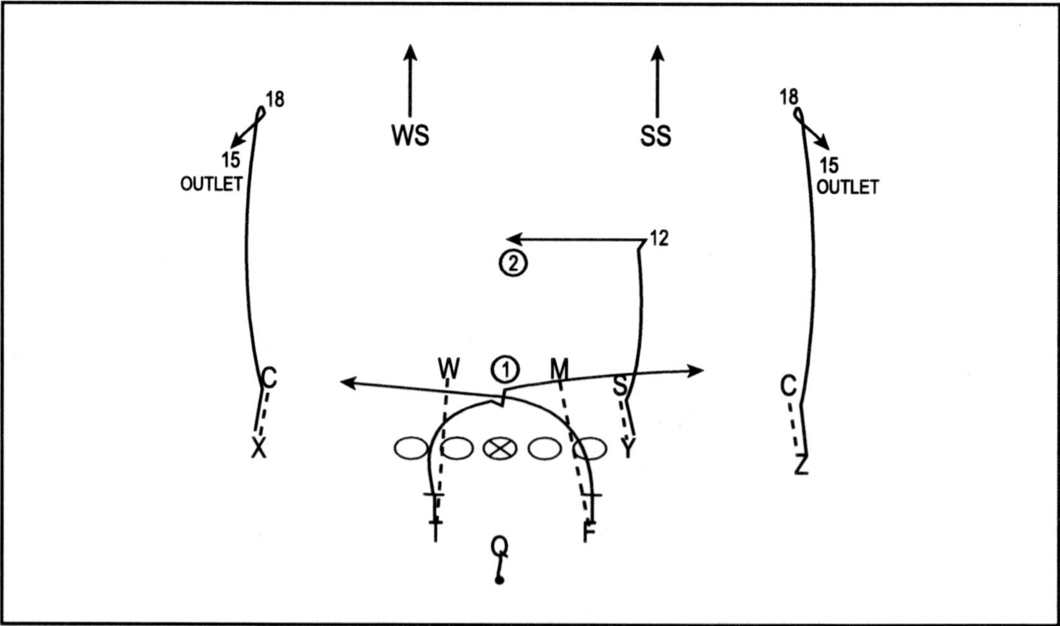

Diagram 5-37. Backs-cross concept versus cover-2 man under

In backs-fake cross, the backs fake backs-cross action once the linebackers start to play the cross action and man-break back out toward the sidelines. Again, the quarterback reads to see if one (or both) of the backs pop open. If not, the tight end's short-dig route then becomes the come-open-late route to go to. The backs-fake-cross concept versus cover-2 man under is shown in Diagram 5-38.

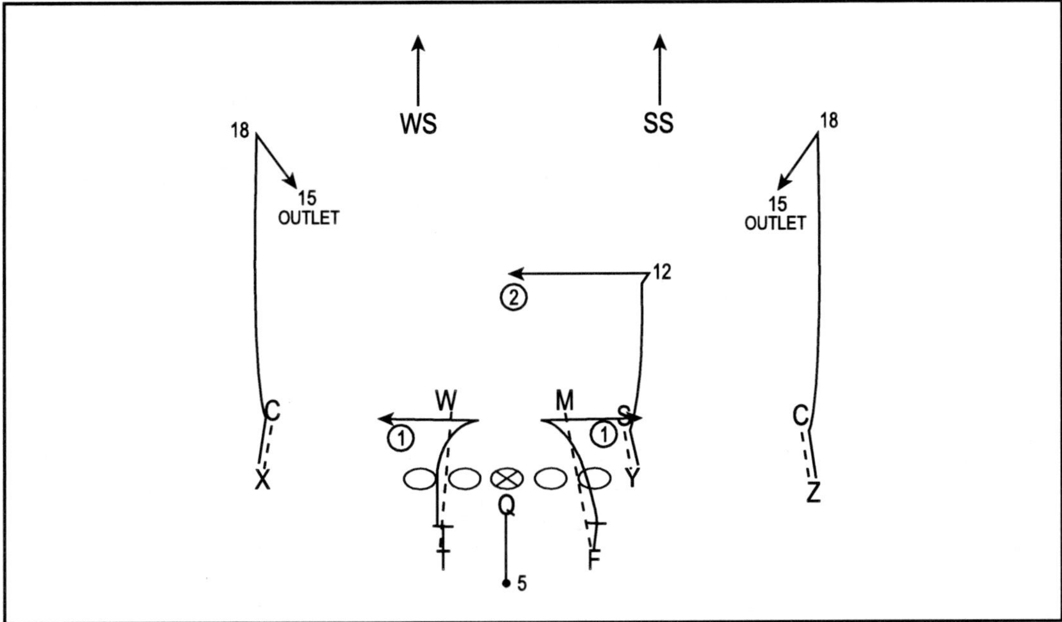

Diagram 5-38. Backs-fake-cross concept versus cover-2 man under

Pick and Rub Concepts

Pick and rub concepts can be excellent cover-2 man-under man-beater route combinations. Of course, any pick or rub must be legally executed. Receivers cannot run into and/or block coverage defenders as a part of the pick or rub concept. Diagram 5-39 shows a pick-route combination with an inside receiver working to the outside versus cover-2 man under.

An interesting idea is to have the receiver who actually sets up the pick for the prime pick, rub, or slice route (Diagrams 5-39 to 5-41) run a modified option route if the quarterback snaps his eyes late to that receiver. In this fashion, if the pick, rub, or slice receiver is covered, the quarterback has a delayed-timed option route to work to as an outlet.

Diagram 5-40 shows a rub-route combination with an outside receiver working to the inside. In rub action, the offense always has to be worried about the depth and activity of the deep-half cover-2 safety to the side of the rub. Diagram 5-41 shows a slice-route combination with an inside receiver working off a pick set-up and executing a fade route.

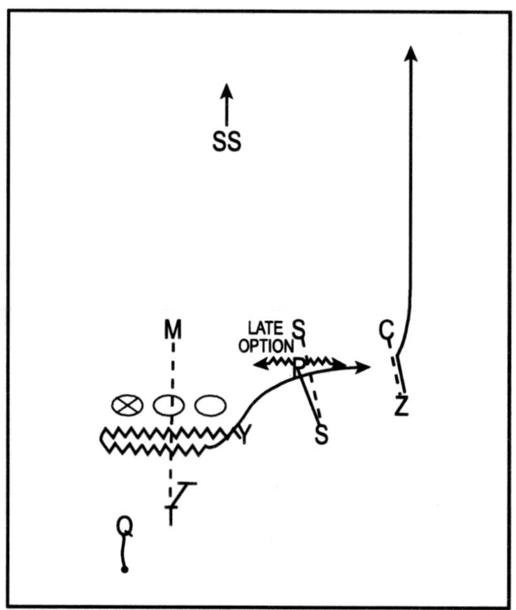

Diagram 5-39. Pick-route combination versus cover-2 man under

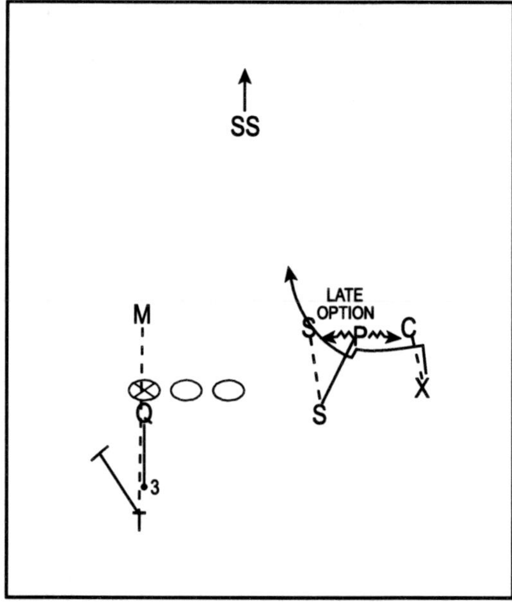

Diagram 5-40. Rub-route combination versus cover-2 man under

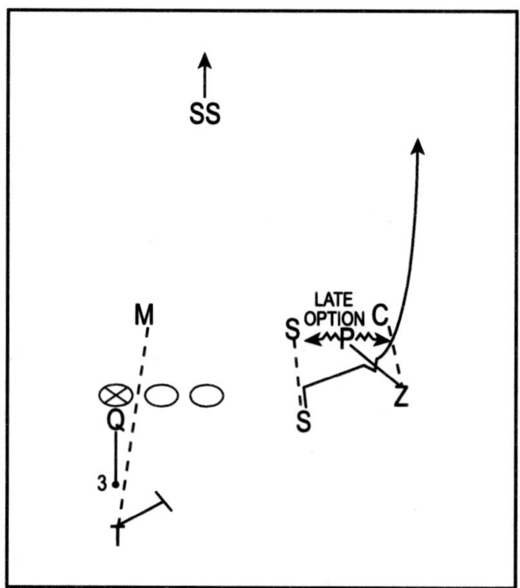

Diagram 5-41. Slice route combination versus cover-2 man under

Picking Screens

Picking-type screens, legal when the ball is thrown behind the line of scrimmage, is a very effective concept to use versus cover-2 man under. Diagram 5-42 shows a wide-receiver screen with the tight end blocking out on the cover-2 cornerback man-covering the flanker (Z). Diagram 5-43 shows a pick screen to a back versus cover-2 man under as the tight end blocks the linebacker assigned to man cover the back.

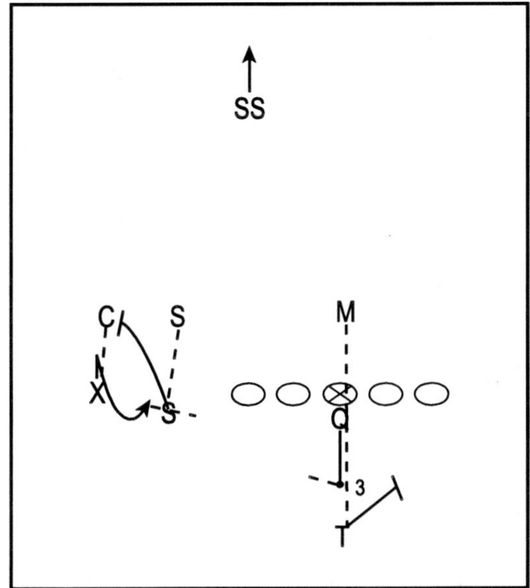

Diagram 5-42. Wide-receiver pick screen versus cover-2 man under

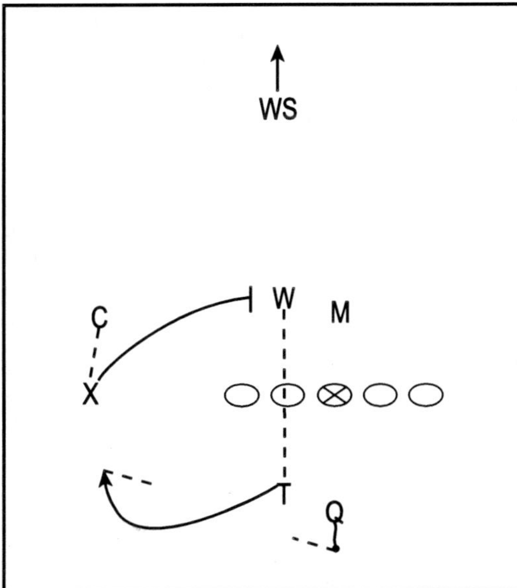

Diagram 5-43. Back pick screen versus cover-2 man under

6

Pass Attack of Quarters Coverage

Quarters coverage is a commonly-used coverage in the two-safeties family. Two deep safeties are in the middle of the field. However, unlike the deep-halves play of cover-2 safeties aligned on or near the hashes at about 14 yards, the quarters-coverage safeties align up tighter toward the line of scrimmage, 10 to 12 yards deep. The safeties align in a position that will allow them to be excellent off-tackle or alley-run-support defenders. Their depth and horizontal-alignment positioning allows the quarters safeties to be responsible for covering the two inside deep quarters of the field.

The quarters-coverage cornerbacks—unlike the low, squatted cover-2 cornerbacks—align off the ball 9 to 11 yards deep. They are normally aligned head-up to outside of the widest receiver. The cornerbacks will probably be in more of a straight-legged, squared-up zone stance looking through the wide receiver on whom they are aligned in an effort to "peek in" towards the next receiver (in case the coverage is brackets/inside-out/combo-type coverage). The depth and horizontal-alignment positioning allows the quarters cornerbacks to be responsible for covering the two outside deep quarters of the field. Diagram 6-1 shows quarters (four across deep, three under) zone coverage.

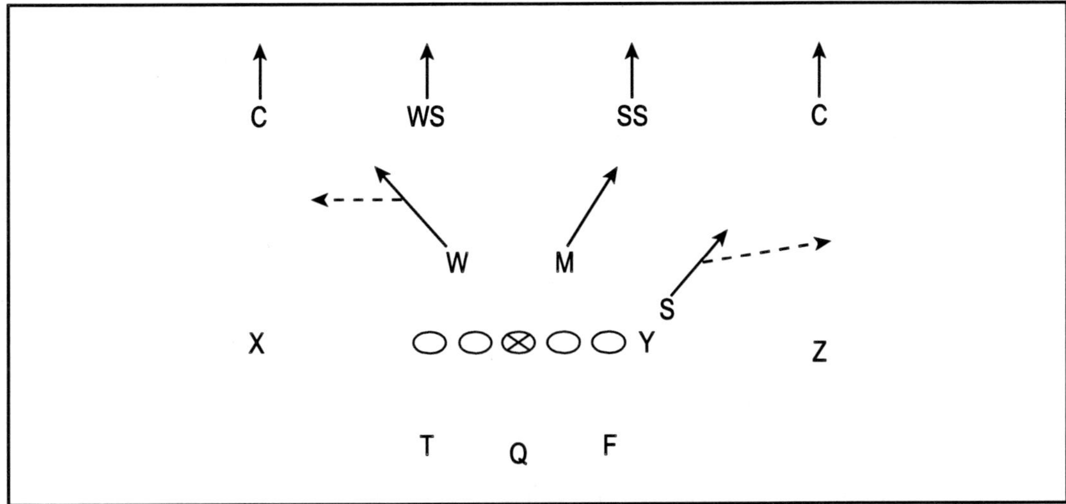

Diagram 6-1. Quarters (four across deep, three under) zone coverage

Quarters-Coverage Pass-Game Strengths

- The four-across, deep-quarters coverage is the strength of quarters coverage. Each deep defender (the two cornerbacks and two safeties) each zone cover one-fourth of the field deep.
- With the low positioning of the cornerbacks and their ability to quickly work upfield to defend versus quick-flat pass game and outside runs, quarters coverage mostly acts like a tilted cover-2 coverage.
- The cornerback and safety to each side can work in combination with one another (brackets/combo/inside-out technique), reading and reacting to the first (widest) receiver and second (next receiver to the inside) to their side. Such brackets/combo/inside-out combination-coverage techniques are shown in Diagram 6-2.
- The low positioning of the safeties allows for excellent extra edge (off-tackle) run support from the secondary. Such an extra run-support defender helps, in design, to produce an eight-man front when given a run read to one side of the offensive formation or the other.
- The relatively low, four-across positioning of the four defensive backs in the 9- to 11-yard range allows for excellent alignments to rotate to most any other type of man or zone coverage.
- Depending on the deep threat that a quarters-coverage cornerback is facing, a cornerback can give a low enough alignment look to help confuse a quarterback into thinking he's facing cover 2.

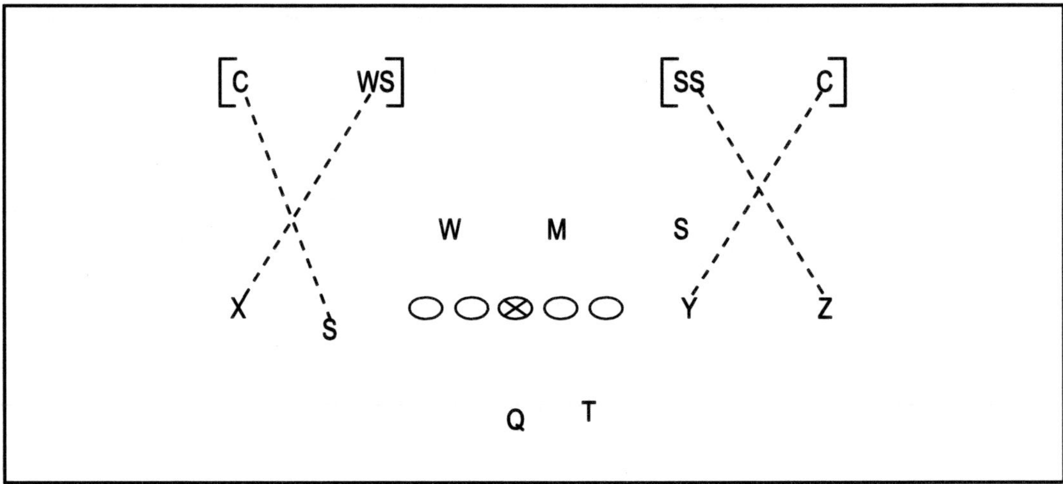

Diagram 6-2. Brackets/combo/inside-out combination quarters-coverage techniques

Quarters-Coverage Pass-Game Weakness

- Quarters coverage gives up easy underneath throws—especially to the outside flat-zone areas. These quarters-coverage voids are shown in Diagram 6-3.
- As a result of the outside-flat quarters-coverage voids, the coverage is extremely susceptible to hitch and any level of out-type routes, which is true both to the strongside and weakside of the formation.
- If the quarters coverage tries to make up for its flat-zone hitch and out-route vulnerability by having its cornerbacks work upfield fast and hard, the coverage

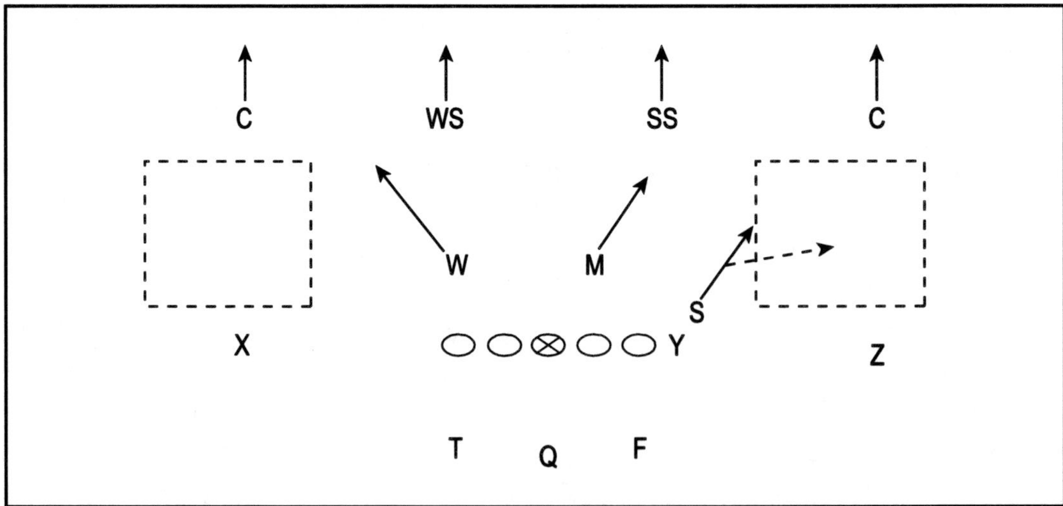

Diagram 6-3. Quarters-coverage voids

becomes extremely vulnerable to deep, double-move routes off of the hitch and out routes.

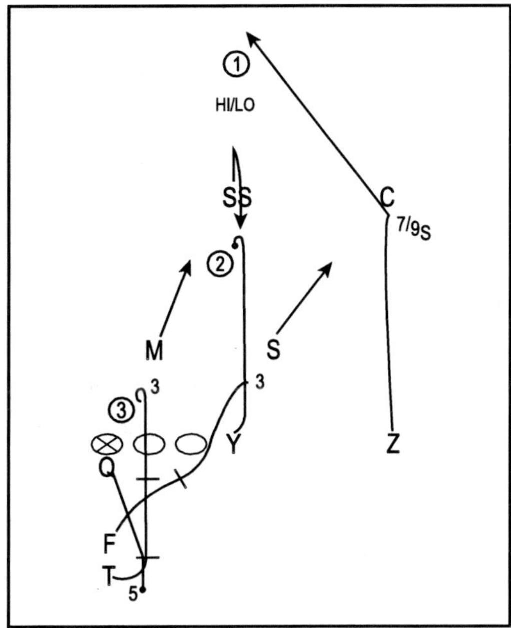

Diagram 6-4. Play-action to throw over the top of an influenced quarters safety

- Hard supporting quarters-coverage safeties versus the run game make the coverage vulnerable to play-action passing. Diagram 6-4 shows a play-action fake sucking up a safety, enabling an over-the-top post throw over the head of the influenced safety.
- Quarters coverage is susceptible to high-low-read concepts, especially to the inside versus quarters-coverage safeties.
- Dig concepts with deep middle-zone clear-out routes can be very effective versus quarters coverage. Three-tiered patterns with such a deep middle-zone clear-out route helps to produce effective high-low reads on the quarters-coverage inside linebackers.
- Quarters coverage has only three underneath-zone (linebacker) defenders. As a result, it puts tremendous coverage strain on the weakside linebacker, the only true underneath-coverage defender to that side. And, it puts tremendous strain on the field/strongside outside linebacker, who must cover the curl to the flat zone, depending on how he is being threatened. Such quarters-coverage underneath-linebacker coverage problems are shown in Diagram 6-5.
- With the different coverage responsibilities of the field/strongside linebacker (curl/flat), the two inside linebackers are susceptible to high-low isolations, option isolations and/or flood concepts.
- Drive- and cross-route concepts are very effective in creating three-on-two flood isolations on the two inside quarters-coverage linebackers.
- Naked-bootleg action can be very effective versus quarters-coverage—both weak and strong. The play-action does much to hold and influence the three underneath-zone linebackers. And, the play-action can help to influence the safeties to suck up for possible deep throws over their heads. Diagram 6-6 shows naked-bootleg action versus quarters coverage.
- Screens can be very effective versus quarters coverage. Much like cover 2, formationing can help to create screen numbers (i.e., three-on-two) mismatches.

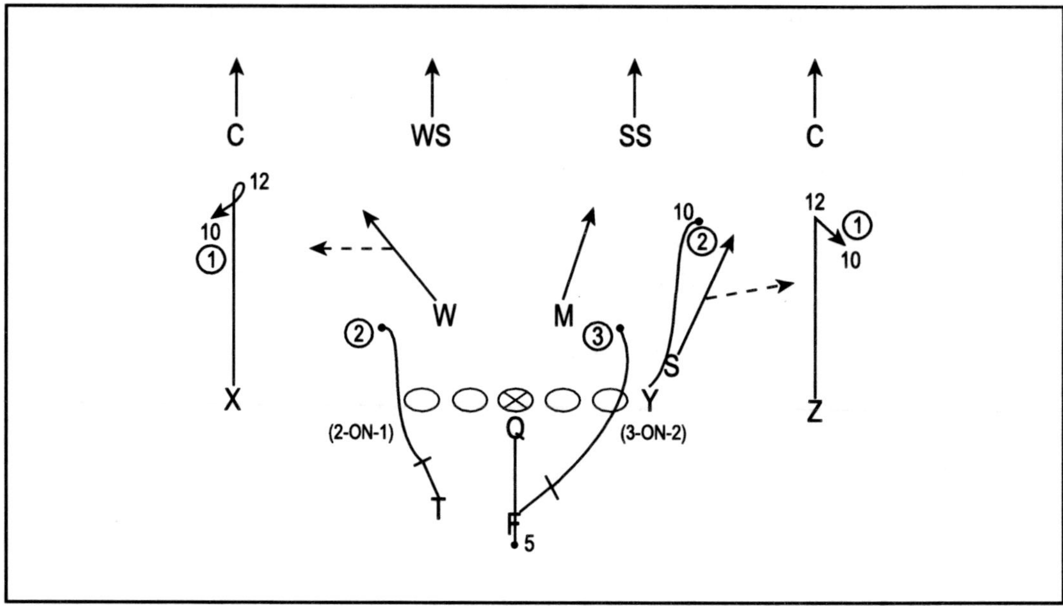

Diagram 6-5. Quarters-coverage underneath-zone linebacker-coverage problems

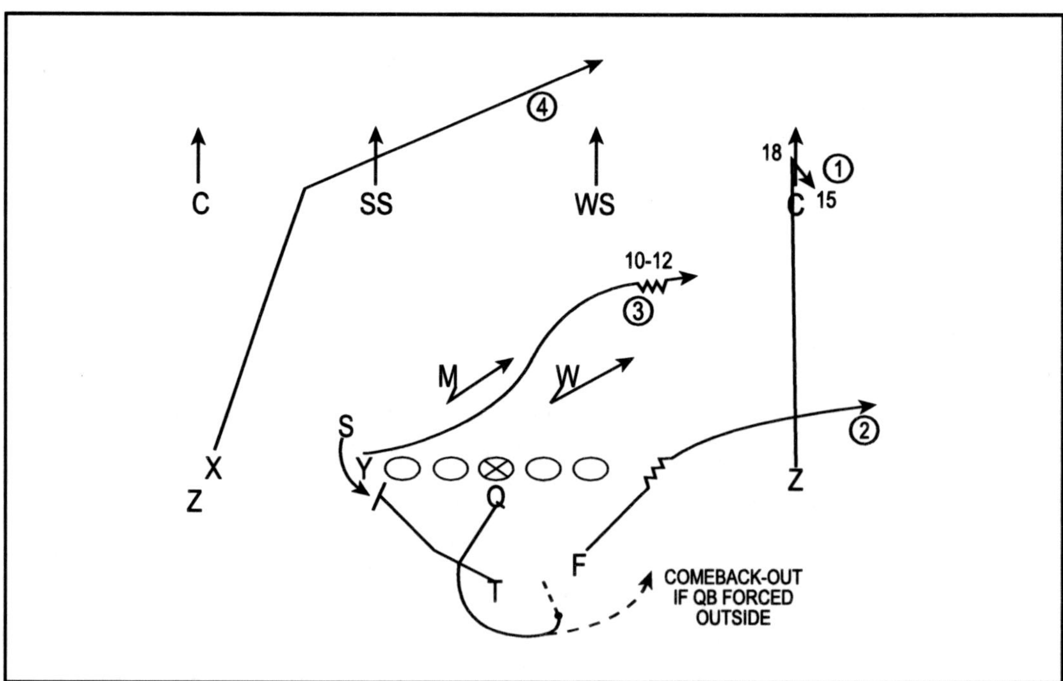

Diagram 6-6. Naked-bootleg action versus quarters coverage

Route Combination and Pass-Pattern Attack of Quarters Coverage

Quick-Game Hitch

The quick-game (three-step-drop-timed throw by the quarterback) hitch route is an excellent route concept versus quarters coverage. The hitch route helps to exploit the quarters-coverage flat-zone-coverage void. Diagram 6-7 shows double-hitch action versus quarters coverage to help hold the outside linebacker and create a lateral-read-throw action.

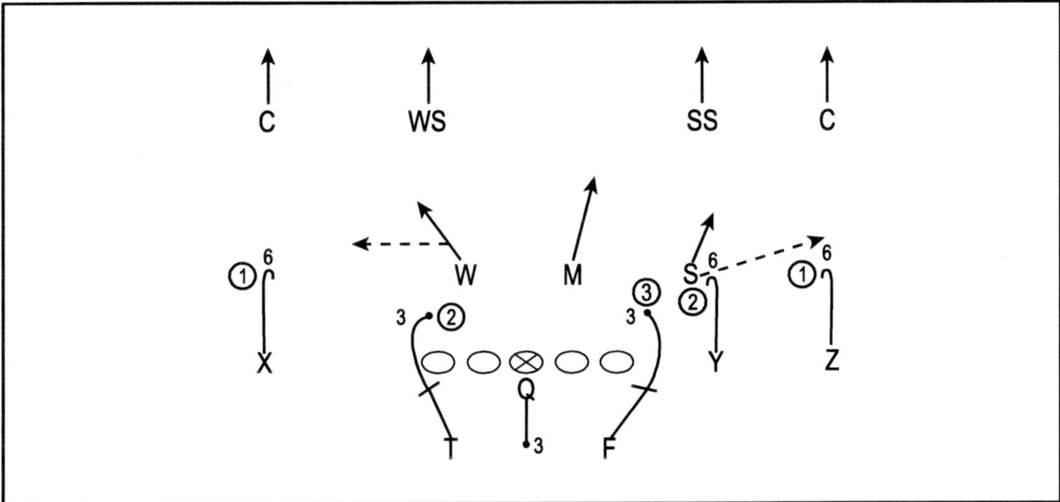

Diagram 6-7. Quick-game double-hitch action versus quarters coverage

Quick-Game Speed-Out

The quick-game speed-out route is an excellent route concept versus quarters coverage. Just like the hitch route, the speed-out route helps to exploit the quarters-coverage flat-zone-coverage void, as shown in Diagram 6-8.

Quick-Game Inside-Receiver Speed-Out

The quick-game inside-receiver speed-out route combination creates an excellent clear-out route to push the quarters-coverage cornerback deep while bringing the inside receiver to the outside underneath the clear-out action. Diagram 6-9 shows a slot-inside-receiver quick speed-out-route combination with quick play-action to hold the outside linebacker from getting out to the speed-out route and a tight-end (Y) one-on-one isolation to the backside.

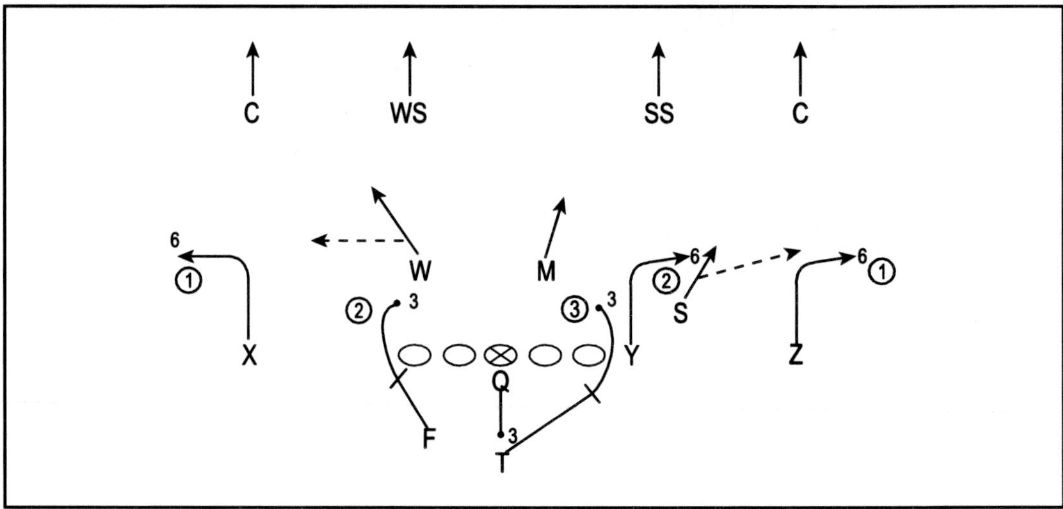

Diagram 6-8. Quick-game speed-out versus quarters coverage

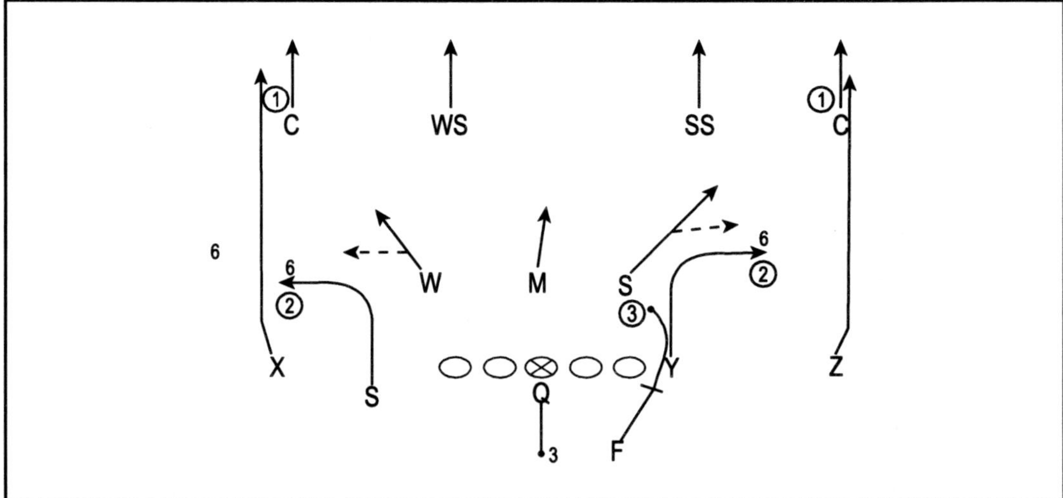

Diagram 6-9. Quick-game inside-receiver speed-out concept versus quarters coverage

The quick-game inside-receiver speed-out concept is also an excellent concept to execute off of five-step-timed quarterback-drop action. The deeper speed-out route, however, becomes more of a square-out route at 10 yards, as shown in Diagram 6-10.

Quick-Game Weakside Play-Action Slant Isolation

The quick-game weakside-slant isolation is an excellent concept to use in the attack of quarters coverage. Play-action away from the slant action helps to influence the weakside linebacker from dropping underneath the slant, as seen in Diagram 6-11.

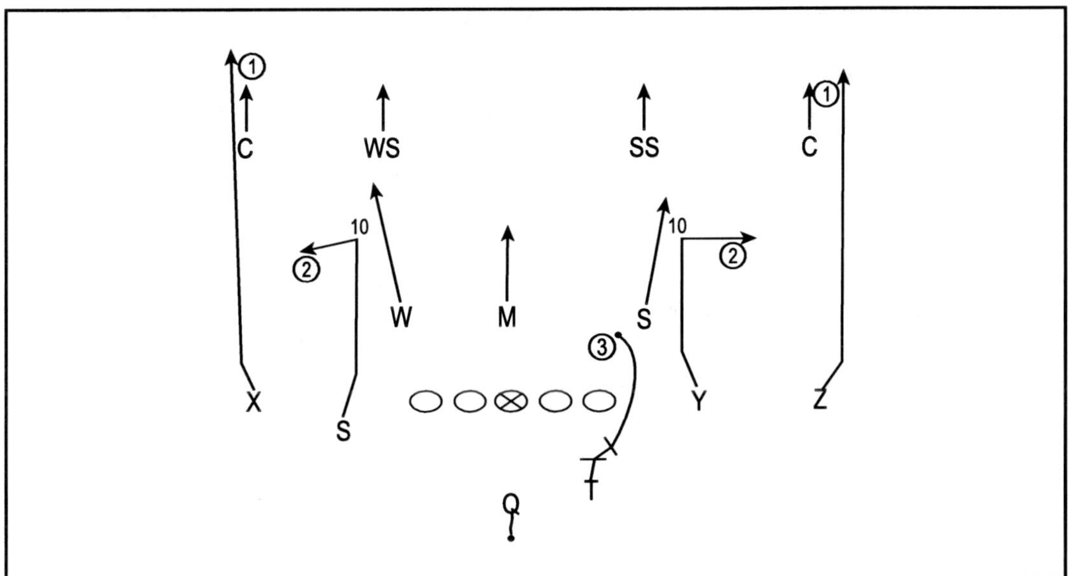

Diagram 6-10. Inside-receiver square-out concept versus quarters coverage

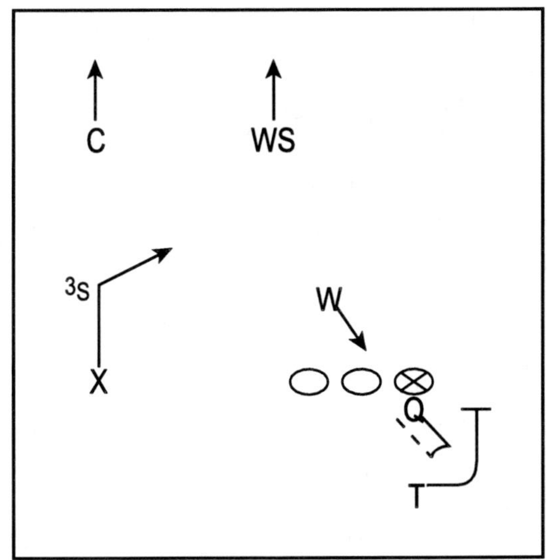

Diagram 6-11. Quick-game weakside play-action slant isolation versus quarters coverage

Quick-Game Double-Slant Concept

The quick-game double-slant concept is an excellent means of attacking quarters coverage. The concept places a two-on-one lateral-read-action on the outside linebacker, as seen in Diagram 6-12 with quick play-action faking.

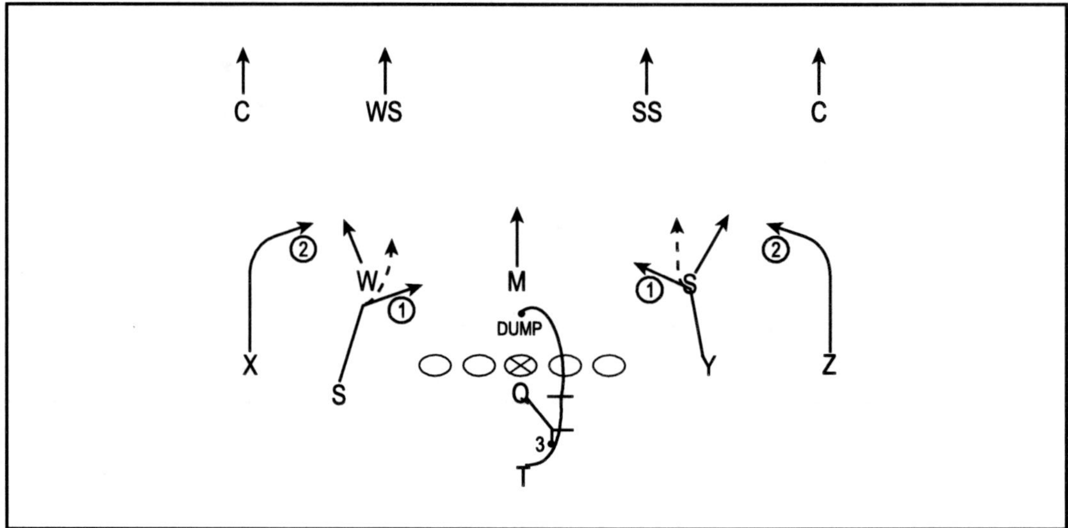

Diagram 6-12. Double-slant versus quarters coverage

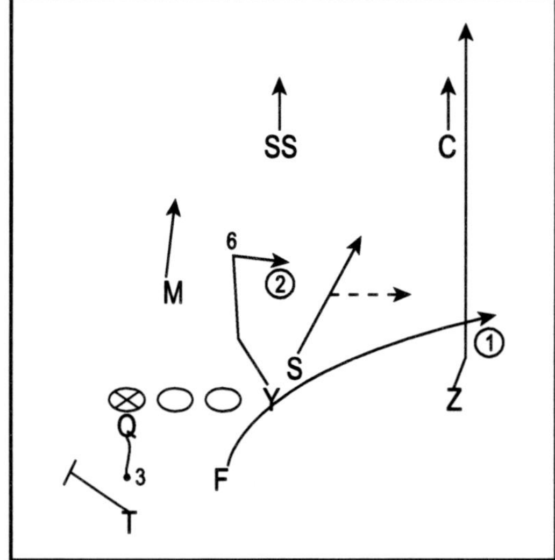

Diagram 6-13. Quick-game stick isolation versus quarters coverage

Quick-Game Inside-Receiver Stick-Route Isolation

The quick-game inside-receiver stick-route isolation can be very effective strong or weak versus quarters coverage. If run strong, a flat route by the back can help to create a one-on-one isolation on the inside linebacker. Diagram 6-13 shows both a strongside and weakside stick-route isolation.

Quick-Game Double-Move-Route Isolations

Double-move action off of quick-game pass routes is an excellent way to attack quarters-coverage cornerbacks who try to jump the quick-game prime routes. Double-move route isolations off of the hitch and quick speed-out routes to produce hitch-and-go and quick speed-out-and-up routes are shown in Diagram 6-14.

The quick-game slant-and-go double-move route by the outside slant receiver is an excellent concept to utilize if a quarters safety tries to jump an outside slant. The outside-slant route breaks his slant deep over the top of the quarters safety, as shown in Diagram 6-15.

The quick-game Y-stick-and-go double-move route is an excellent concept to utilize if a quarters-coverage safety tries to jump a tight-end (Y) stick route. The Y-stick-and-go route concept is shown in Diagram 6-16.

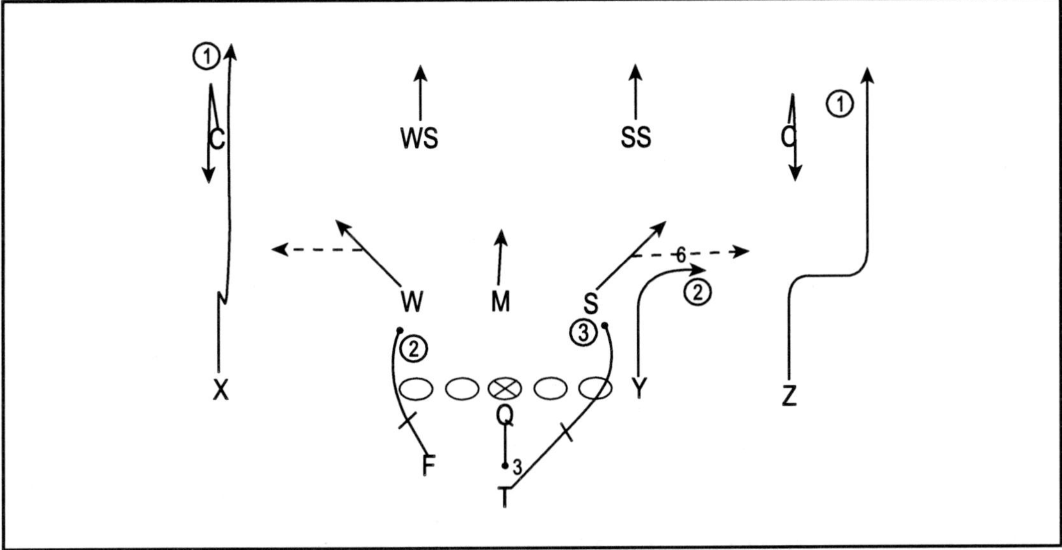

Diagram 6-14. Quick-game double-move hitch-and-go and speed-out-and-go routes versus quarters coverage

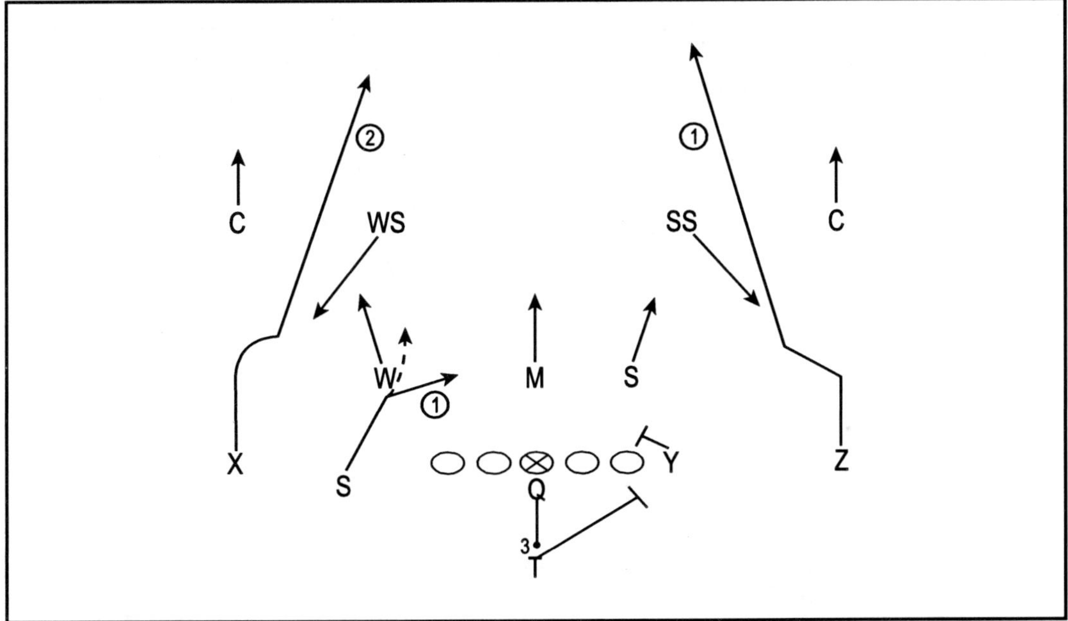

Diagram 6-15. Slant-and-go double-move route versus quarters coverage

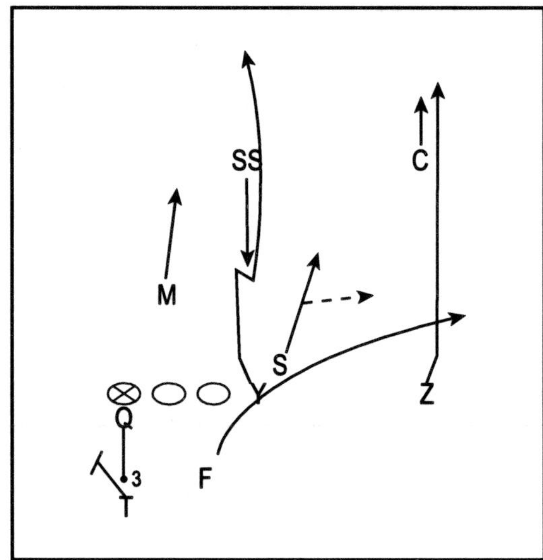

Diagram 6-16. Y-stick-and-go route versus quarters coverage

Speed-Out/Rollaway Lateral-Read Combinations

The five-step quarterback drop-timed speed-out and rollaway lateral-read-route combinations are excellent ways to attack quarters coverage. Both the prime route speed-out and rollaway routes attack the true-coverage voids of quarters coverage, the flat zones. As shown in Diagram 6-17, the tight-end (Y) alley route helps to create a true lateral read on the outside linebacker, while the weakside back's seam route helps to hold the weakside linebacker from getting out to the rollaway route. The rollaway

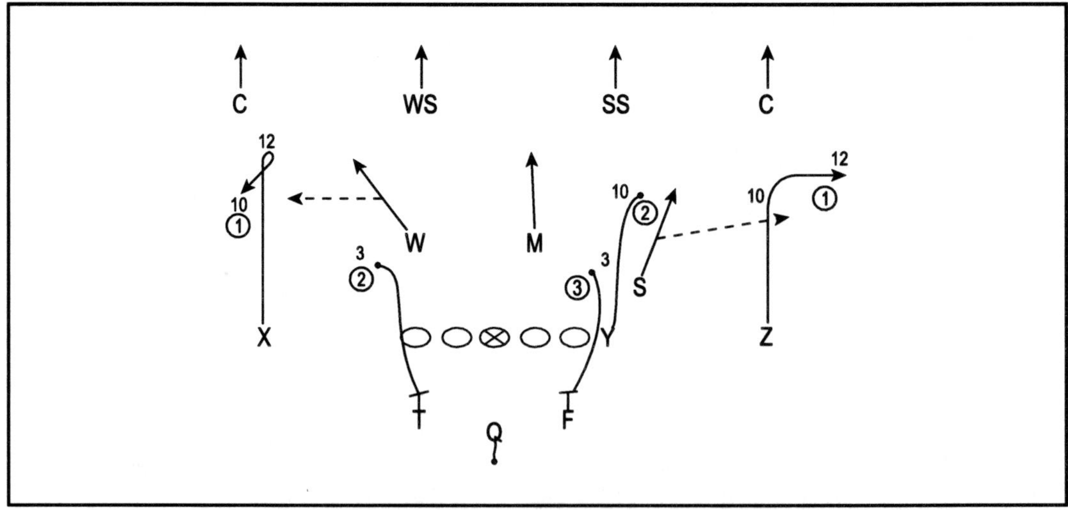

Diagram 6-17. Speed-out and rollaway lateral-read concepts versus quarters coverage

route is an excellent concept to use when the ball is on the hash into the boundary where the speed-out may not have enough room to operate. Diagram 6-18 shows a similar lateral-read concept with deeper, seven-step quarterback drop-timed comeback-out and deep rollaway routes.

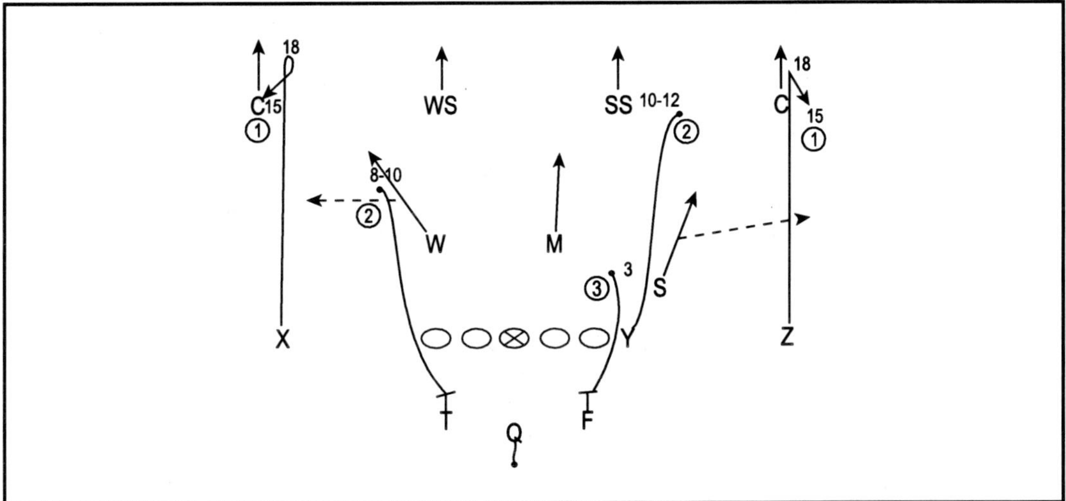

Diagram 6-18. Comeback-out and deep rollaway lateral-read concepts versus quarters coverage

Curl (or Hook)/Flat Lateral-Read Concept

The curl/flat (or deeper hook/flat) lateral-read concept is an excellent way to attack the lack of underneath coverage of quarters coverage. To the weakside, the lateral-read action isolates on the weakside linebacker, as shown by the split-end (X) curl route and the back's flat route in Diagram 6-19. To the strongside, the lateral-read action isolates on the strongside outside linebacker as shown by the flanker (Z) hook route and the tight-end (Y) flat route, also shown in Diagram 6-19. (The only difference between the curl and hook routes is the depths of the routes and the need for seven-step drop-timed action by the quarterback for the deeper hook route).

Speed-Out, Rollaway, Curl Double-Move-Route Concepts

As has been shown, speed-outs, rollaways, and curl-route concepts are excellent ways to attack quarters coverage. Quite often, the quarters-coverage cornerback will try to jump those routes by the widest receiver. As a result, double-move-route concepts can be very effective to create "home-run" deep-ball threats to combat aggressive cornerback play on these five-step-timed quarterback drop actions. Diagram 6-20 shows a rollaway- (fake-) and-go double-move action by the split end (X) and speed-out-and-up double-move action by the flanker (Z). Diagram 6-21 shows a curl-and-go double-move action by the split end (X) and a flat-and-up double-move action by the tight end (Y).

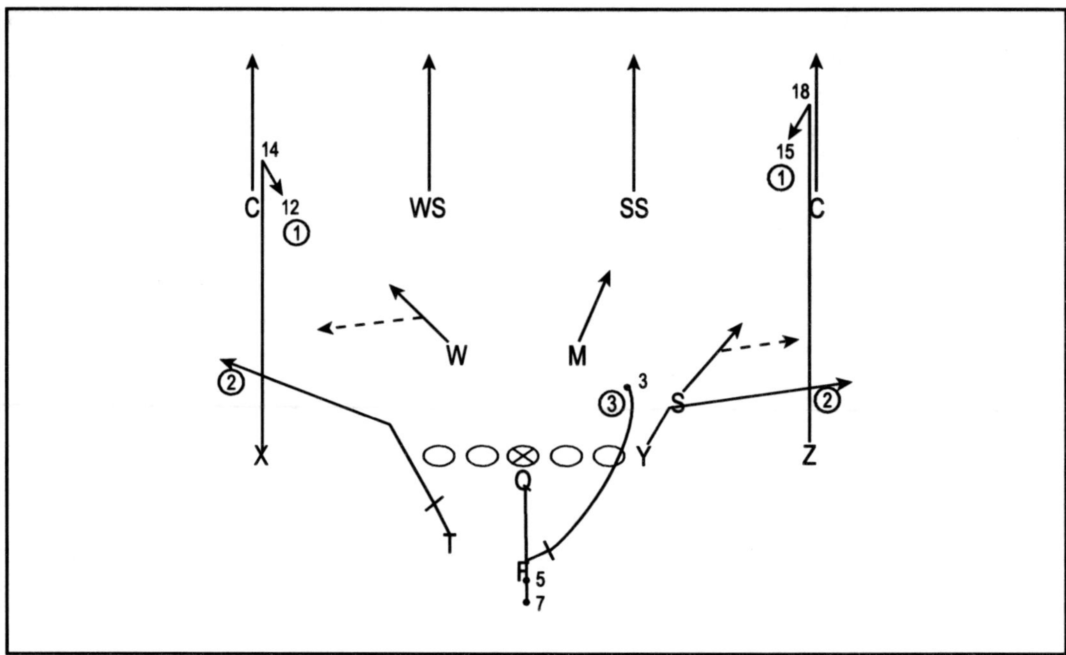

Diagram 6-19. Curl/flat or hook/flat lateral-read concept versus quarters coverage

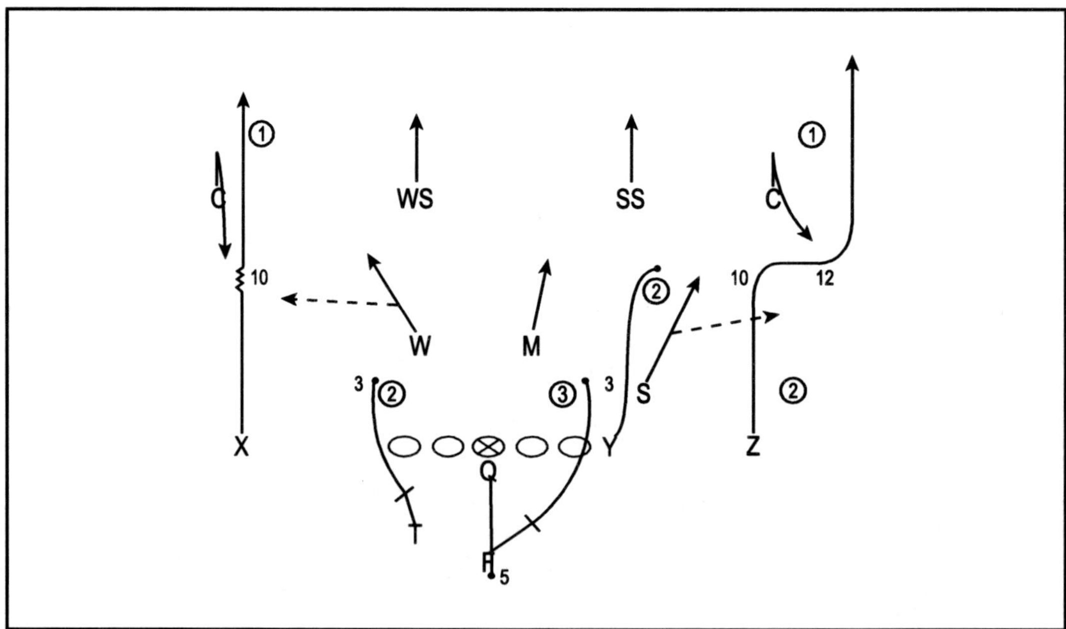

Diagram 6-20. Rollaway-and-go/speed-out-and-up double-move concepts versus quarters coverage

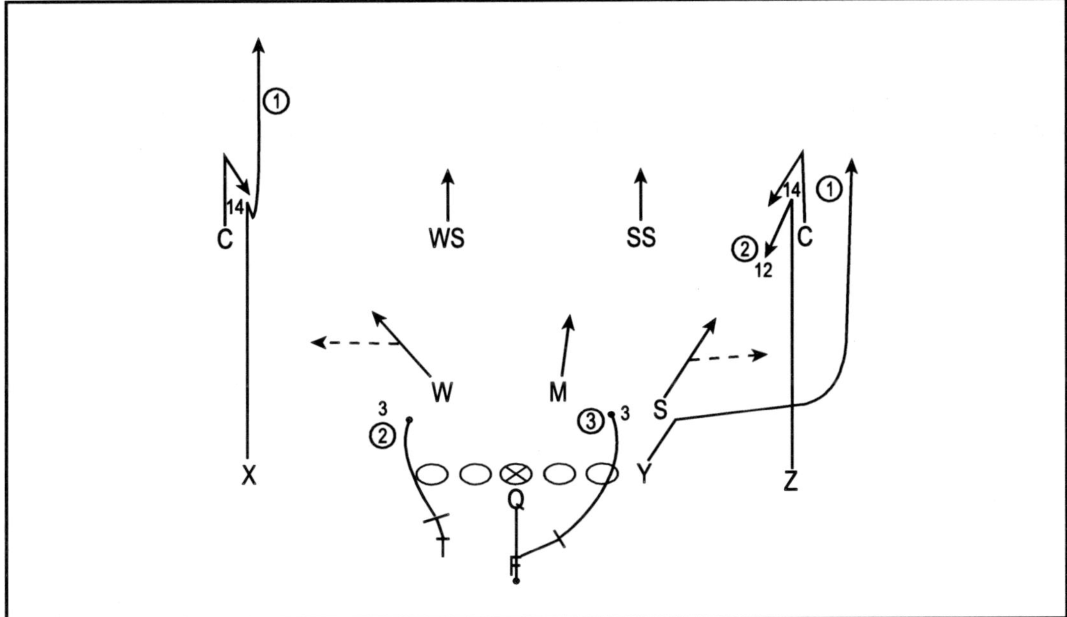

Diagram 6-21. Curl-and-go and flat-and-up double-move concepts versus quarters coverage

High-Low Fish-Isolation Concept

The high-low fish-isolation concept is an excellent way to attack quarters coverage in an effort to produce deep throw yardage. The fish concept puts a (low) short hook-up route in front of the patternside safety (the bait) in an effort to throw (high) to the deep, over-the-top post route (the fishing pole). The read is a high-low read with the hope of influencing the patternside safety to suck up on the (low) short hook-up route, as shown in Diagram 6-22.

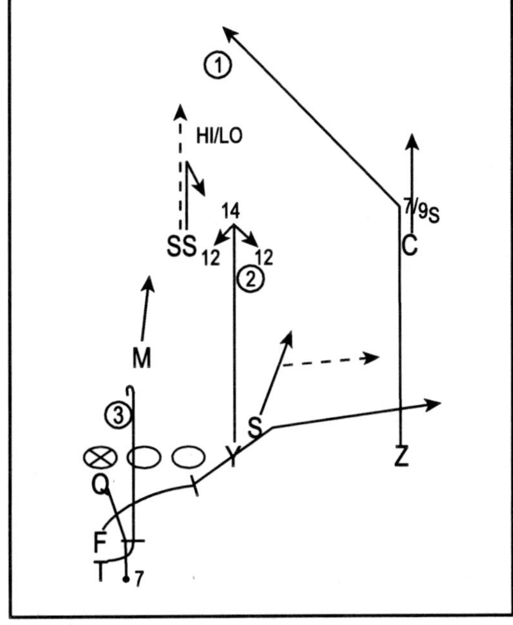

Diagram 6-22. High-low-read fish concept versus quarters coverage

Backside Post/Clear-Out-Route Combination Isolation

A two-on-one route isolation on the backside safety from a trips to the flanker (Z) formation can help to produce deep, big-yardage capabilities versus quarters coverage. Very often, quarters coverage will man-cover the third receiver to the opposite trips side if that receiver runs a vertical route. As a result, a backside post route by the widest backside wide receiver can help to produce an excellent, deep two-on-one isolation on the backside quarters-coverage weak safety, as shown in Diagram 6-23.

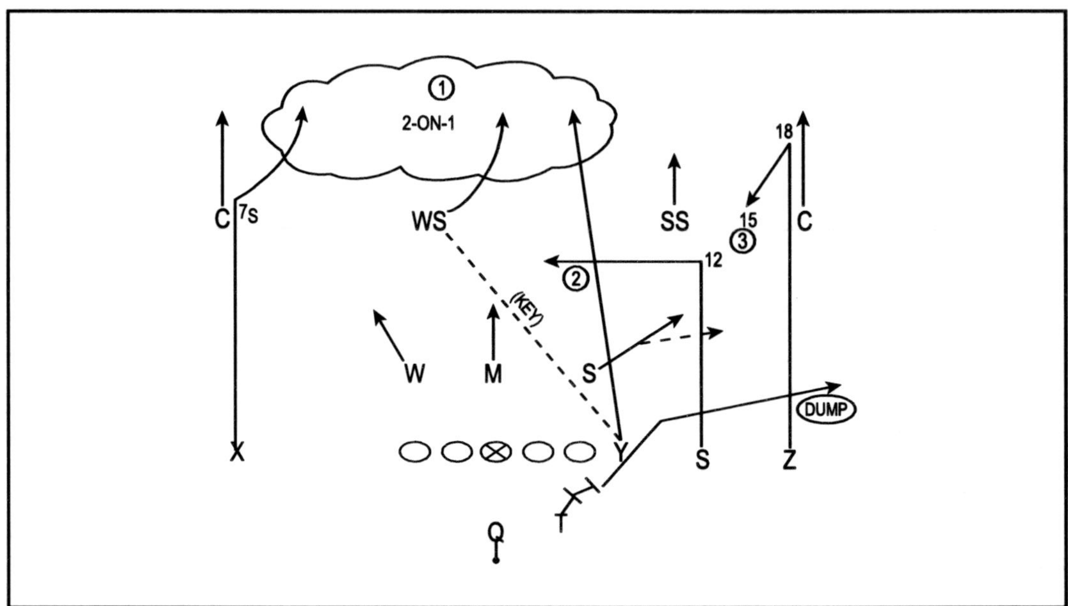

Diagram 6-23. Backside post/clear-out two-on-one isolation versus quarters coverage

Smash High-Low Isolation

The smash high-low isolation concept is a decent concept to utilize versus quarters coverage. The problem with the concept is that the deep quarters coverage of the cornerbacks can force the smash high-low read to consistently turn into hitch-route throws. The smash concept versus quarters coverage is shown in Diagram 6-24.

Seal Concept

The seal concept is an excellent deep-throw potential isolation on the field/formationside safety versus quarters coverage. As shown in Diagram 6-25, the backside quarters-coverage safety is held by the post-corner route of the backside split-end (X) receiver. To the prime patternside, the slot and flanker receivers place a two-on-one isolation of the field/formation side safety. The slot (S) runs a quick, inside vertical route as the flanker (Z) runs an over-the-top post. The quarterback throws off of the coverage reaction of the field/formation side safety to either the slot or the flanker.

Three-Tiered Dig/Square-In High-Low Isolation

The three-tiered dig/square-in high-low isolation concept presents an excellent high-to-low read action for the quarterback versus quarters coverage. As shown in Diagram 6-26, the slot (S) receiver runs a clear-out route through the patternside safety. The flanker (Z) runs a square-in inside of the clear-out route to produce a high-low read for the quarterback on the playside, inside linebacker.

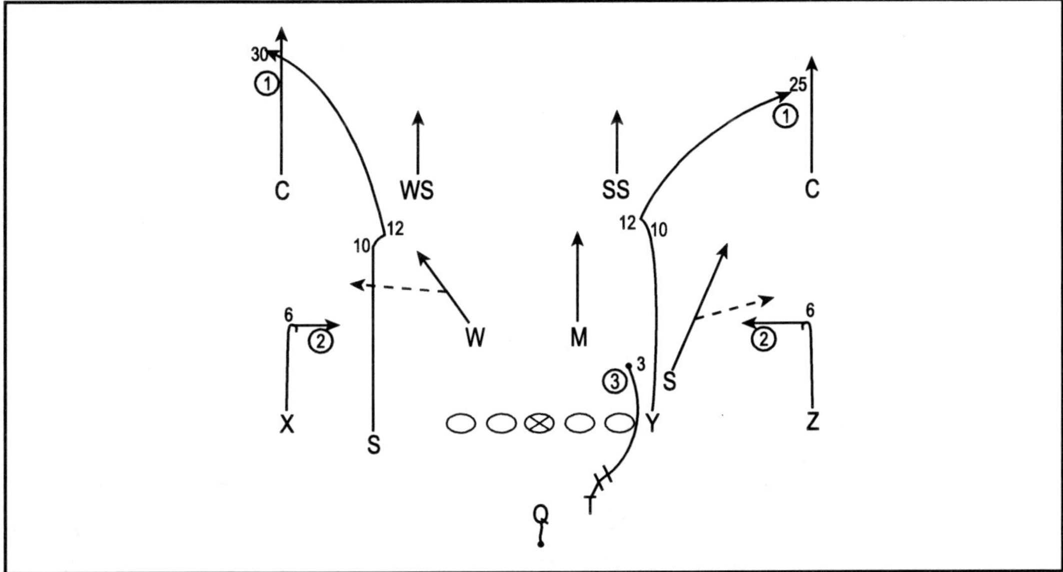

Diagram 6-24. Smash concept versus quarters coverage

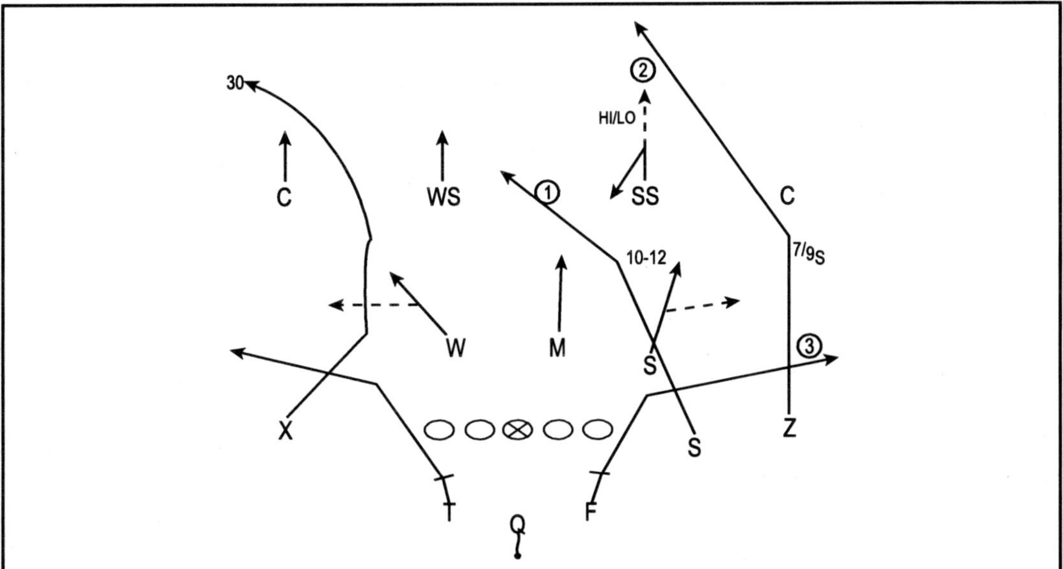

Diagram 6-25. Seal two-on-one isolation concept versus quarters coverage

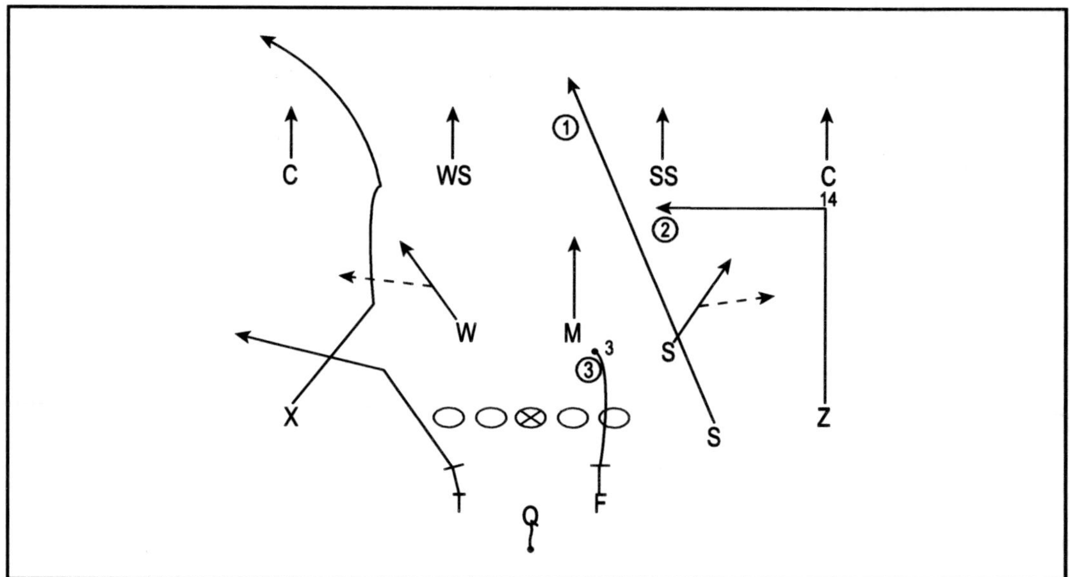

Diagram 6-26. Three-tiered dig/square-in concept versus quarters coverage

Four-Streaks Concept with Comeback-Outs or Deep Rollaways

The four streaks concept can be an effective way of attacking quarters coverage. However, the outside receivers may be better off running deep rollaway routes or comeback-out routes as outlets rather than streak routes if the cornerbacks are aligned deeply, as shown in Diagram 6-27. The deep rollaways or comeback-out routes do, however, still come off of the deep-streak threat.

The key to the four-streaks concept is the read of the slot receiver (S) on his read route versus the safety to his side. If the slot finds that the safety is playing him with a shallow alignment, the read-route receiver (the slot) should keep on going and blow past the safety. If the safety stays deep and head up to outside of the slot, the slot should adjust to a broken-arrow (skinny-post) route. If the safety aligns deep and to the inside, the slot breaks his route to the inside with a square-in route adjustment. If the slot is covered, the quarterback can dump the ball off to the back or go to the outside to the outlet deep rollaways or comeback-outs.

Under Concept

The under concept is a decent concept versus quarters coverage. Often, the lack of flat coverage has the under route turn into a hitch route as the under route stays out wide in the coverage void rather than unnecessarily working to the inside to produce a high-low read on the outside linebacker. The under-route receiver will work inside, however, if the outside linebacker drives out hard to the flat. The under concept versus quarters coverage is shown in Diagram 6-28 from a no-backs set—both weak and strong.

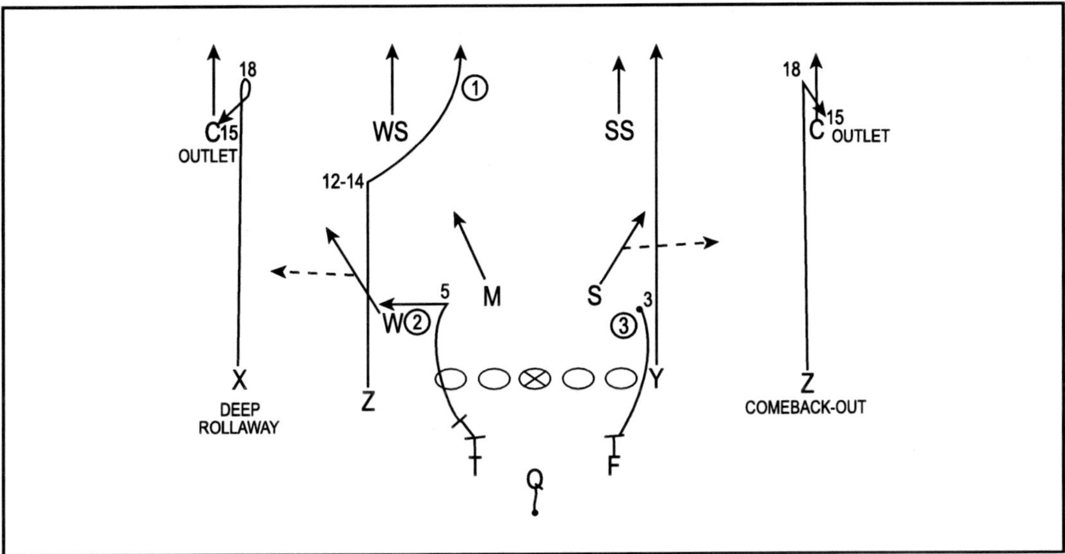

Diagram 6-27. Four-streaks concept with outside comeback-outs or deep rollaways versus quarters coverage

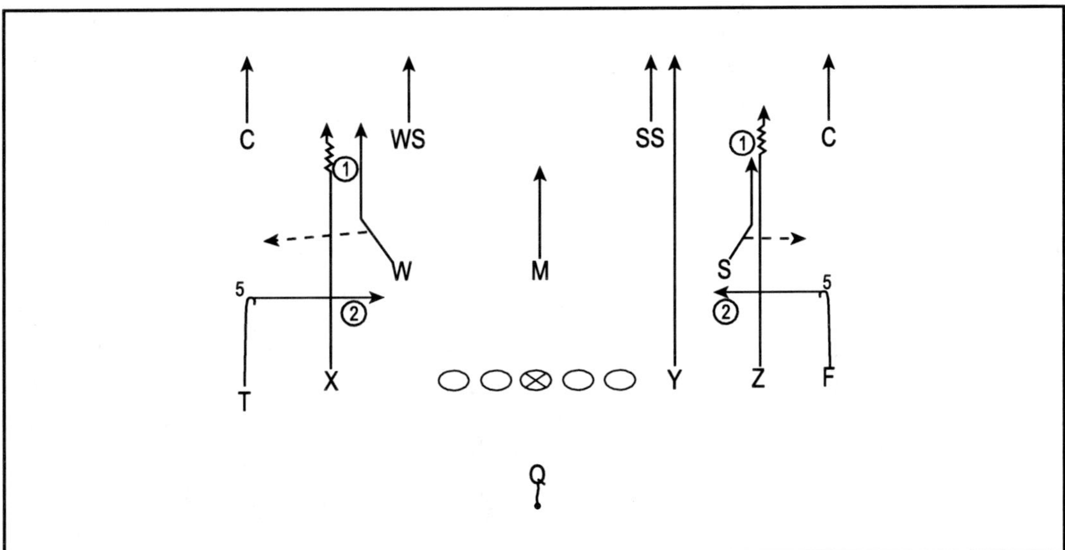

Diagram 6-28. Under concept versus quarters coverage

Drive Concept

The drive concept helps to create a three-on-two flood isolation on the two inside quarters-coverage linebackers. The drive-route wide receiver, the tight end, and the back form a triangle position to help create the three-on-two advantage. The drive concept versus quarters is shown in Diagram 6-29.

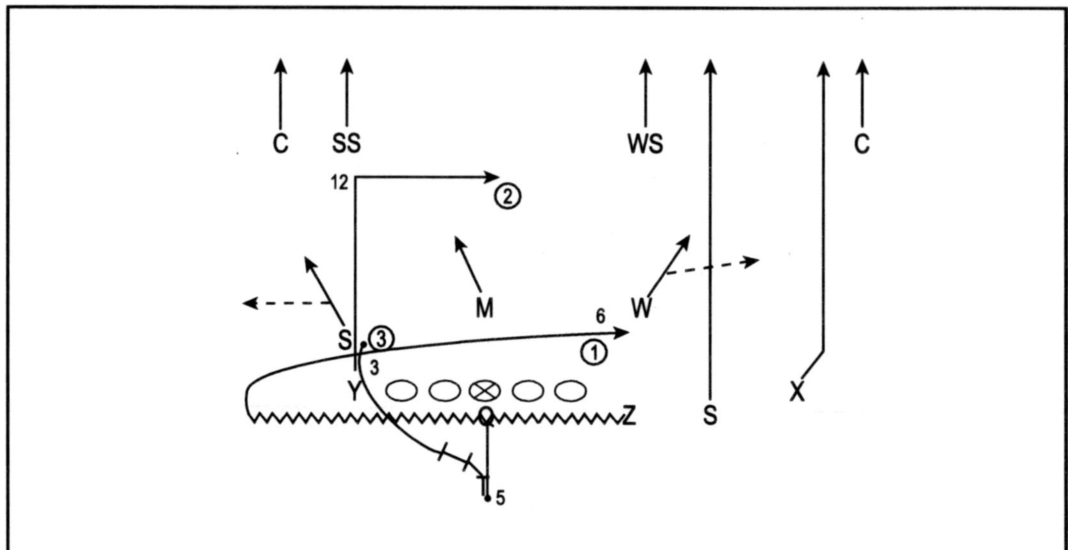

Diagram 6-29. Drive concept versus quarters coverage

Cross Concept

The cross concept also helps to create a three-on-two flood isolation on the two inside quarters-coverage linebackers. The slot receiver, tight end, and back form a triangle position to help create the three-on-two advantage. The cross concept, from a balanced, doubles set with a tight-end cross, slot-short-dig action is shown in Diagram 6-30.

Texas Concept

The Texas concept helps to create a two-on-one crossing isolation on the quarters-coverage inside linebacker. The underneath cross route stretches the quarters-coverage outside linebacker with an initial flat-route stem and threat. He then breaks underneath and crosses the square-out action of the tight end. If the inside linebacker runs out with the tight end's square-out route, the underneath cross route should be wide open. If the tight end is able to wall the inside linebacker off, the quarterback can stick a tight throw in to the tight end before the tight end works out wide into the quarters-coverage outside linebacker. The Texas concept versus quarters coverage is shown in Diagram 6-31.

Option-Isolation Concept

Option isolation routes help to produce excellent one-on-one isolations on quarters coverage linebackers. Option routes can help to produce one-on-one size, talent, and speed mismatches. As previously mentioned, option routes are best run off of five-step drop-timing by the quarterback. Five-step drop-timing by the quarterback allows for option routes run in the 8- to 12-yard range, giving the option-route receivers time to properly maneuver and execute their option routes for man- or zone-separation techniques. Diagram 6-32 shows a tight-end (Y) option and a halfback (H) option versus quarters coverage.

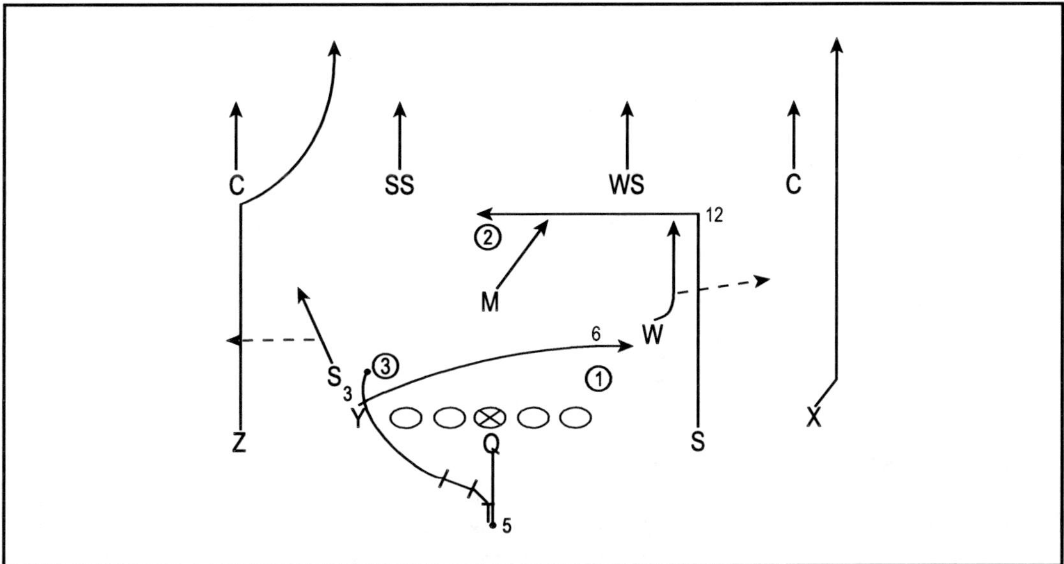

Diagram 6-30. Y-cross concept versus quarters coverage

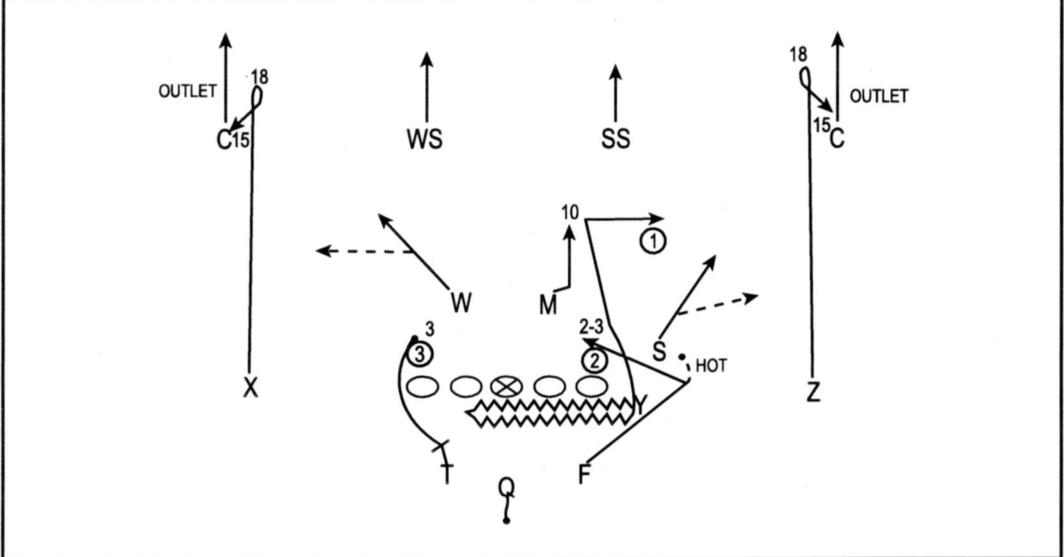

Diagram 6-31. Texas concept versus quarters coverage

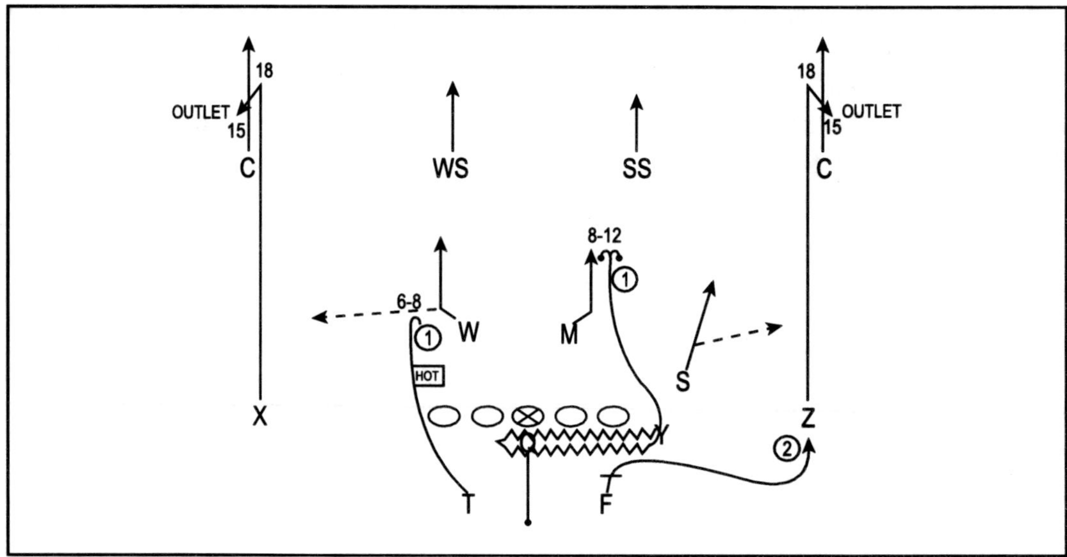

Diagram 6-32. Option-isolation routes versus quarters coverage

High-Low Delay-Route Isolations

High-low delay-route isolations can be very effective against quarters coverage. With vertical broken-arrow routes splitting the quarters-coverage safeties and a delay route working underneath, the quarterback simply throws off of the two-on-one coverage reaction of the isolated strong, inside linebacker. A high-low-read tight-end (Y) delay versus quarters coverage is shown in Diagram 6-33.

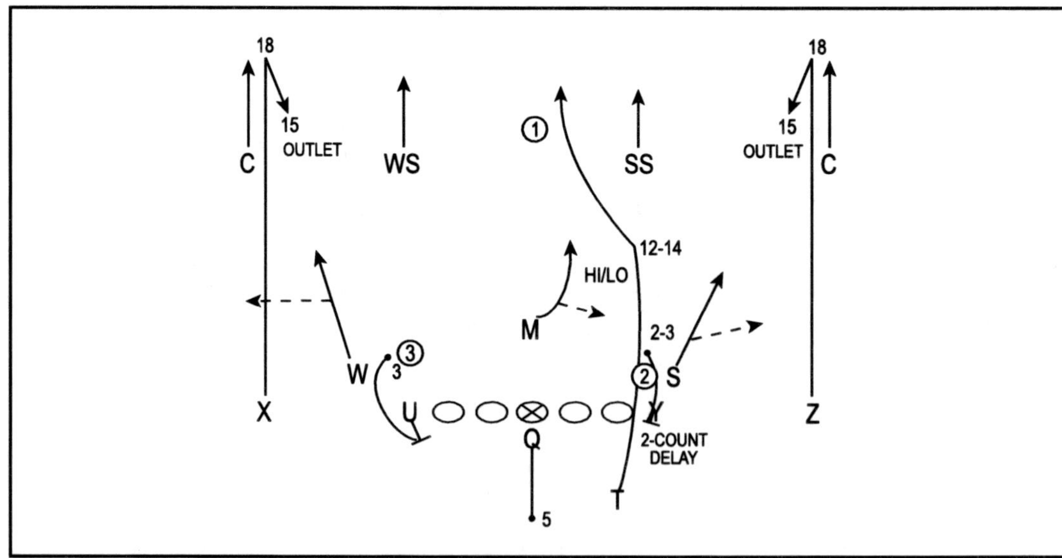

Diagram 6-33. High-low-read Y-delay-route isolation versus quarters coverage

High-Low Pivot- and Break-Route Isolations

Just like delay-route high-low isolations, tight-end (Y) pivot- and break-route isolations can be very effective versus quarters coverage. With a vertical broken-arrow route by a back splitting the deep quarters-coverage safeties and a tight-end (Y) pivot or break route, the quarterback simply throws off of the two-on-one coverage reaction of the isolated strong, inside linebacker. The pivot and break routes are run in the six- to seven-yard range. Diagram 6-34 shows a Y-pivot high-low-read isolation action to attack quarters coverage. Diagram 6-35 shows Y-break action versus quarters coverage.

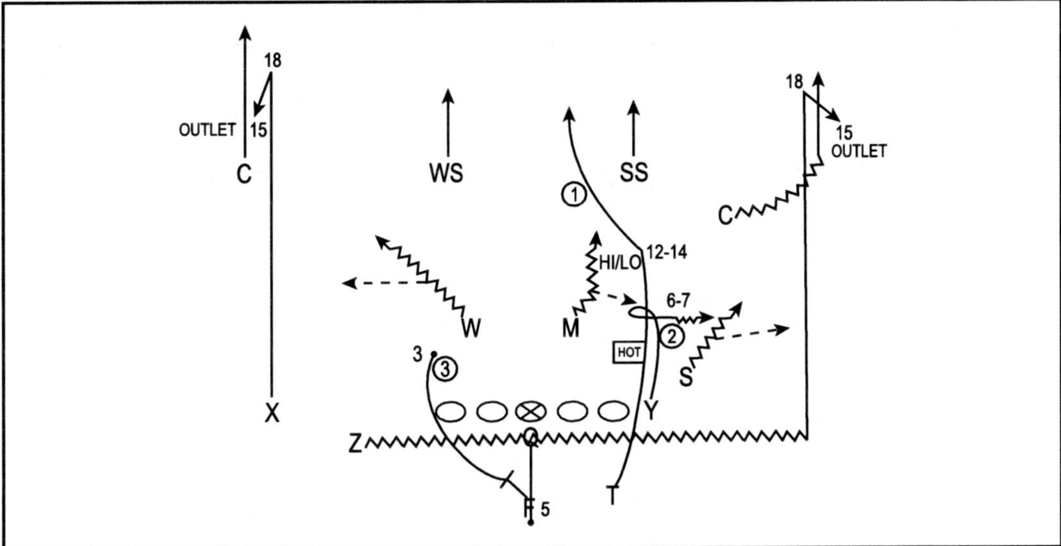

Diagram 6-34. High-low-read Y-pivot isolation versus quarters coverage

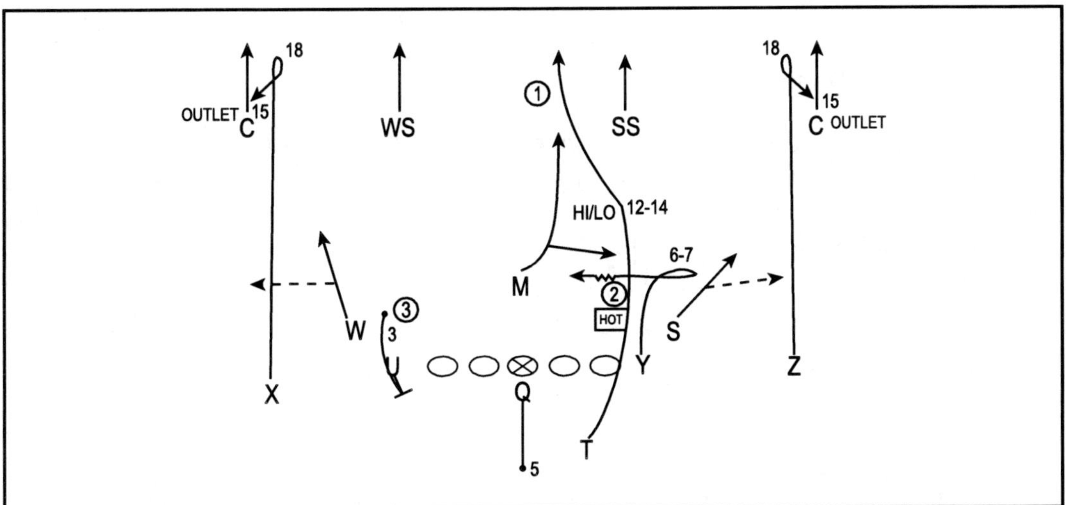

Diagram 6-35. High-low-read Y-break isolation versus quarters coverage

Deep Curl/Hook Outlets

Deep curl/hook outlet routes can be very effective concepts in attacking quarters coverage. Deep, longer-developing curl/hook routes that push the deep quarters-coverage cornerbacks vertically can find quarters-coverage-void pockets to work such deep curl/hook routes into to act as effective late outlets. Such action is especially true if a receiver is used to the inside of the deep curl/hook outlet route to clear out the adjacent quarters-coverage safety. Diagram 6-36 shows such deep curl/hook action used as a late-developing pass-pattern outlet versus quarters coverage. An inside Y-option route-pattern concept is used as the prime-route example.

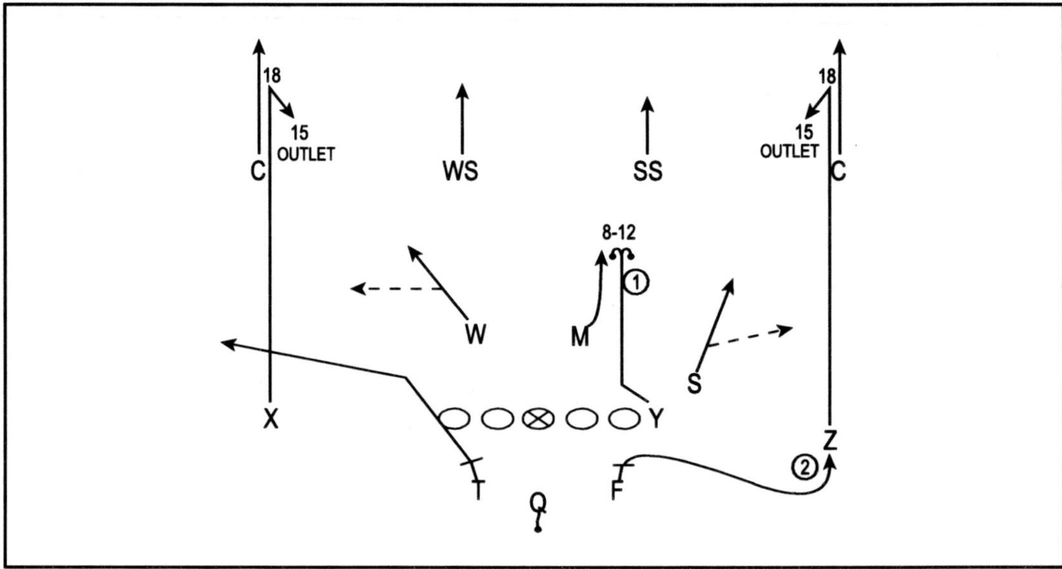

Diagram 6-36. Deep curl/hook outlet action versus quarters coverage

Naked-Bootleg Concept

The naked-bootleg concept can be an effective way to attack quarters coverage. (Naked-bootleg action refers to the fact that no fakeside lineman is pulling to the backside to block protect the bootlegging quarterback.) The naked-bootleg patterns that are most effective versus quarters coverage are the ones that attack the aggressive run-support action of the quarters-coverage safeties. Naked-bootleg action is shown in Diagram 6-37 in its effort to attack quarters coverage with a comeback-out concept to isolate on the play of the weakside cornerback.

Wide-Receiver Screens

Wide-receiver screens are very effective versus quarters coverage, which can be especially true from spread formations if the front tries to keep six front defenders in the box. As a result, the offense can gain a three-on-two advantage to, say, a trips-type set with a wide-receiver screen concept. Such wide-receiver screen action is shown in Diagram 6-38 versus quarters coverage.

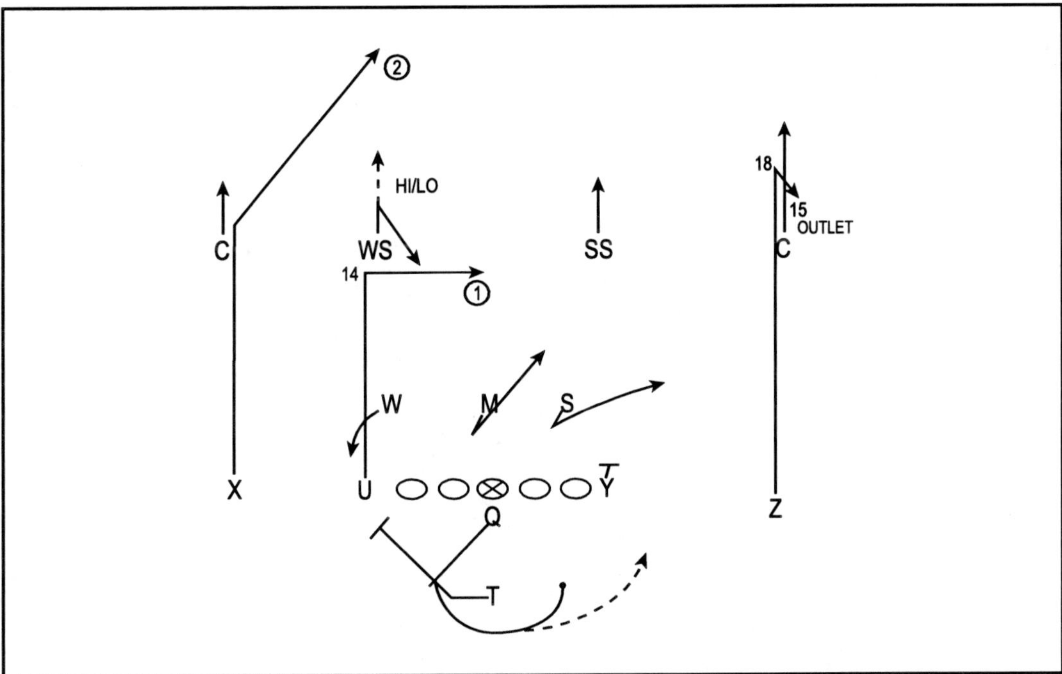

Diagram 6-37. Naked-bootleg action versus quarters coverage

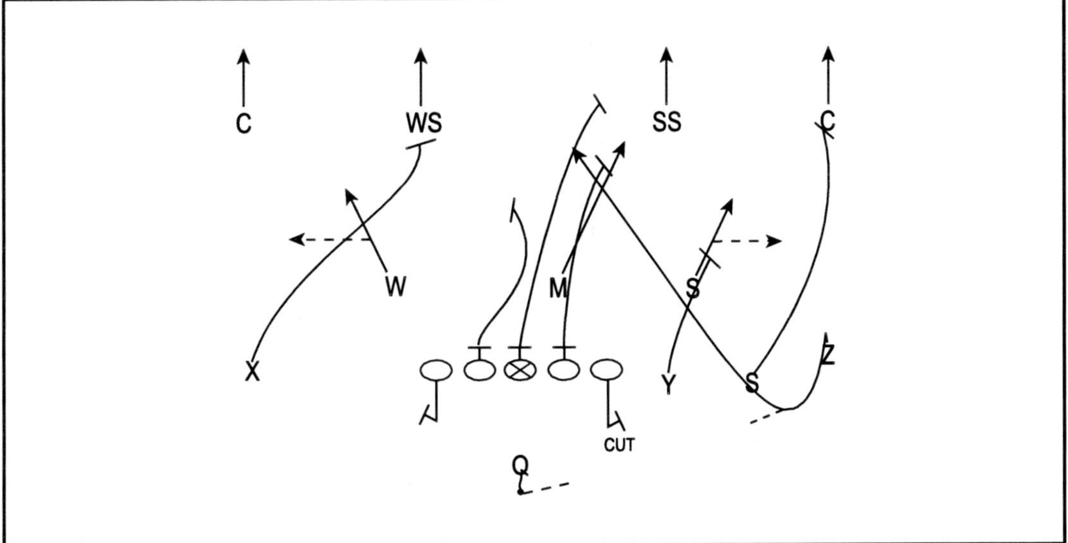

Diagram 6-38. Wide-receiver screen versus quarters coverage

Back Screens

Back screens can be very effective versus quarters coverage—especially if the linebackers are spot droppers. Back-screen action can allow the linebacker spot droppers to get depth to allow for the back-screen blockers to work up to the linebackers to block for the back's screen action, as seen in Diagram 6-39.

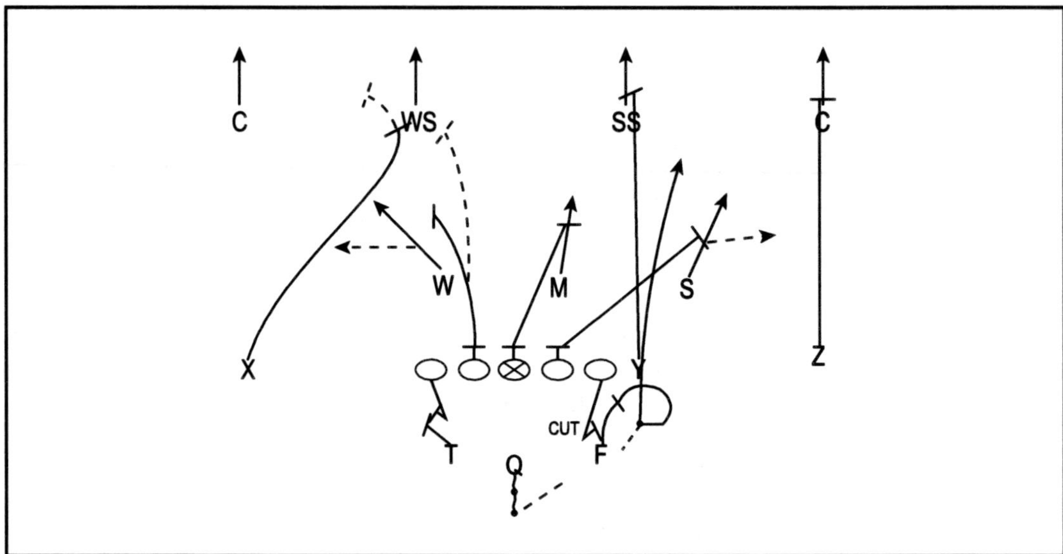

Diagram 6-39. Back screen versus quarters coverage

7

Pass Attack of Quarter-Quarter-Half Coverage

Quarter-quarter-half coverage is another commonly used coverage in the two-safeties family. Two deep safeties are in the middle of the field. Quarter-quarter-half coverage is, basically, a combination of cover 2 and quarters coverage. Quarter-quarter-half coverage plays cover 2 into the boundary away from formation strength and quarters coverage to the field and formation strength. The cover-2 safety, however, knowing that he has greater safety help from the field-quarters safety, will often cheat off the hash towards the boundary sideline four yards or more. As a result, with the hard-squat action of the cover-2 weakside cornerback, quarter-quarter-half coverage often acts more like a one-safety family, cover-3 weak-roll coverage than a true two-safeties family coverage. Diagram 7-1 shows quarter-quarter-half (combination cover 2/quarters coverage with four-under zone coverage).

Quarter-Quarter-Half Coverage Pass-Game Strengths

- The strength of quarter-quarter-half coverage is the three-deep weak-roll aspect of the coverage. The coverage plays cover 2 weak with the safety cheated off the hash to provide greater deep outside coverage abilities. As a result, normal deep outside post-corner/smash route high-low-read combinations are eliminated.

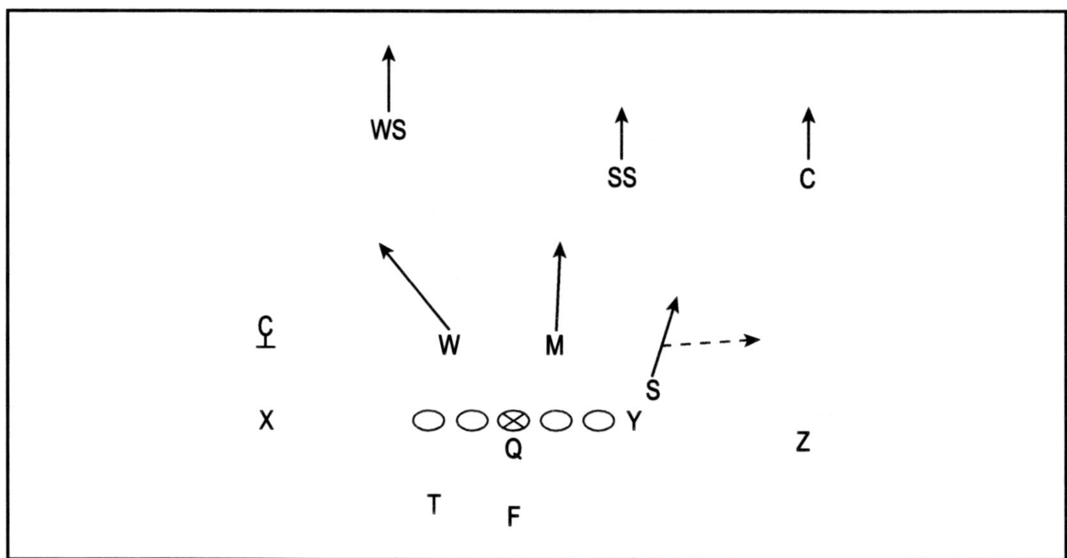

Diagram 7-1. Quarter-quarter-half coverage (combination cover 2/quarters coverage with four-under zone coverage)

- The squatted, weakside cover-2-type cornerback can do a great job of disrupting pass-route releases—especially routes that attack upfield vertically.
- The weakside, cover-2 aspect of the quarter-quarter-half coverage takes away easy, quick, or short pass-game routes and patterns.
- The weakside, cover-2 aspect of the quarter-quarter-half coverage eliminates side-by-side, lateral-read-route combinations, which are a big part of many offensive designs. Diagram 7-2 shows how a side-by-side lateral-read rollaway/Y-square-out-route combination is covered by the underneath-zone-coverage aspect of the cover 2 part of the quarter-quarter-half coverage.
- The weakside cover-2 aspect of quarter-quarter-half coverage does a good job of eliminating out-route concepts due to the squatted cornerback-coverage play. Diagram 7-3 shows the elimination of a speed-out route due to squatted cover-2 coverage of the cornerback.
- The weakside cover-2 cornerback can help to do a great job of containing and pushing pass-pattern routes to the inside toward the weakside cover-2 hash-mark safety.
- The cornerback and safety to the strongside quarters coverage side can work in combination with one another (brackets/combo/inside-out technique), reading and reacting to the first (widest) receiver and second (next receiver to the inside) to their side. Such brackets/combo/inside-out combination-coverage techniques for the strongside of quarter-quarter-half coverage is shown in Diagram 7-4.

- The low positioning of the strong/fieldside quarter-quarter-half strong safety allows for excellent extra edge (off-tackle) run support from the secondary. Such an extra run support defender helps, in design, to produce an eight-man front to the strong/fieldside when given a run read.
- Depending on the deep threat that the strongside quarters coverage cornerback of the quarter-quarter-half coverage is facing, the fieldside cornerback can give a low enough alignment look to help confuse a quarterback into thinking he's facing cover 2.

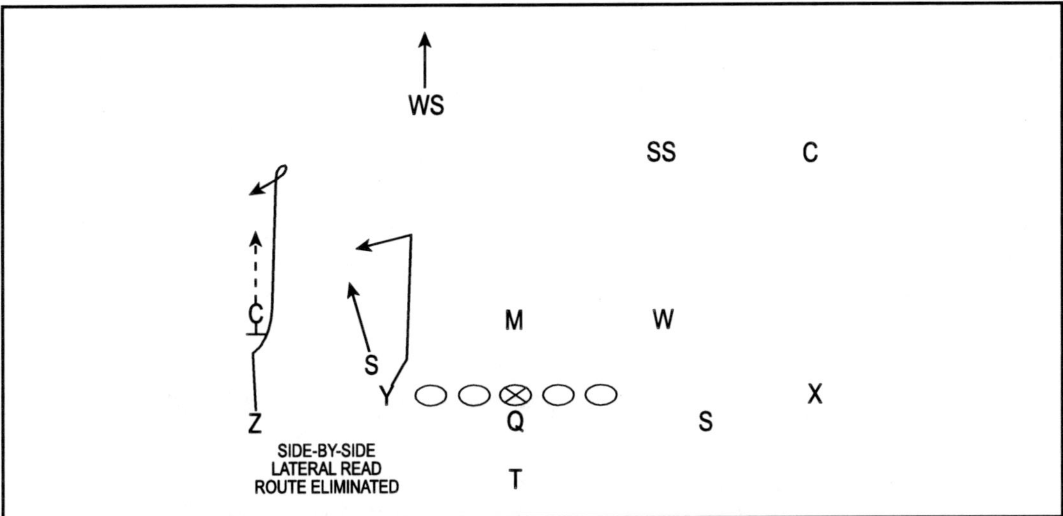

Diagram 7-2. Side-by-side lateral-read-route combination taken away by quarter-quarter-half coverage to weakside

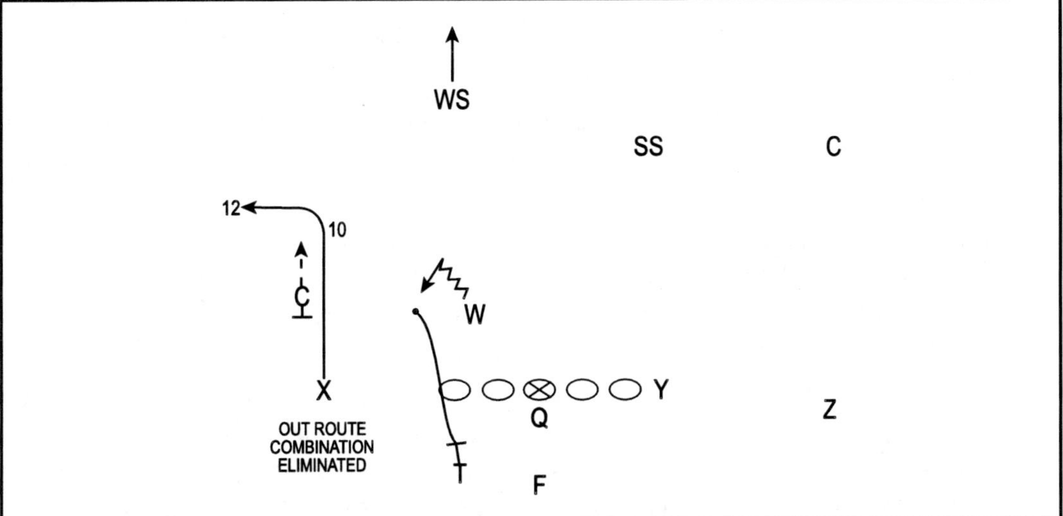

Diagram 7-3. Cover-2 aspect of quarter-quarter-half-coverage elimination of out routes

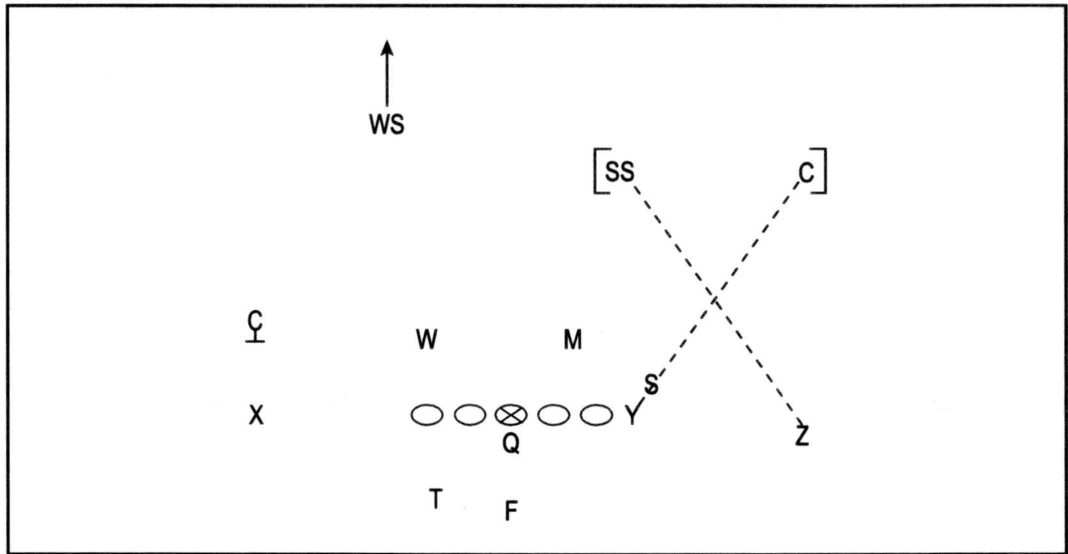

Diagram 7-4. Strongside brackets/combo/inside-out combination quarter-quarter-half-coverage techniques

Quarter-Quarter-Half Pass-Game Weaknesses

- The pass-game weaknesses of quarter-quarter-half coverage definitely focus on the strong/fieldside-quarters aspect of the coverage. The weakside, almost weak-roll aspect of the coverage makes the halves aspect of the coverage very difficult to attack.
- The strongside, field-quarters-coverage aspect of quarter-quarter-half coverage gives up easy underneath throws—especially to the outside flat-zone areas. This quarters-coverage void is shown in Diagram 7-5.
- As a result of the outside-flat quarters-coverage void in quarter-quarter-half coverage, the coverage is extremely susceptible to hitch and any level of out-type routes.
- If the strongside quarters-coverage aspect of the quarter-quarter-half coverage tries to make up for its flat-zone hitch and out-route vulnerability by having its cornerback work upfield fast and hard, the coverage becomes extremely vulnerable to deep double-move routes off of the hitch and out routes.
- The hard supporting strong/fieldside quarters-coverage safety versus the run game makes the quarter-quarter-half coverage vulnerable to strong/fieldside play-action passing. Diagram 7-6 shows a play-action fake sucking up the strong/fieldside quarter-quarter-half safety enabling an over-the-top post throw over the head of the influenced safety.

- The strong/fieldside quarters-coverage aspect of quarter-quarter-half coverage is susceptible to high-low-read concepts—especially to the inside on the safety. Diagram 7-7 shows a high-low-read isolation to the inside on the quarters coverage safety.

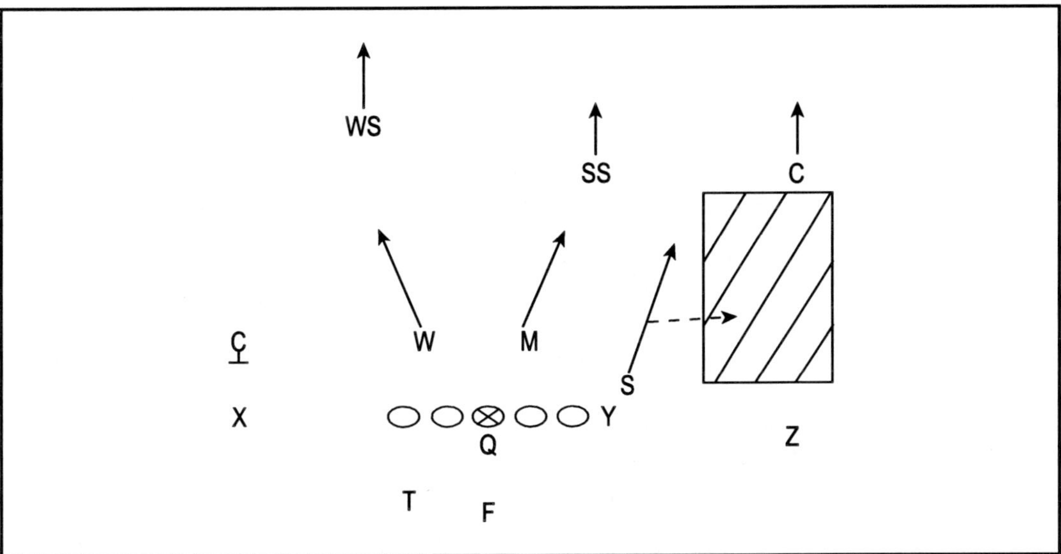

Diagram 7-5. Strongside flat quarters coverage void in quarter-quarter-half coverage

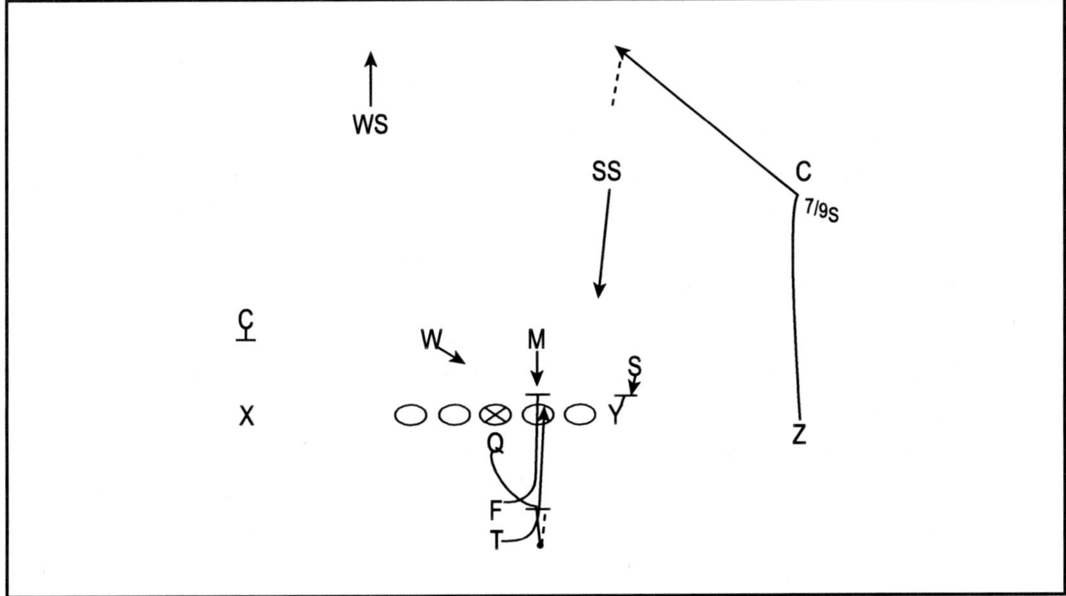

Diagram 7-6. Play-action to throw over the top of the influenced quarters-coverage-aspect safety of the quarter-quarter-half coverage

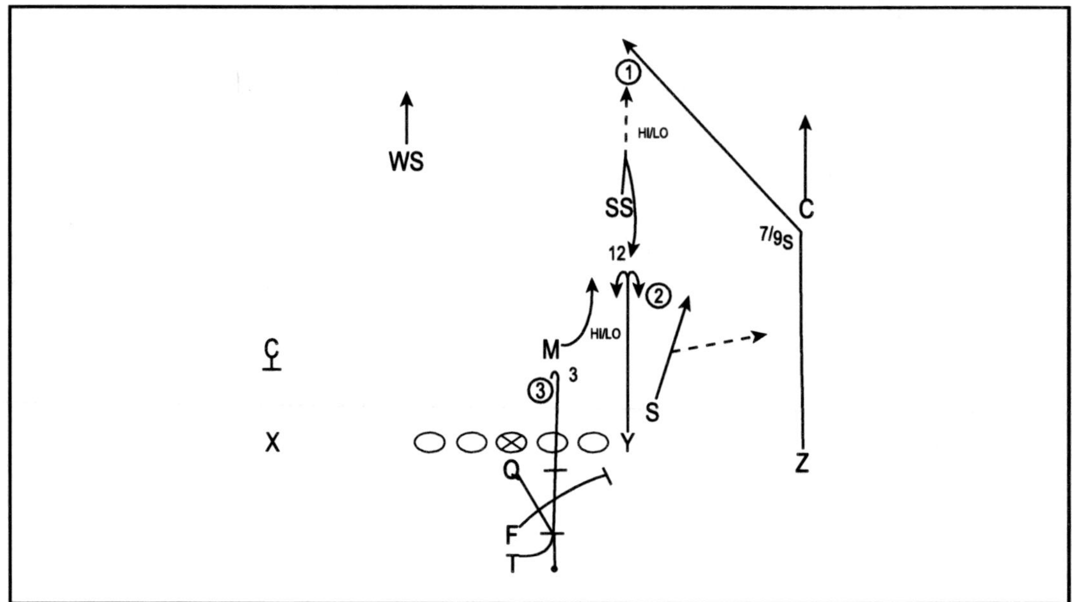

Diagram 7-7. High-low-read isolation on quarters-coverage-aspect safety of the quarter-quarter-half coverage

- Quarter-quarter-half coverage has only two underneath-zone (linebacker) defenders to the strong/fieldside quarters-coverage side. This alignment puts tremendous strain on the field/strongside outside linebacker who must cover curl zone to flat zone, depending on how he is being threatened.
- With the pressing coverage responsibilities of the strong/fieldside linebacker (curl/flat), the strong/fieldside inside linebacker is susceptible to high-low isolations, option isolations, and/or flood concepts.
- Dig and square-in concepts with a deep clear-out-route action through the safeties can be very effective versus quarter-quarter-half coverage. Three-tiered patterns with such a deep clear-out route helps to produce an effective high-low read on a quarter-quarter-half inside linebacker.
- Drive- and cross-route concepts are very effective in creating three-on-two flood isolations on the two inside quarter-quarter-half-coverage linebackers.
- Naked-bootleg action can be very effective versus quarter-quarter-half coverage—both weak and strong. The play-action does much to hold and influence the three underneath-zone linebackers—and play-action can help to influence the strong/fieldside quarters-coverage safety to suck up for possible deep throws over his head.
- Screens can be very effective versus quarter-quarter-half coverage. Much like cover 2, formationing can help to create screen numbers (i.e., three-on-two) mismatches versus quarter-quarter-half coverage.

Route Combination and Pass-Pattern Attack of Quarter-Quarter-Half Coverage

Quick-Game Hitch

The quick-game (three-step drop-timed throw by the quarterback) hitch route is an excellent route concept versus quarter-quarter-half coverage to the strong/fieldside quarters-coverage side. The hitch route helps to exploit the quarters-coverage flat-zone-coverage void. Diagram 7-8 shows hitch action versus the quarters-coverage aspect of quarter-quarter-half coverage.

Quick-Game Speed-Out

The quick-game speed-out route is an excellent route concept versus quarter-quarter-half coverage to the strong/fieldside quarters-coverage side. Just like the hitch route, the speed-out route helps to exploit the quarters-coverage flat-zone-coverage void as shown in Diagram 7-9.

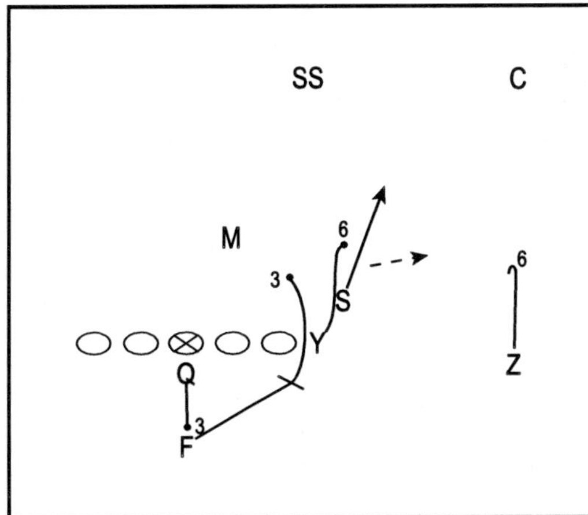

Diagram 7-8. Quick-game hitch versus quarters-coverage aspect of quarter-quarter-half coverage

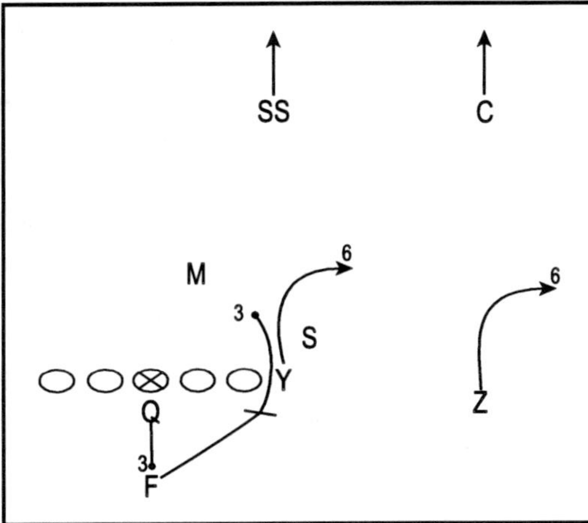

Diagram 7-9. Quick-game speed-out versus quarters-coverage aspect of quarter-quarter-half coverage

Quick-Game Inside-Receiver Speed-Out

The quick-game inside-receiver speed-out route combination creates an excellent clear-out route to push the quarters-coverage cornerback and the squatted, cover-2 cornerback deep while bringing the inside receiver to the outside underneath the clear-out action. Diagram 7-10 shows a quick, slot-inside-receiver speed-out route combination to the field and a quick tight-end inside-receiver speed-out-route combination to the backside versus quarter-quarter-half coverage.

The quick-game inside-receiver speed-out concept is also an excellent concept to execute off of five-step-timed quarterback drop action. The deeper speed-out route, however, becomes more of a square-out route at 10 yards versus the quarters-coverage aspect of the quarter-quarter-half coverage as shown in Diagram 7-11.

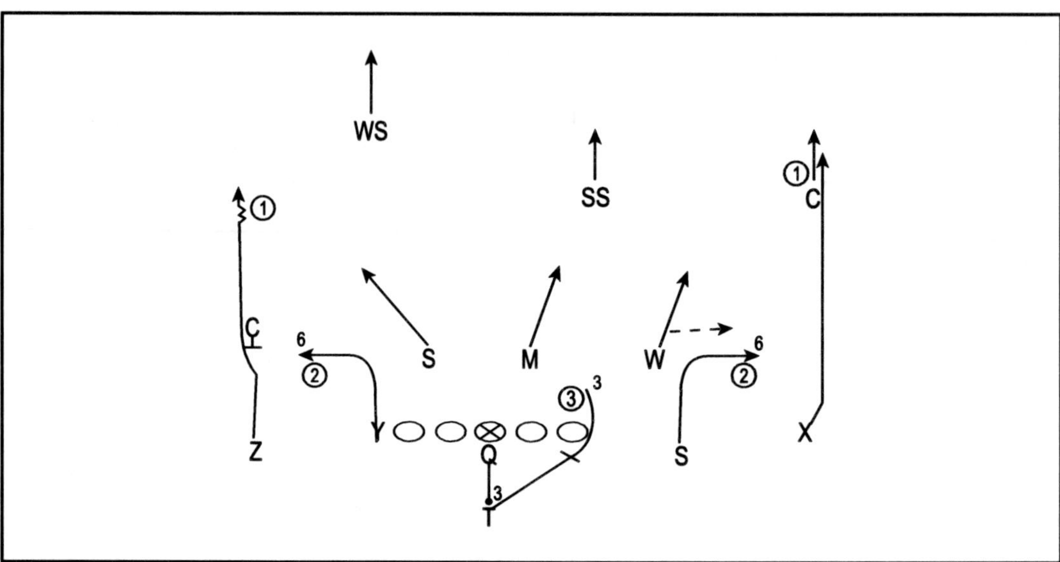

Diagram 7-10. Quick-game inside-receiver speed-out concept versus quarter-quarter-half coverage

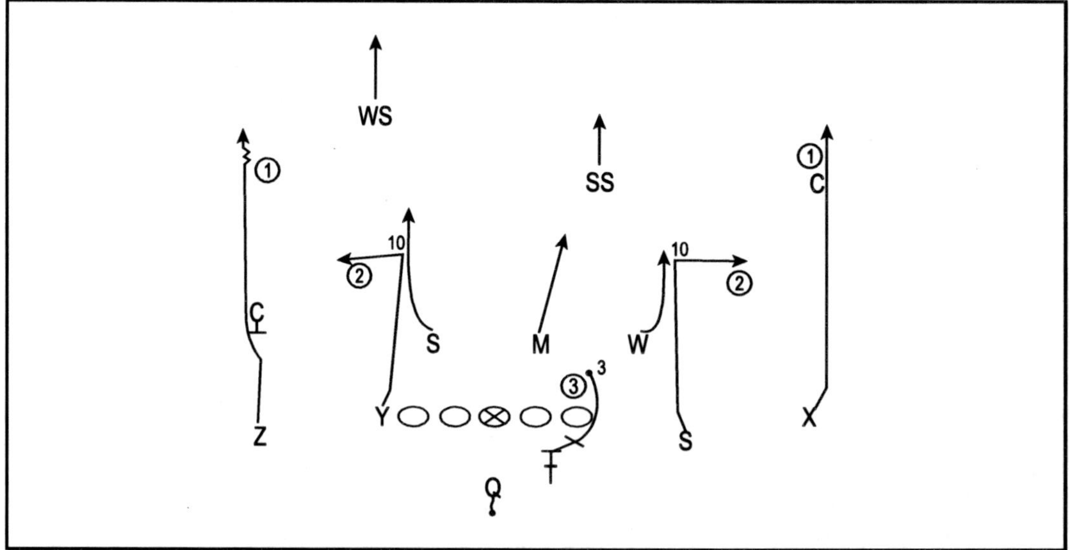

Diagram 7-11. Inside-receiver square-out concept versus quarters-coverage aspect of quarter-quarter-half coverage

Quick-Game Double Slant

The quick-game double-slant-route combination places a two-on-one isolation on the strong/fieldside quarters-outside linebacker of the quarter-quarter-half coverage. If the linebacker (S) in Diagram 7-12 follows the inside slant, a throw lane is opened up to the outside slant. If the linebacker tries to work outside to the outside slant, the inside slant receiver bends his slant upfield to make the reception. The quick-game double-slant-route combination action is shown in Diagram 7-12 to the quarters-coverage side of the quarter-quarter-half coverage.

Quick-Game Inside-Receiver Stick-Route Isolation

The quick-game inside-receiver stick-route isolation can be very effective to the strong/fieldside versus the quarters-coverage aspect of the quarter-quarter-half coverage. The flat route by the back can help to create a one-on-one isolation on the inside linebacker. Diagram 7-13 shows a strong/fieldside stick-route isolation versus quarter-quarter-half coverage.

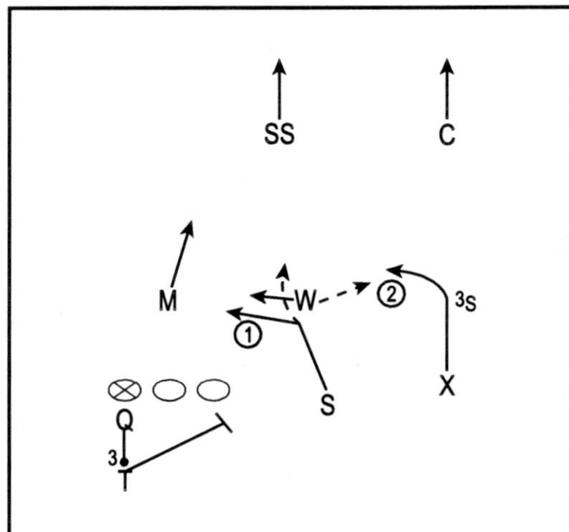

Diagram 7-12. Quick-game double-slant-route combination to the quarters-coverage aspect of quarter-quarter-half coverage

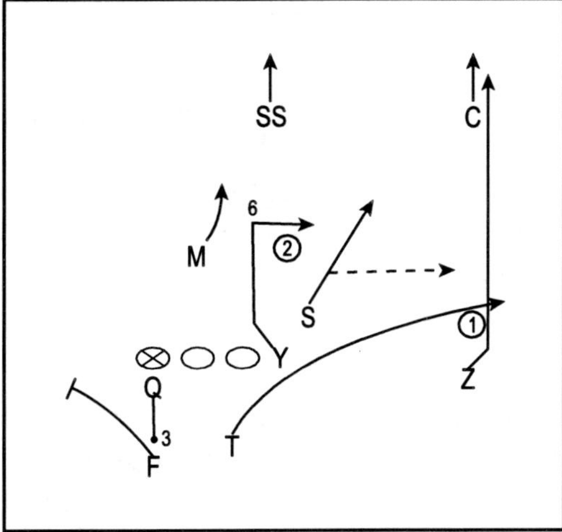

Diagram 7-13. Quick-game stick isolation to the quarters-coverage aspect of quarter-quarter-half coverage

Quick-Game Double-Move-Route Isolations

Double-move action off of quick-game pass routes is an excellent way to attack the strong/fieldside quarters-coverage aspect cornerback of quarter-quarter-half coverage who try to jump the quick-game prime routes. This aspect is shown in Diagram 7-14 via the hitch-and-go and speed-out-and-up routes.

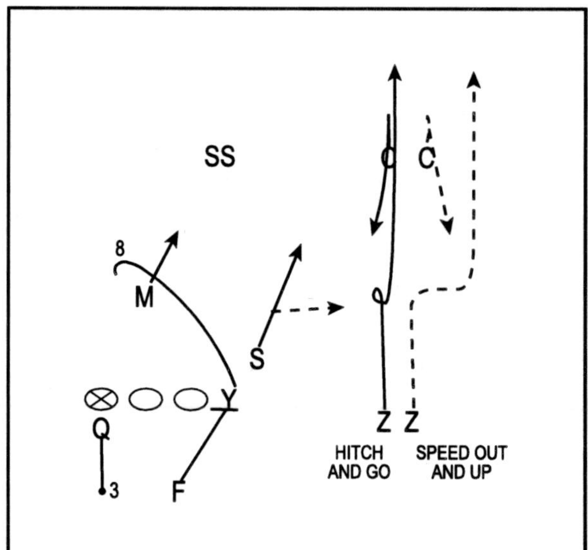

Diagram 7-14. Quick-game double-move routes versus quarters-coverage aspect of quarter-quarter-half coverage

Speed-Out Lateral-Read Combination

The five-step quarterback drop-timed speed-out lateral-read-route combination is an excellent way to attack the strong/fieldside quarters-coverage aspect of quarter-quarter-half coverage. The prime-route speed-out route attacks the one true-coverage void of quarter-quarter-half coverage: the field flat zone. As shown in Diagram 7-15, the tight end's seam route helps to create a true lateral read on the outside linebacker.

Diagram 7-16 shows a similar lateral-read concept with deeper, seven-step quarterback drop-timed comeback-out (could use deep rollaway route) versus the strong/fieldside quarters-coverage aspect of quarter-quarter-half coverage.

Curl (or Hook)/Flat Lateral-Read Concept

The curl/flat (or, deeper hook/flat) lateral-read concept is an excellent way to attack the lack of underneath coverage of the strong/fieldside of the quarters-coverage aspect of quarter-quarter-half coverage. To the strong/fieldside, the lateral-read action isolates on the strongside outside linebacker, as shown by the flanker (Z) curl and hook routes, and the tight-end flat route, as shown in Diagram 7-17. (The only difference between the curl and hook routes is the depths of the routes and the need for seven-step drop-timed action by the quarterback for the deeper hook route.)

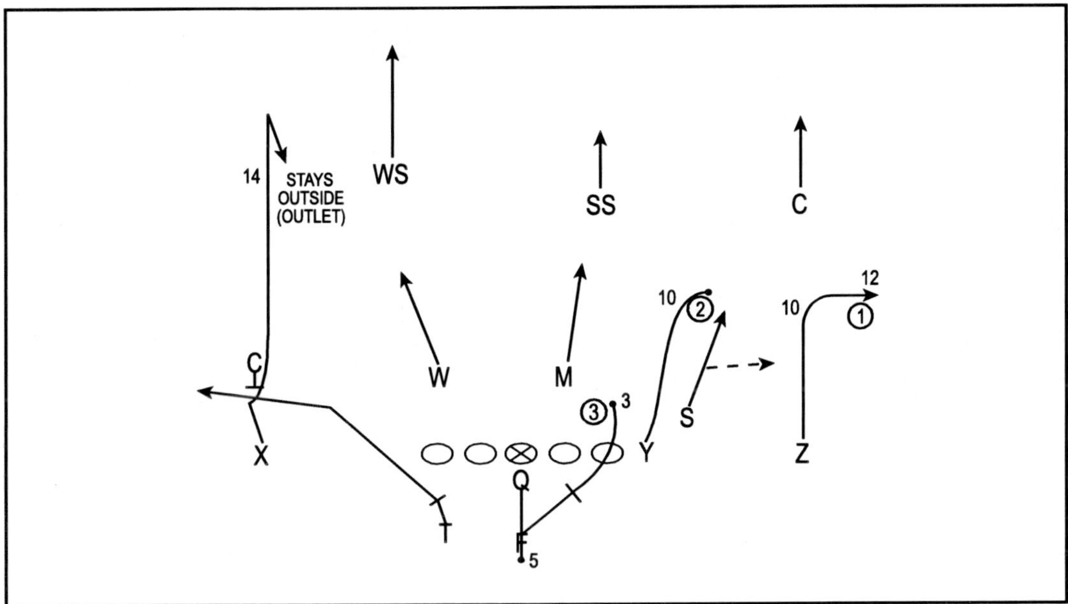

Diagram 7-15. Speed-out lateral-read concept versus quarters-coverage aspect of quarter-quarter-half coverage

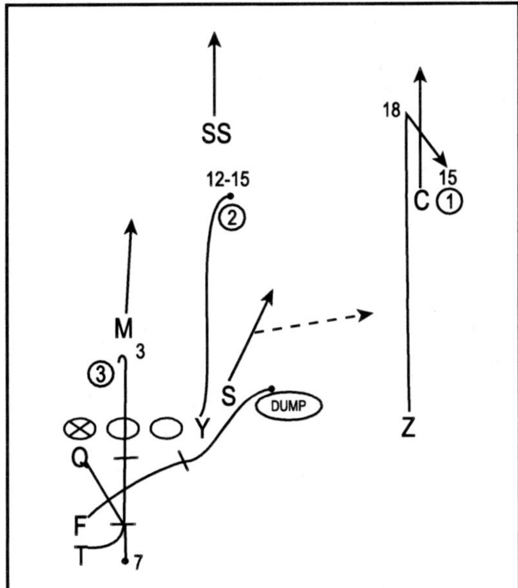

Diagram 7-16. Comeback-out and deep rollaway lateral-read concepts versus quarters-coverage aspect of quarter-quarter-half coverage

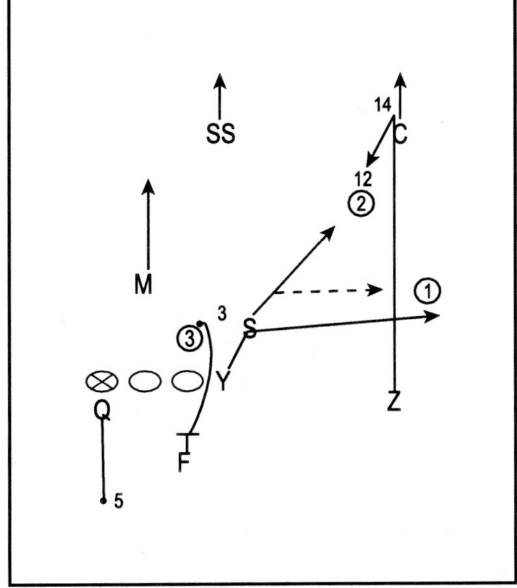

Diagram 7-17. Curl/flat or hook/flat lateral-read concept versus the quarters-coverage aspect of quarter-quarter-half coverage

Speed-Out and Curl Double-Move-Route Concepts

As has been shown, speed-outs and curl-route concepts are excellent ways to attack the strong/fieldside quarters-coverage aspect of quarter-quarter-half coverage. Quite often, the quarters-coverage cornerback will try to jump those routes by the widest receiver. As a result, double-move-route concepts can be very effective to create "home-run" deep-ball threats to combat aggressive cornerback play on these five-step-timed quarterback-drop actions. Diagram 7-18 shows a speed-out-and-up double-move action by the flanker (Z) versus the strong/fieldside quarters-coverage aspect of quarter-quarter-half coverage. Diagram 7-19 shows a curl-and-go double-move action by the flanker (Z) and a flat-and-up double-move action by the tight end (Y).

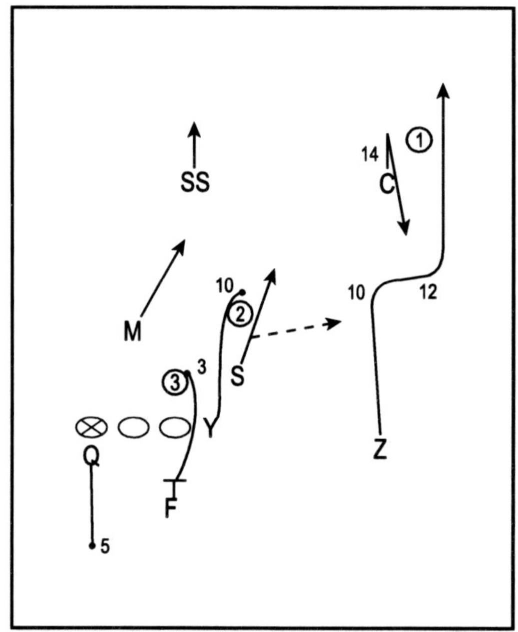

Diagram 7-18. Speed-out-and-up double-move concept versus quarters-coverage aspect of quarter-quarter-half coverage

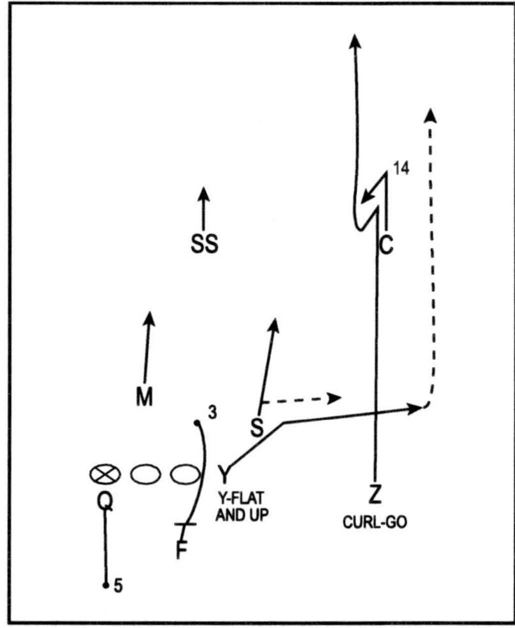

Diagram 7-19. Curl-and-go/flat-and-up double-move concepts versus quarters-coverage aspect of quarter-quarter-half coverage

High-Low Fish-Isolation Concept

The high-low fish-isolation concept is an excellent way to attack the strong/fieldside of the quarters-coverage aspect of quarter-quarter-half coverage in an effort to produce deep-throw yardage. The fish concept puts a low short hook-up route in front of the strong/fieldside safety (the bait) in an effort to throw high to the deep, over-the-top post route (the fishing pole). The read is a high-low read with the hope of influencing the strong/fieldside safety to suck up on the low, short hook-up route, as shown in Diagram 7-20.

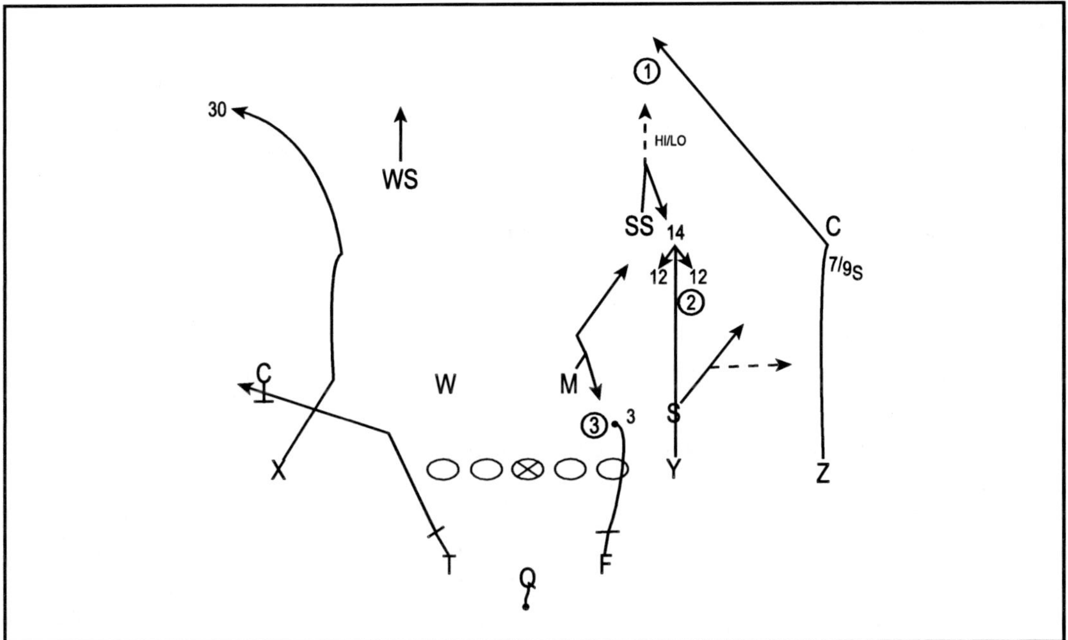

Diagram 7-20. High-low-read fish concept versus quarters-coverage aspect of quarter-quarter-half coverage

Smash High-Low Isolation

The smash high-low isolation concept is a decent concept to utilize versus the strong/fieldside quarters-coverage aspect of quarter-quarter-half coverage. The problem with the concept is that the deep quarters-coverage cornerback can force the smash high-low read to consistently turn into hitch-route throws. The smash concept versus the strong/fieldside quarters-coverage aspect of quarter-quarter-half coverage is shown in Diagram 7-21.

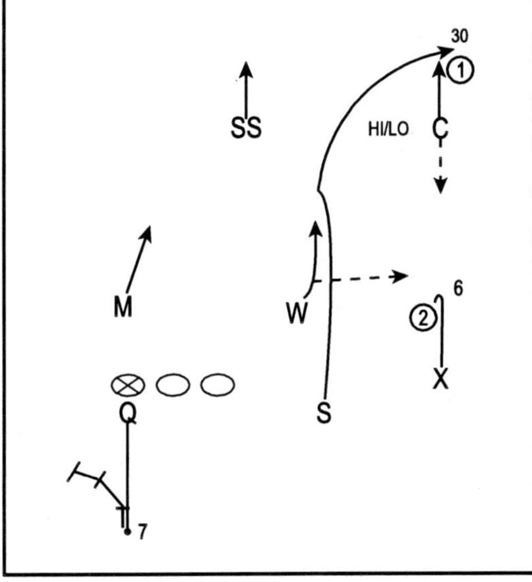

Diagram 7-21. Smash concept versus quarters-coverage aspect of quarter-quarter-half coverage

Seal Concept

The seal concept is an excellent deep-throw-potential isolation on the field/formationside safety of the quarters-coverage aspect of quarter-quarter-half coverage. As shown in Diagram 7-22, the backside cover-2 weak safety is held by the cover-2 post-corner adjustment route of the backside flanker (Z) receiver. To the prime patternside, the slot (S) and split-end (X) receivers place a two-on-one isolation of the field/formationside quarters-coverage strong safety. The slot (S) runs a quick, inside vertical route as the split end (X) runs an over-the-top post. The quarterback throws off of the coverage reaction of the field/formationside quarters-coverage strong safety to either the slot or the split end.

Three-Tiered Dig/Square-In High-Low Isolation

The three-tiered dig/square-in high-low-isolation concept presents an excellent high-low-read action for the quarterback to the strong/fieldside quarters-coverage aspect of quarter-quarter-half coverage. As shown in Diagram 7-23, the slot receiver (S) runs a clear-out route through the strong/fieldside quarters-coverage strong safety. The flanker (Z) runs a square-in inside of the clear-out route to produce a high-low read for the quarterback on the strong/fieldside, inside quarters-coverage linebacker.

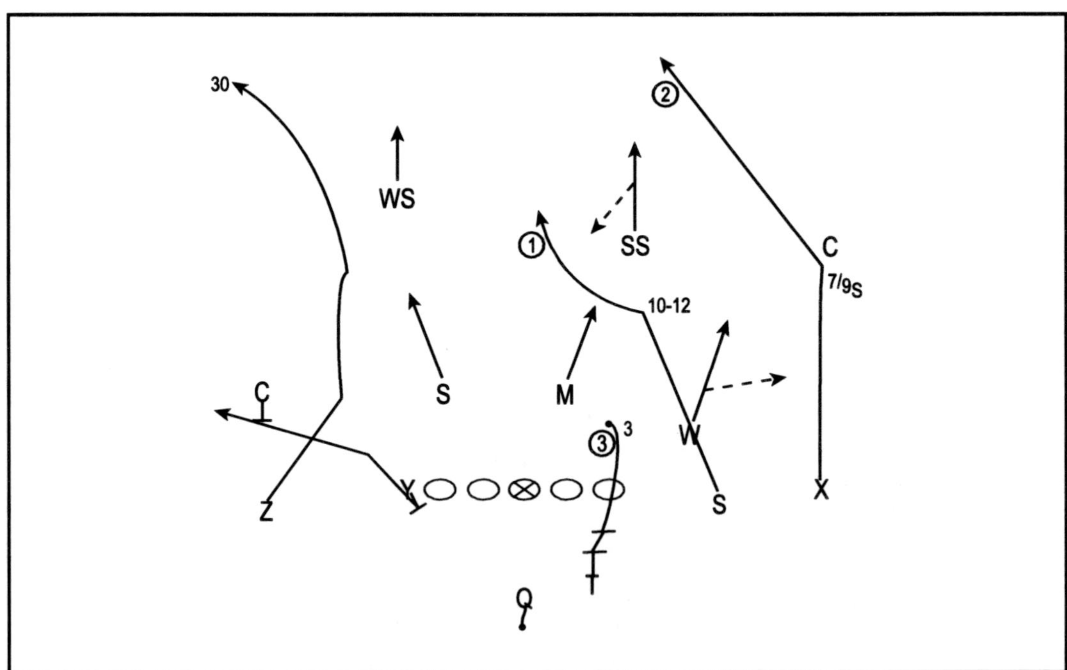

Diagram 7-22. Seal two-on-one isolation concept versus quarters-coverage aspect of quarter-quarter-half coverage

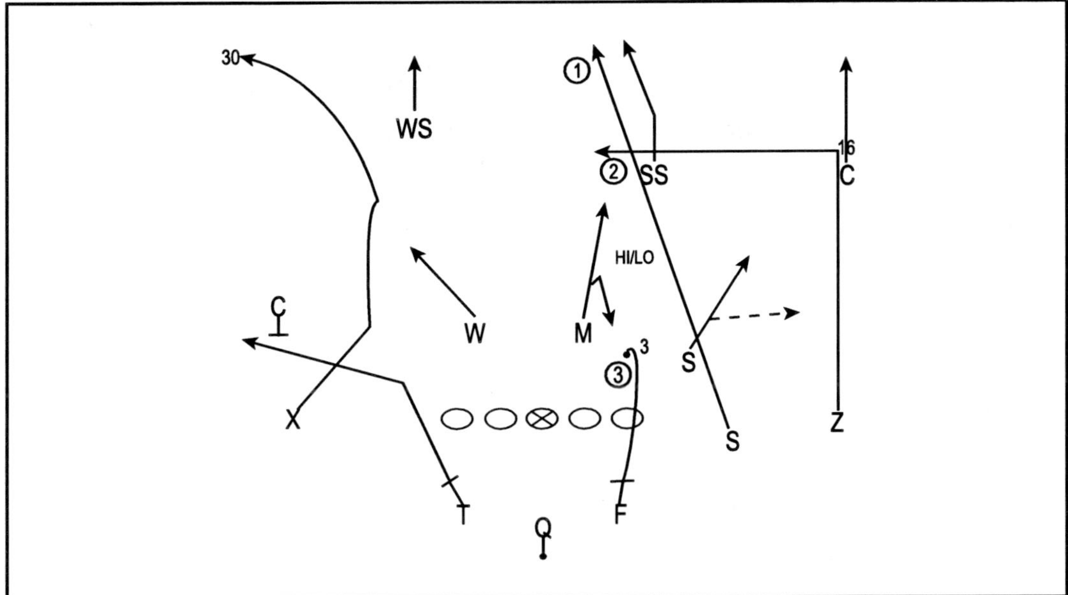

Diagram 7-23. Three-tiered dig/square-in concept versus quarters-coverage aspect of quarter-quarter-half coverage

Under Concept

The under concept is a decent concept versus quarter-quarter-half coverage. Often, the lack of flat coverage to the strong/fieldside quarters coverage of quarter-quarter-half coverage has the under route turn into a hitch route as the under route stays out wide in the coverage void rather than unnecessarily working to the inside to produce a high-low read on the outside linebacker. The under-route receiver will work inside, however, if the outside linebacker drives out hard to the flat. The under concept to the weak, boundary side helps produce a quick, high-low read on the inside linebacker versus the backside cover-2 aspect of the coverage. Both concepts are shown in Diagram 7-24.

Drive Concept

The drive concept helps to create a three-on-two flood isolation on the two inside quarter-quarter-half-coverage linebackers. The drive-route wide receiver, the tight end, and the back form a triangle position to help create the three-on-two advantage. The drive concept versus quarter-quarter-half coverage is shown in Diagram 7-25.

Cross Concept

The cross concept also helps to create a three-on-two flood isolation on the two inside quarter-quarter-half coverage linebackers. The slot receiver, tight end, and back form a triangle position to help create the three-on-two advantage. The cross concept, from a balanced doubles set with a tight-end cross, slot-short-dig action is shown in Diagram 7-26 versus quarter-quarter-half coverage. Note that the post route, normally opposite the side of the short-dig route, is on the same side as the short-dig route. The purpose of this placement is to set up a possible over-the-top "home-run"-type throw to the post route if the quarters-coverage side strong safety jumps the short-dig route.

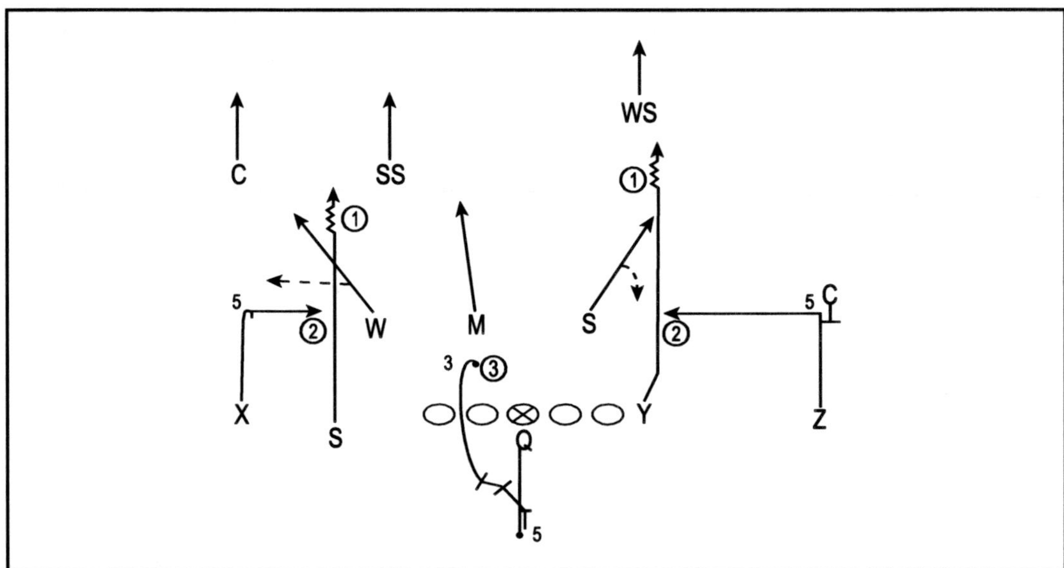

Diagram 7-24. Under concept versus quarter-quarter-half coverage

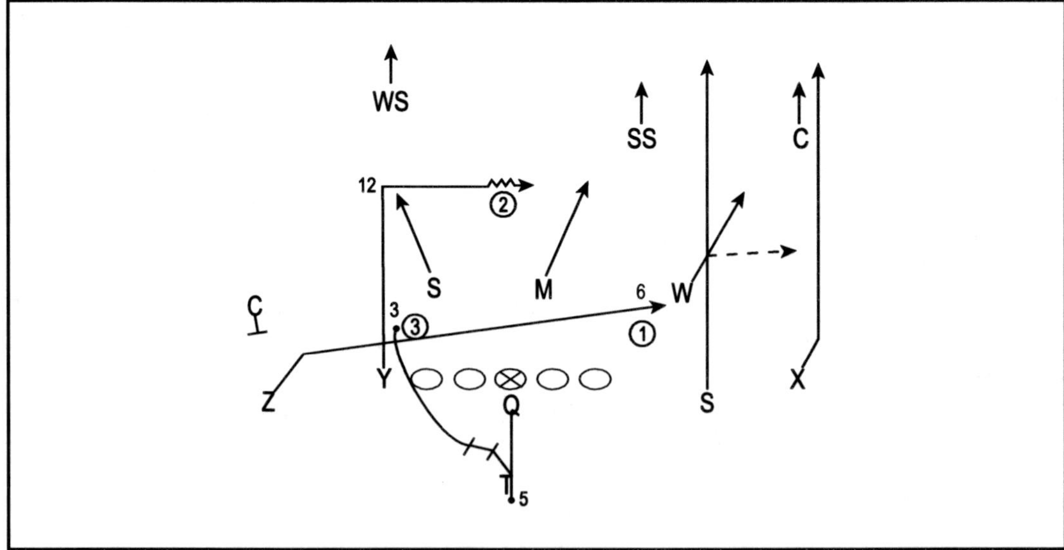

Diagram 7-25. Drive concept versus quarter-quarter-half coverage

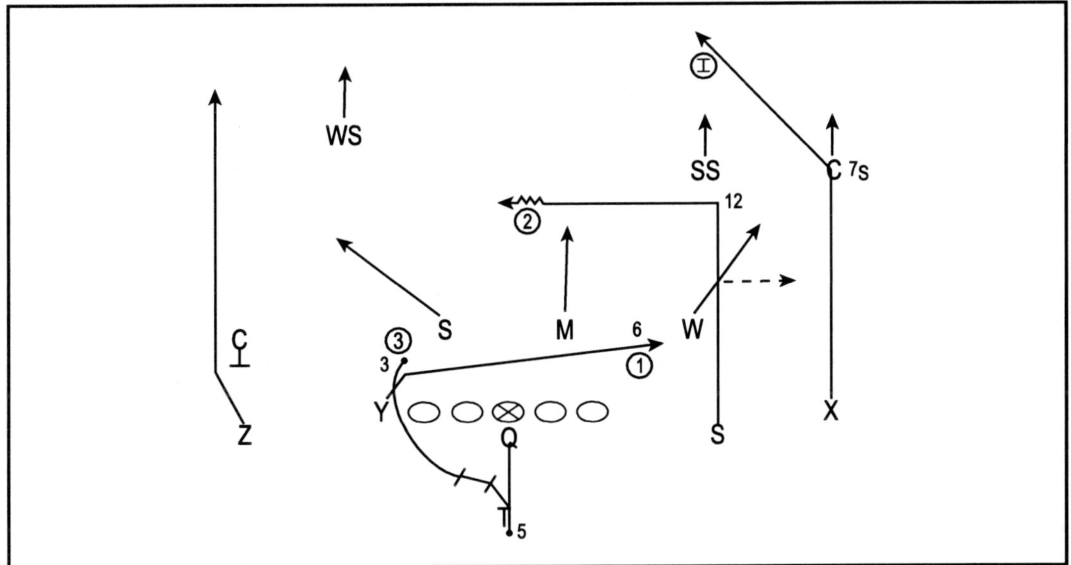

Diagram 7-26. Cross concept versus quarter-quarter-half coverage

Texas Concept

The Texas concept helps to create a two-on-one crossing isolation on the quarter-quarter-half-coverage inside linebacker. The underneath cross route stretches the quarter-quarter-half coverage outside linebacker with an initial flat-route stem and threat. He then breaks underneath and crosses the square-out action of the tight end. If the inside linebacker runs out with the tight end's square-out route, the underneath cross route should be wide open. If the tight end is able to wall the inside linebacker off, the quarterback can stick a tight throw in to the tight end before the tight end works out wide into the quarter-quarter-half-coverage outside linebacker. The Texas concept versus quarter-quarter-half coverage is shown in Diagram 7-27.

Option-Isolation Concept

Option-isolation routes help to produce excellent one-on-one isolations on quarter-quarter-half-coverage linebackers. Option routes can help to produce one-on-one size, talent, and speed mismatches. As previously mentioned, option routes are best run off of five-step drop-timing by the quarterback. Five-step drop-timing by the quarterback are for option routes run in the 8- to 12-yard range, giving the option-route receivers time to properly maneuver and execute their option-route man- or zone-separation techniques. Diagram 7-28 shows a tight-end (Y) option and a halfback (H) option versus quarter-quarter-half coverage.

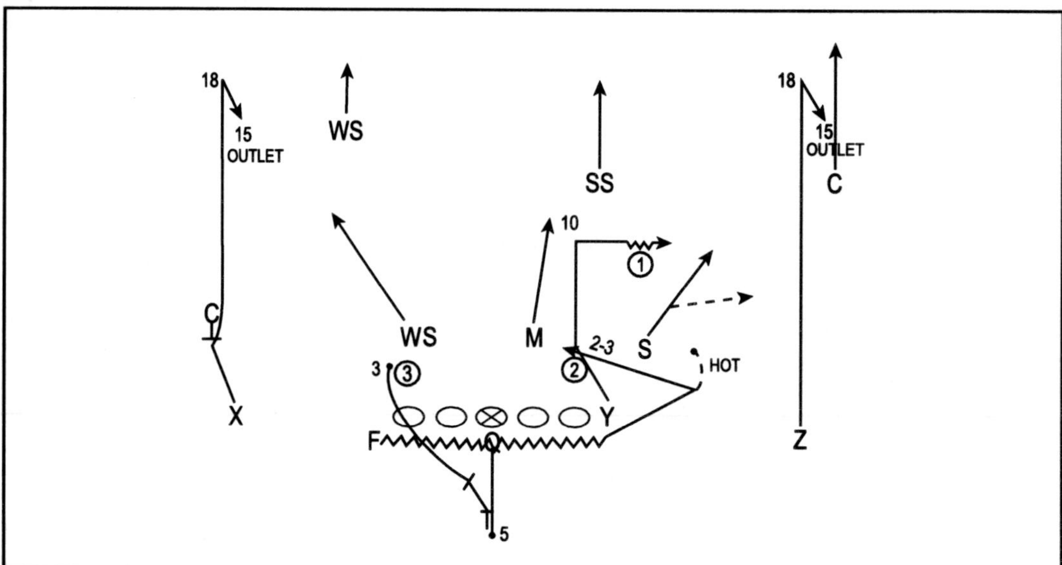

Diagram 7-27. Texas concept versus quarter-quarter-half coverage

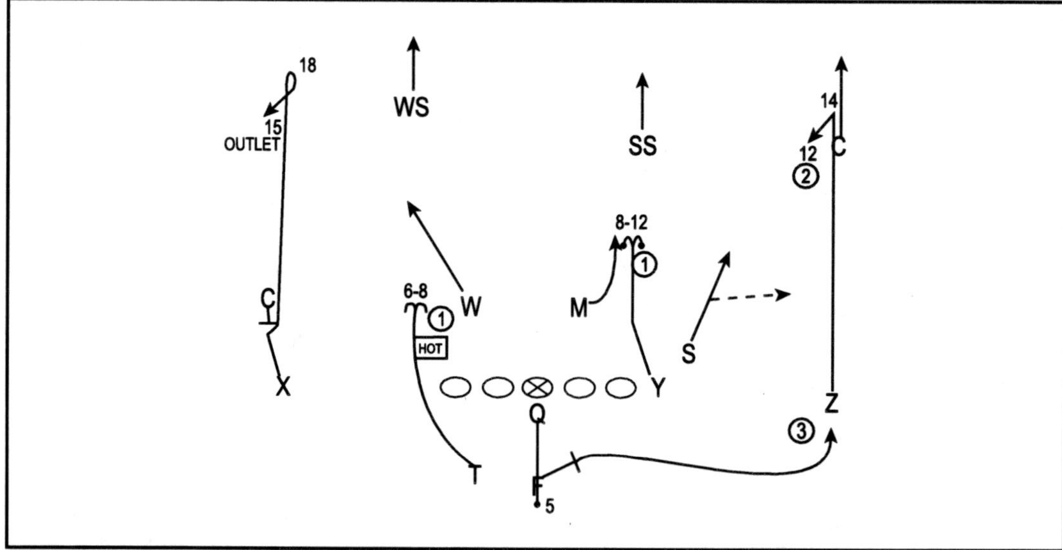

Diagram 7-28. Option-isolation routes to attack quarter-quarter-half coverage

High-Low Delay-Route Isolations

High-low delay-route isolations can be very effective against quarter-quarter-half coverage. With vertical broken-arrow routes splitting the quarter-quarter-half-coverage safeties and a delay route working underneath, the quarterback simply throws off of the two-on-one coverage reaction of the isolated strong, inside linebacker. A high-low-read tailback delay versus quarter-quarter-half coverage is shown in Diagram 7-29.

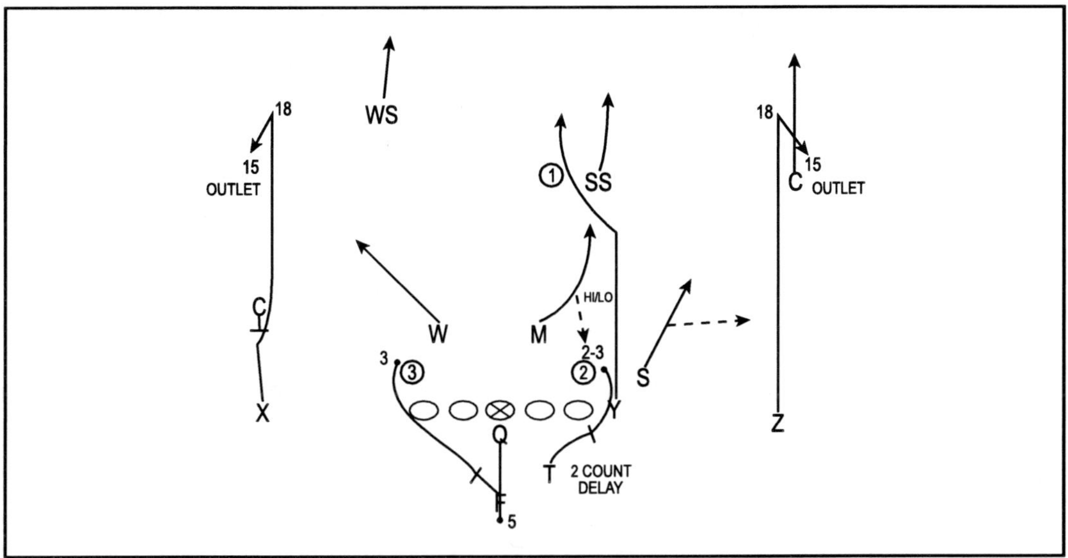

Diagram 7-29. High-low-read tailback delay-route isolation versus quarter-quarter-half coverage

High-Low Pivot- and Break-Route Isolations

Just like delay-route high-low isolations, tight-end (Y) pivot- and break-route isolations can be very effective versus quarter-quarter-half coverage. With a vertical broken-arrow route by a back splitting the deep quarter-quarter-half-coverage safeties and a tight-end (Y) pivot or break route, the quarterback simply throws off of the two-on-one coverage reaction of the isolated strong, inside linebacker. The pivot and break routes are run in

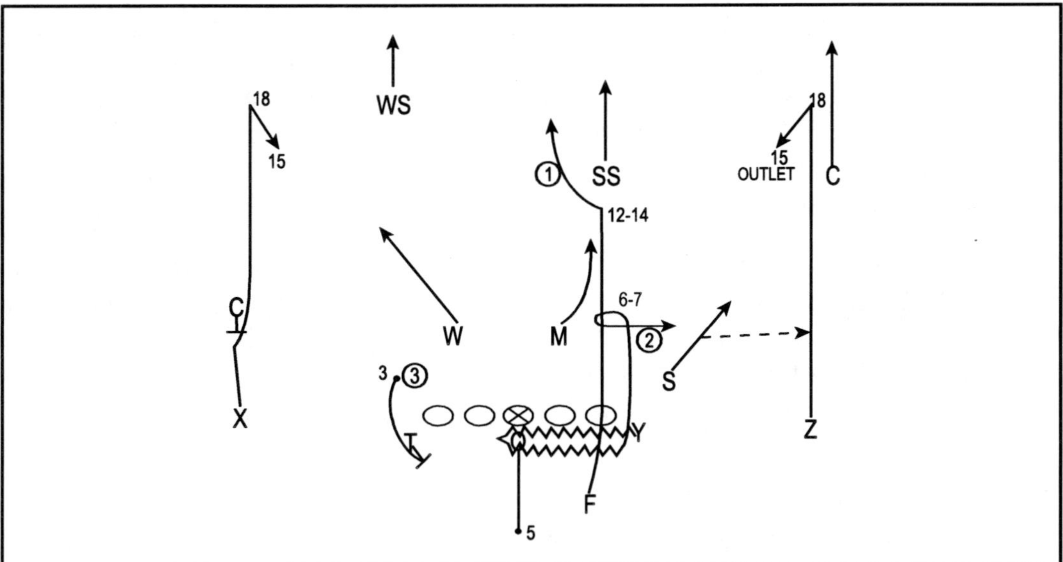

Diagram 7-30. High-low-read Y-pivot isolation versus quarter-quarter-half coverage

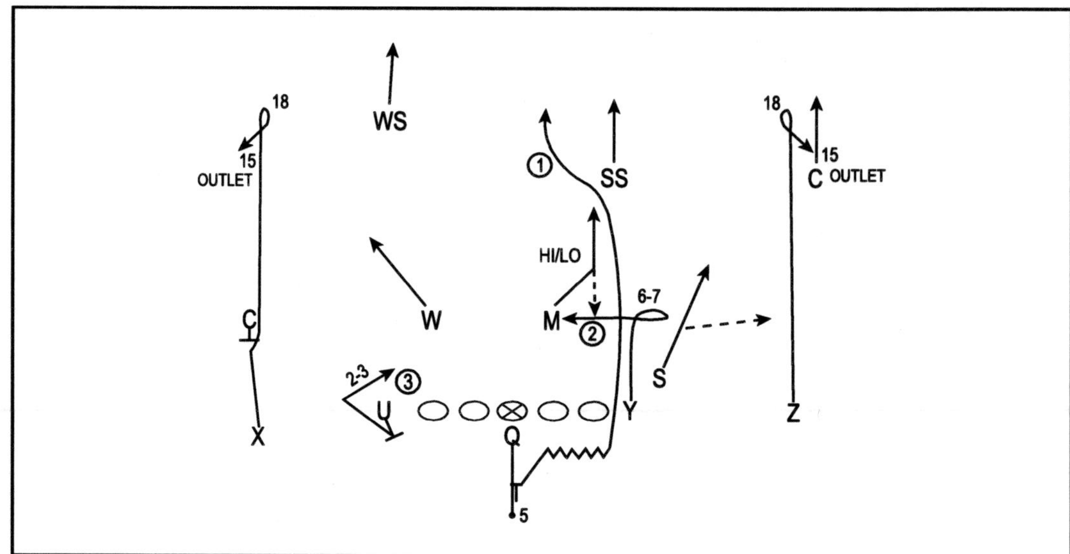

Diagram 7-31. High-low-read Y-break isolation versus quarter-quarter-half coverage

the six- to seven-yard range. Diagram 7-30 shows a Y-pivot high-low-read-isolation action to attack quarter-quarter-half coverage. Diagram 7-31 shows Y-break action versus quarter-quarter-half coverage.

Naked-Bootleg Concept

The naked-bootleg concept can be an effective way to attack quarter-quarter-half coverage. The naked-bootleg patterns that are most effective versus quarter-quarter-half coverage are the ones that work back into the quarters-coverage aspect of the quarters coverage. Naked-bootleg action is shown in Diagram 7-32 in its effort to attack the quarters-coverage aspect of the quarter-quarter-half coverage with a fish-pattern-type concept to isolate on the aggressive run-support play of the quarters-side safety.

Wide-Receiver Screens

Wide-receiver screens are very effective versus quarter-quarter-half coverage. These screens can be especially effective from spread formations if the front tries to keep six front defenders in the box. As a result, the offense can gain a three-on-two advantage to, say, a trips-type set with a wide-receiver-screen concept. Such wide-receiver-screen action is shown in Diagram 7-33 versus quarter-quarter-half coverage.

Back Screens

Back screens can be very effective versus quarter-quarter-half coverage—especially to the strong, formation, fieldside where less underneath coverage is present per the amount of lateral distance the inside and outside linebackers have to cover. Back-screen action can allow the linebacker spot droppers to get depth to allow for the back-screen blockers to work up to the linebackers to block for the back's screen action off of play-action passing, as seen in Diagram 7-34.

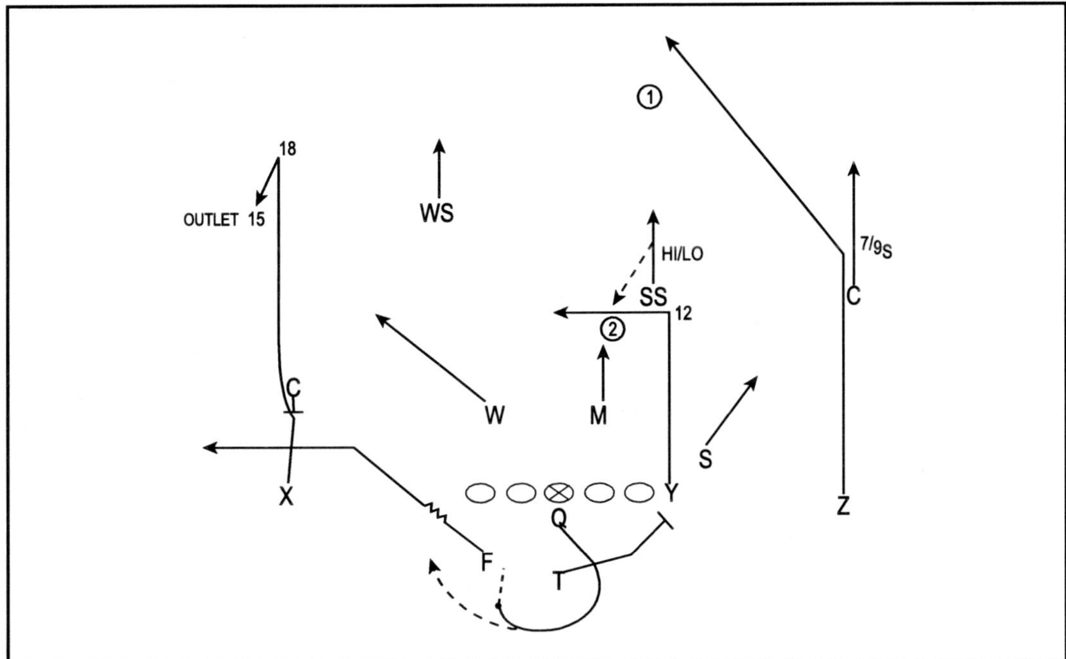

Diagram 7-32. Naked-bootleg action versus quarter-quarter-half coverage

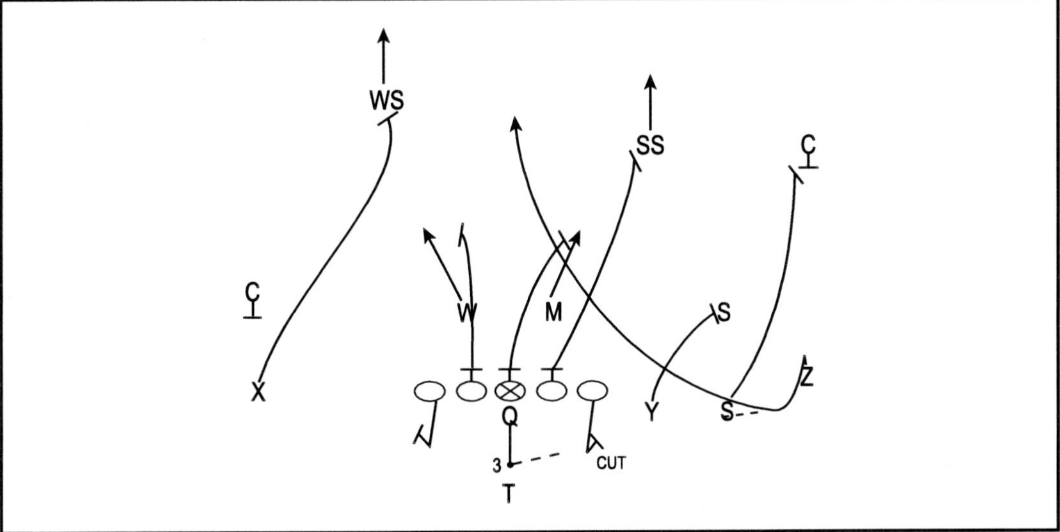

Diagram 7-33. Wide-receiver screen versus quarter-quarter-half coverage

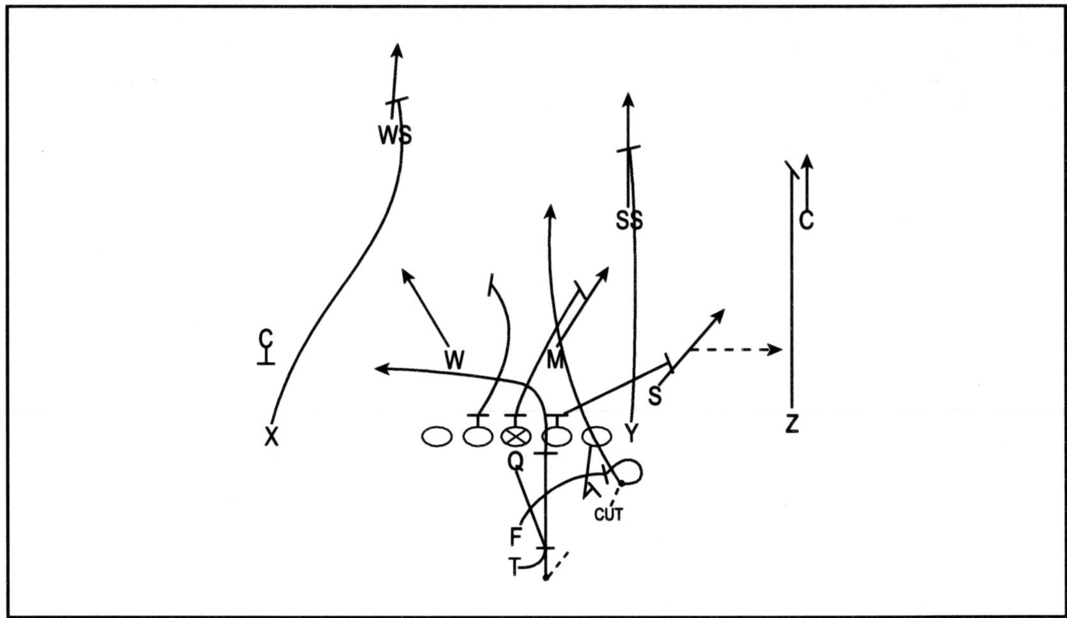

Diagram 7-34. Back screen versus quarter-quarter-half coverage

8

Pass Attack of Four-Across Man (Cover Zero)

Four-across man (or cover zero, as it is also commonly called) is a man-to-man coverage that supports frontal stunts of up to six frontal rushers. ("Stunts" is a term used to signify pressure-type action of the linebackers in combination with pressure action of the defensive line.) As a result, the four secondary-coverage defenders cover four potential receivers with one of the frontal defenders covering the fifth potential receiver, as shown in Diagram 8-1.

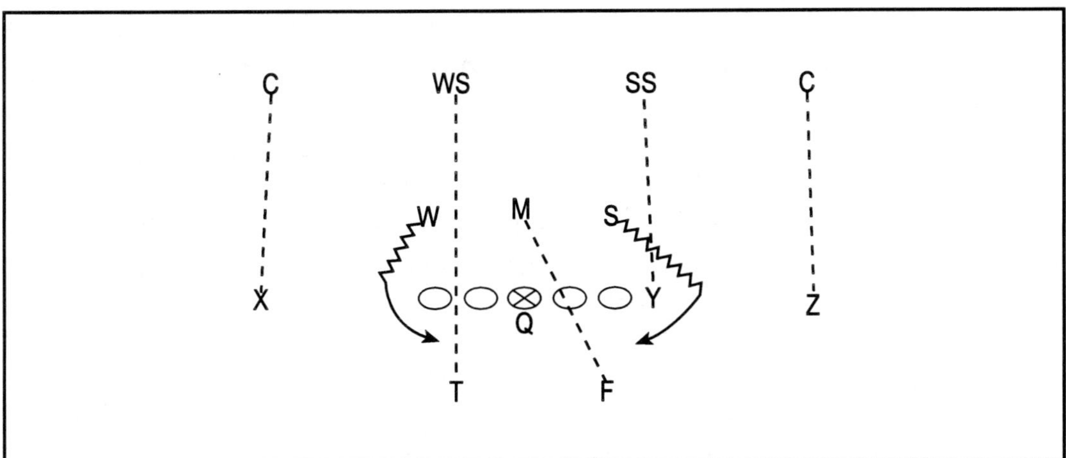

Diagram 8-1. Four-across man shown with six frontal stunters

A front that is tied into four-across man can stunt all seven frontal defenders. However, this would be done at the possible expense of one of the five potential receivers being left uncovered.

Four-across-man coverage can be played with a variety of press-coverage techniques, as was shown in Chapter 3 for attacking man-free coverage and in Chapter 5 for cover-2 man-under coverage. However, this chapter will focus on the attack of the off-man-coverage techniques more commonly associated with four-across-man coverage. Since no deep-zone-safety-coverage defender(s) are used (as you would find in man free and cover-2 man under) to back up the four secondary-man-coverage defenders, most defenses that utilize four-across-man play with off-man-coverage techniques for the purpose of deep-pass-completion prevention. The off-man-to-man-coverage techniques allow the secondary man-coverage defenders a cushion of distance to help the defenders not get beat deep easily.

Four-Across-Man Pass-Game Strengths

- Four-across-man coverage blends efficiently with frontal stunts of up to six frontal defenders. With the pass coverage of the one remaining frontal defender, all five potential receivers of the offense can be man-to-man covered.
- Four-across-man coverage defenders easily fit to any offensive formation, shift, or motion variation.
- Four-across man has the flexibility of fortifying its man-coverage abilities by playing with a fifth (nickel) secondary defender to better help man-cover the fifth potential pass receiver.
- The off-man-to-man-coverage techniques help the four-across-man-coverage defenders to prevent from getting beat deep.
- The deepened off-man-to-man-coverage techniques of the four-across-man-coverage defenders help to make up for the fact that the coverage has no deep-zone safety help to back it up.
- If the offense's backs and/or tight ends don't release into pass routes, covering safeties can help to act as robber-type coverage defenders. At their safety-coverage depths, the safeties can help support deep, inside, crossing-type routes.
- The off-man-to-man coverage techniques of four-across man helps the coverage take on a "bend-but-don't-break" philosophy, which can be true even though as many as six frontal defenders may be involved in some form of a pressure stunt with only five defenders left to man-to-man cover.
- Four-across-man coverage does have the flexibility of press-man-covering specific receivers. The concern here is the lack of any deep backup coverage to support such press-coverage alignments and techniques.

Four-Across-Man Pass-Game Weaknesses

- Two of the most basic premises of attacking man (man-to-man) coverage holds true for the attack of four-across-man coverage: isolate and cross. In both concepts, it is extremely important for the receivers to man-separate and then to be sure to maintain such separation from the man-to-man coverage.
- Beating off-man coverage can easily lead to big gains. A major reason for such gains is that the other coverage defenders may be chasing (or covering) other receivers. As a result, the area around the receiver making the reception may be well cleared out, allowing the receiving ballcarrier to run for big gains. In addition, with no deep-zone safety behind the four-across-man coverage, no deep-zone help is available to support receptions by the receivers.
- The total man-coverage design can only be as strong as the weakest man-coverage defender, much as a chain is only as strong as its weakest link. An offense can quickly focus on attacking (or isolating) the weakest man-coverage defender(s).
- The commonly-used off-man-coverage techniques of four-across-man coverage can lead to a "bend-but-don't-break" philosophy by the defense. As a result, a patient, short-pass, ball-control-type of pass attack can be very effective versus four-across man and its related frontal-stunt pressures.
- Since four-across man is often tied into heavy frontal-stunt activity, good stunt-beating pass actions can be very effective, which can be true whether the offense is using quick, stunt-beater-type routes and patterns, hot-route concepts, or maximum protections. Diagram 8-2 shows a backside drag route acting as a stunt-beater route.

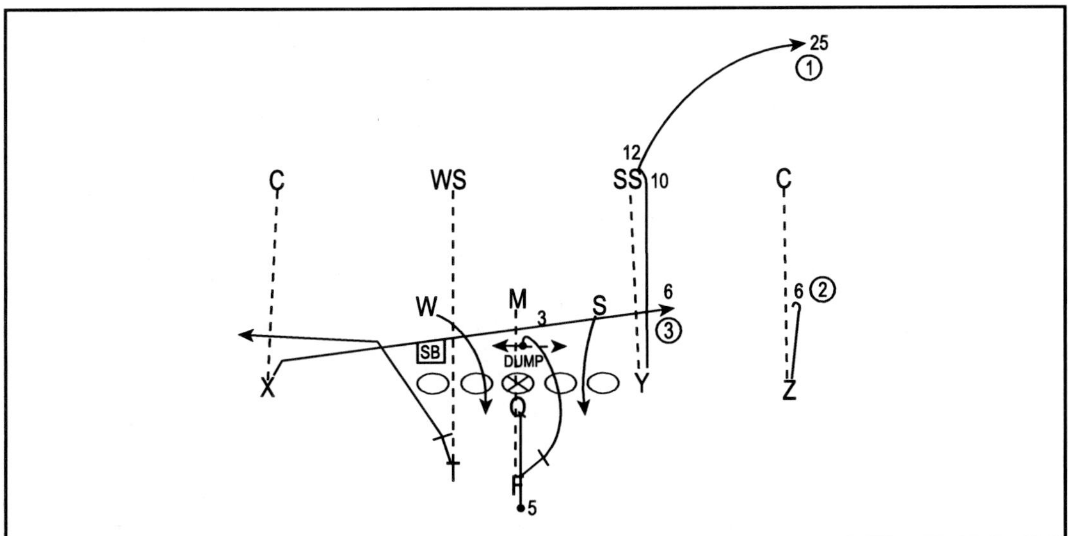

Diagram 8-2. Backside drag stunt-beater route versus four-across man

- Throwing quickly is, perhaps, the best way to beat frontal-stunt pressure. Whether it's the quick-pass game, the use of hot routes, or any other form of throwing quickly, getting a pass off before the rush pressure can get to the quarterback is one of the best ways of defeating four-across man and its related frontal-stunt pressures.
- Quick-game isolations, such as slants, inside-receiver speed-outs, and hitches can all be very effective versus four-across-man off-man coverage.
- Hot-route concepts can effectively help control—and beat—the execution of many of the frontal stunts associated with four-across-man coverage. Diagram 8-3 shows a fullback's hot route to control inside-linebacker stunt action.
- Quarterback-move action can greatly help a pass offense to combat the frontal-stunt action that is associated with four-across-man coverage. Moving the quarterback helps to disturb the stunt-execution action of the front and helps the quarterback to move away from one side of the front's rush. Diagram 8-4 shows quarterback-sprint action to combat the front's stunt action and a crossing post-corner/smash pattern to combat the four-across-man coverage.
- The off-man-to-man-coverage techniques of four-across man can be extremely vulnerable to outside acute, rollaway, and comeback-out routes off of deep-streak-threat action.
- Outs (square-outs) can be very effective versus four-across-man coverage, which is especially true when executing such square-out routes by inside receivers.
- The off-man-coverage techniques of four-across man can be extremely susceptible to deep, double-move-type route isolations, which is true whether the double-move action is off of quick-game three-step drop-timed routes (quick hitch, slants, speed-outs) or five-step drop-timed routes (outs, flats, curls, rollaways). The

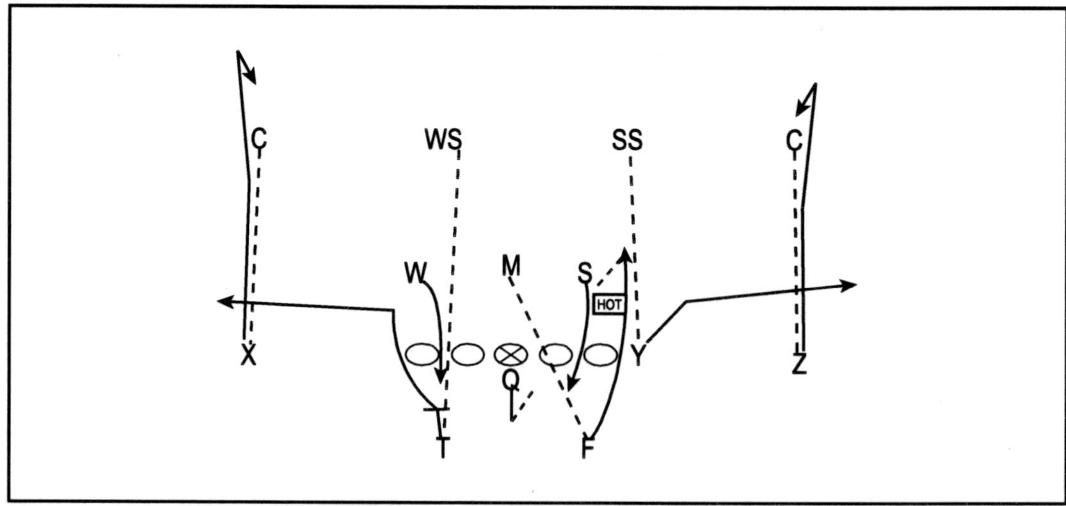

Diagram 8-3. Hot-route action of strongside back versus inside-linebacker stunt and four-across man

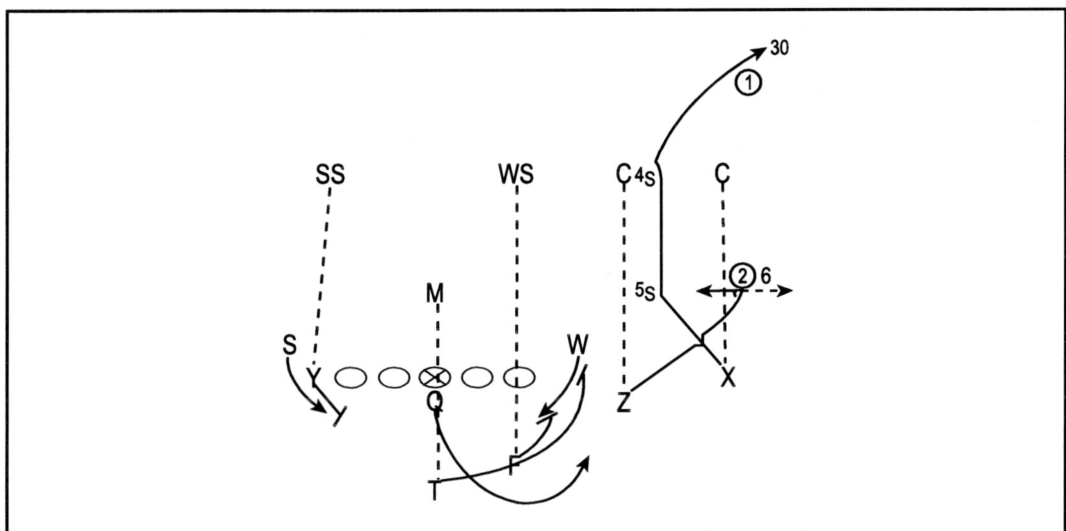

Diagram 8-4. Sprint-out action to combat a weakside stunt and four-across man

concern, however, is the protection time that may be needed to allow the quarterback to get a double-move pass off—especially true for five-step-timed double-move routes.

- Underneath-smash isolations and under-route isolations offer the offense quick, inside crossing routes to help beat the off-man coverage of four-across man.
- Option-isolation routes (Y-options, H-options, slot-options) help to exploit possible one-on-one mismatches in favor of the offense in the attack of four-across man.
- Y-pivot and Y-break routes also help create one-on-one isolation routes in favor of the offense versus four-across man. Stick routes and the square-out route on a Texas concept can also do the same. The quickness ability of the tight end to execute such routes (especially if five-step-timed in relation to the quarterback's drop) must be considered in regard to combating frontal-stunt pressures.
- Post-corner isolations by both outside- and inside-aligned receivers can help to exploit the one-on-one off-man outside coverage of four-across man. Such deep post-corner-isolation action by an inside receiver to the outside (as well as the excellent underneath lateral dragging action of the smash route versus the off-man coverage) is shown in Diagram 8-5. However, it must be kept in mind that due to the longer-developing prime-pass routes, the offense does have to account for the possibility of extra pass-protection needs versus the frontal-stunt combinations associated with four-across-man coverage.
- Deeper digs and square-ins can help to isolate the off-man coverage and utilize the deeper crossing actions of such routes. This is especially true since no deep-zone safety help is available in the middle for four-across-man coverage. Versus heavy

frontal-stunt-pressure possibilities, maximum pass-protection schemes should be strongly considered due to the pass-protection time needed for such longer-developing routes. Diagram 8-6 shows a split-end (X) dig-route-pattern principle with a maximum pass-protection design.

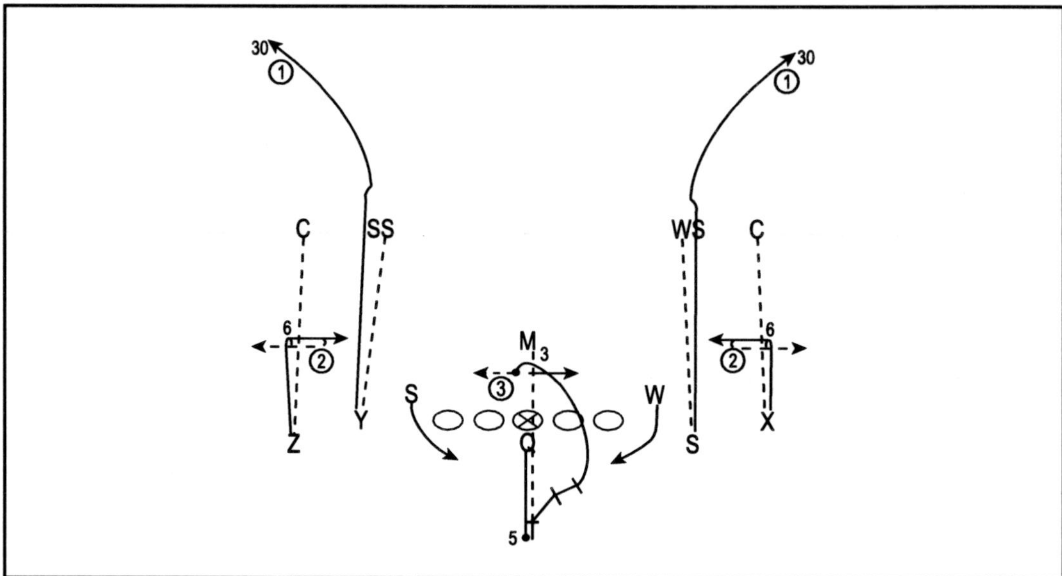

Diagram 8-5. Smash-pattern attack of four-across-man outside voids plus underneath smash-route drag action

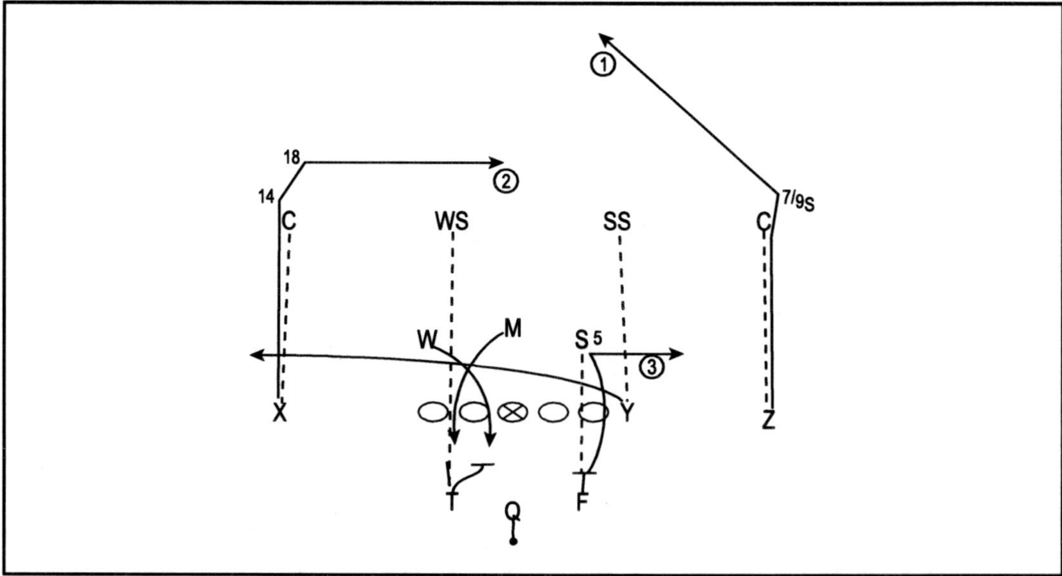

Diagram 8-6. Split-end (X) dig pattern versus four-across man with maximum pass-protection design

- Cross-the-field route actions, such as drives and drag routes, can be very effective four-across-man underneath-isolation routes to help act as stunt-pressure-beater routes. Such routes have much (or all) of the width of the field to beat the off-man coverage and get open to receive a pass.
- Crossing action is an excellent way to attack the off-man aspect of four-across-man coverage. Cross-route-pattern concepts and the Texas concepts are excellent examples. Diagram 8-7 shows a Texas crossing-pattern action.

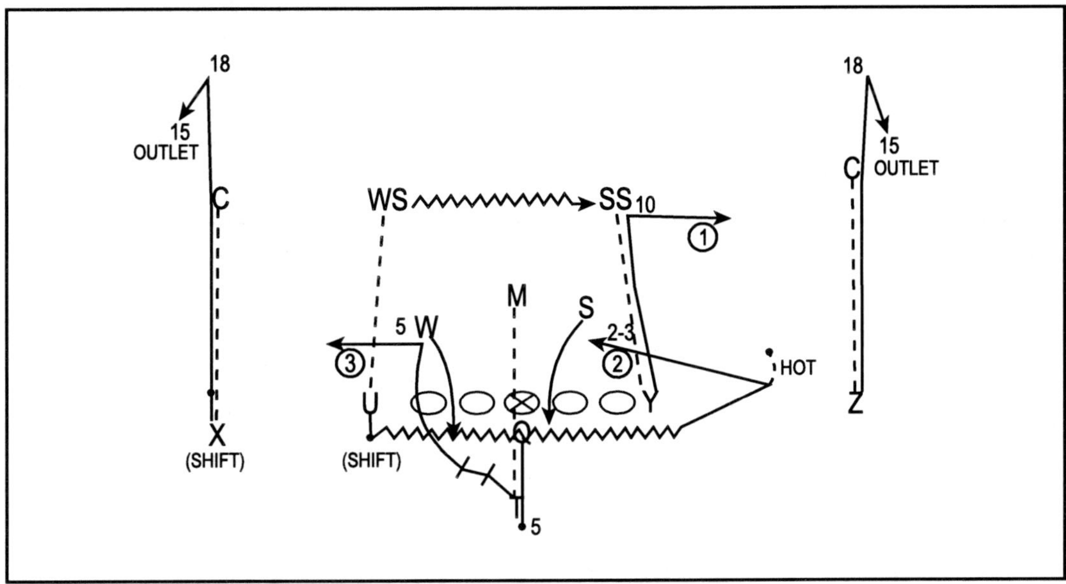

Diagram 8-7. Texas crossing-pattern action versus four-across man

- Backs-cross and back-fake-cross action can be good man-attack concepts that can be used versus four-across man, even though the safeties are in off positions. The concern, however, is the backs being forced to block versus the frontal-stunt pressures associated with four-across man.
- Picks and rubs can be excellent route combinations to attack four-across man. The concern for such picks and rubs may be the depths of the defensive backs' off alignments. Of course, such pick and rub action must all be executed off of legal picking action. A tight-end (Y) pick-route combination from a trips to the split-end (X) formation is shown in Diagram 8-8.
- Picking screens thrown to backs and receivers behind the line of scrimmage can also be very effective in defeating the off-man aspect of four-across-man coverage. Diagram 8-9 shows a wide-receiver pick screen versus four-across man.

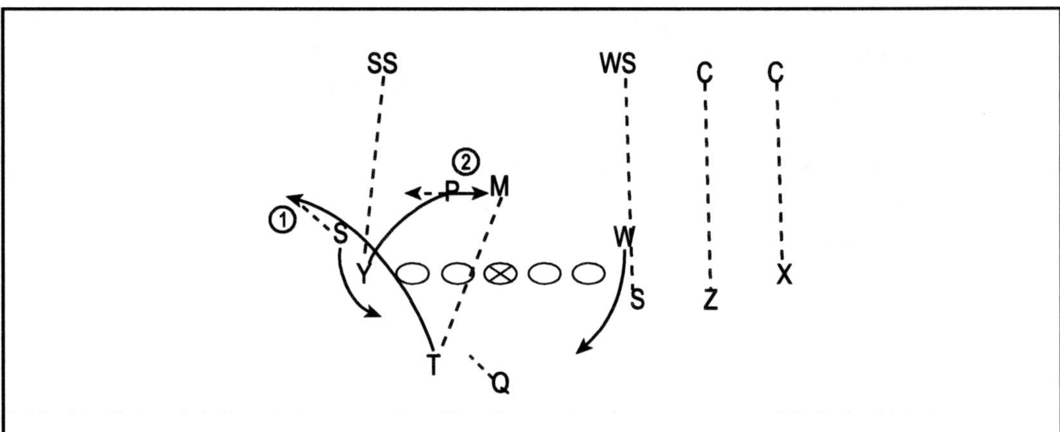

Diagram 8-8. Y-pick action versus four-across man

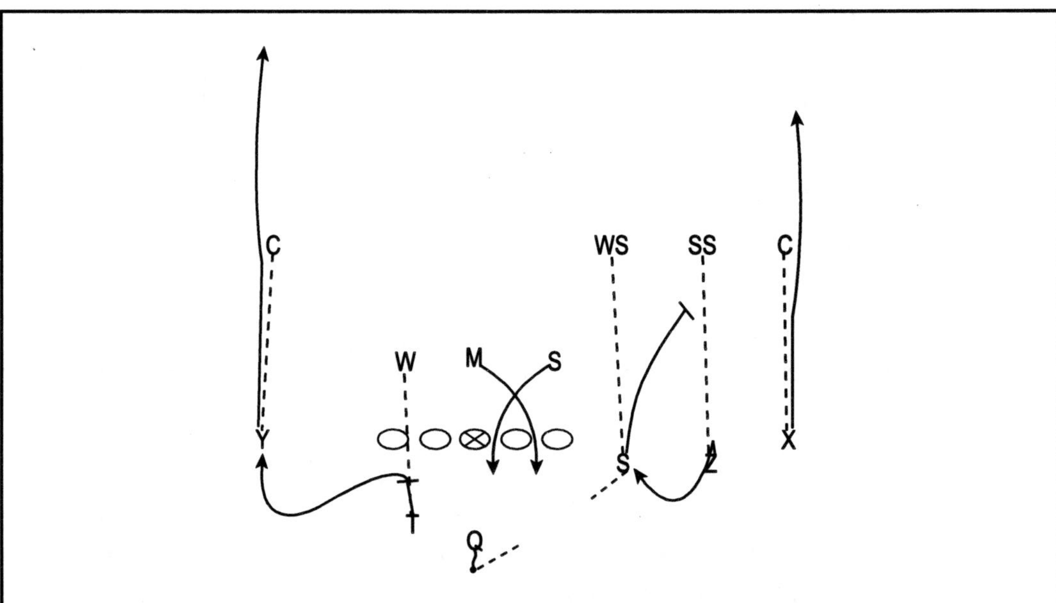

Diagram 8-9. Wide-receiver pick screen versus four-across man

Route Combination and Pass-Pattern Attack of Four-Across Man

Quick-Game Hitch

The quick-game hitch route is a very effective quick-game pass concept versus four-across-man off-man coverage as are most of the concepts of the quick-pass game. The quick-pass game, in general, helps in the effort to combat frontal-stunt pressure by throwing quickly. The hitch receiver works hard to produce a six-yard hitch stem off of a streak threat to push the off-man-coverage defender backwards. Quick-game hitch action versus four-across-man coverage is shown in Diagram 8-10.

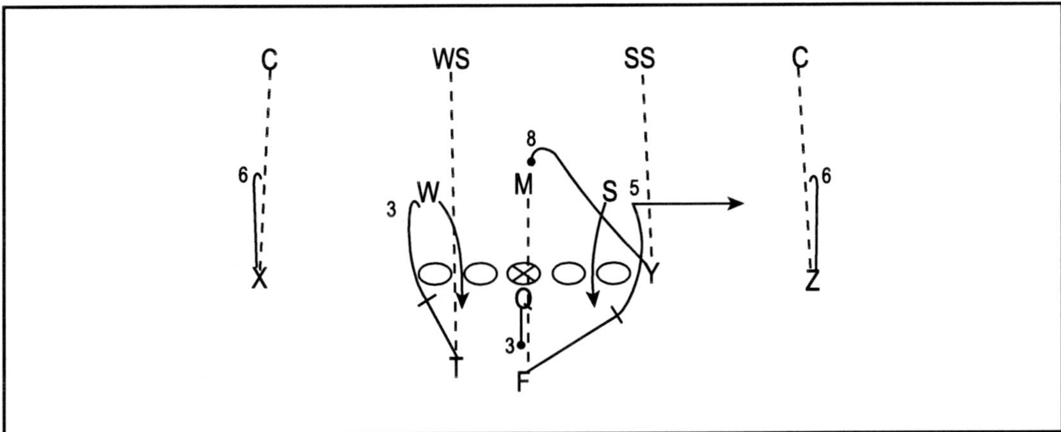

Diagram 8-10. Quick-game hitch route versus four-across man

Quick-Game Slant

Slant-route isolations and double-slant actions can be very effective versus four-across-man coverage. Once the quarterback and receivers recognize four-across man, they should be thinking frontal-stunt pressure. One of the best ways to beat frontal-stunt pressure is to throw the ball quickly before the rush can get to the quarterback. As a result, the quick-pass game provides an offense with a natural stunt-beater package.

The slant receiver must initially be sure to attack the technique of his man-covering defender, even though that defender will probably be in an off-position alignment. The slant receiver then breaks his slant action hard to the inside to get separation and stay on the move at top speed to be sure to maintain such man-separation. Slant and double-slant action versus four-across-man coverage is shown in Diagram 8-11.

Diagram 8-12 shows slant/arrow action versus four-across man. The crossing action of the slant and arrow routes can help to actually produce a quick crossing action of the two routes, helping to free one route or the other versus the off-man coverage.

Quick-Game Speed-Out

The quick-game speed-out route can be an excellent concept versus the loose off-man coverage of four-across-man coverage, as shown in Diagram 8-13.

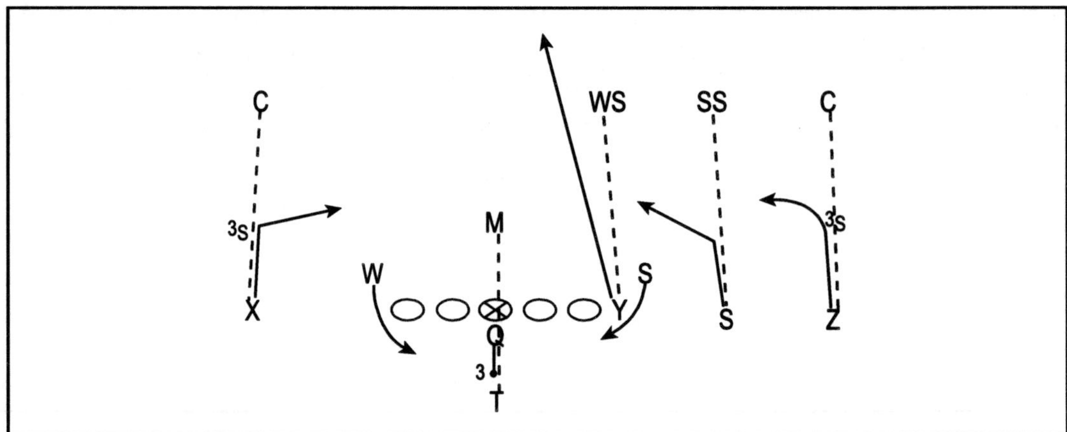

Diagram 8-11. Quick-game slant-route and double-slant-route action versus four-across man

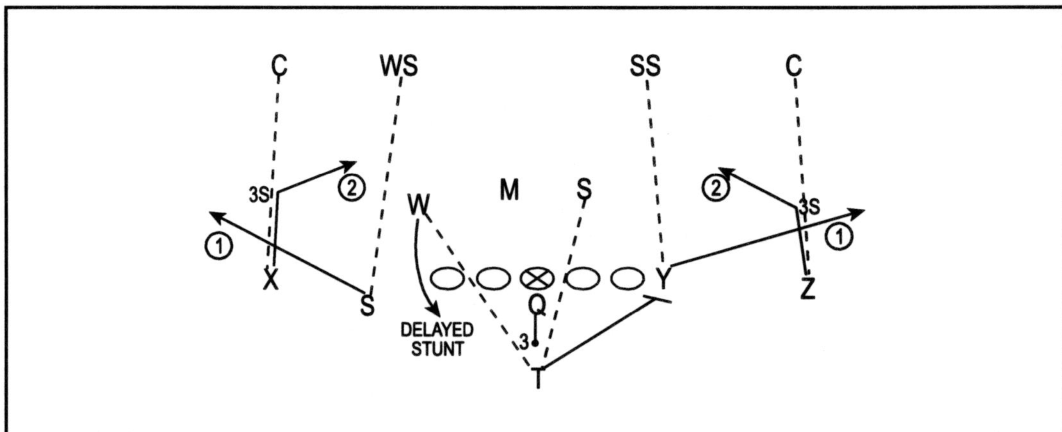

Diagram 8-12. Quick-game slant/arrow-route combination versus four-across man

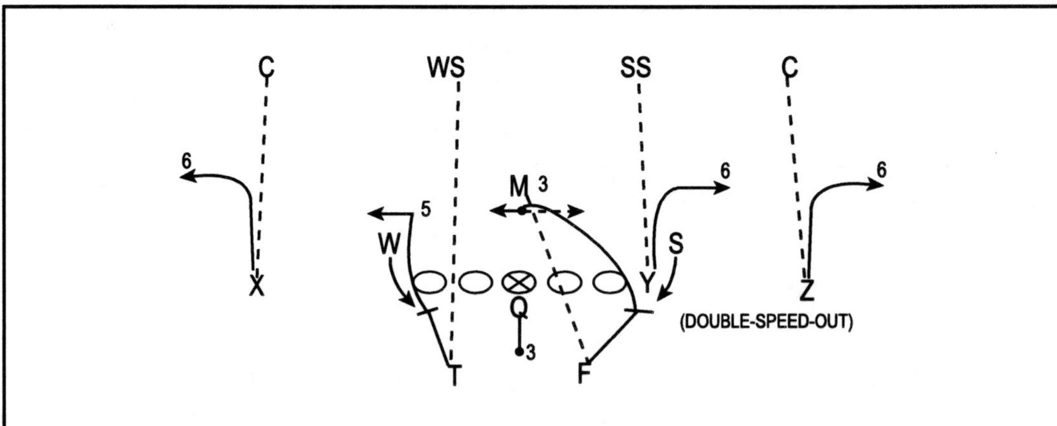

Diagram 8-13. Quick-game speed-out versus four-across man

Quick-Game Inside-Receiver Speed-Out-and-Fade

The quick-game inside-receiver speed-out-and-fade-route combination creates an excellent off-man coverage isolation to help defeat four-across man. The wide receiver works a fade route to clear the cornerback, while the inside receiver runs his speed-out route. The off-man coverage will probably allow the inside receiver to run a normal, zone-type speed-out route rather than a needed quick-game square-out route. Such quick-game inside-receiver speed-out action versus cover zero is shown in Diagram 8-14.

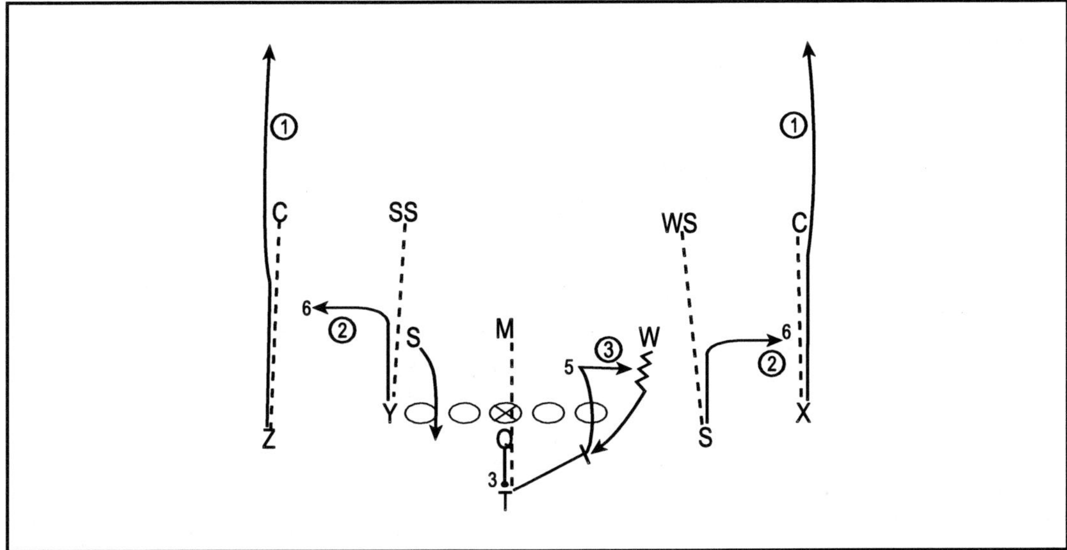

Diagram 8-14. Quick-game inside-receiver speed-out action versus four-across man

An excellent supplemental concept to utilize when a four-across-man-coverage defender starts to overplay a quick-game speed-out is the spin route, as shown in Diagram 8-15. The speed-out receiver simply plants his upfield foot and spins back to the inside versus the defender's overplay action. Although a slower quick-pass-game concept, the route action still should have enough time to execute the pass pattern effectively versus stunt-pressure potentials. Diagram 8-15 shows maximum pass protection to help provide the quarterback with the needed time to get the pass off efficiently.

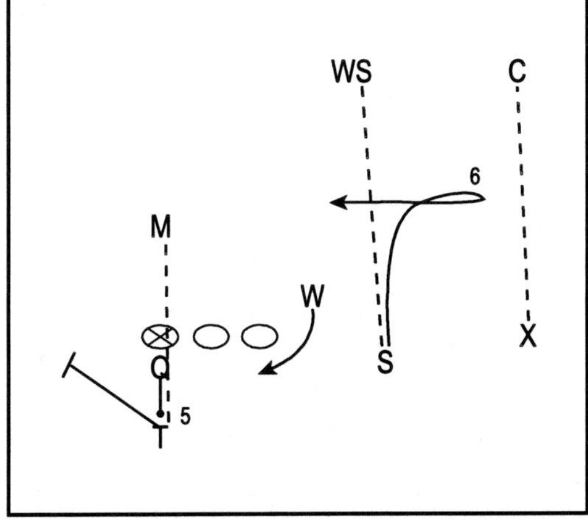

Diagram 8-15. Quick-game spin route versus four-across man

Versus the off-man coverage of four-across man, deeper, five-step quarterback-drop-timed square-outs by an inside receiver are also very effective. The inside receiver attacks the technique of the off-man defender covering him, separates, and squares out to the sideline. As on all man-coverage wide-receiver-separation techniques, the inside receiver must get separation and then be sure to run at top speed to maintain such separation. The deeper, five-step drop-timed square-out concept versus four-across man is shown in Diagram 8-16.

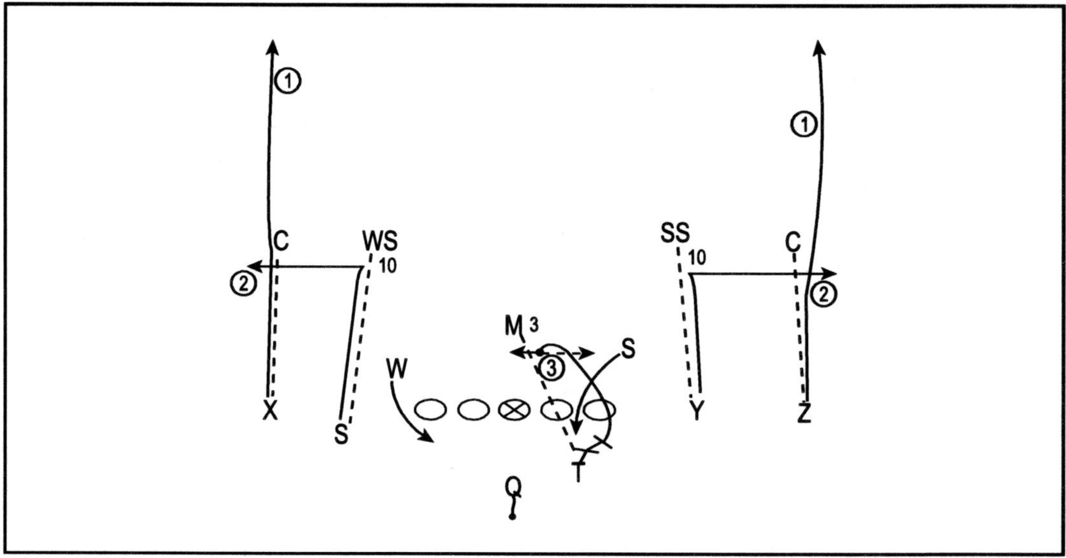

Diagram 8-16. Five-step drop-timed inside-receiver speed-out concept versus four-across man

Quick-Game Stick

The quick-game stick route concept is an excellent isolation-type route versus four-across-man coverage. The flat route in front of the stick route helps to open up the stick area for the stick-route receiver to man-separate into. The stick receiver initially works tightly into the technique of the defender man-covering him and then snaps to the outside to get man-separation. The stick receiver must then be sure to work hard to the outside, losing ground slightly, to help maintain such separation. The quick-game stick-route concept versus four-across man is shown in Diagram 8-17.

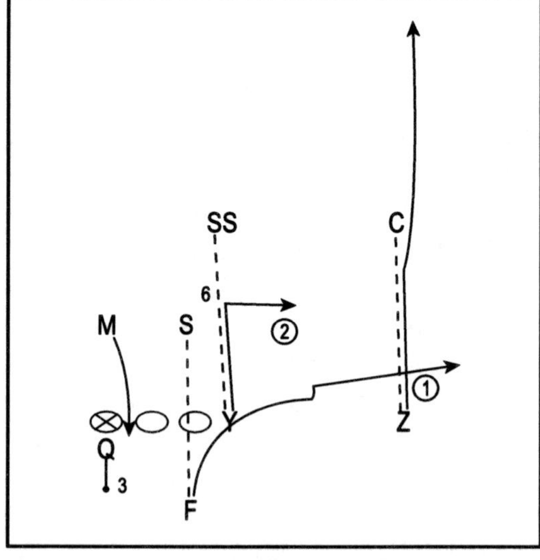

Diagram 8-17. Quick-game stick route versus four-across man

Quick-Game Double-Move Routes

Quick-game double-move routes can be very effective versus four-across-man coverage once the defensive backs start jumping the short, prime quick-game routes. Hitch-and-go and speed-out-and-go routes are shown in Diagram 8-18.

Diagram 8-19 shows slant-and-go action and Y-stick-and-go action versus four-across man. To ensure enough time for the quarterback to get this slightly delayed three-step drop-pass action off, a maximum pass protection could be utilized.

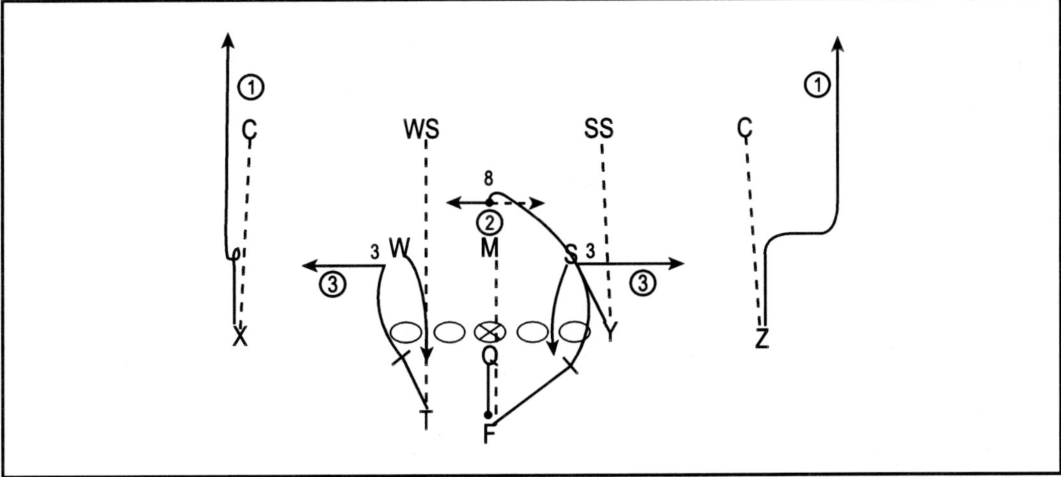

Diagram 8-18. Quick-game double-move hitch-and-go and speed-out-and-go routes versus four-across man

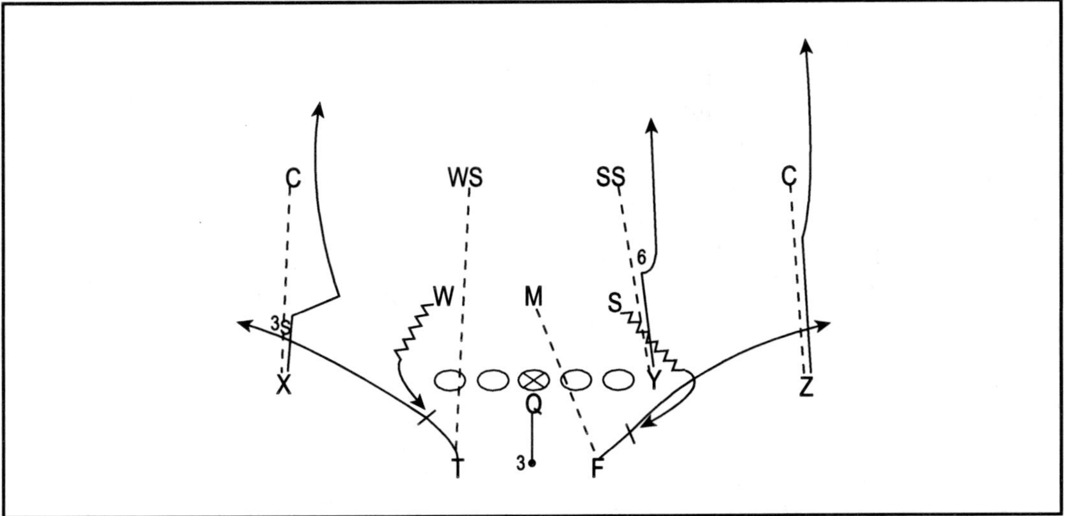

Diagram 8-19. Quick-game double-move slant-and-go and Y-stick-and-go action versus four-across man

Hot Routes to Combat Frontal-Stunt Pressures

Before going into actual five- to seven-step-timed drop and route actions, it is first necessary to explore the use of hot-route actions. Hot-route actions can help control the frontal stunt pressures that are so often tied into four-across-man coverage. Actually, such hot-route action need not be just tied into four-across man. Chapter 9 will cover the use of hot routes to control the frontal-stunt pressures that are so commonly tied into secondary blitzes. Such hot concepts can as easily be tied into the zone-blitz concepts that were discussed in Chapter 2 concerning the pass attack of cover 3.

Versus defenses that utilize four-across-man hot routes by the backs and tight ends can be utilized to help control the frontal stunts that are often tied into the man-to-man coverage. Simply, a back (or a tight end) can be put on a free-release assignment (no blocking assignment). If the defender that the free releaser is normally assigned to block rushes as part of the frontal stunt, or if a part of the frontal stunt vacates an area that a free releaser is releasing through, the quarterback can quick-pass-dump the ball off hot to that free-releasing receiver. Examples of such hot throwing are shown in Diagrams 8-20 to 8-22. Diagram 8-20 shows a weakside back's hot action versus a weakside inside linebacker's stunt action. Diagram 8-21 shows tight-end (Y) hot action versus a strongside linebacker's stunt action. Diagram 8-22 shows a strongside back's hot action versus a strongside outside linebacker's stunt action.

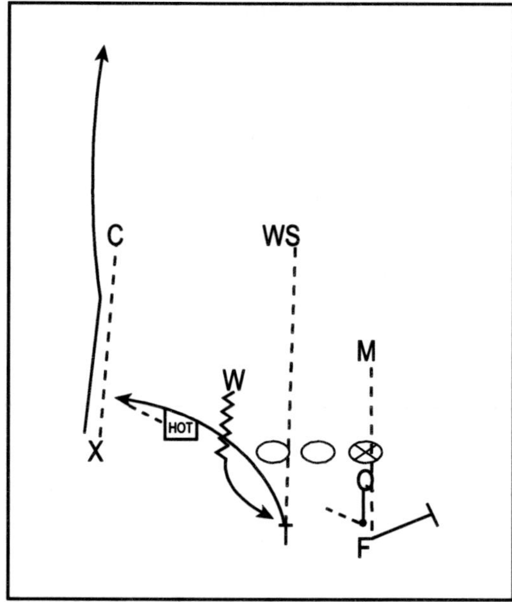

Diagram 8-20. Weakside-back hot action versus weakside-inside-linebacker stunt with four-across man

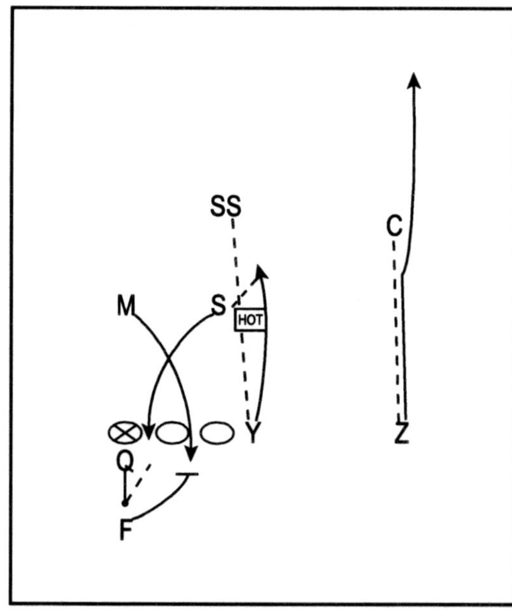

Diagram 8-21. Tight-end (Y) hot action versus strongside-inside-linebacker stunt with four-across man

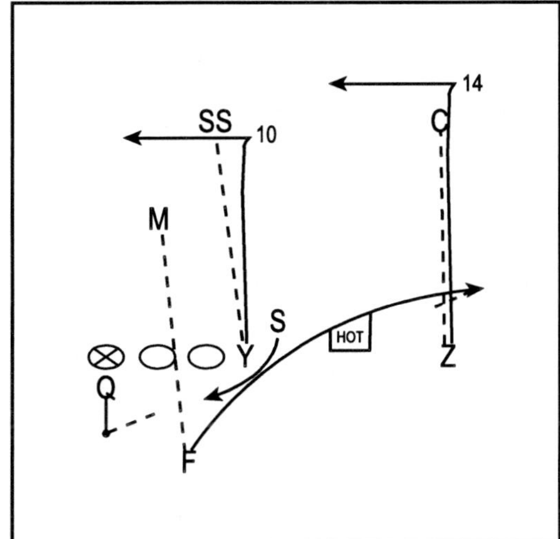

Diagram 8-22. Strongside back hot action versus strongside-outside-linebacker stunt with four-across man

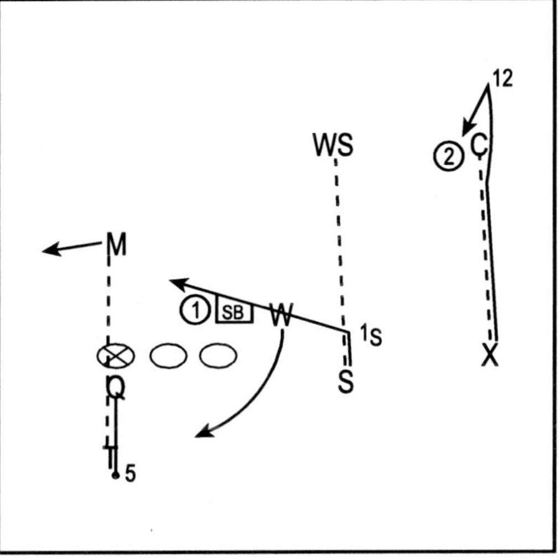

Diagram 8-23. Shallow-cross route acting as a stunt-beater route versus four-across man

Stunt-Beater Routes to Combat Frontal-Stunt Pressure

Much like the use of hot routes to control frontal-stunt pressures that are so often tied into four-across-man coverage, the designation (and use) of stunt-beater routes within the actual design of a pass pattern can be equally effective. Actually, such stunt-beater routes within the designs of specific pass patterns need not be just tied into four-across man. Chapter 9 will cover the use of stunt-beater routes (where they will be referred to as blitz-beater routes) to control the frontal-stunt pressures that are so commonly tied into secondary blitzes. Such stunt-beater concepts can also be easily tied into the zone-blitz concepts that were discussed in Chapter 2 concerning the pass attack of cover 3.

A stunt-beater route is, simply, a route within a pass pattern that the quarterback can scan (or go) to once he realizes that the pass coverage is four-across man and that the defense is utilizing some sort of frontal stunt. A stunt-beater route is a route that, by design, has the ability to effectively beat man-to-man-coverage techniques. A stunt-beater route may be a crossing drag-type route, a flat route, some form of a speed-out or square-out route, or a shallow route. Diagram 8-23 shows a shallow-cross route acting as a stunt-beater route, as part of a shallow-cross/curl-pass pattern.

Under Concept

The under concept presents an excellent underneath isolation of a wide receiver working underneath a clear route by the adjacent receiver to the inside versus four-across-man coverage. The clear route may very well get eaten up by the off-man coverage of the safety. However, the under route has an excellent opportunity to beat the man coverage by man-separating and maintaining such separation to the inside underneath the clear route by staying on the move. Diagram 8-24 shows an under-route isolation versus four-across-man coverage.

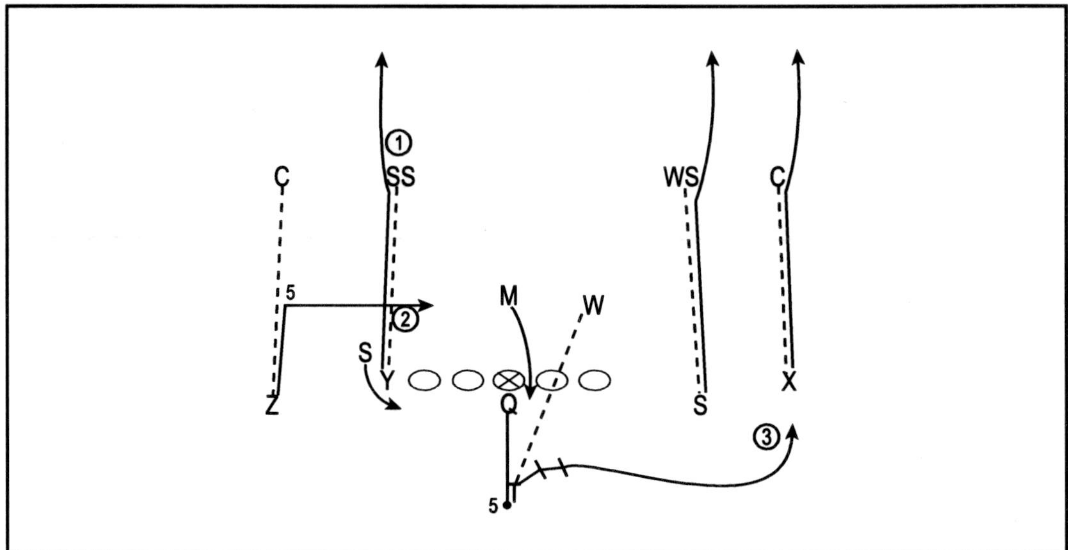

Diagram 8-24. Under concept versus four-across man

High-Low-Read Smash Isolation

The high-low-read smash isolation gives an offense an excellent ability to attack four-across man. The inside-receiver post-corner route must beat the off-man coverage. However, he does have a good amount of room to the outside to do so. When run as a hitch-option route, the smash route has the ability to beat the off-man coverage across the field to the inside or back outside to the sideline if the man-coverage cornerback overplays the inside break of the smash route. Such man-breaking action of the smash concept versus four-across man is shown in Diagram 8-25. As you progress to the utilization of the deeper and longer developing smash-route combination, the necessity for more protection time and (perhaps) maximum protections should become serious considerations.

Bunch-Formation Post-Corner Flood-Isolation Concept

A bunch-formation post-corner flood-isolation concept is an excellent way of attacking four-across man. You might normally think of flood action to overload zone coverages. However, the picking/crossing action of the post-corner bunch-flood concept helps to condense four-across man and actually outflank the coverage with the outside, man-breaking flood-route action, as shown in Diagram 8-26.

Post-Corner High-Low Isolation

A very similar concept to the smash high-low isolation versus four-across man is the post-corner high-low isolation. The post-corner isolation of the widest receiver helps to produce an excellent deep isolation versus four-across man, as shown in Diagram 8-27. This action gives the pass offense a chance to attack the coverage in the deep

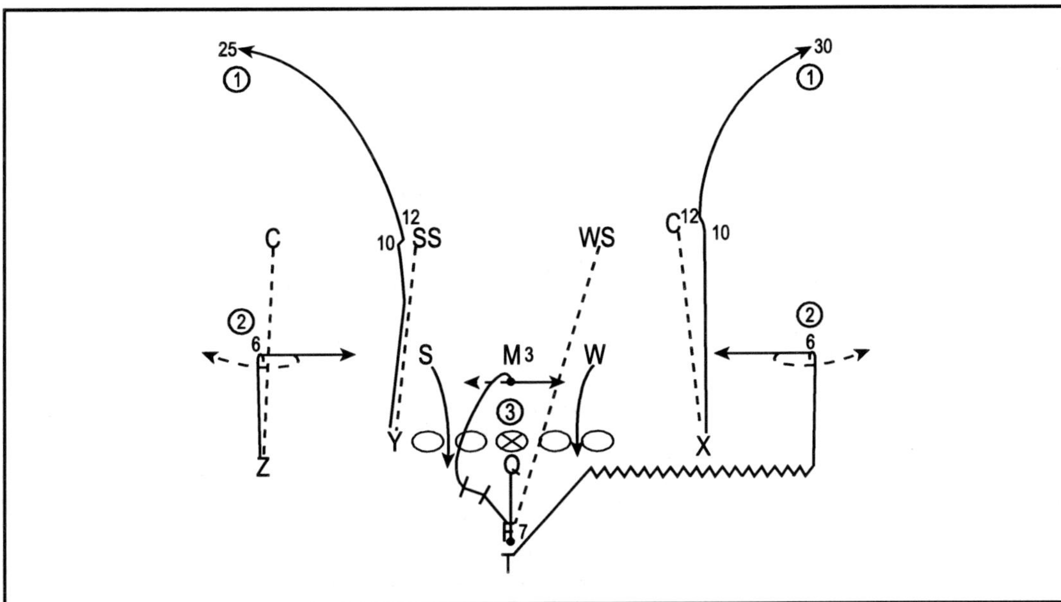

Diagram 8-25. Smash concept versus four-across man

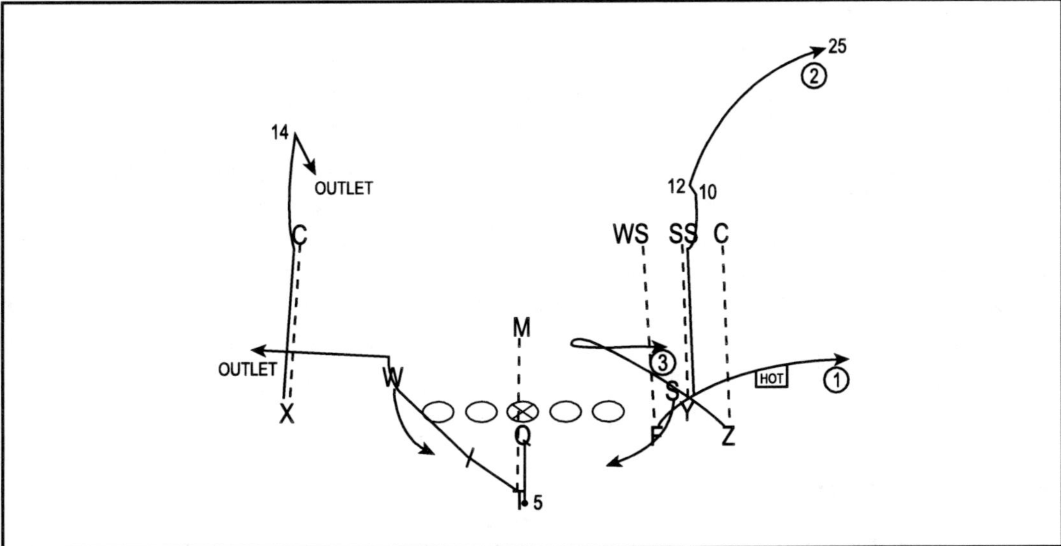

Diagram 8-26. Bunch-formation post-corner flood-isolation concept versus four-across man

outside zone. However, the offense must start thinking, at this point, that the slower-developing post-corner-route combination may have difficulty holding up to the potential of six-frontal-defender stunt action that is so often tied into four-across man. Maximum-protection schemes, such as the one shown in Diagram 8-27, should be given careful consideration for such longer-developing route actions.

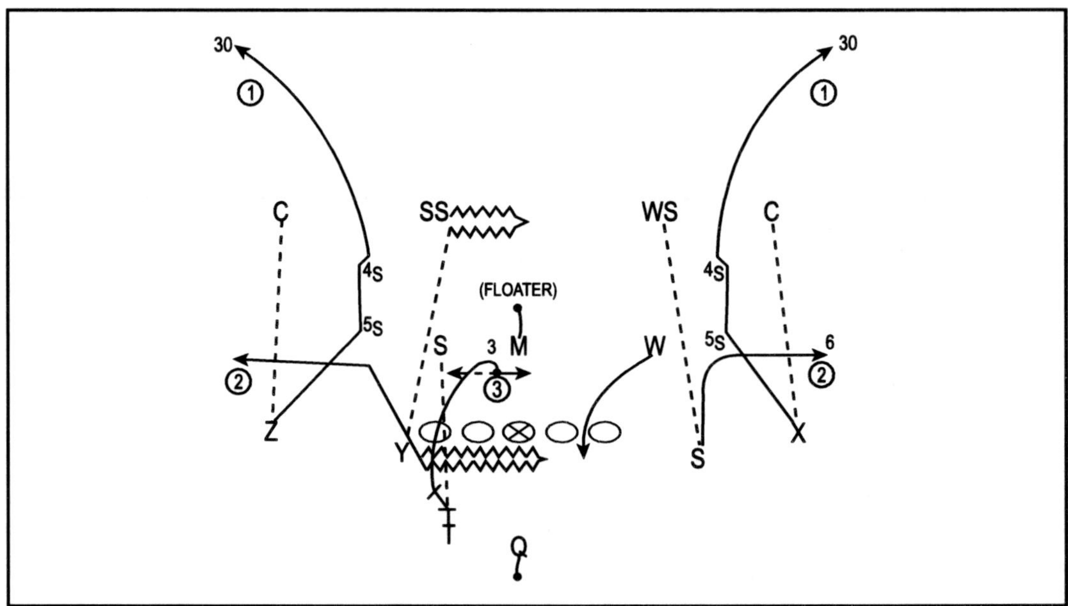

Diagram 8-27. Post-corner high-low isolation concept versus four-across man

Three-Tiered-Dig Concept

Versus four-across man, the three-tiered-dig concept is set up by having the wide receiver opposite the dig run through the middle of the field to open up a deep-middle void for the dig route to work into. This technique helps the dig receiver to focus on beating the one-on-one off-man coverage without having to worry about deep-middle-safety support. The major concern for the three-tiered-dig concept is, once again, the possible problem of lack of time due to the fact that four-across man is so heavily tied into heavy frontal-stunt pressures. Maximum pass protections should definitely be given consideration. Some offenses will adjust the depth of their dig routes to shorter 10- to 12-yard square-ins as a result. The quarterback must also realize that the tight-end (Y) crossing route can be an excellent stunt-beater route. The pattern concept versus four-across man with shortened square-in action is shown in Diagram 8-28.

Four-Streaks Concept

The four-streaks concept is a good way of attacking four-across-man coverage, especially when the off-man coverage starts to clamp down on underneath, control-pass-game completions. Since no middle, deep-zone safety help is available in cover zero, the quarterback is able to look for his best one-on-one isolation. The four-streaks concept versus cover zero is shown in Diagram 8-29.

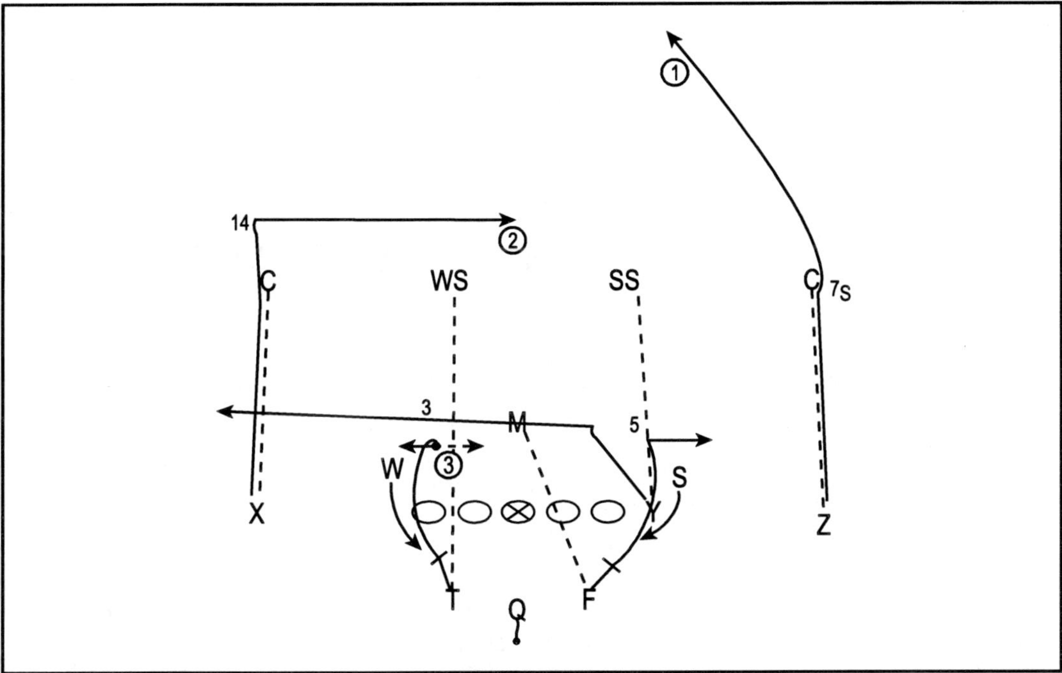

Diagram 8-28. Three-tiered X dig concept (with X square-in action) versus four-across man

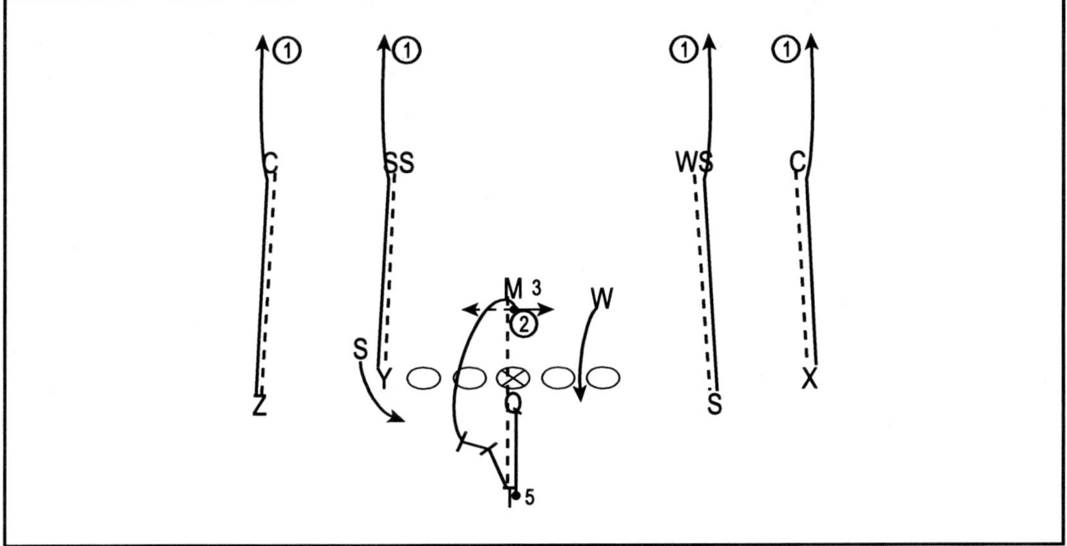

Diagram 8-29. Four-streaks concept versus four-across man

Rollaway/Acute Routes

Rollaway and acute routes are excellent isolation actions versus four-across man. These routes are especially effective when they develop off of strong streak-threat fakes pushing the four-across-man off-man-coverage cornerbacks deep. Rollaway/acute route action versus four-across man is shown in Diagram 8-30 from a four-streaks design.

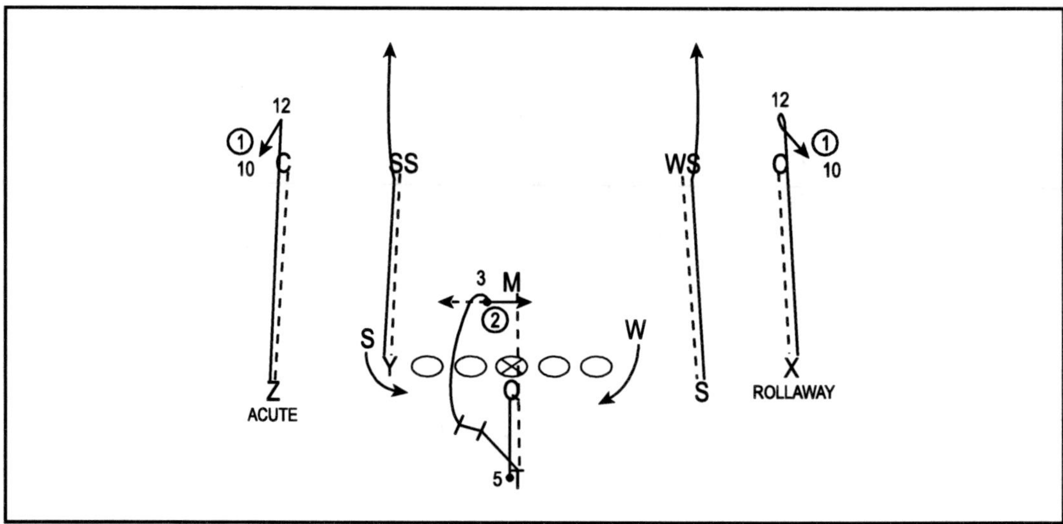

Diagram 8-30. Rollaway/acute routes versus four-across man

Speed-Outs

Speed-out routes can be very effective route concepts versus four-across man—especially when the cornerbacks are in deep off alignments. However, it is important to note that if speed-outs are called versus tighter off-man coverage, the speed-out routes must be adjusted to square-out routes "on the run," as shown in Diagram 8-31.

Switch Acute

The switch-acute concept can be an excellent concept versus four-across man. The switching action on the stem of the two receivers involved in the route combination helps to produce a crossing action. Such a crossing action can help combat the off-man coverage, as shown in Diagram 8-32 with sprint-out quarterback action. The sprint-out action of the quarterback and the frontside (or backside) gap protection can help to provide more time for the slightly slower-developing five-step-timed switch-acute pass-route combination.

Curl

The curl-route concept can be very effective versus four-across man—with or without flat-route thinking in combination. The key is the beating of the off-man coverage by the curl route. The receivers must learn to throw their defenders by them as they aggressively work back inside to the quarterback and "body up" on the ball. Curl-route action versus four-across man is shown in Diagram 8-33. The hook route, which is deepened curl-route action, can also be utilized in the attack of four-across man. Once again, however, is the concern for quicker throwing versus the frontal-stunt pressure so often associated with four-across man.

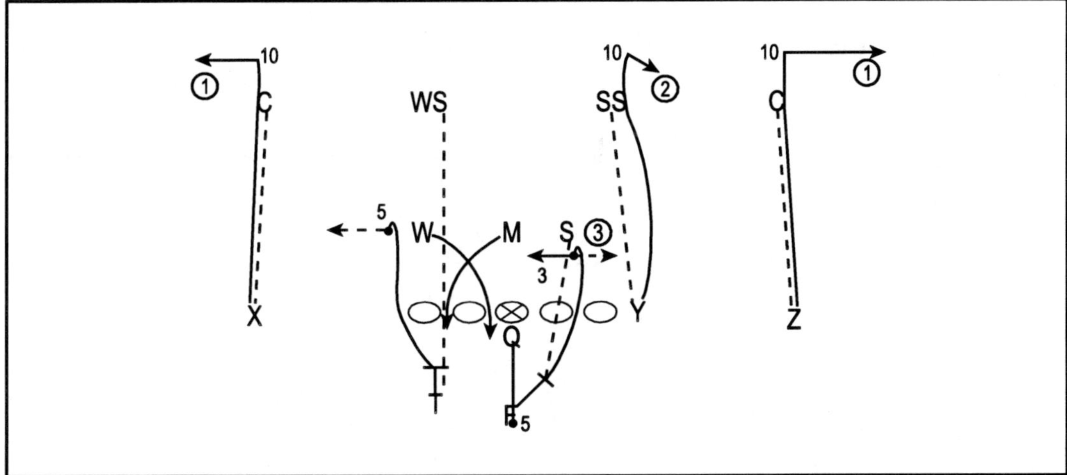

Diagram 8-31. Adjusting speed-outs into square-outs versus tightened off-man four-across-man techniques

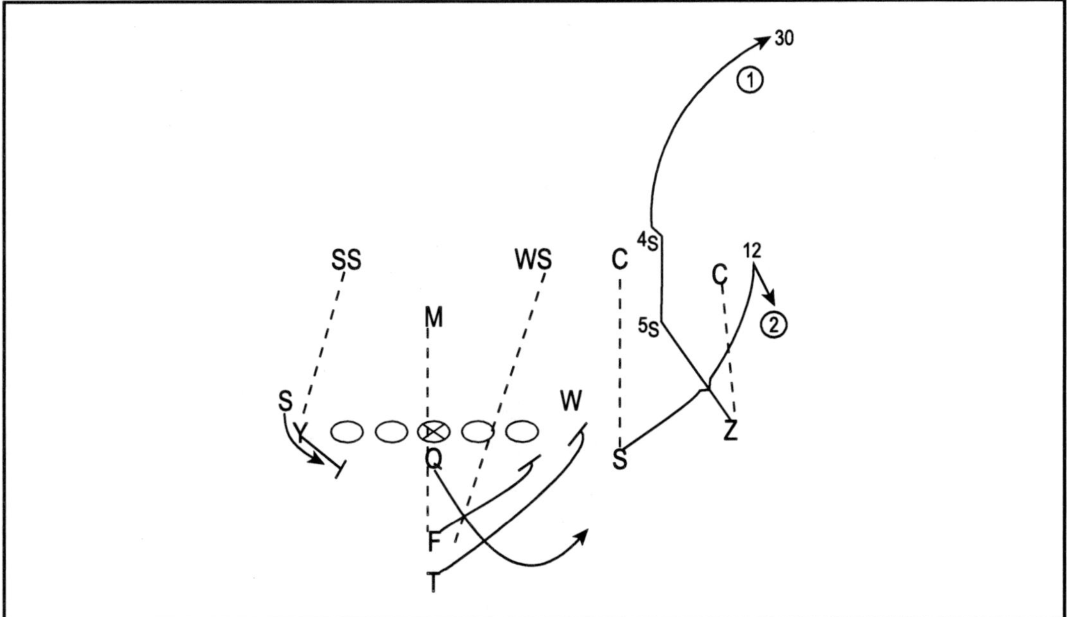

Diagram 8-32. Switch-acute-route combination versus four-across man

Diagram 8-34 shows sprint-out curl action versus four-across man. Note that the curl route must work to the outside if the pass is late-developing so that the receiver works in special coordination with the quarterback as the play takes more time to develop. Once again, sprint-out move action of the quarterback can help greatly to give more time for the quarterback to throw versus frontal-stunt pressures.

Square-In/Flat Combination

Many coaches prefer running square-ins versus four-across man rather than curls and hooks. The feeling is that the receiver has a better chance of producing man-to-man

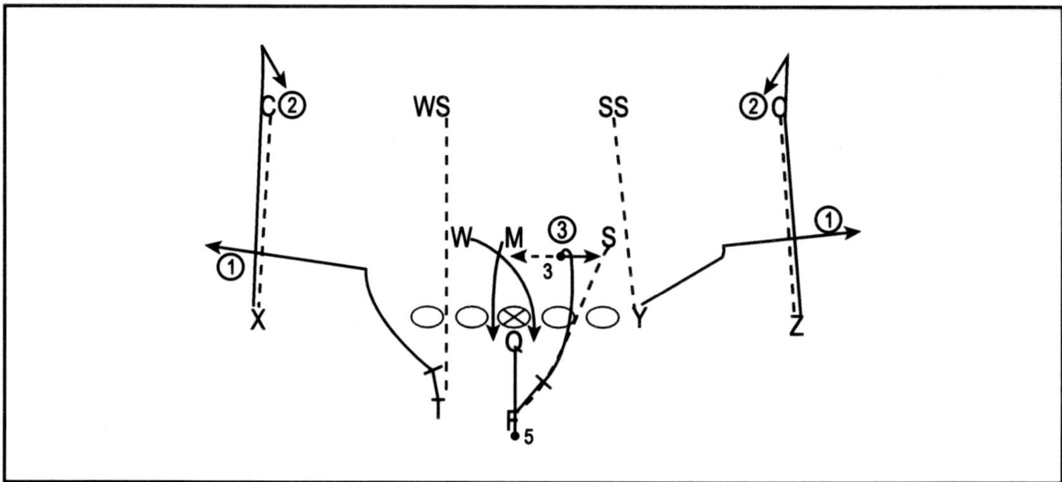

Diagram 8-33. Curl- route action versus four-across man

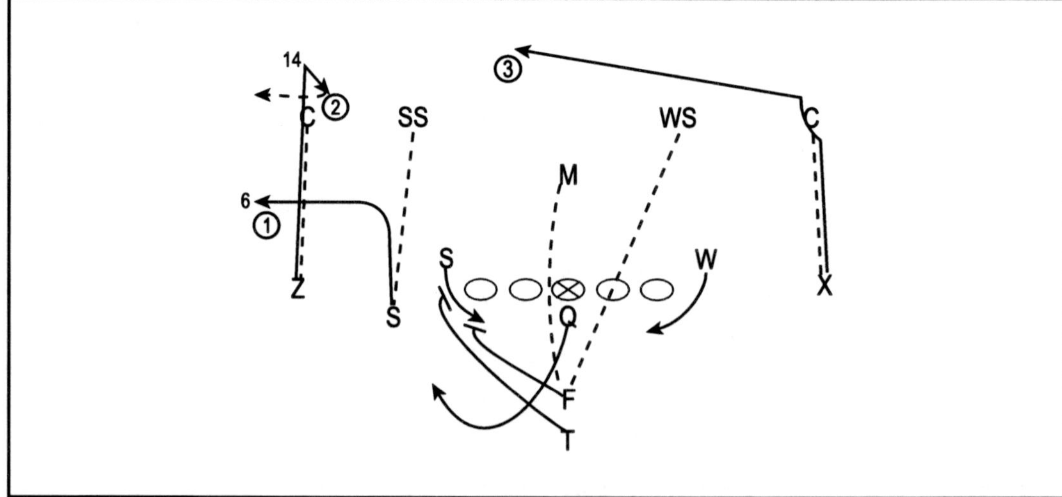

Diagram 8-34. Sprint-out curl action versus four-across man

separation versus the off-man coverage with square-in routes, as shown in Diagram 8-35. Diagram 8-36 shows double square-in action versus four-across man.

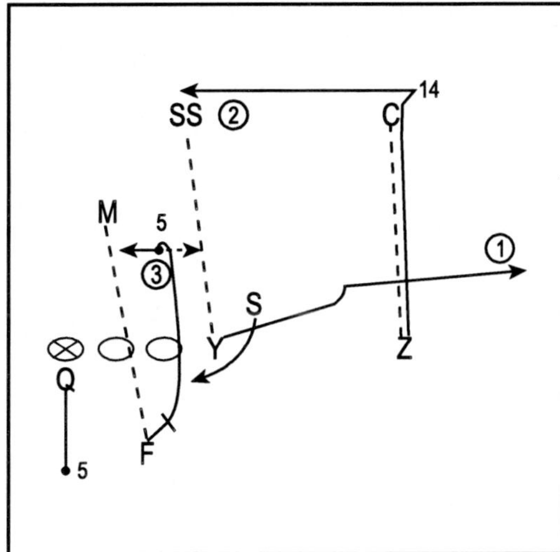

Diagram 8-35. Square-in/flat-route combination versus four-across man

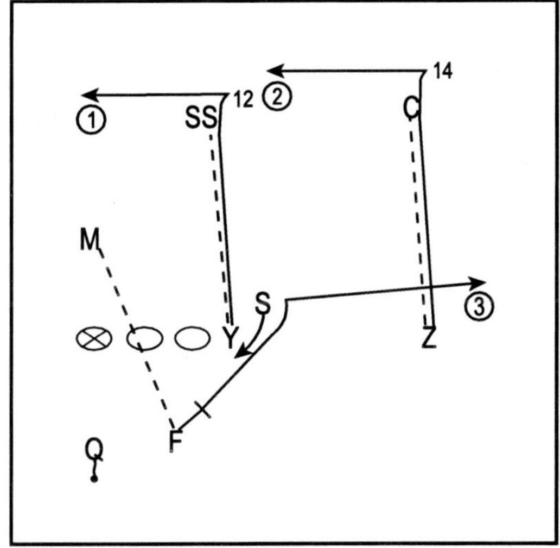

Diagram 8-36. Double square-in action versus four-across man

Shallow Cross/Replacement Curl

The shallow cross/replacement curl concept helps to produce an excellent crossing/picking action to attack four-across man. The inside, hard-breaking shallow route helps to produce an excellent man- and stunt-beater-type route. The replacement curl (replacing the original alignment of the outside receiver) has an excellent chance of man-separating to break back into the quarterback due to the crossing/picking action of the two receivers. The replacement curl is shortened to 10 yards to help produce consistent quarterback drop-timing. The shallow cross/replacement curl combination route concept versus four-across man is shown in Diagram 8-37.

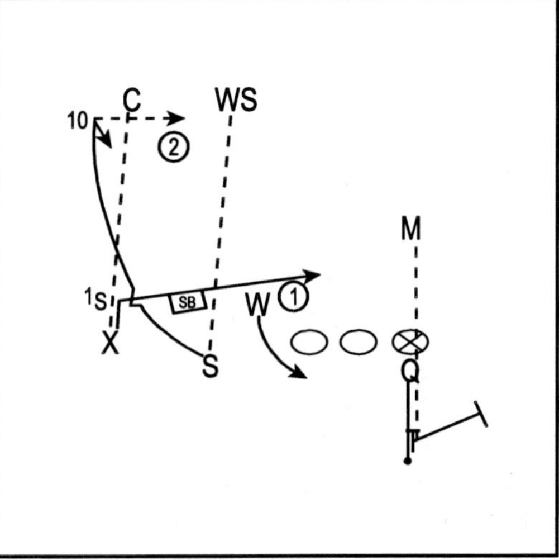

Diagram 8-37. Shallow cross/replacement curl concept versus four-across man

Curl/Hook/Square-In Routes as Outlets

Curls, hooks, and square-in routes can be very effective outlet routes to the backside of a pattern versus four-across man. Although such routes can have a tough time separating from the off-man coverage, those routes are often given more time to accomplish such tasks as a result of being outlets. Once such receivers are able to separate, they are given plenty of room to maneuver as they work across the field to the inside, as shown in Diagram 8-38.

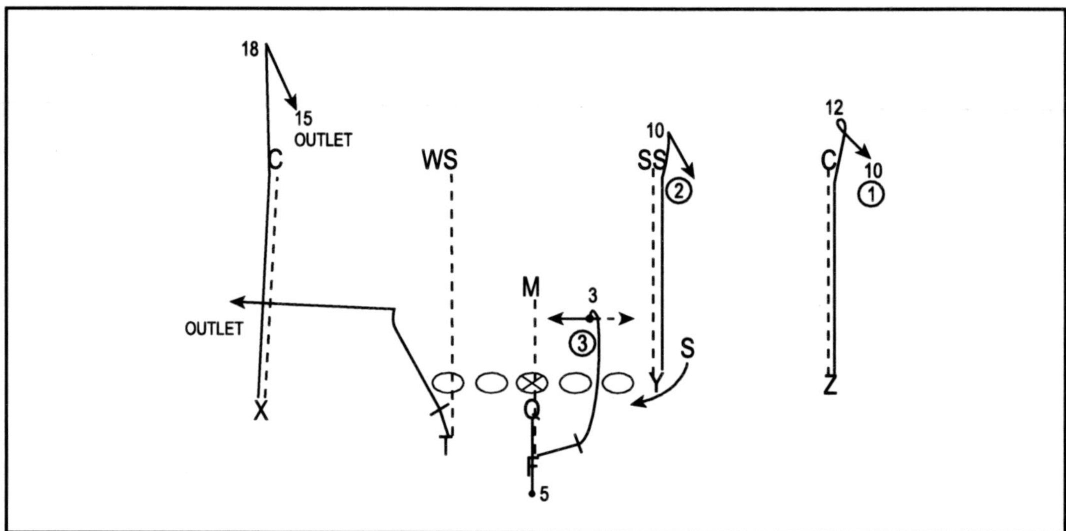

Diagram 8-38. Curls, hooks, and square-ins as backside outlets versus four-across man

Drive Concept

The drive concept helps to create three excellent man-to-man-coverage isolations on two of the inside four-across-man linebackers and a similar isolation on one of the cornerbacks. The drive route by one of the wide receivers is, in itself, an excellent man- and stunt-beater route. The tight-end (Y) short-dig route is an excellent man-beater route. The back, on his break-to-the-inside aspect of his sit route (which he must be sure to execute patiently to be sure to allow the execution of the tight end's short-dig route to be spaced in front of him), also presents an excellent man-beater route for the quarterback to go to, as shown in Diagram 8-39.

Cross Concept

The crossing-route action of the cross concept is an excellent four-across-man man- and stunt-beater action. As in the drive concept, the cross, short-dig, and man-adjustment aspects of the sit route help to create excellent man-under beater possibilities—and crossing receivers, themselves, are excellent man- and stunt-beater actions, as shown in Diagram 8-40 versus four-across man.

Texas Concept

The Texas concept helps to create a crossing isolation on two of the underneath-man-coverage four-across-man defenders. The tight end (Y) works to pin the strongside inside linebacker to the inside for his outside square-out-type man-break. The back drives to the flat to produce hard outside flow by his covering linebacker, and then works back inside hard underneath to separate from that linebacker. The major concern

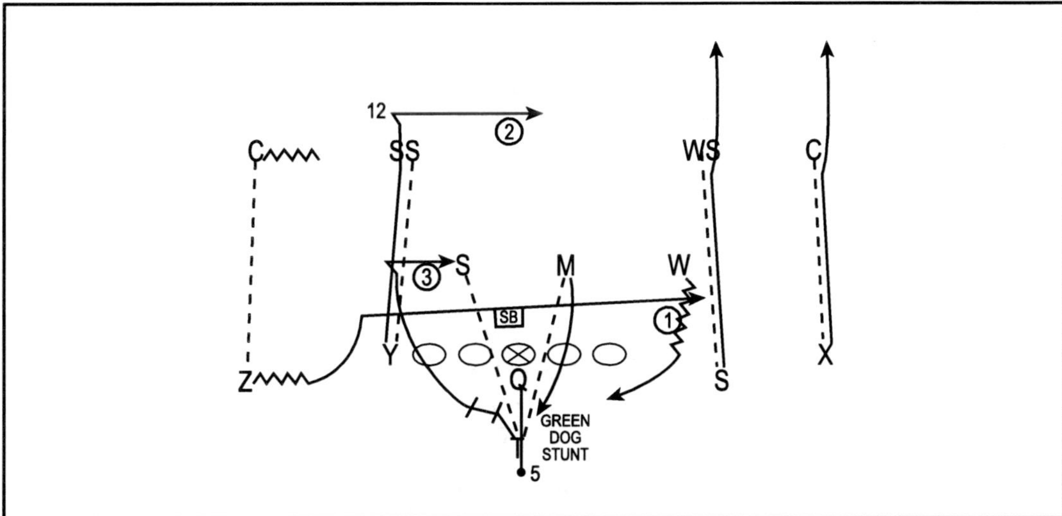

Diagram 8-39. Drive concept versus four-across man

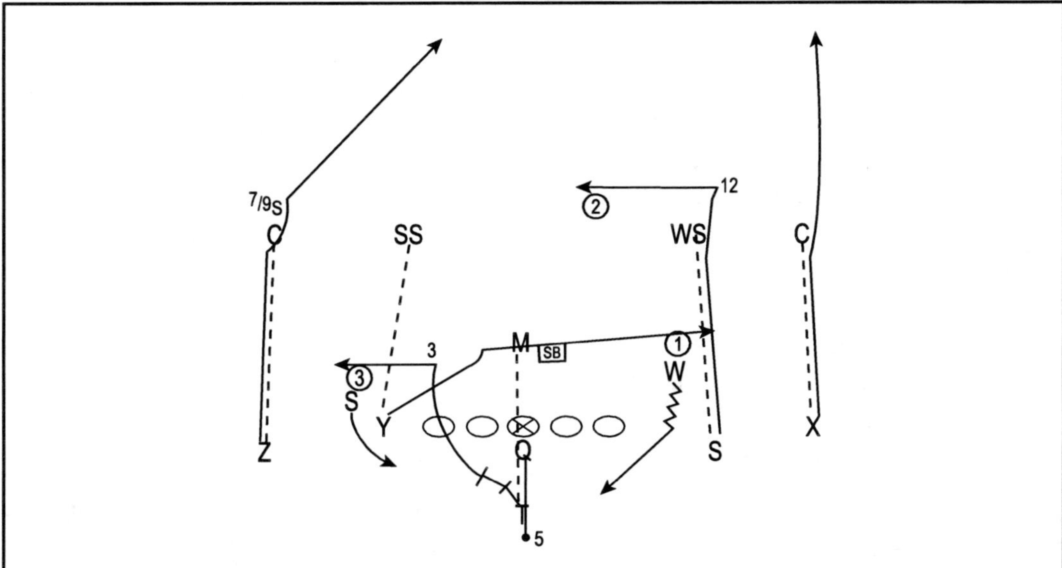

Diagram 8-40. Cross pattern versus four-across man

for the Texas concept versus four-across man is the associated frontal-pressure stunts that may be tied into four-across man. On his inside Texas release, the tight end (Y) can check for any quick (hot) dump-type pass action by the quarterback over a possible vacated strongside linebacker area. The Texas concept versus four-across man is shown in Diagram 8-41. Note that outside comeback-out routes are shown to act as excellent outside one-on-one outlet isolations versus four-across man.

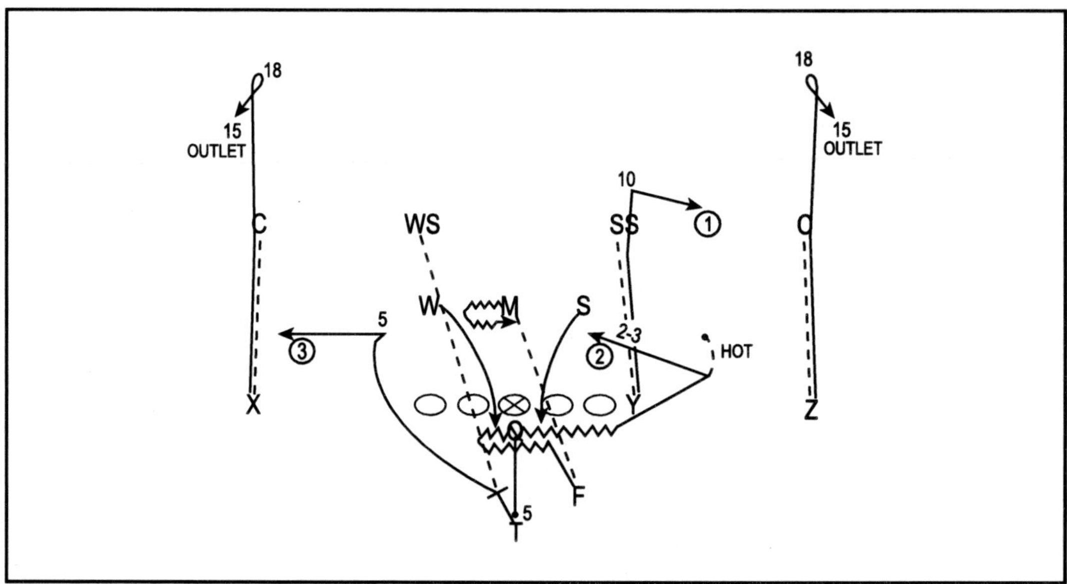

Diagram 8-41. Texas pattern versus four-across man

Option-Isolation Concept

Option-isolation routes help to produce excellent one-on-one isolations on four-across-man-under coverage defenders. Option routes can help to produce one-on-one size, talent, and speed mismatches. Option routes are best run off of five-step drop-timing by the quarterback. Five-step drop-timing by the quarterback allows for option routes run in the 8- to 12-yard range, giving the option-route receivers time to properly maneuver and execute their option-route man- or zone-separation techniques. Diagram 8-42 shows a tight-end (Y) option and a halfback (H) option versus four-across man. Note that to the outside of the option routes, deep rollaway and comeback-out routes are shown to act as excellent late-developing outlet routes versus four-across man.

Pivot- and Break-Route Isolations

Tight-end (Y) pivot- and break-route isolations can be very effective versus four-across man. Such routes can often help produce mismatches in favor of the offense—especially if the linebacker is bigger and more physical than the four-across man strongside safety who may be covering him.

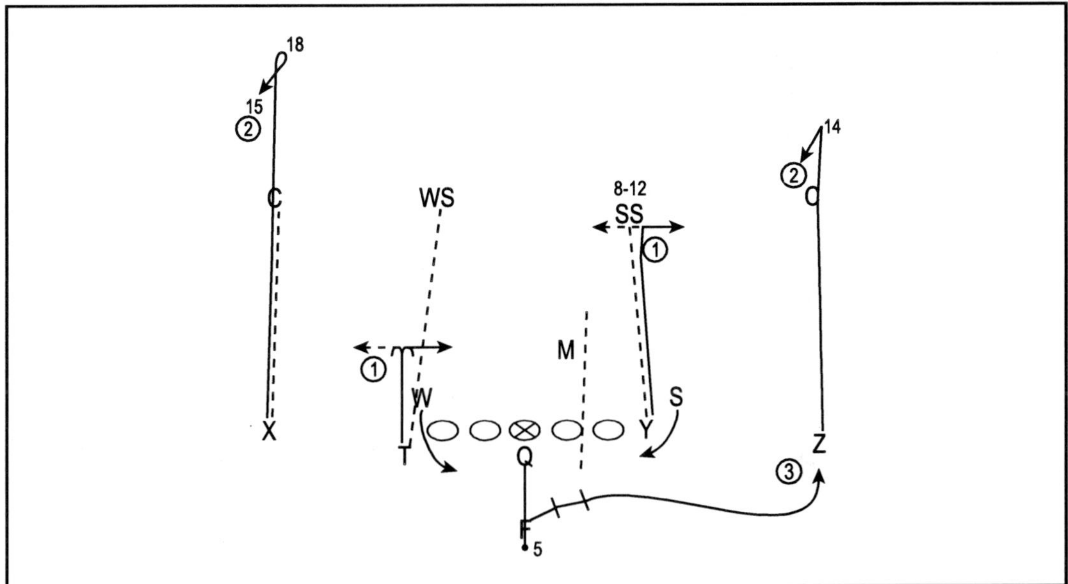

Diagram 8-42. Option-isolation routes versus four-across man

The pivot and break routes are run in the six- to seven-yard range. Versus a normal inside-out man-coverage alignment by the covering strong safety, the Y-pivot route may be the better route of the two, allowing the tight end to wall off the covering defender by alignment. However, versus an active, fast-flowing covering strong safety, the break route can help the tight end to separate by breaking back to the inside. Diagram 8-43 shows a Y-pivot high-low-read isolation action to attack four-across man.

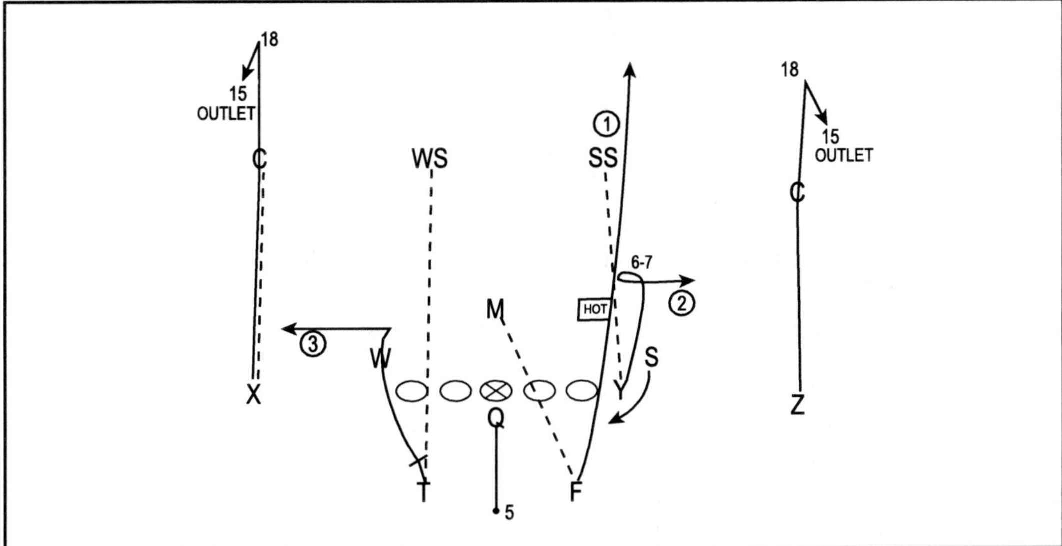

Diagram 8-43. Y-pivot isolation versus four-across man

Diagram 8-44 shows a Y-break action to attack four-across man. More often than not, the back's route becomes a clear-type route on both the Y-pivot and Y-break actions due to the fact that the back is not given the option to man-break to the inside since he has to start from a deepened backfield alignment.

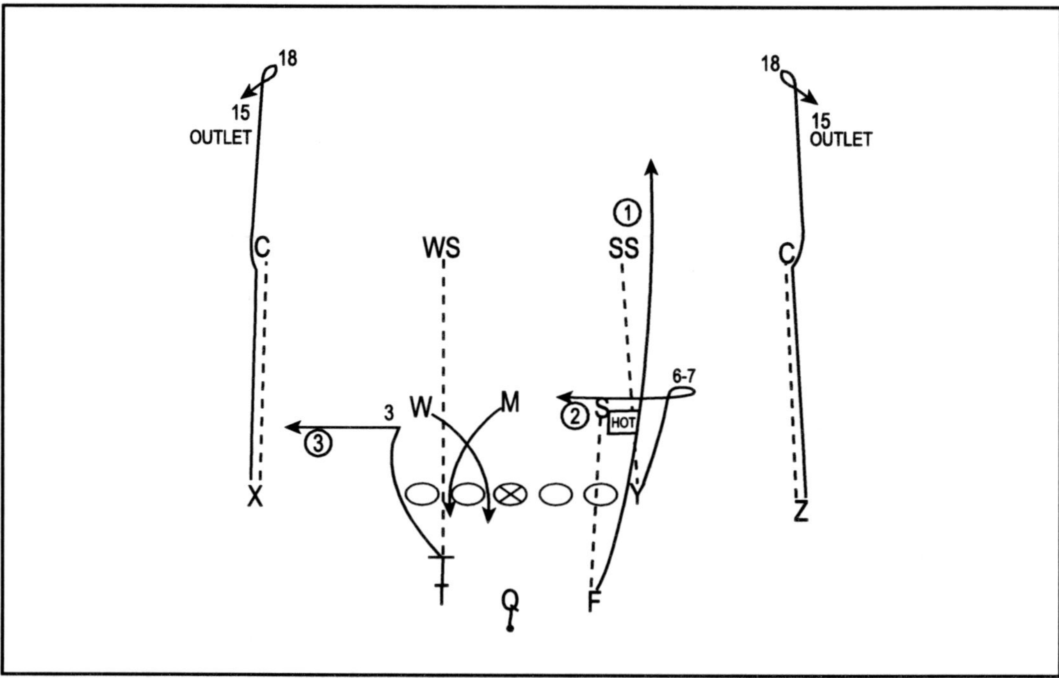

Diagram 8-44. Y-break isolation versus four-across man

Backs-Cross and Fake-Cross Isolations

Short inside backs-cross and fake-cross isolations can be very effective versus four-across man—even if man-to-man covering safeties are in off-coverage alignments. On backs cross, the quarterback reads the mesh of the crossing backs to see if one (or both) of the backs pop open versus the man-under coverage. If they don't, the tight-end route over the middle becomes the come-open-late route to go to. Between the crossing/picking action of the backs and the man-separating short-dig route of the tight end, it is likely that at least one of the three receivers will pop open. The backs-cross concept versus four-across man is shown in Diagram 8-45.

In backs-fake cross, the backs fake cross action once the linebackers start to play the cross action and man-break back out toward the sidelines. Again, the quarterback reads to see if one (or both) of the backs pop open. If not, the tight end's short-dig route then becomes the come-open-late route to go to. The backs-fake-cross concept versus four-across man is shown in Diagram 8-46.

Pick and Rub Concepts

Pick and rub concepts can be excellent four-across-man route combinations to beat the four-across-man coverage. Of course, any pick or rub must be legally executed. Receivers cannot run into and/or block coverage defenders as a part of the pick or rub concept. Diagram 8-47 shows a pick-route combination with an inside receiver working to the outside versus four-across man.

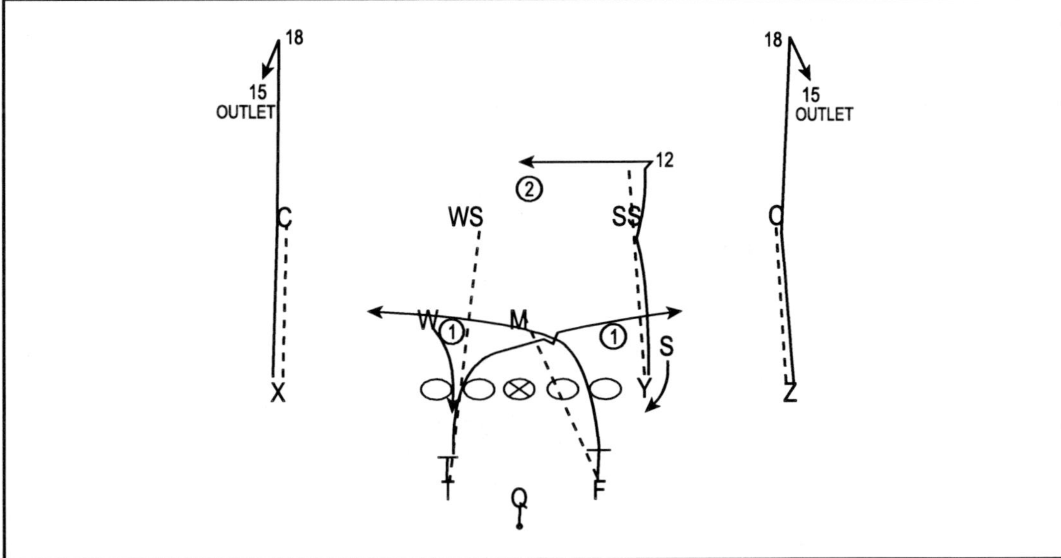

Diagram 8-45. Backs-cross concept versus four-across man

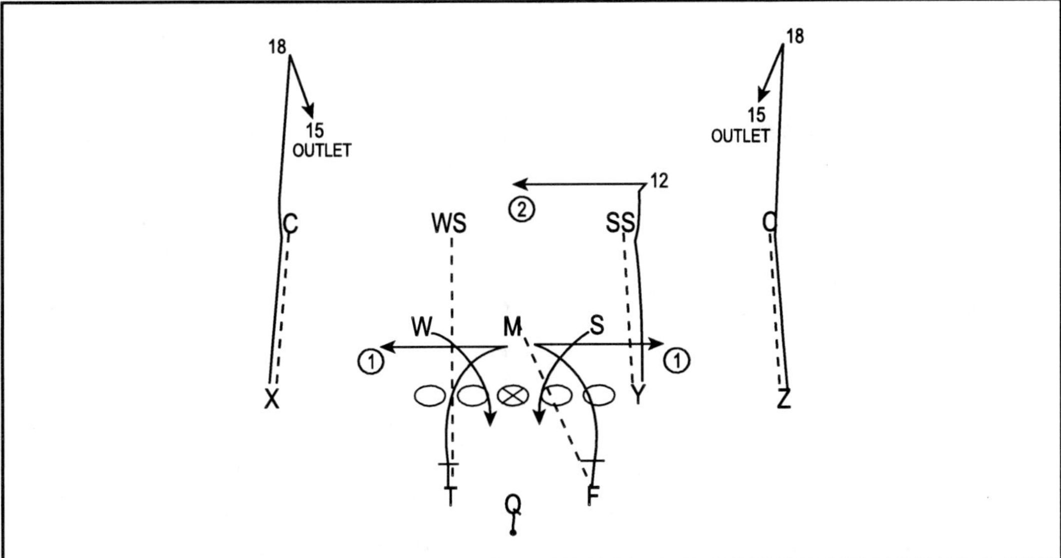

Diagram 8-46. Backs-fake-cross concept versus four-across man

An interesting idea is to have the receiver who actually sets up the pick for the prime pick, rub, or slice route run a modified option route if the quarterback snaps his eyes to that receiver. In this fashion, if the pick, rub, or slice receiver is covered, the quarterback has a delayed timed route to work to as an outlet. Diagram 8-48 shows a rub-route combination with an outside receiver working to the inside. Diagram 8-49 shows a slice-route combination with an inside receiver working off a pick set-up and executing a fade route.

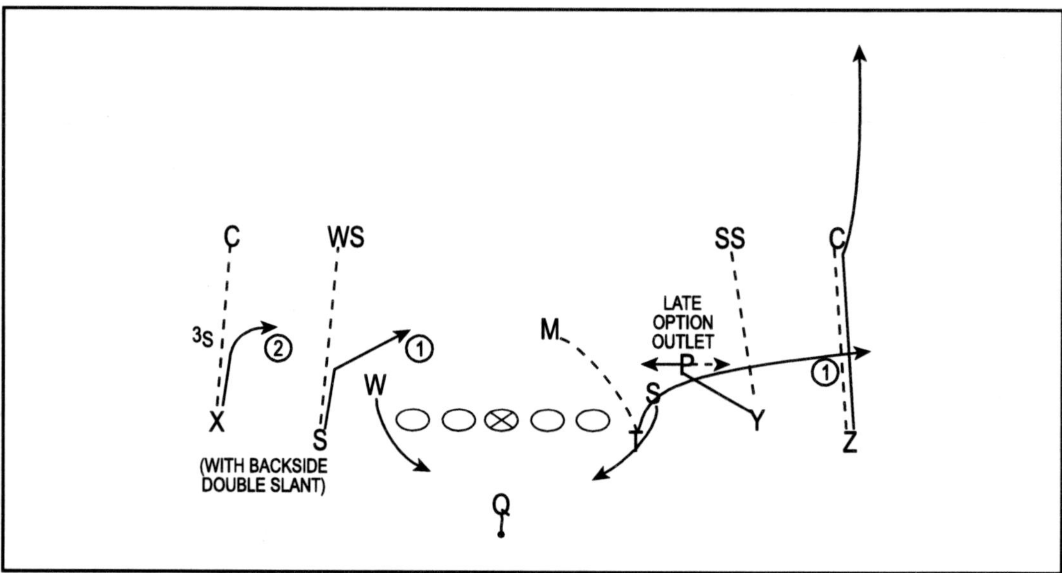

Diagram 8-47. Pick-route combination versus four-across man

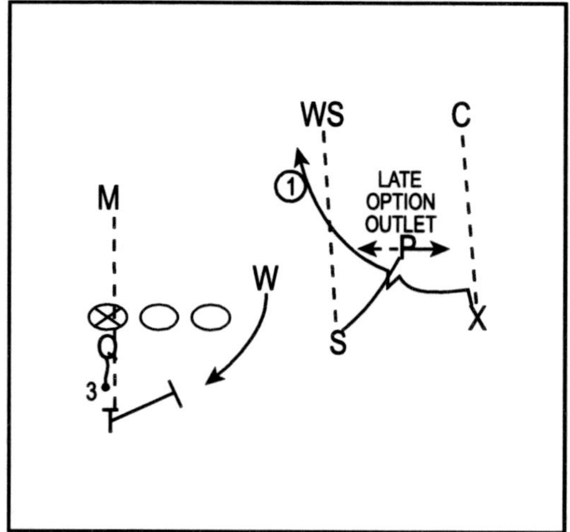

Diagram 8-48. Rub-route combination versus four-across man

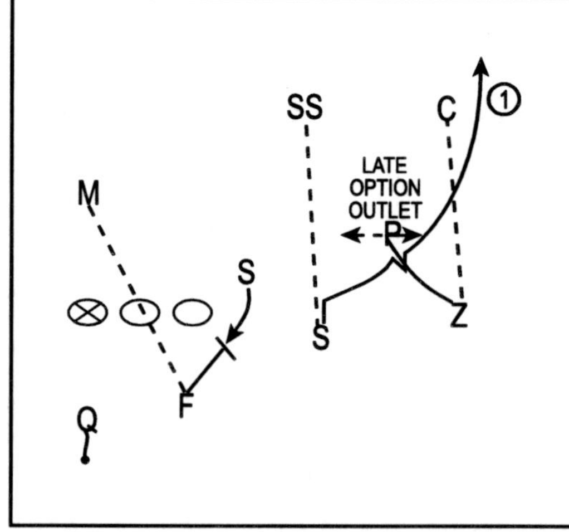

Diagram 8-49. Slice-route combination versus four-across man

Picking Screens

Picking screens, legal when the ball is thrown behind the line of scrimmage, is a very effective concept to use versus four-across man. Diagram 8-50 shows a double-screen action from a balanced doubles formation versus four-across man. The quarterback reads the rush of the end-of-line defender to the tight end (Y) side to see if he can throw a flare screen to the flaring back as the tight end (Y) actually blocks (picks) the strongside inside linebacker (such action is legal since the ball is thrown *behind* the line of scrimmage). The quarterback throws to the back if the end-of-line rusher rushes the quarterback. If the end-of-line rusher peels to the outside to cover the back, the quarterback works backside to throw to the picking split-end (Y) screen.

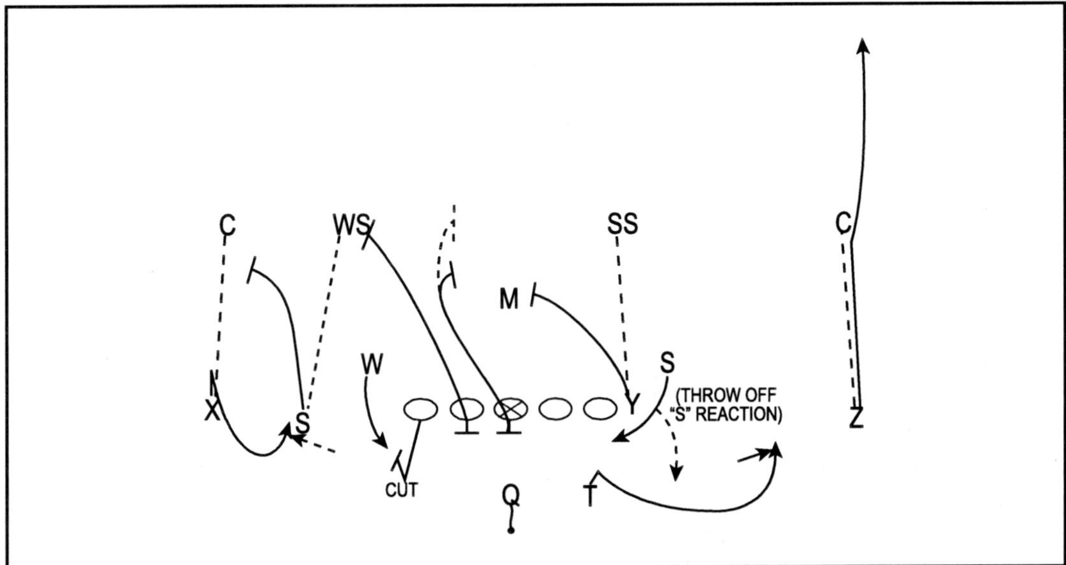

Diagram 8-50. Double screen with pick action versus four-across man

9

Pass Attack of Blitz-Man Coverage

Blitz-man coverage (or "three-across man," as it is also commonly called) is a man-to-man coverage that supports a secondary blitzer usually in combination with some form of frontal stunt. "Blitz" is a term used to signify pressure-type action from one of the secondary defenders (a cornerback or a safety). As a result, the three remaining secondary-coverage defenders man-to-man-cover three of the potential receivers. The front can now stunt up to five defenders with the two remaining frontal defenders man-to-man-covering the fourth and fifth potential receivers. Blitz-man coverage with a five-man frontal stunt is shown in Diagram 9-1.

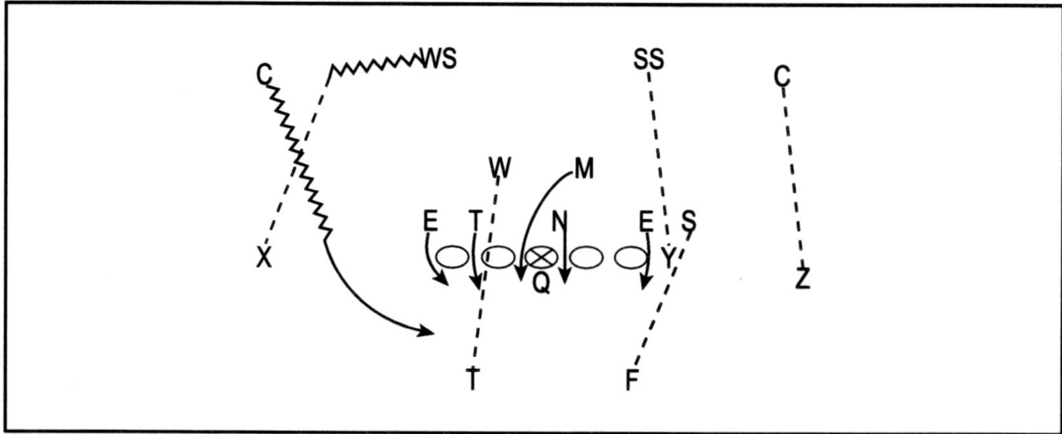

Diagram 9-1. Blitz-man coverage shown with a weak-corner blitz and linebacker stunt

The defense can stunt more than five frontal defenders when blitzing while using blitz-man coverage. However, this stunt can only be done at the expense of leaving one (or two) of the potential pass receivers uncovered.

Blitz-man coverage is normally played from off-man-coverage alignments. Since no deep-zone-coverage defender(s) are used (as you would find in man free or cover-2 man under) to back up the three remaining secondary-man-coverage defenders, most defenses will utilize off-man coverage techniques for the purpose of deep pass-completion prevention. Diagram 9-2 shows an outside weak-safety blitz in combination with a weakside frontal stunt. Diagram 9-3 shows a strong-safety blitz in combination with a strongside frontal stunt. Field (or strongside) cornerback blitzes are rare, due to the great distance the field that the strongside cornerback has to cover to get to the quarterback on blitz action.

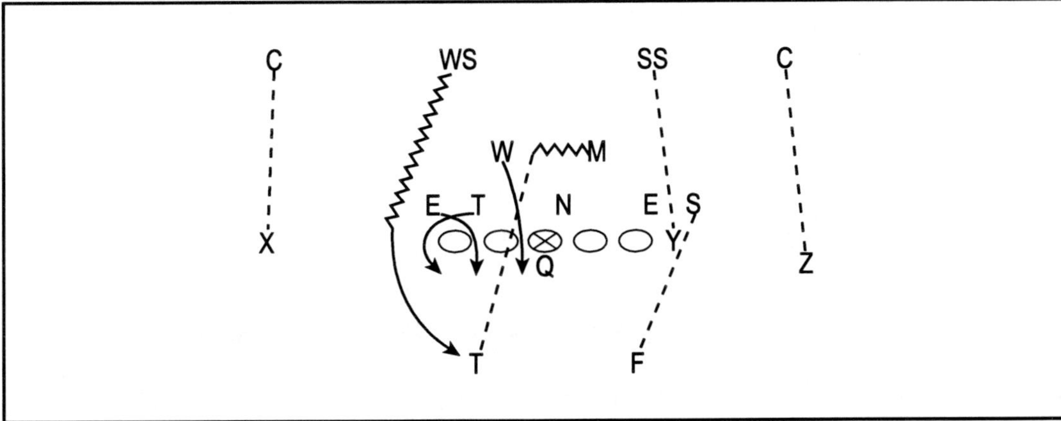

Diagram 9-2. Blitz-man coverage shown with a weak-safety blitz outside and a weak-linebacker stunt inside

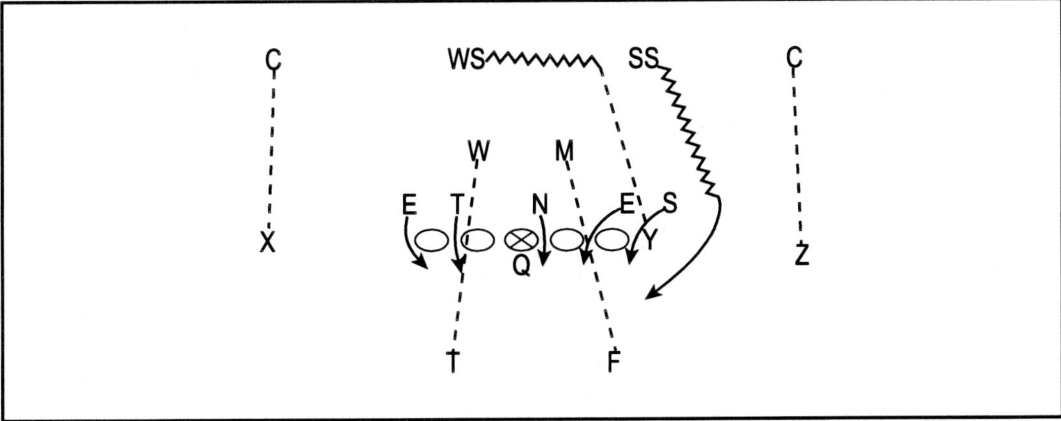

Diagram 9-3. Blitz-man coverage shown with a strong-safety blitz outside and a strongside linebacker stunt outside

Blitz-Man Pass-Coverage Strengths

- Blitz-man coverage blends efficiently with secondary blitz action and frontal stunts of up to five frontal defenders. With the coverage of two of the remaining frontal defenders, all five potential receivers of the offense can be covered man-to-man.
- The blitz-man-coverage defenders easily fit to any offensive formation, shift, and motion variations.
- The off-man-to-man-coverage techniques help the blitz-man-coverage defenders to prevent from getting beat deep.
- The deepened off-man-to-man-coverage techniques of blitz-man coverage defenders help to make up for the fact that the coverage has no deep-zone safety help to help back it up.
- The off-man-to-man-coverage techniques of blitz man help the coverage take on a "bend-but-don't-break" philosophy, which can be true even though a secondary blitzer and as many as five frontal defenders may be involved in some form of a pressure stunt with only five defenders left to cover man-to-man.
- Blitz-man coverage does have the flexibility of press-man-covering specific receivers. The concern here is the lack of any deep backup coverage to support such press-coverage alignments and techniques.

Blitz-Man Coverage Pass-Game Weaknesses

- Since blitz-man coverage is tied into secondary blitz and heavy frontal-stunt activity, good blitz-beating pass actions can be very effective, which can be true whether the offense is using quick, blitz-beater-type routes and patterns, hot- and sight-adjust-route concepts, or maximum protections. Diagram 9-4 shows a frontside shallow-cross-route pattern to help provide an excellent blitz-beater route in the form of the shallow-cross route.
- Throwing quickly is, perhaps, the best way to beat blitz with frontal-stunt pressure. Whether it is the quick-pass game, the use of hot or sight-adjust routes, or any other form of throwing quickly, getting a pass off before the rush pressure can get to the quarterback is one of the best ways of defeating blitz-man coverage and its related blitz and frontal-stunt pressures.
- Quick-game isolations—such as slants, inside receiver speed-outs, and hitches—can all be very effective versus blitz-man off coverage. The quick-game pass package is an excellent blitz-beater package in general. Even if the defense decides to press cover, fade-adjustment routes become extremely effective weapons. Tell your quarterbacks to never check out of quick-game-pass action. He may signal for a better route isolation (i.e., fade). However, he should be told to never check out of the quick-pass game versus blitz because the quick-pass game *is* blitz-beater action.

- Hot-route concepts can effectively help control (and beat) the execution of blitz-man coverage and the blitz and frontal stunts that may be associated with it. Diagram 9-5 shows a strongside back's hot-route action to control a strongside strong-safety blitz and inside-linebacker stunt.
- Sight-adjust route concepts can be extremely effective in helping to combat blitz-man coverage with its secondary-blitz action. On sight-adjust action, receivers adjust

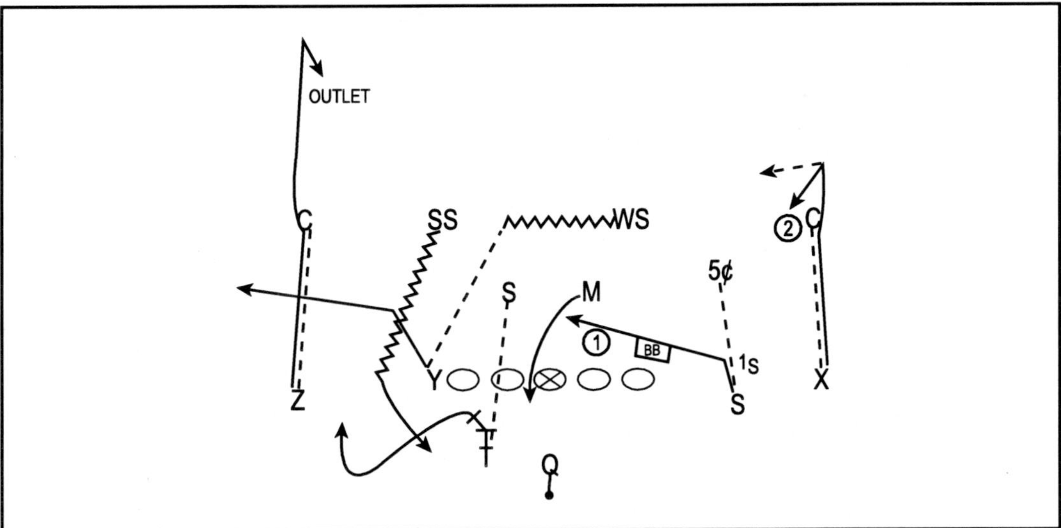

Diagram 9-4. Using shallow-cross route to combat blitzes and blitz-man coverage

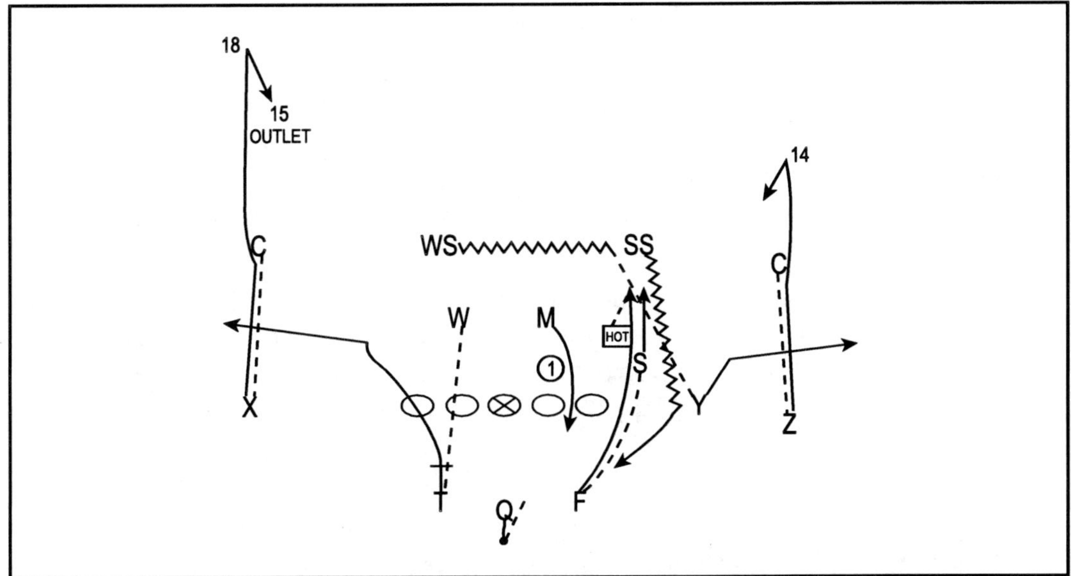

Diagram 9-5. Hot-route action of strongside back versus an inside-linebacker stunt and strong-safety blitz with blitz-man coverage

their normally deeper five- to seven-step-timed routes to slants, one-step hitches, or fade routes upon seeing (sighting) a secondary blitz unfold in front of them. The quarterback also sights the blitz action and adjusts to make the quick sight-adjust throw. Sight-adjust action is shown in Diagram 9-6 in which the split-end (X) receiver sight-adjusts to a slant route versus a weak-safety blitz.

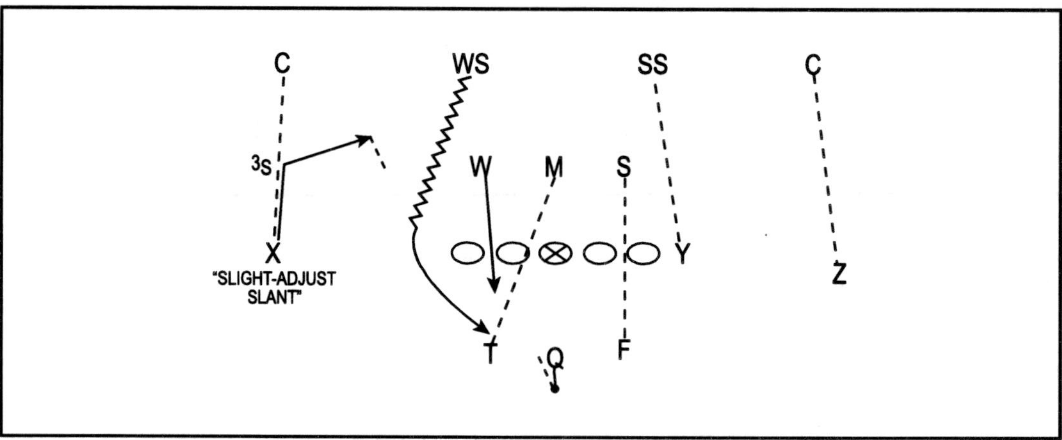

Diagram 9-6. Split-end (X) sight-adjustment action versus weak-safety blitz and blitz-man coverage

- Two of the most basic premises of attacking man-to-man coverage holds true for the attack of blitz-man coverage: isolate and cross. In both concepts, it's extremely important for the receivers to man-separate and then to be sure to maintain such separation from the man-to-man coverage.
- Beating off-man coverage can easily lead to big gains. A major reason for this is that the other coverage defenders may be chasing/covering other receivers. As a result, the area around the receiver making the reception may be well cleared out, allowing the receiving ballcarrier to run for big gains. In addition, with no deep-zone safety behind the blitz-man coverage, no deep help is available to support receptions by the receivers.
- The total man-coverage design can only be as strong as the weakest man-coverage defender, much as a chain is only as strong as its weakest link. An offense can quickly focus on attacking (or isolating) the weakest man-coverage defender(s).
- Quarterback-move action can greatly help a pass offense to combat the blitz and corresponding frontal-stunt action associated with blitz-man coverage. Moving the quarterback—especially away from the blitz/stunt action—helps to disturb the stunt execution of the front and helps the quarterback to move away from one side of the front's rush. Being able to check to a sprint-out pass to the fieldside, or to the weakside, versus a team that is predominantly a weakside (or strongside) blitz team can be a very effective offensive anti-blitz weapon. Diagram 9-7 shows weakside

quarterback-sprint-action to combat a strong-safety blitz/stunt action by the defense and its blitz-man coverage.

- The off-man-to-man-coverage techniques of blitz man can be extremely vulnerable to outside acute, rollaway, and comeback-out routes off of deep-streak-threat action. The quarterback can definitely think about making maximum-pass-protection calls when he sees such good one-on-one isolation throws versus the blitz so that he can get the time to effectively get his pass off.
- Outs (square-outs) can be very effective versus blitz-man coverage—especially when executing such square-out routes by inside receivers.
- The off-man-coverage techniques of blitz-man coverage can be extremely susceptible to deep, double-move-type route isolations, which is true whether the double-move action is off of quick-game three-step drop-timed routes (quick hitch, slants, speed-outs) or five-step drop-timed routes (outs, flats, curls, rollaways). The concern, however, is the protection time that may be needed to allow the quarterback to get a double-move pass off, which is especially true for five-step-timed double-move routes.
- Underneath-smash isolations and under-route isolations offer the offense quick, inside crossing routes to help beat the off-man coverage of blitz man .
- Option-isolation routes (Y-options, H-options, slot-options) can help to exploit possible one-on-one mismatches in favor of the offense in the attack of blitz-man coverage. The receivers, however, must see the blitz threat as it develops and run such option routes with great urgency. Protection here is, again, a serious concern.
- Post-corner isolations—by both outside- and inside-aligned receivers—can help to exploit the one-on-one off-man outside coverage of blitz-man coverage. Such deep

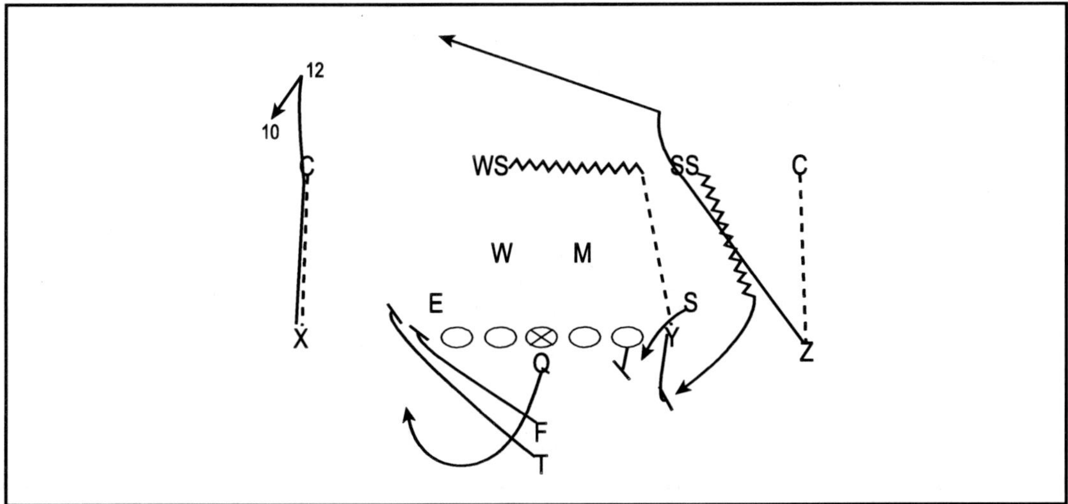

Diagram 9-7. Sprint-out action to combat a strong-safety blitz and blitz-man coverage

post-corner-isolation action by an inside receiver to the outside (as well as the excellent underneath lateral dragging action of the smash route versus the off-man coverage) is shown in Diagram 9-8 with a maximum-pass-protection-block scheme. It must be kept in mind that due to the longer-developing prime-pass routes, the offense does have to account for the possibility of extra pass-protection needs versus the blitz and corresponding frontal-stunt combinations associated with the blitz-man coverage. In addition, the underneath lateral dragging action of the smash route can help the quarterback "get-off-the-hook" by acting as an excellent blitz-beater route.

- Although definitely not a blitz-beater route, or route-combination thought, deeper digs and square-ins can help to isolate the off-man coverage and utilize the deeper crossing actions of such routes, which is especially true, since no deep-zone safety help is available in the middle for blitz-man coverage. Versus the blitz and (possibly) the heavy frontal-stunt-pressure possibilities, maximum-pass-protection schemes should be strongly considered, due to the pass-protection time needed for such longer-developing routes. Diagram 9-9 shows a flanker (Z) square-in route-pattern principle with a maximum-pass-protection design to combat the inside strong-safety blitz.
- Cross-the-field route actions, such as drives and drag routes, can be very effective blitz-man-coverage underneath-isolation routes to help act as blitz-, stunt-, and man-to-man-beater routes. Such routes have much (or all) of the entire width of the field to beat the off-man coverage and get open to receive a pass.

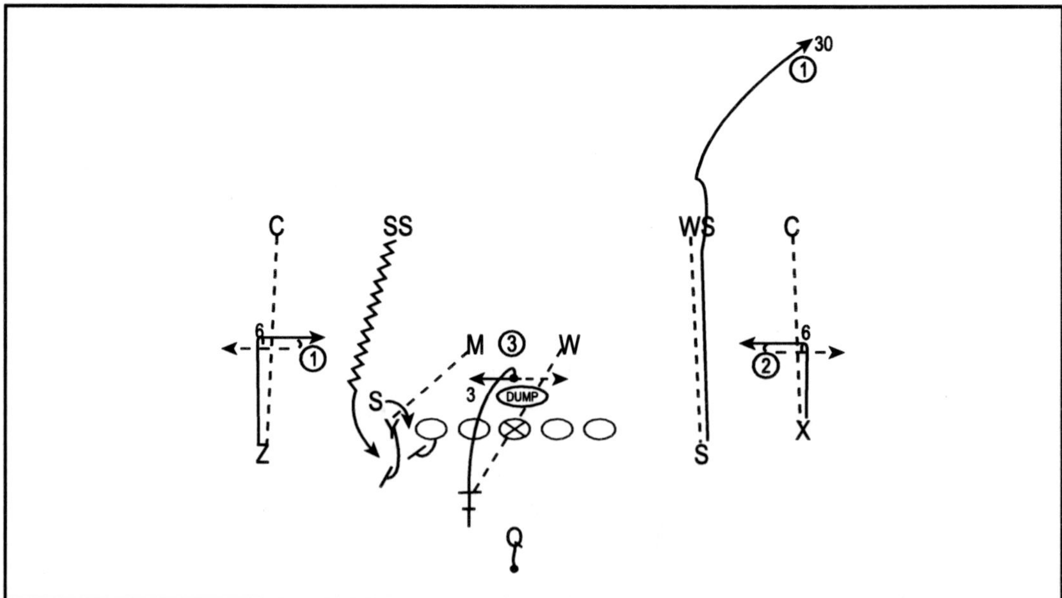

Diagram 9-8. Smash-pattern attack of blitz-man-coverage outside voids plus underneath smash-route drag action

- Crossing action is an excellent way to attack the off-man aspect of blitz-man coverage. The cross routes, themselves, help to provide the quarterback with excellent blitz-beater routes.
- Picks and rubs can be excellent routes combinations to attack blitz-man coverage. The concern for such picks and rubs may be the depths of the defensive backs' off alignments. Of course, such pick and rub action must all be executed off of legal picking action. A fullback pick route from a bunch set is shown in an effort to combat blitz action and blitz-man coverage in Diagram 9-10.

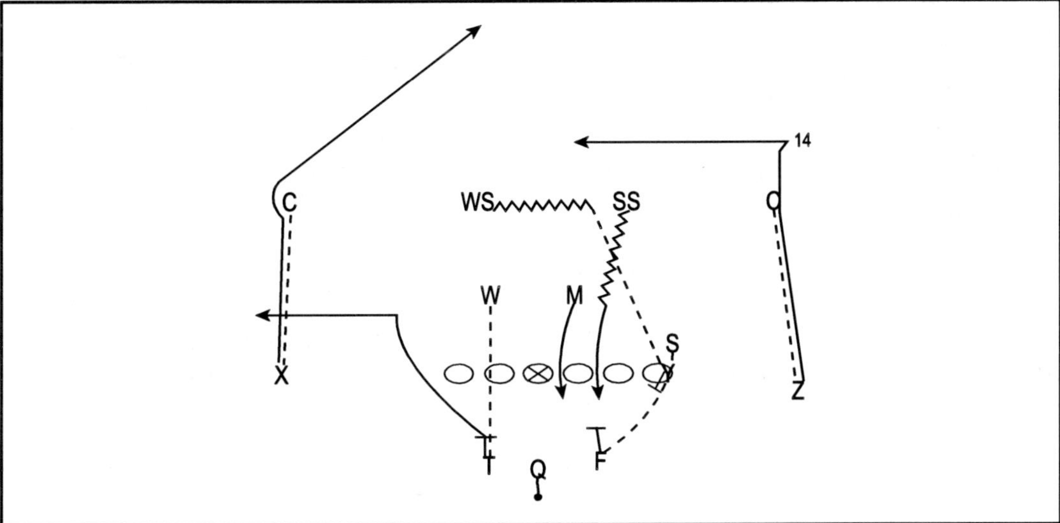

Diagram 9-9. Flanker (Z) square-in pattern versus blitz man with maximum-pass-protection design for the strong-safety blitz

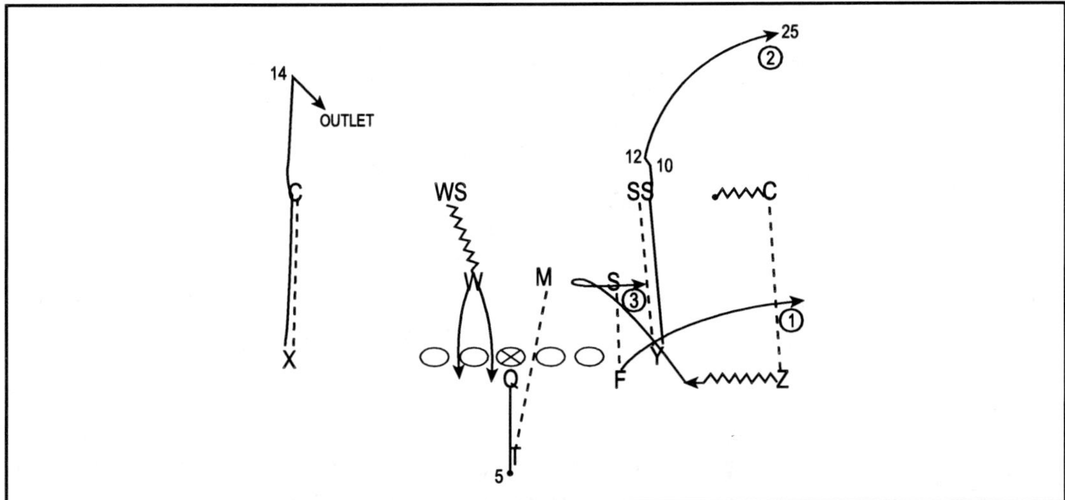

Diagram 9-10. Fullback pick action from a bunch set versus blitz and blitz-man coverage

- Picking screens thrown to backs and receivers behind the line of scrimmage can also be very effective in defeating the off-man aspect of blitz-man coverage and its related blitzes and stunts.

Route Combinations and Pass-Pattern Attack of Blitz Man

Quick-Game Hitch/Fade

The quick-game hitch route is a very effective quick-game-pass concept versus blitz-man coverage (as are most of the concepts of the quick-pass game in the effort to beat the blitz by throwing quickly). One of the best ways to beat frontal-stunt pressure is to throw the ball quickly before the rush can get to the quarterback. As a result, the quick-pass game provides an offense with a natural blitz-beater package.

The hitch receiver works hard to produce a six-yard hitch stem off of a streak threat to push the off-man coverage defender deep. Since defenses may try to aggressively jump the wide receivers with press coverage, the hitch's fade-adjustment aspect can help to exploit the weakness of such press coverage with a deep-fade throw. Quick-game hitch/fade action versus blitz-man coverage is shown in Diagram 9-11.

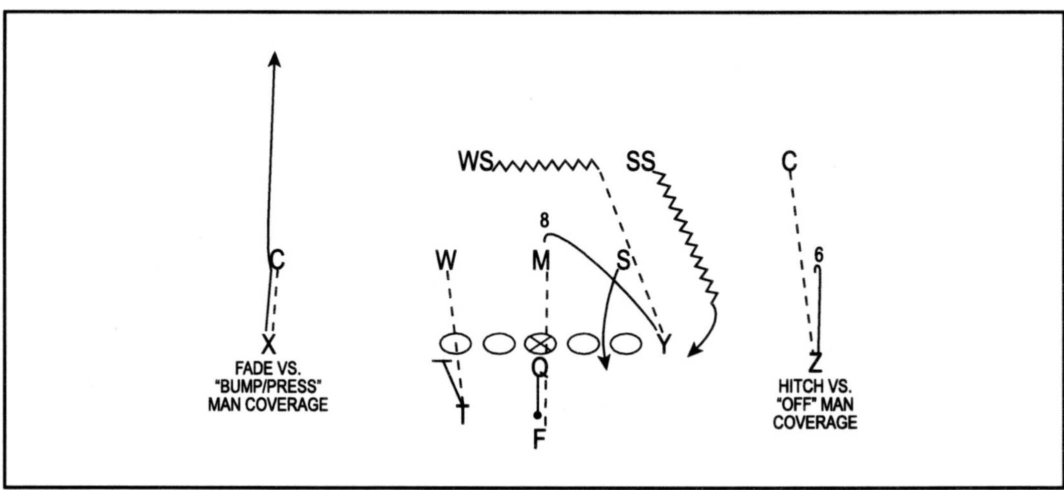

Diagram 9-11. Quick-game hitch/fade route versus blitz-man coverage

Quick-Game Slant

Slant-route isolations and double-slant actions can be very effective versus blitz-man coverage. Once the quarterback and receivers recognize blitz-man coverage, they should be thinking blitz pressure with the possibility of related frontal-stunt action. The slant receiver must initially be sure to attack the technique of his man-covering defender, even though that defender will probably be in an off-position alignment. The slant receiver then breaks his slant action hard to the inside to get separation and stay on the move at top speed to be sure to maintain such man-separation. Slant and double-slant action versus blitz-man coverage is shown in Diagram 9-12.

Diagram 9-13 shows slant/arrow action versus blitz-man coverage. The crossing action of the slant and arrow routes can help to actually produce a quick crossing action of the two routes helping to free one route or the other versus the man coverage (whether it is off-man coverage or press-man coverage).

Quick-Game Speed-Out

The quick-game speed-out route can be an excellent concept versus the loose off-man coverage of blitz-man coverage. This route is shown in Diagram 9-14.

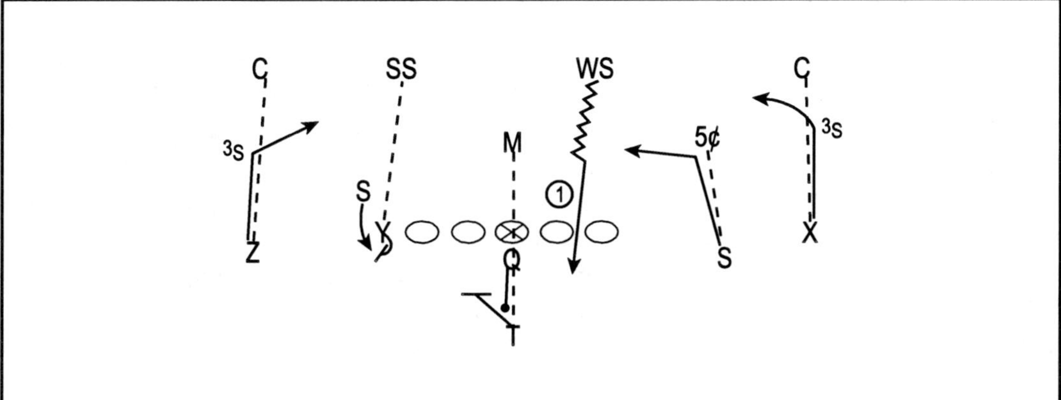

Diagram 9-12. Quick-game slant-route and double-slant-route action versus blitz-man coverage

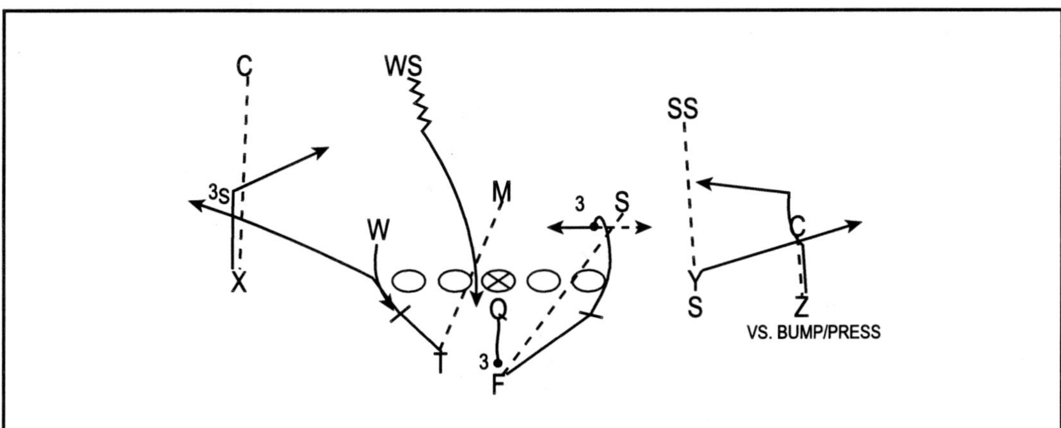

Diagram 9-13. Quick-game slant/arrow route combination versus blitz-man coverage

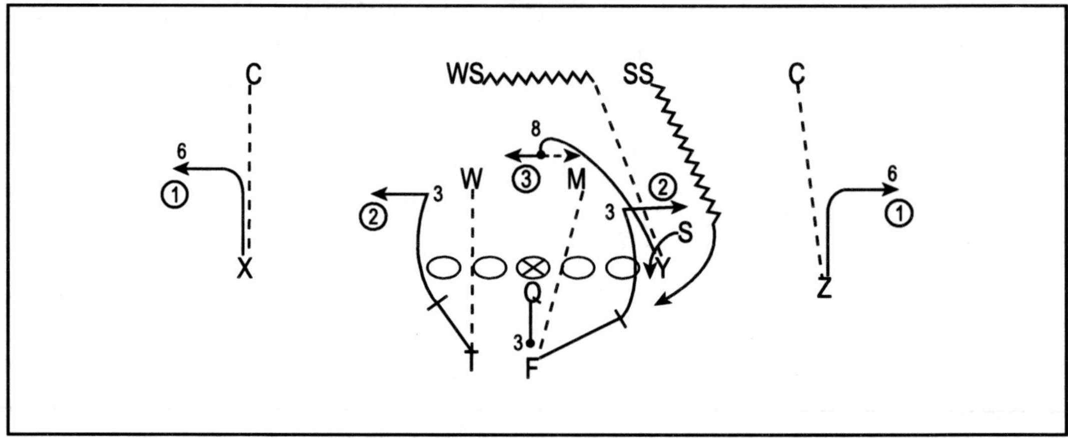

Diagram 9-14. Quick-game speed-out versus blitz-man coverage

Quick-Game Inside-Receiver Speed-Out-and-Fade

The quick-game inside-receiver speed-out-and-fade-route combination creates an excellent off-man-coverage isolation to help defeat blitz-man coverage. The wide receiver works a fade route to clear the cornerback, while the inside receiver runs his quick speed-out route. The off-man coverage will probably allow the inside receiver to run a normal zone-type speed-out route rather than a needed quick-game square-out route. The quick-game inside-receiver speed-out-and-fade concept is also excellent if the secondary defenders jump up to play press-man coverage. The only change versus the press-man coverage is that the inside speed-out receiver will press his press-man-coverage defender on his release and then square his quick-pass-game speed-out

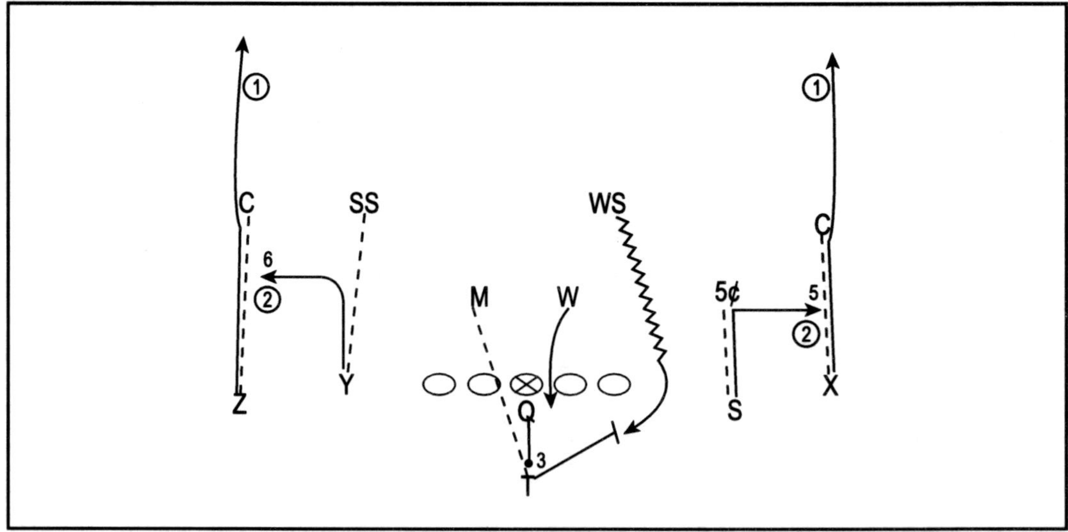

Diagram 9-15. Quick-game inside-receiver speed-out action versus blitz-man coverage

route to the sideline. Such quick-game inside-receiver speed-out action versus blitz-man coverage is shown in Diagram 9-15.

Versus the off-man coverage of blitz-man coverage, deeper, five-step quarterback-drop-timed square-outs by an inside receiver are also very effective. The inside receiver attacks the technique of the off-man defender covering him, separates, and squares out to the sideline. As on all man-coverage wide-receiver-separation techniques, the inside receiver must get separation and then be sure to run at top speed to maintain such separation. The deeper, five-step drop-timed square-out concept versus blitz-man coverage is shown in Diagram 9-16 with a maximum-protection scheme called by the quarterback to combat the defenses' blitz and stunt efforts.

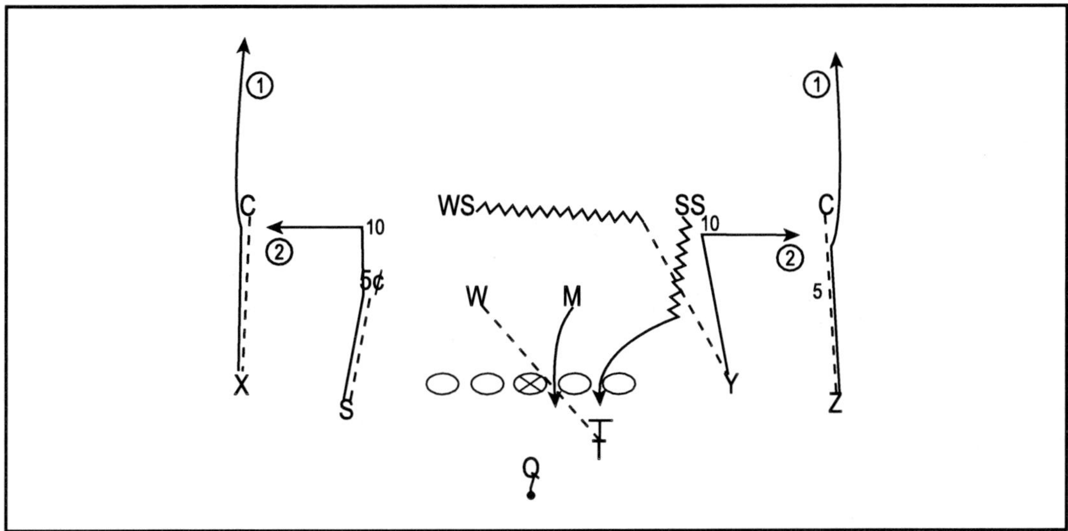

Diagram 9-16. Five-step-timed inside-receiver square-out concept versus blitz-man coverage

Quick-Game Stick

The quick-game stick-route concept is an excellent isolation-type route versus blitz-man coverage. The flat route in front of the stick route helps to open up the stick area for the stick-route receiver to man-separate into. The stick receiver initially works tightly into the technique of the defender man-covering him and then snaps to the outside to get man-separation. The stick receiver must then be sure to work hard to the outside, losing ground slightly, to help maintain such separation. The quick-game stick-route concept versus blitz-man coverage is shown in Diagram 9-17.

Quick-Game Double-Move Routes

Quick-game double-move routes can be very effective versus blitz-man coverage once the defensive backs start jumping the short, prime quick-game routes. Such routes help to take advantage of aggressive secondary play to help produce big-play pass capabilities. Hitch-and-go and speed-out-and-go routes are shown in Diagram 9-18. To ensure enough time for the quarterback to get this slightly delayed three-step drop-pass action off, a maximum-pass-protection scheme could be utilized, as shown in the diagram. Diagram 9-19 shows slant-and-go action and Y-stick-and-go action versus blitz-man coverage.

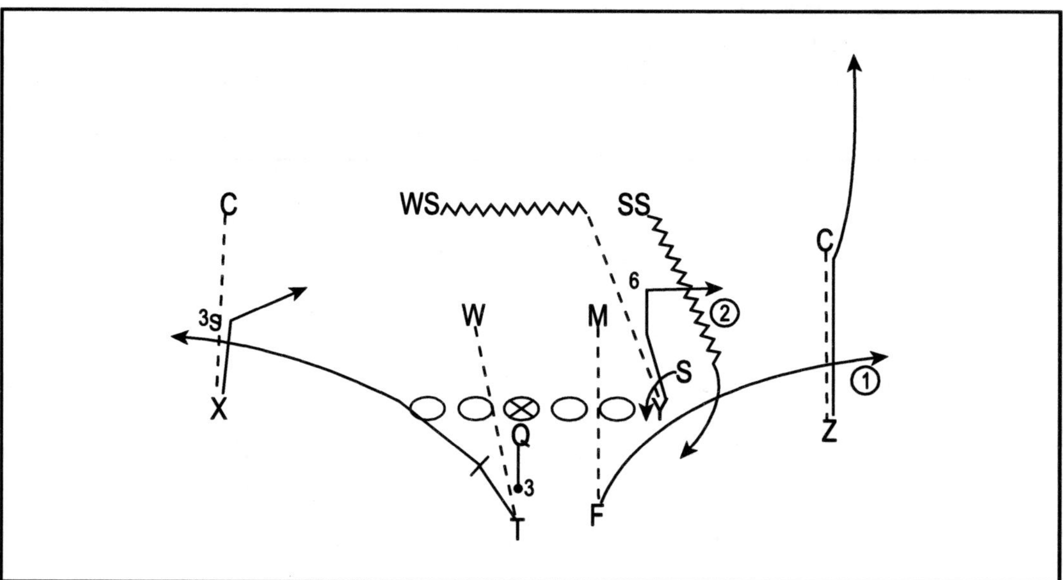

Diagram 9-17. Quick-game stick route versus blitz-man coverage

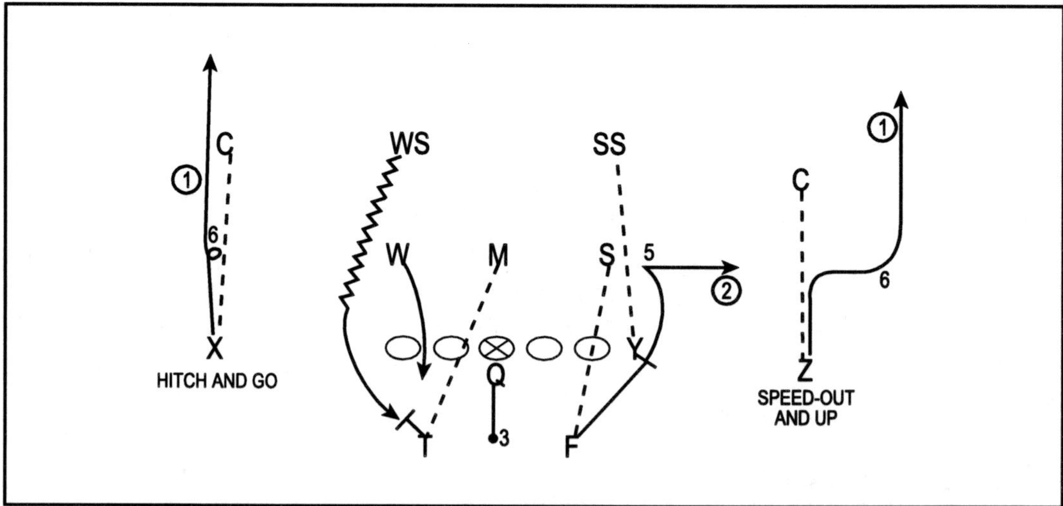

Diagram 9-18. Quick-game double-move hitch-and-go and speed-out-and-go routes versus blitz-man coverage

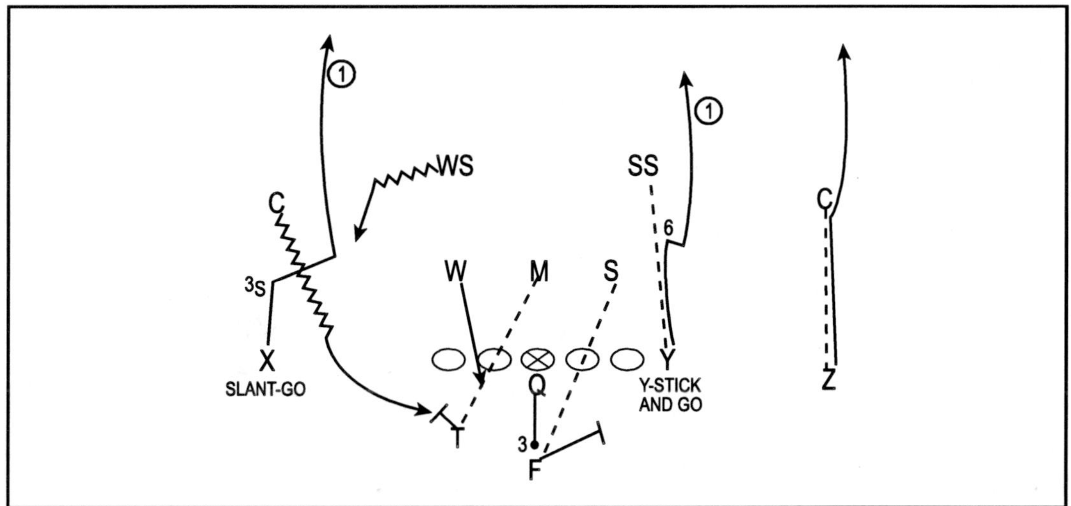

Diagram 9-19. Quick-game double-move slant-and-go and Y-stick-and-go action versus blitz-man coverage

Hot Routes to Combat Blitz/Frontal-Stunt Pressures

Before going into actual five- to seven-step-timed quarterback-drop and route actions to attack blitz-man coverage, it is first necessary to explore the use of hot-route action to help control the combination of blitzes and frontal-stunt pressures that are so often tied into blitz-man coverage. Actually, such hot-route action need not be just tied into blitz-man coverage. Chapter 8 discussed the use of hot routes to control the frontal-stunt pressures that are so commonly tied into four-across man. Such hot concepts can also easily be tied into the "zone-blitz" concepts that were discussed in Chapter 2 concerning the pass attack of cover 3.

Versus defenses that utilize blitz-man coverage, hot routes by the backs and tight ends can be utilized to help control the blitzes and corresponding frontal stunts that are often tied into the man-to-man coverage. Simply, a back or a tight end can be put on a free-release assignment (no blocking assignment). If the defender that the free releaser is normally assigned to block rushes as part of the frontal stunt or if a part of the frontal stunt vacates an area that a free releaser is releasing through, the quarterback can quickly dump the ball off hot to that free-releasing receiver. In this manner, the quarterback is taking what the defense is giving him in the effort to control both the blitz and stunt actions that can go along with the blitz-man coverage. Examples of such hot throwing versus blitz-man coverage are shown in Diagrams 9-20 to 9-22. Diagram 9-20 shows a weakside back's hot action versus a weakside-cornerback crash blitz and inside-linebacker stunt action. Diagram 9-21 shows tight-end (Y) hot action versus a strong-safety blitz and an outside linebacker's stunt action. Diagram 9-22 shows a strongside back's hot action versus a strong-safety blitz and an outside linebacker's stunt action.

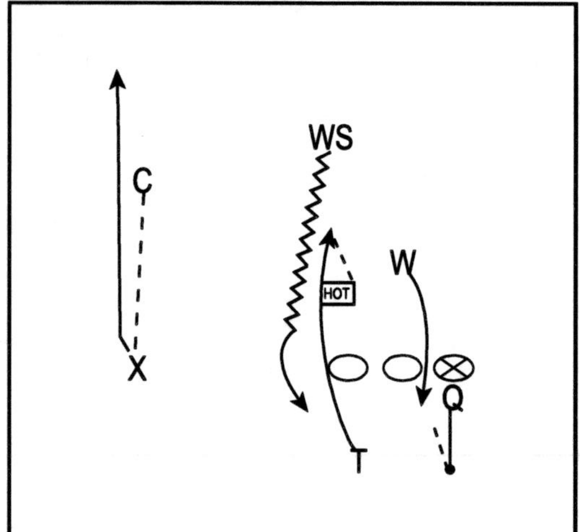

Diagram 9-20. Weakside-back hot action versus weakside inside-linebacker stunt and weak-corner blitz with blitz-man coverage

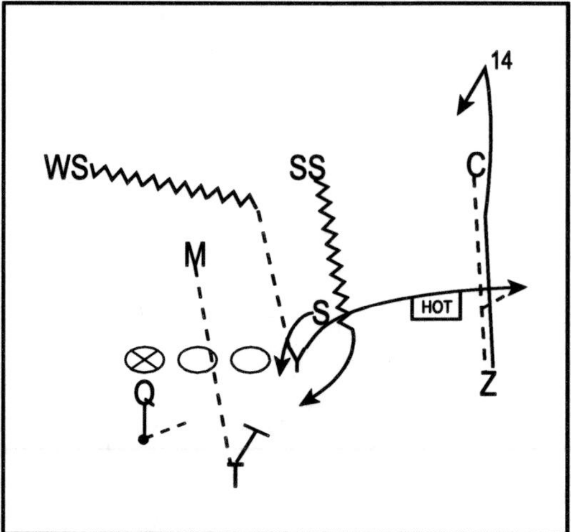

Diagram 9-21. Tight-end (Y) hot action versus strongside inside-linebacker stunt and strong-safety blitz with blitz-man coverage

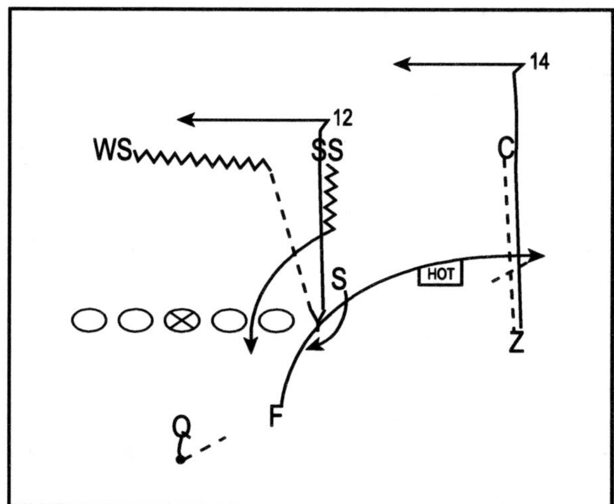

Diagram 9-22. Strongside-back hot action versus strongside outside-linebacker stunt with strong-safety blitz with blitz-man coverage

Blitz-Beater Routes to Combat Blitz/Frontal-Stunt Pressures

Much like the use of hot routes to help control frontal-stunt pressures that are so often tied into blitz-man coverage, the designation (and use) of blitz-beater routes within the actual design of a pass pattern can be equally effective to help control blitzes and associated stunts tied in with blitz-man coverage. In reality, blitz-beater routes and stunt-beater routes are conceptually the same thought. Stunt-beater routes (such as drags, shallow crosses, flats, and speed-outs) are routes that can be utilized to combat stunts from a defensive front. Blitz-beater routes are the same type of routes. The only difference is the designation of their use in being called blitz-beater routes to help beat blitzes along with the probable frontal stunts associated with such blitzes. Such a conceptual differentiation is made only to help the quarterback and the receivers understand the difference between frontal stunts by themselves and secondary blitzes that can be associated with frontal stunts.

A blitz-beater route is, simply, a route within a pass pattern that the quarterback can scan (or go) to once he realizes that the pass coverage is blitz man and that the defense is utilizing some of secondary blitz. A blitz-beater route is a route that, by design, has the ability to effectively beat man-to-man-coverage techniques. Diagram 9-23 shows how a slot-cross route acts as a blitz-beater route as part of a slot-cross-pass pattern.

Sight-Adjust Routes to Combat Blitz

Sight-adjusting is a very common system used by pass-oriented teams to control blitzing. On sight-adjust action, receivers adjust their normally deeper five- to seven-step-timed routes to slants, one-step hitches, or fade routes upon seeing (sighting) a secondary blitz unfold in front of them. The quarterback also sights the blitz action and adjusts to make the quick sight-adjust throws. Usually, sight-adjust teams start with the rule of "slanting till you can't" with regard to adjusting a five- or seven-step-timed route to a quickly timed sight-adjust slant route. Sight-adjust slant-route action is shown in Diagram 9-24, in which the flanker (Z) receiver sight-adjusts to a slant route versus a strong-safety blitz with blitz-man coverage.

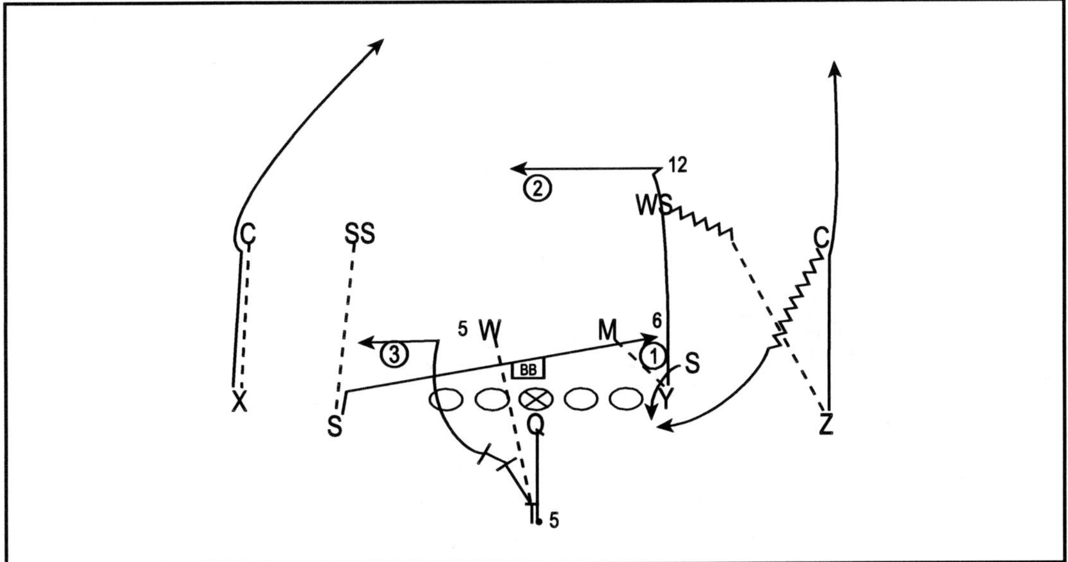

Diagram 9-23. Cross route acting as a blitz-beater route versus blitz-man coverage

If a safety sits down in the slant hole in an effort to take away a slant sight-adjustment route, the sight-adjust receiver can execute a one-step hitch route one yard deep and one yard wide off the line of scrimmage. Such action is shown in Diagram 9-25 off of a weakside cornerback blitz. If a safety drives down hard on a wide receiver's one-step hitch sight-adjust route, the quarterback can quickly arm pump the receiver. Such arm-pump action tells the wide receiver to adjust his hitch route by taking off from his hitch route to execute a fade-route adjustment for an upfield throw. The arm-pump hitch/fade action is shown off of a weakside cornerback blitz in Diagram 9-26.

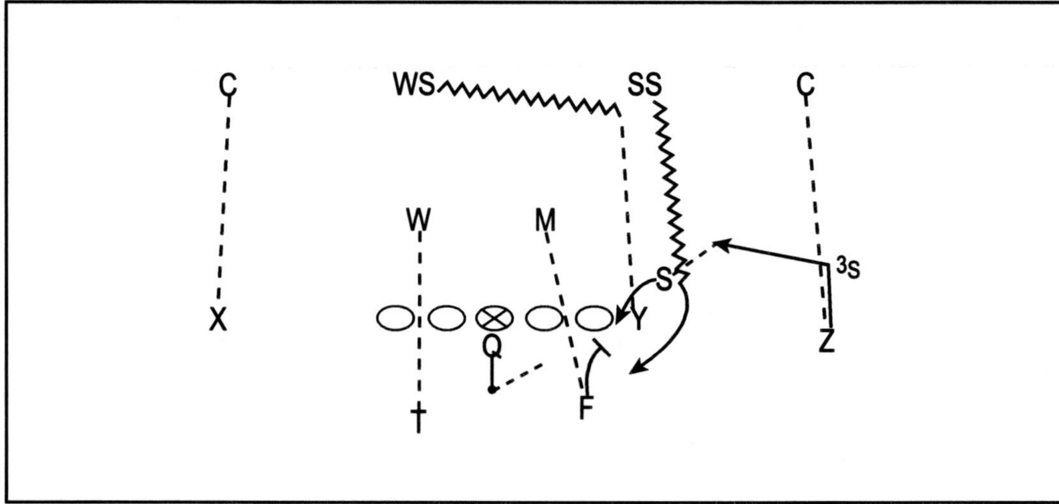

Diagram 9-24. Flanker (Z) sight-adjust slant action versus strong-safety blitz and blitz-man coverage

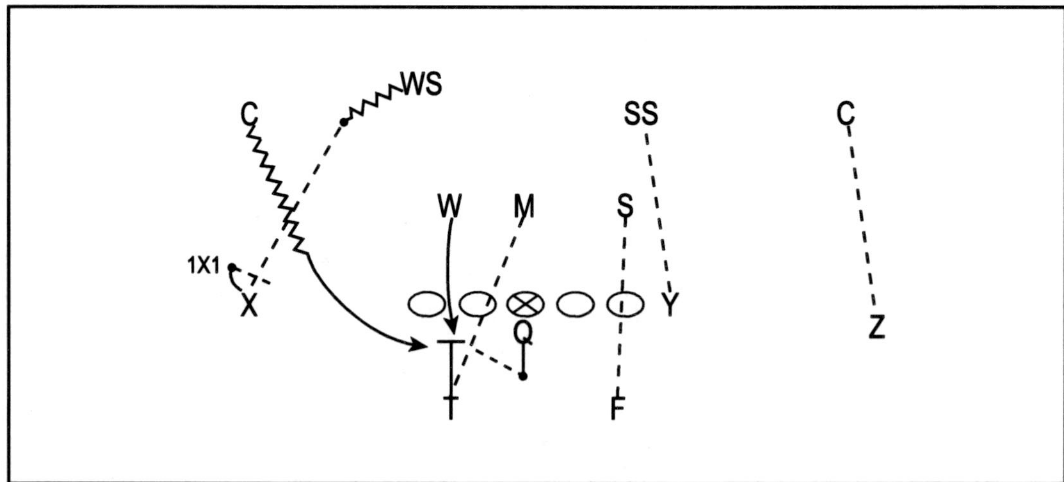

Diagram 9-25. Split-end (X) sight-adjust one-step hitch action versus weak-corner blitz and blitz-man coverage

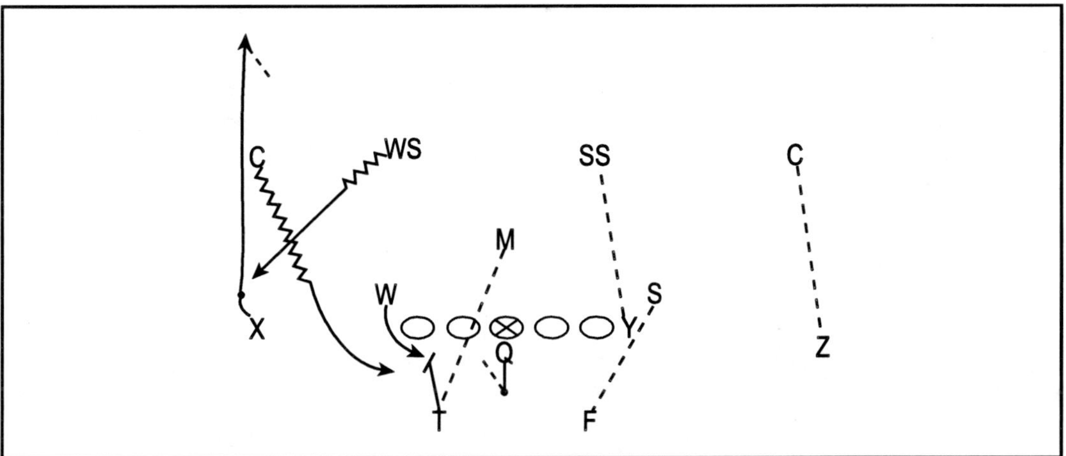

Diagram 9-26. Split-end (X) sight-adjust pump hitch/fade action versus weak-corner blitz and blitz-man coverage

Under Concept

The under concept presents an excellent underneath isolation of a wide receiver working underneath a clear route by the adjacent receiver to the inside versus blitz-man coverage. The clear route may very well get eaten up by the off-man coverage of the safety. However, the under route has an excellent opportunity to beat the man coverage by man-separating and maintaining such separation to the inside underneath the clear route by staying on the move. Diagram 9-27 shows an under-route isolation versus blitz-man coverage.

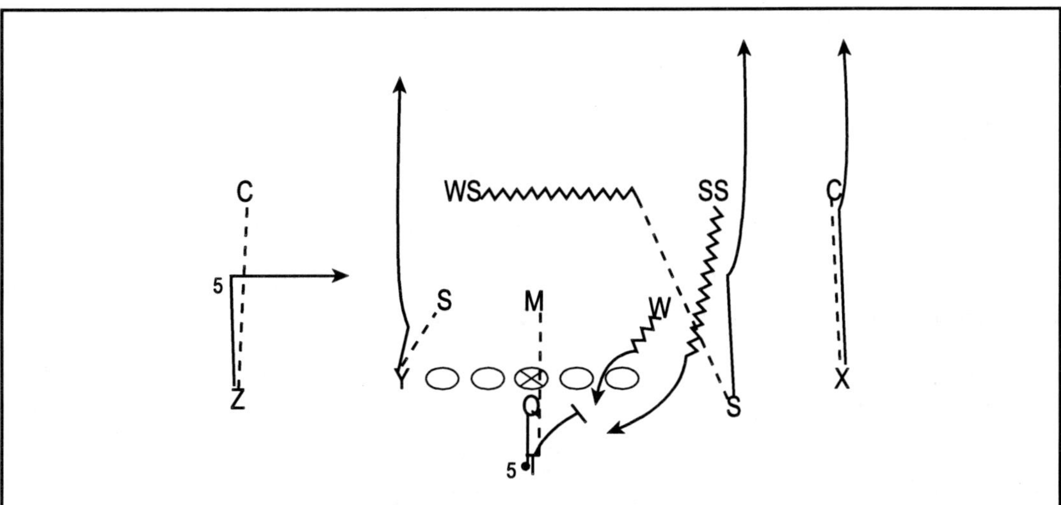

Diagram 9-27. Under concept versus blitz-man coverage

High-Low-Read Smash Isolation

The high-low-read smash isolation could give an offense an excellent ability to attack blitz-man coverage. The major concern for the smash-route combination is the time the post-corner route might take versus the defense's blitz activity. As a result, an offense may want to call for a maximum protection or have the quarterback check to such a protection. The inside-receiver post-corner route must beat the off-man coverage. However, he does have a good amount of room to the outside to do so.

The smash route, run as a hitch-option route, gives the smash route the ability to beat the off-man coverage across the field to the inside, acting as an excellent blitz-beater route. Such man-breaking actions of the smash concept versus blitz-man coverage with a maximum-pass-protection scheme is shown in Diagram 9-28.

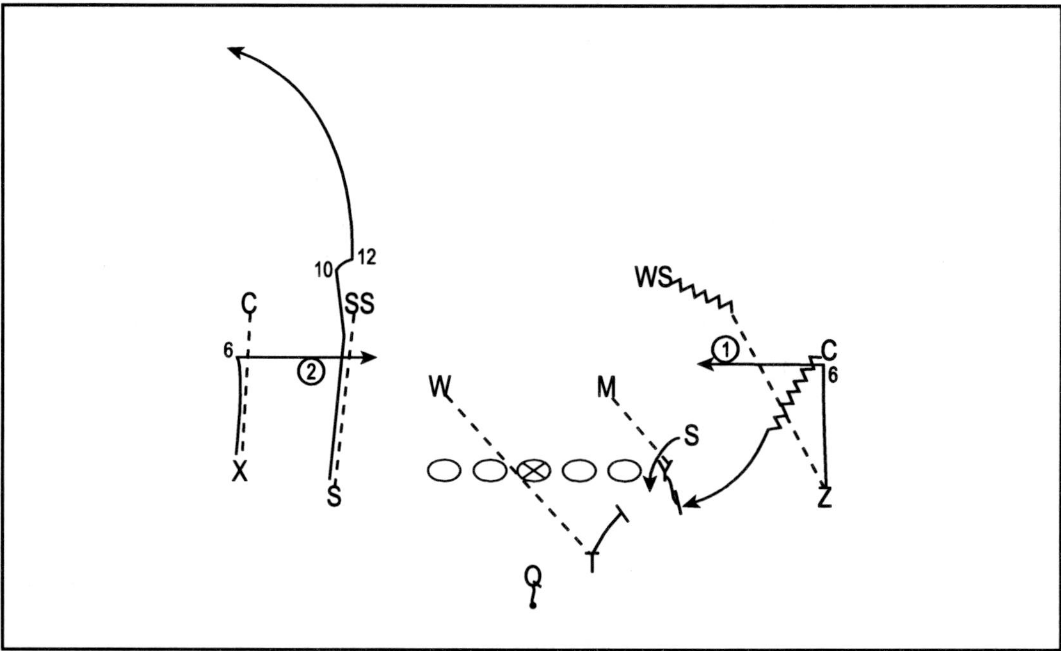

Diagram 9-28. Smash concept versus blitz-man coverage with maximum pass protection

Bunch-Formation Post-Corner Flood-Isolation Concept

A bunch-formation post-corner flood-isolation concept is an excellent way of attacking blitz-man coverage. You might normally think of flood action to overload zone coverages. However, the picking/crossing action of the post-corner bunch concept helps to condense blitz-man coverage and actually outflank the coverage with the outside man-breaking flood action, as shown in Diagram 9-29. Note that the flat route by the third inside receiver acts as an excellent blitz-beater route.

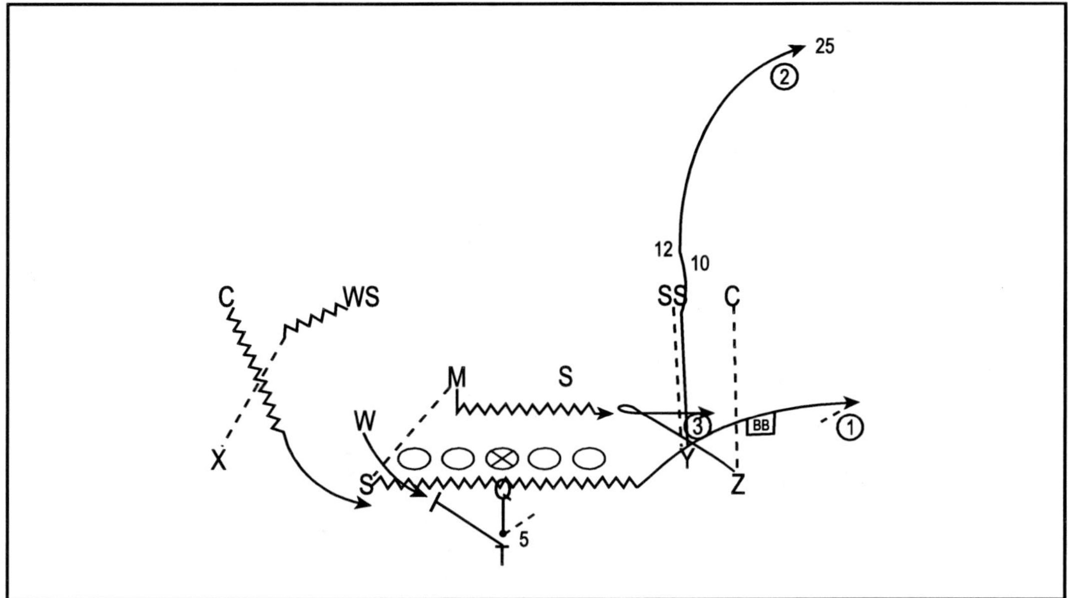

Diagram 9-29. Bunch-formation post-corner flood-isolation concept versus blitz-man coverage

Post-Corner/Dig-Route Combination

The post-corner/dig-route-pattern combination is an excellent man-beater concept to utilize versus blitz-man coverage. The quarterback initially checks the post-corner isolation and then scans back to the dig route if the post-corner-isolation read doesn't look good. Once again, the major concern is pass-protection needs versus the blitz. However, on a critical third-and-long situation in which the offense *must* maintain possession of the ball, the post-corner/dig-route concept is an excellent pattern to utilize to get deep-yardage needs—and this pass-pattern concept fits very well with maximum-pass-protection needs, as seen in Diagram 9-30 versus blitz-man coverage.

Four-Streaks Concept

The four-streaks concept is a good way of attacking blitz-man coverage—especially when the off-man coverage starts to camp down on underneath, control pass-game completions. Since no middle deep-zone safety help is available in blitz-man coverage, the quarterback is able to look for his best one-on-one isolation. The four-streaks concept versus blitz-man coverage is shown in Diagram 9-31 with the tight-end (Y) streak isolation on the middle linebacker (M) being the best quick one-on-one isolation.

Rollaway/Acute Routes

Rollaway and acute routes are excellent isolation actions versus blitz-man coverage. They are especially effective when they develop off of strong streak-threat fakes pushing the blitz-man off-man-coverage cornerbacks deep. Rollaway/acute-route action versus blitz-man coverage is shown in Diagram 9-32 from a three-streaks design with maximum protection.

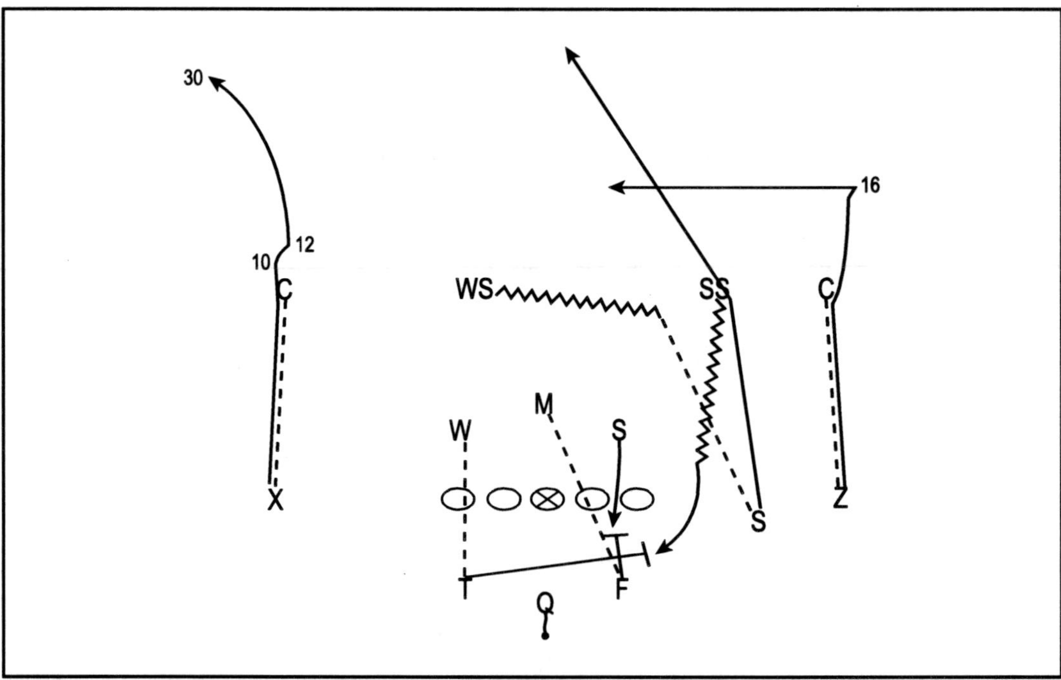

Diagram 9-30. Post-corner/dig concept versus bliz-man coverage

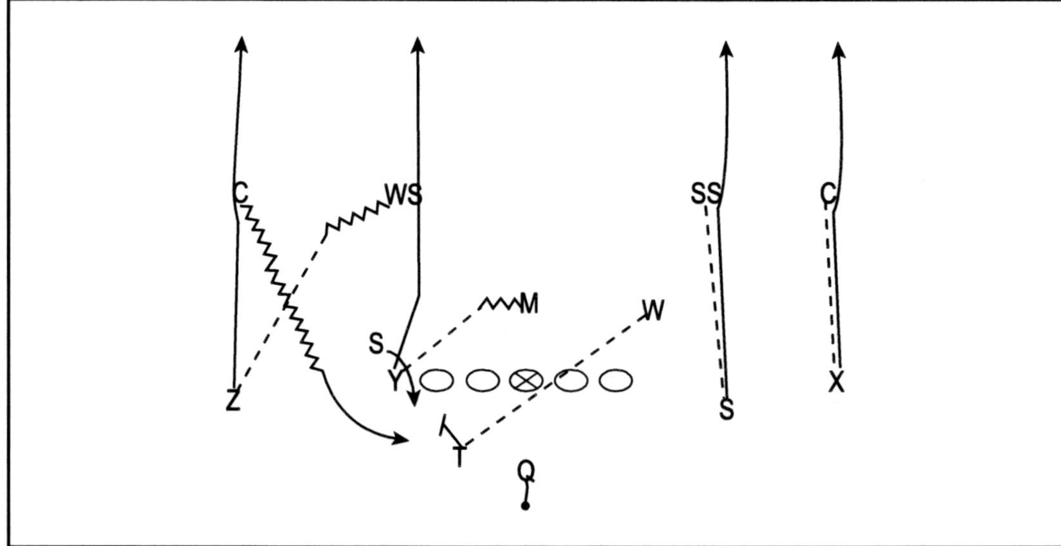

Diagram 9-31. Four-streaks concept versus blitz-man coverage

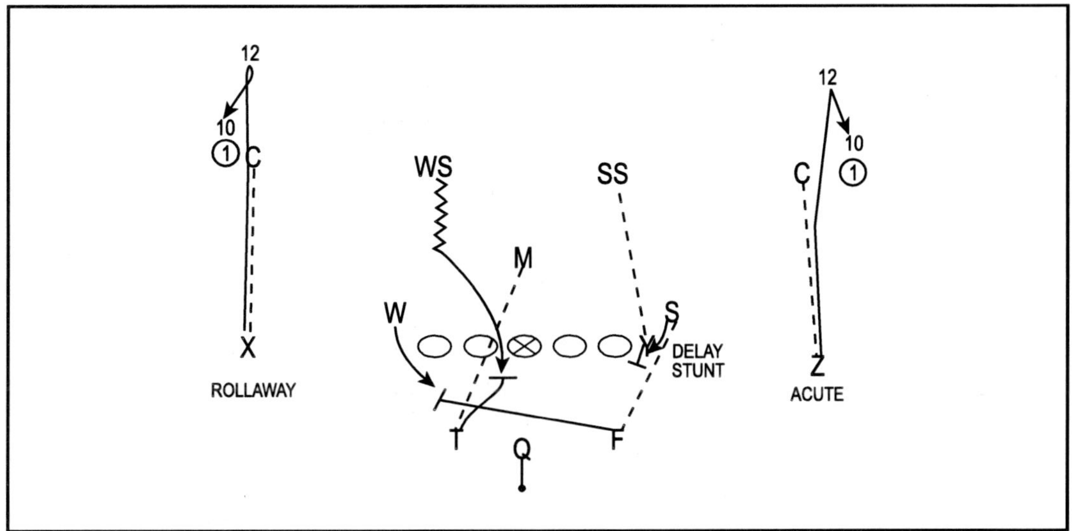

Diagram 9-32. Rollaway/acute routes versus blitz-man coverage

Speed-Outs

Speed-out routes can be very effective route concepts versus blitz-man coverage—especially when the cornerbacks are deep in off alignment. However, it is important to note that if speed-outs are called versus tighter off-man coverage, the speed-out routes must be adjusted to square-out routes "on the run," as shown in Diagram 9-33.

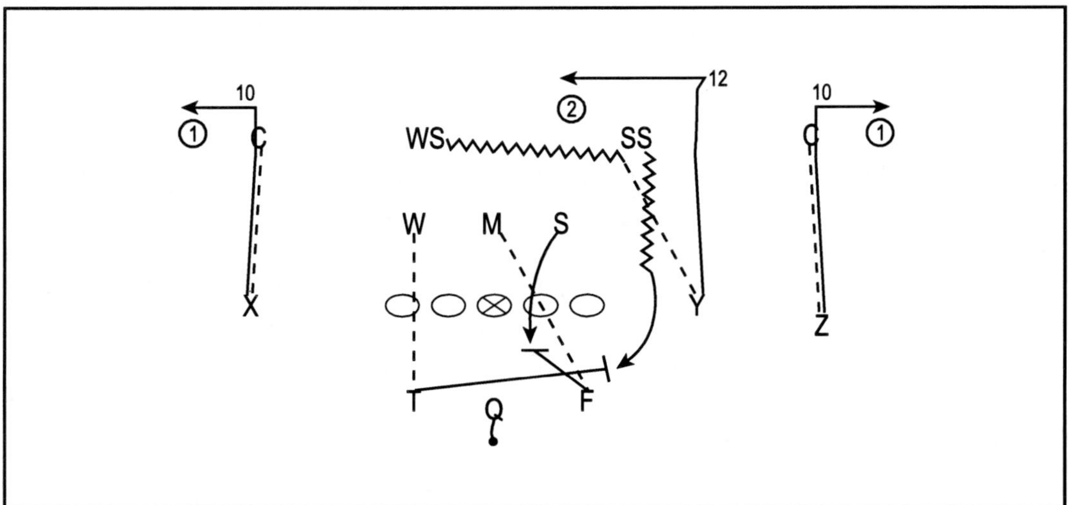

Diagram 9-33. Adjusting speed-outs into square-outs versus tightened off-blitz-man-coverage techniques

Sprint-Out With Curl/Flat Pattern

Diagram 9-34 shows sprint-out curl/flat action versus blitz-man coverage. Frontside (or backside) gap-protection sprint-out action—especially when the sprint-out action is away from the defensive-blitz action—is an excellent concept to use to block blitzes and the corresponding frontal stunts that are often associated with blitzes. Note that the curl route must work to the outside if the pass is late-developing so that the receiver works in special coordination with the quarterback as the play takes more time to develop. The quarterback should think "throw the flat until you can't." The quick speed-out route in Diagram 9-34 acts as an excellent blitz-beater route.

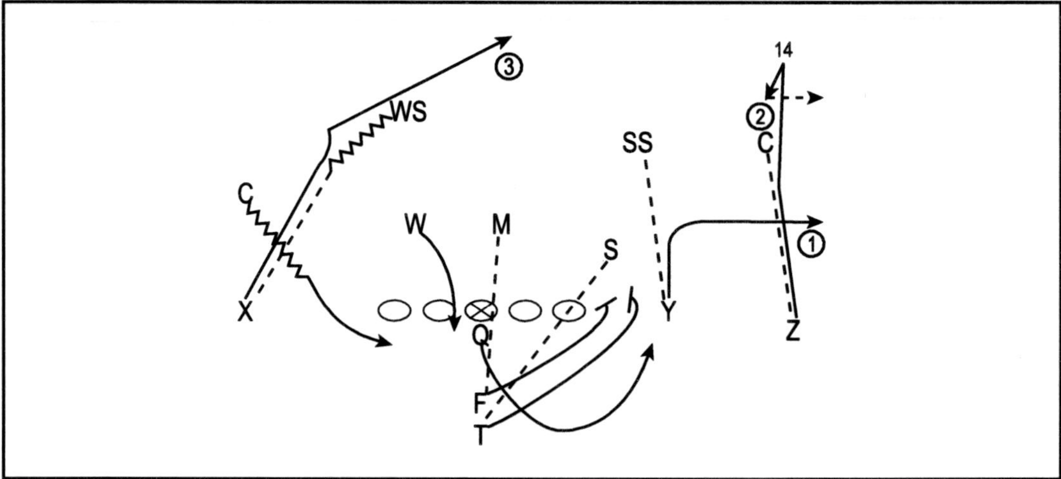

Diagram 9-34. Sprint-out action with curl/flat-route combination versus blitz-man coverage

Square-In/Flat Combination

Many coaches prefer running short square-ins versus blitz-man coverage rather than curls and hooks. The feeling is that the receiver has a better chance of producing quick man-to-man separation versus the off-man coverage with short square-in routes, as shown in Diagram 9-35. Once again, the flat route can act as an excellent blitz-beater route. In addition, a maximum-pass-protection scheme can be utilized to help the quarterback get the pass off versus any blitz threat.

Shallow Cross/Replacement Curl

The shallow cross/replacement curl concept helps to produce an excellent crossing/picking action to help attack blitz-man coverage. The inside hard-breaking shallow route helps to produce an excellent man- and blitz-beater-type route. The replacement curl (replacing the original alignment of the outside receiver) has an excellent chance of man-separating to break back into the quarterback due to the crossing/picking action of the two receivers. The replacement curl is shortened to 10 yards to help produce consistent quarterback-drop-timing. The shallow cross/replacement-curl-combination route concept versus blitz-man coverage is shown in Diagram 9-36.

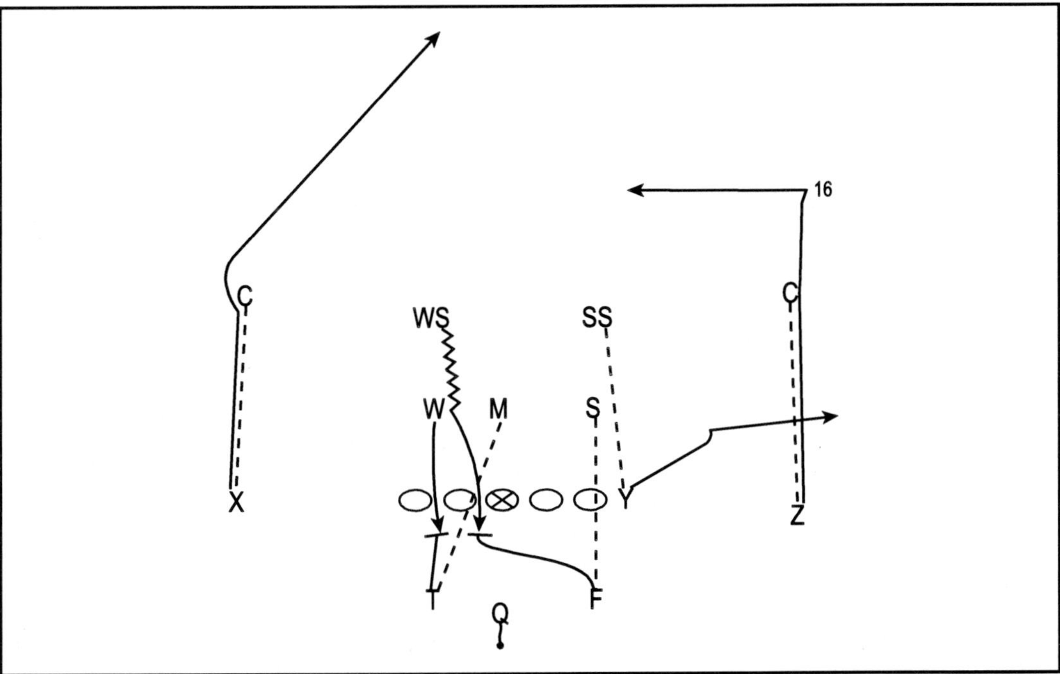

Diagram 9-35. Square-in/flat-route combination versus blitz-man coverage

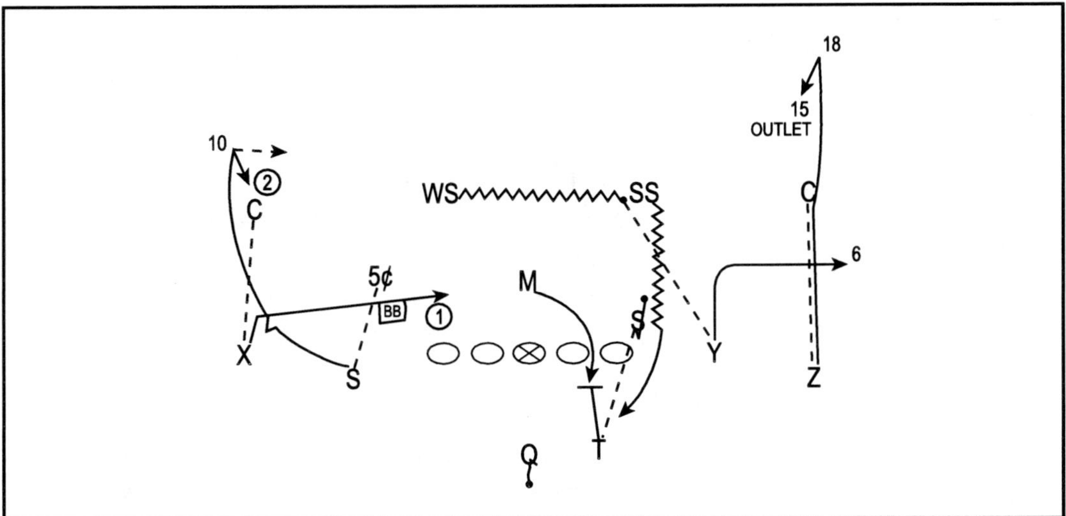

Diagram 9-36. Shallow cross/replacement-curl pattern versus blitz-man coverage

Diagram 9-37 shows the shallow-cross/curl pattern as a shallow-cross pattern alternative to attack blitz-man coverage. Once again, the shallow-cross route helps to act as an excellent blitz- and man-beater route.

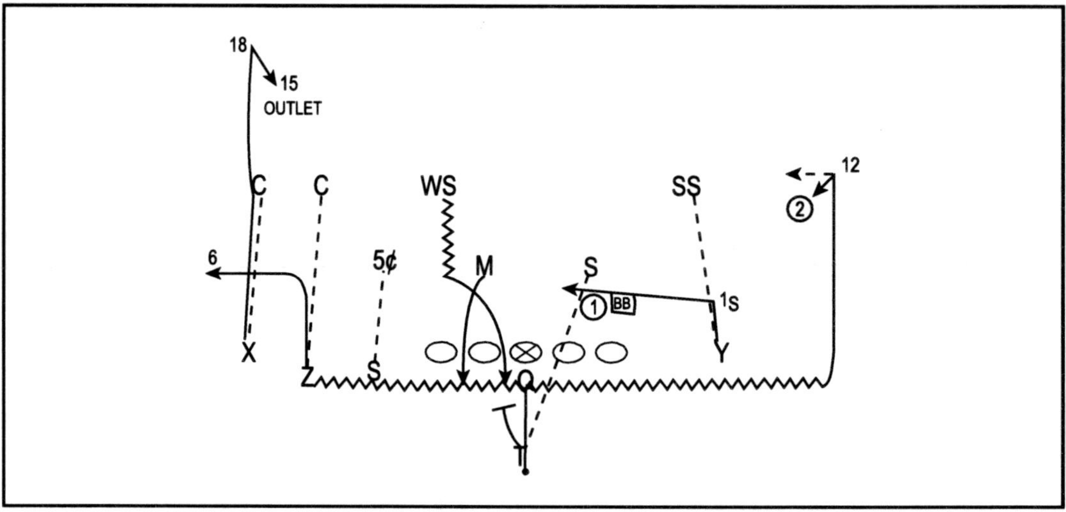

Diagram 9-37. Shallow cross/curl pattern versus blitz-man coverage

Drive Concept

The drive concept helps to create an excellent blitz-beater concept to attack blitz-man coverage. The prime route of the drive pattern, the actual drive route itself, is an excellent man- and blitz-beater route in its crossing-the-field drag action. If the drive route is covered, the short-dig route of the tight end (Y) and the back's delayed drag-type adjustment of his sit route give the quarterback three excellent man-to-man route beaters to help attack the blitz-man coverage, as shown in Diagram 9-38.

Cross Concept

The crossing-route action of the cross-pattern concept is an excellent blitz-man-coverage beater. As in the drive concept, the cross, short dig, and the man-adjustment aspect of the back's sit route help to create excellent man-beater possibilities—and crossing receivers, themselves, are excellent man-beater actions, as shown in the slot-cross pattern in Diagram 9-39. The dragging-cross route itself is an excellent blitz-beater route.

Texas Concept

The Texas concept helps to create a crossing isolation on two of the underneath blitz-man-coverage defenders. The tight end works to pin the strongside inside linebacker to the inside for his outside square-out-type man-break. The back drives to the flat to produce hard outside flow by his covering linebacker and then works back inside hard underneath to separate from that linebacker. The major concern for the Texas concept versus blitz-man coverage is the associated frontal-pressure stunts that may be tied into blitz man. On his inside Texas release, the tight end (Y) can check for any quick-dump pass-type action by the quarterback over a possible vacated strongside linebacker area. In addition, the crossing Texas back can turn quickly to receive a hot-route dump pass

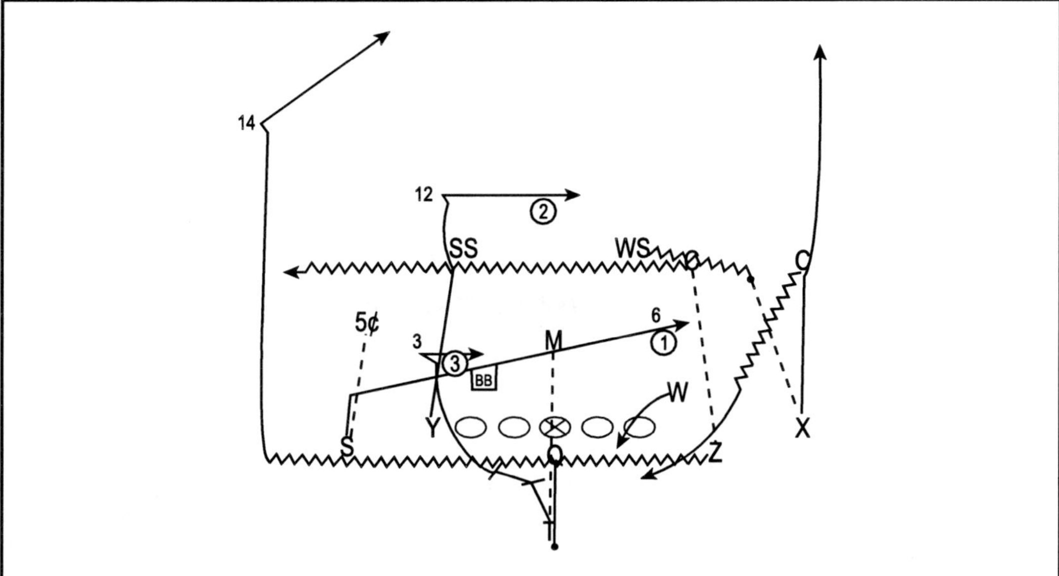

Diagram 9-38. Drive concept versus blitz-man coverage

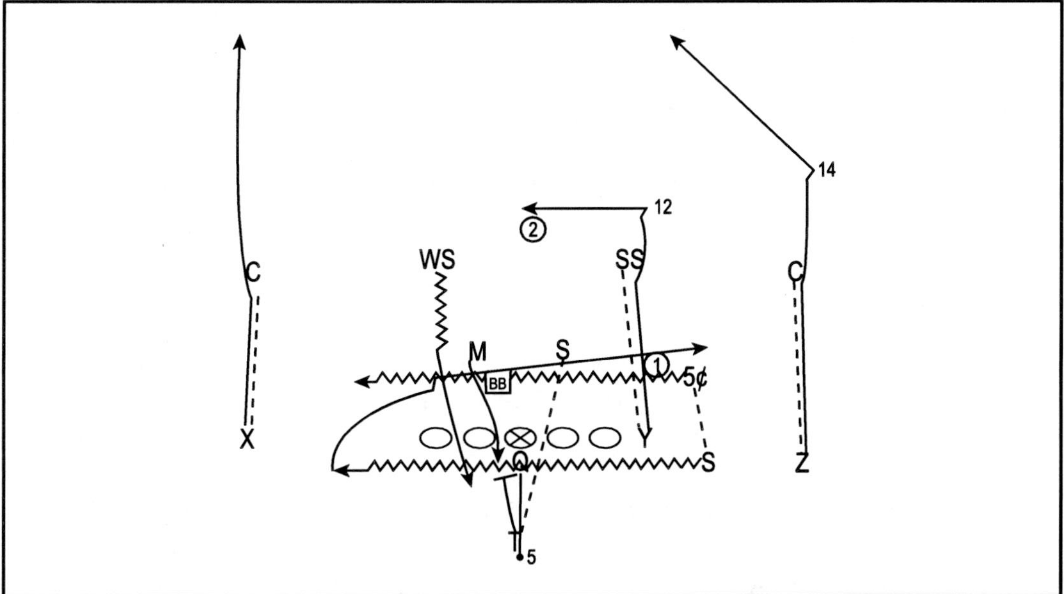

Diagram 9-39. Slot-cross pattern concept versus blitz-man coverage

from the quarterback at the end of his initial flat-route stem if he reads any outside stunt or blitz pressure, as seen in Diagram 9-40.

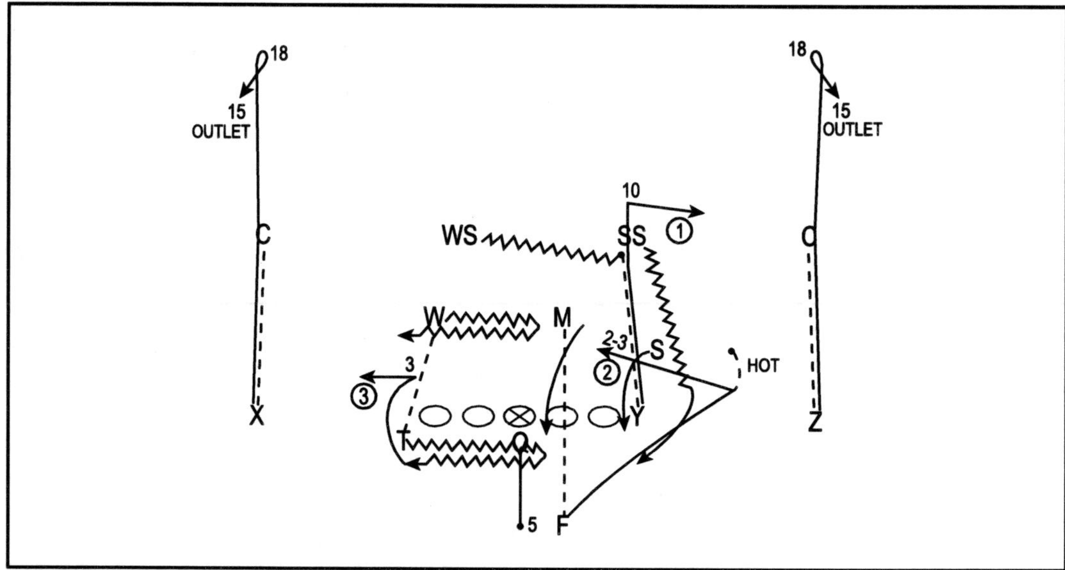

Diagram 9-40. Texas concept versus blitz-man coverage with hot-route dump pass to back

Option-Isolation Concept

Option-isolation routes help to produce excellent one-on-one isolations on the off blitz-man-coverage defenders. Option routes can help to produce one-on-one size, talent, and speed mismatches. Versus blitz-man coverage, the key is for the option receiver(s) to recognize blitz and think to execute his man-separation techniques quickly to "get open quickly." Diagram 9-41 shows a tight-end (Y) option and a slot (S) option versus blitz-man coverage. Note that to the outside of the option routes, a rollaway and an acute route are shown to act as excellent initial-read blitz-beater routes for the quarterback if he were to recognize the blitz looks early enough.

Pick and Rub Concepts

Pick and rub concepts can be excellent route combinations to beat the blitz-man coverage. Of course, any pick or rub must be legally executed. Receivers cannot run into and/or block coverage defenders as a part of the pick or rub concept. Diagram 9-42 shows a pick-route combination with an inside receiver working to the outside versus blitz-man coverage. Diagram 9-43 shows a rub-route combination with an outside receiver working to the inside. Diagram 9-44 shows a slice-route combination with an inside receiver working off a pick set-up and executing a fade route.

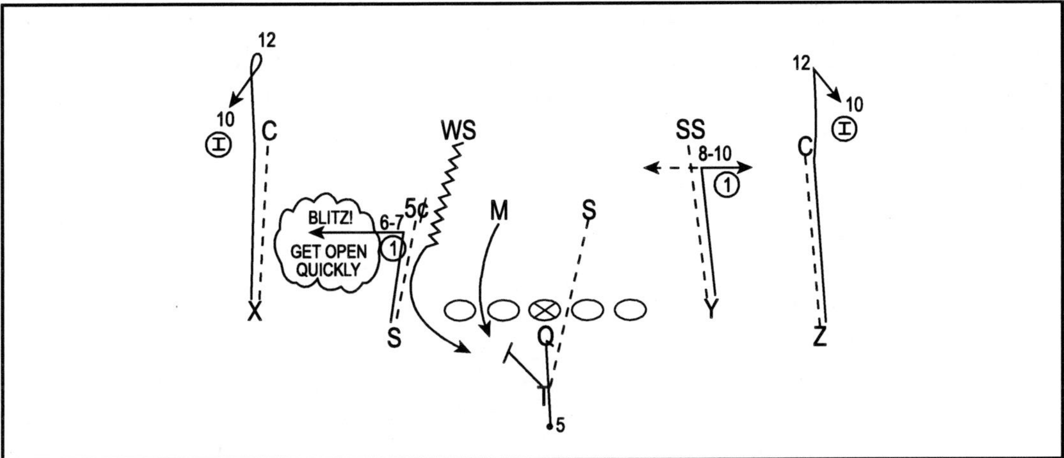

Diagram 9-41. Option-isolation routes versus blitz-man coverage

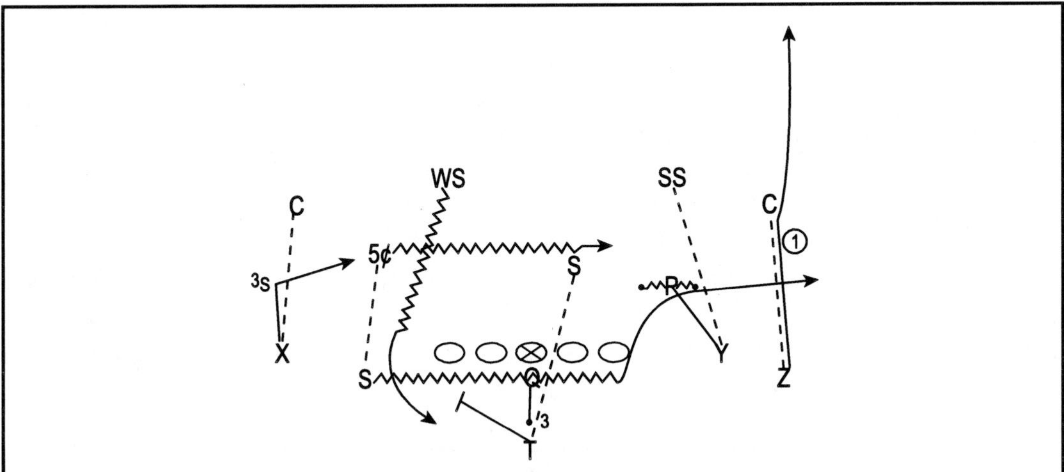

Diagram 9-42. Pick-route combination versus blitz-man coverage

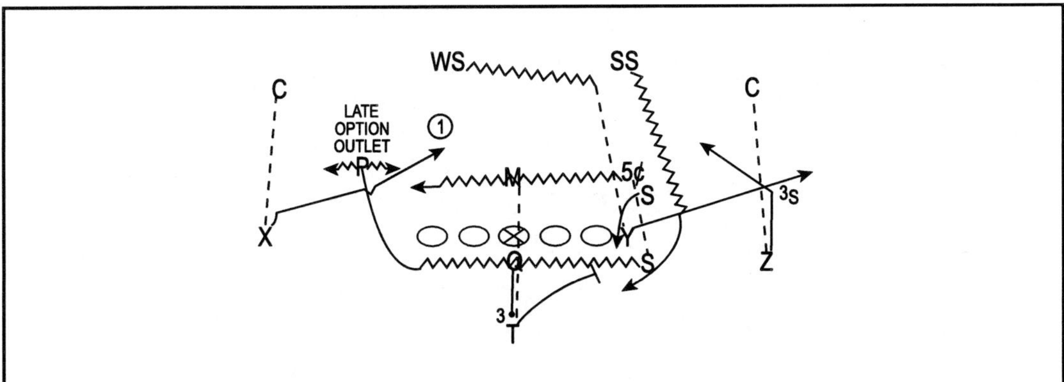

Diagram 9-43. Rub-route combination versus blitz-man coverage

An interesting idea is to have the receiver who actual sets up the pick for the prime pick, rub, or slice route run a modified option route if the quarterback snaps his eyes to that receiver. In this fashion, if the pick, rub, or slice receiver is covered, the quarterback has a delayed timed route to work to as an outlet.

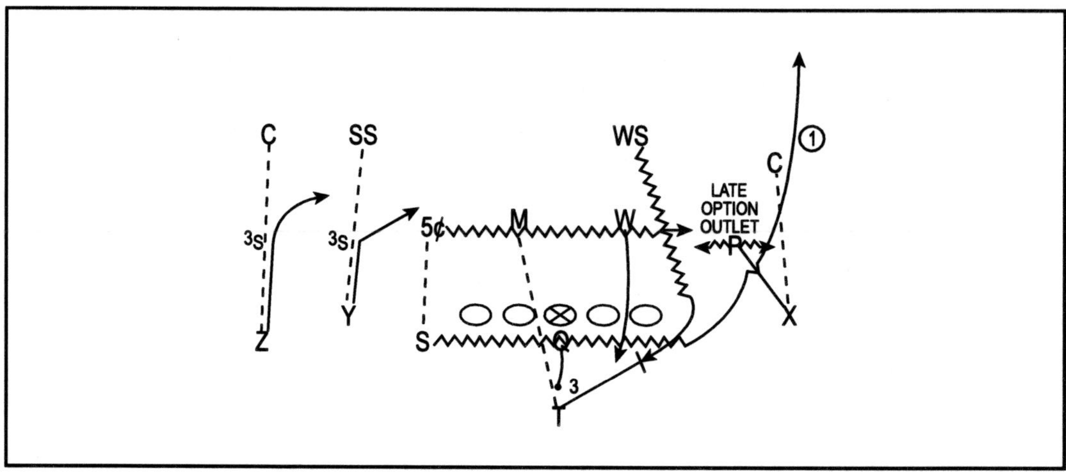

Diagram 9-44. Slice-route combination versus blitz man coverage

Picking Screens

Picking screens, legal when the ball is thrown behind the line of scrimmage, is a very effective concept to use versus blitz-man coverage. Diagram 9-45 shows a back pick-screen action from a slotted tight-end set versus blitz-man coverage. The tight end (Y) blocks (picks) the strongside inside linebacker.

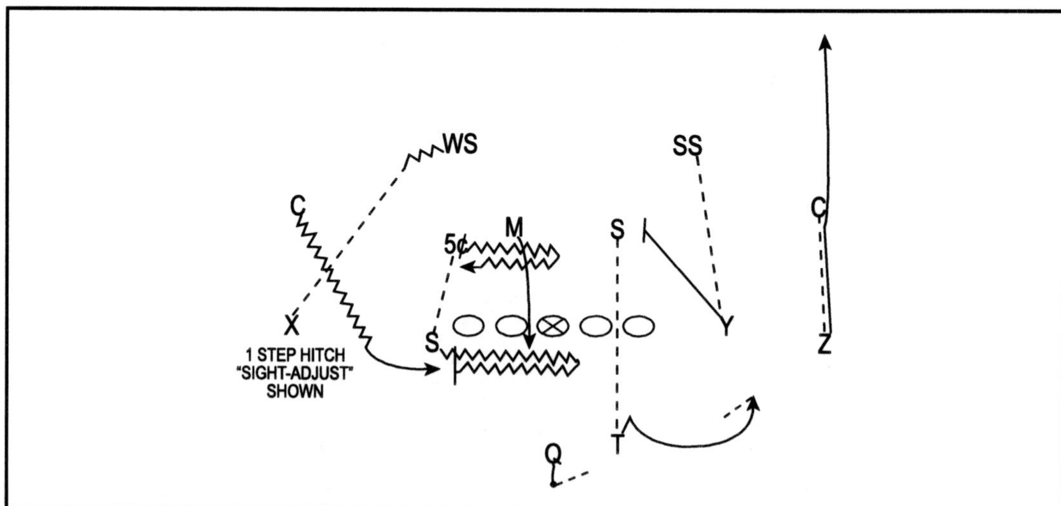

Diagram 9-45. Back pick screen versus blitz-man coverage

About the Author

Steve Axman is the quarterbacks coach at the University of Montana. Previously Axman was the wide receivers coach at the University of Washington, a position he assumed prior to the 2004 season. It was Axman's second stint on the Huskies staff. Previously, he served as the assistant head coach, wide receivers coach, and quarterbacks coach at the University of Washington (1999-2002). As the Huskies quarterbacks coach, Axman oversaw the work of UW record-setting quarterbacks Marques Tuiasosopo and Cody Pickett. During the 2003 season, he was the offensive coordinator and quarterbacks coach at UCLA.

Axman is no stranger to wide-open, multiple offense football or producing top-flight collegiate quarterbacks. During his career, he has worked at four Pac-10 schools (UCLA, Arizona, Stanford, and Washington). Among his former collegiate pupils are Troy Aikman and Drew Olson (UCLA), Neil O'Donnell (Maryland), and Jeff Lewis and Travis Brown (Northern Arizona).

In 1998 (prior to joining the UW staff the first time), Axman served as the quarterbacks coach at Minnesota under Glen Mason. Before that, Axman was the head coach at Northern Arizona from 1990-97. He inherited a NAU program that had experienced just three winning seasons during the 1980s and had never qualified for the Division I-AA postseason playoffs. During his eight years with the Lumberjacks, Axman guided the team to a 48-41 record, making him the second-winningest coach in Northern Arizona's history.

Axman's NAU teams were known for their offensive fireworks. During his eight-year career, Axman's teams averaged 30 points per game. His 1996 Lumberjack squad set or tied 14 national records and averaged 43.2 points per game en route to a 9-3 overall record and a 6-1 record in the Big Sky Conference. That season produced a second-place finish in the Big Sky, the school's first postseason appearance, and a school-best No. 6 national ranking. In 1989, Axman served as quarterbacks coach for Maryland, where he worked with O'Donnell. In 1987-88, he was the offensive coordinator at UCLA, where he coached Aikman. Prior to UCLA, Axman coached at Stanford (1986), with the Denver Gold of the United States Football League (1985), and at the University of Arizona (1980-84), as the offensive coordinator and quarterbacks coach. Axman previously spent a year at Illinois, three seasons at Army, and one season at Albany State. Prior to that, Axman's first collegiate coaching assignment was at East Stroudsburg State in 1974. A 1969 graduate of C.W. Post in Greenvale, NY, Axman went on to earn his first master's degree from Long Island University in 1972 and his second in 1975 while coaching at East Stroudsburg State.

Axman has authored nine instructional books on football. He has also been featured on seven well-received instructional videos on football. He is nationally renowned for his knowledge of offensive fundamentals, schemes, and techniques, particularly quarterback play.

A native of Huntington Station, NY, Axman and his wife, Dr. Marie Axman, an elementary school principal, have four daughters: Mary Beth, Jaclyn, Melissa, and Kimberly.